The Politics of Time
Modernity and Avant-Garde

◆

PETER OSBORNE

VERSO

London • New York

First published by Verso 1995
© Peter Osborne 1995
All rights reserved

Verso
UK: 6 Meard Street, London W1V 3HR
USA: 180 Varick Street, New York NY 10014–4606

Verso is the imprint of New Left Books

ISBN 0–86091–482–8
ISBN 0–86091–652–9 (pbk)

British Library Cataloguing in Publication Data
A catalogue record for this book is available from the British Library

Library of Congress Cataloging-in-Publication Data
Osborne, Peter, 1958–
The politics of time : modernity & avant-garde / Peter Osborne.
p. cm.
Includes bibliographical references and index.
ISBN 0–86091–482–8 (hardback) — ISBN 0–86091–652–9 (pbk)
1. History—Periodization. 2. History—Philosophy. I. Title.
D16. 15.083 1995   95–30097
901—dc20   CIP

Typeset by Keystroke, Jacaranda Lodge, Wolverhampton
Printed in Great Britain by Biddles Ltd, Guildford and King's Lynn

The Politics of Time

Contents

Preface   vii

1 **Modernity: A Different Time**   1

  Modernity as experience and misrecognition:
    Berman and Anderson
  From *Neue Zeit* to *Neuzeit:* Koselleck's
    historical semantics
  The quality of modernity: homogenization,
    differentiation and abstraction
  Modernity as project: Habermas, Foucault,
    Enlightenment
  Differential time and conjunctural analysis:
    Althusser and the *Annales*

2 **One Time, One History?**   30

  Conditions of possibility: the transcendental path
  Let history judge: the immanent road
  Difference against development
  Hegel's failure: end of history, end of time
  Time and Narrative: phenomenological ontology
  Present or instant? The time of the soul and the
    time of the world
  Historical time: ontology and narrative mediation
  Being-towards-death, being-towards-history
  Ordinary time or cosmological time? Nature and
    the social

3   **Death and Recognition**   69

     Being-there-with-others: the dialectic of recognition
     Trial by death
     From recognition to identification: Hegel and Lacan
     'Afterwardsness' and the death drive
     Primary identification: Kristeva's imaginary father
     In the beginning was the bond: Jessica Benjamin or
       Jean Laplanche?
     Timelessness, death, and the unconscious
     Psychoanalysis, temporality, history

4   **Modernity, Eternity, Tradition**   113

     Exteriority and transcendence: Levinas's eschatology
     Outside or end? Totality, infinity, others
     The eternity of the classical: Gadamer's hermeneutics
     Historiography and the shattering of tradition
     Historicism as bad modernity
     Quasi-messianic interruption: images of redemption
     Montage, mediation, apocalypse: towards a new
       narrativity

5   **Avant-Garde and Everyday**   160
     Conservative revolution: fascism as reactionary
       modernism
     Vision and decision: existence as repetition (against
       decisionism)
     Repetition or remembrance?
     From Marxism to Surrealism: 'the mystery in the
       everyday'
     The verso of modernity: from everydayness to
       historical life

Epilogue   197

Notes   202

Select Bibliography   245

Index   261

Preface

Paik once told a story about buying books in Japan: he succeeded in buying all the most important Japanese philosophical works on the subject of time, in order to study them in the original, only to discover on his return to New York that he didn't have time to read them.[1]

By the time we have read all the works announcing the onset of post-modernity, it will probably already be over. Like the crisis theorists of the 1970s, everyone is waiting for the market in postmodernism to collapse. They are likely to be disappointed. Why this is so, is one of the things this book tries to understand – which is not to suggest that the word 'postmodern' is an adequate sign for the times, still less for the kinds of time that they encode; nor, in this instance, is it to insist upon an ideological or sociological analysis of its persistence. Rather, it is a more philosophical explanation that is sought. For it is a curious feature of the literature of and on postmodernism that despite its ostensibly – on occasion, ostentatiously – theoretical character, it contains hardly any philosophical writing about the concept at all. Just what the postmodern might mean, philosophically – in the sense in which, for example, thinkers as opposed as Habermas and Foucault share a general conception of the philosophical discourse of modernity – remains almost totally obscure.

This claim is liable to be misunderstood. It is not that philosophers have not written about postmodernism. Lyotard would be the obvious example. Nor is there a lack of philosophical literature that designates itself, or other such literature, 'postmodern'. What is rare is to find the ideas of postmodernism, postmodernity and the post-modern the object of philosophical attention at the level at which they are constituted, as periodizing concepts of cultural history. The term 'postmodern' is commonly used to refer to any of a loosely related set of philosophical positions, all more or less critical of something that has come to be called 'Enlightenment reason', all more or less post-Nietzschean. Yet most of these positions are compatible with aspects of the work of a far wider range of thinkers than are usually cited, many of whom (including both Hegel and Marx) are assumed to belong on the other side of its divide. For without an account of the philosophically modern – of 'modern' as a philosophical term – let alone the philosophically modernistic, such references are fated to remain little more than empty gestures, labels for the philosophically fashionable, the comfortably up-to-date. If there is a case for viewing Derrida, for example, within the terms of this debate, the balance of such argument as there has been undoubtedly falls on the side of his being a modernist; not a postmodernist, philosophically, at all.[2]

What follows is an attempt to approach all this from another angle, to pick up some current concerns – about time and history and culture, about the present as change, and history as culture – and subject them to another perspective: a perspective that is best summed up by the phrase, *the politics of historical time*. If Aristotle sought to understand time through change, since it is first encountered in entities that change, might we not reverse the procedure, and seek to comprehend change through time? The aim of this book is to contribute to current debates about historical periodization and cultural change by connecting them up to a philosophical literature on time. Once we do this, two things soon become apparent. One is that the whole network of ideas about the postmodern is firmly inscribed within the problematic of the temporal dialectics of modernity. (It may involve a decisive mutation of the field, but it remains within its parameters nonetheless.) The other is that there is a deeper conceptual logic to be found at work in such categories of cultural self-consciousness than is suggested by the way in which they are usually deployed, as markers for chronologically distinct and empirically identifiable periods, movements, forms or styles: a logic of historical totalization which raises questions about the nature of historical time itself.[3]

It is no longer the case, as it was more than a decade ago, before the publication of Berman's pioneering work and Habermas's lectures on the topic, that 'discourse and controversy over the meaning of modernity . . . have virtually ceased to exist' in the wake of a triumphant postmodernism eager only to rediscover itself in history.[4] Yet the revival of interest in modernity has focused more on the idea of reason, and the variety of its social forms, than on the concept of modernity itself. There remains scope for further clarification of what kind of concept modernity is and, in particular, for a more systematic

consideration of the relations between its various aspects than has
characterized the English-language literature to date. Chapter 1 undertakes this task in the form of a critique of the failure to attend
sufficiently closely to the temporal dimension of 'modernity' as a form
of historical time.

'Modernity' and 'postmodernity', 'modernism', 'postmodernism'
and 'avant-garde' are categories of historical consciousness which are
constructed at the level of the apprehension of history as a whole.
More specifically, they are categories of historical totalization in the
medium of cultural experience. As such, each involves a distinct form
of historical temporalization – a distinctive way of temporalizing
'history' – through which the three dimensions of phenomenological
or lived time (past, present and future) are linked together within the
dynamic and eccentric unity of a single historical view. Associated
with such temporalizations are both particular historical epistemo-
logies (defining the temporal forms and limits of knowledge) and
particular orientations towards practice, particular *politics of time*.
Modernism and postmodernism – like conservatism, traditionalism
and reaction – are interventions in the field of the politics of time. The
historical study of cultural forms needs to be rethought within the
framework of competing philosophies and politics of time. In this
way, the deeper structures that underlie and animate a wide variety
of recent work in social and cultural theory might be exposed to
critical scrutiny.

From this perspective, the popularity and tenacity of postmodernism as a diagnostic discourse of 'the times' can be seen to
bespeak a desire for totalization in the medium of cultural experience
which is not currently satisfied by any other critical tendency.
Postmodernism inherits the terrain not only of Marxism but, thereby,
of classical German philosophy as well: the field of the philosophy
of history.[5] Postmodernism, one might say, is the revenge of the
philosophical discourse of modernity upon Marxism for neglecting
problems in the philosophy of history. Yet if postmodernism offers
a new way out of German idealism, via its 'incredulity towards meta-
narratives',[6] consistency demands that it extend this incredulity
towards itself. If there is a single philosophical trait by which postmodernism is marked, for all its avoidance of 'philosophy', it is
surely its susceptibility to the corrosive power of this paradox of self-
referentiality.[7]

But this is not a book about postmodernism; nor, except in an
extended sense, is it about modernism either. Rather, it is a book
about time which grew out of a book about modernity, a book about

the philosophy of time which grew out of a book about the culture of modernity: two books, written as one. Yet they are not so different as this description might suggest. For modernity is a culture of time of which nineteenth- and twentieth-century European philosophy has been a crucial constituent part. Whether one is, like Baudelaire, 'weighed down, every moment, by the conception and sensation of time',[8] or, like the Surrealists, energized and uplifted by its trans-formative power, it has become increasingly hard to be indifferent to either its simple passage or sudden ruptural force. Time imposes itself as a problem within nineteenth- and twentieth-century European philosophy, in a qualitatively different way from that in which it previously appeared as a paradigmatic example of the unchanging character of philosophical questions, in the new twofold form of the problem of *history* and the problem of *death*.[9]

The specific problem posed by modernity as a structure of histori-cal time concerns its totalizing form. This is the topic of chapter 2. Modernity, it is argued in chapter 1, is a totalizing temporalization of history. Yet what justifies such totalization in the face of the future? Or, to put the question another way, what future is there for an emphatic conception of historical experience after the critique of Hegelianism, within which I include the philosophy of history implicit in the political culture of the Communist tradition? Chapter 2 follows Ricoeur, in approaching this question through a rethinking of the relevance of post-Hegelian phenomenology to an understanding of the narrative structure of historical experience. It suggests that we cannot avoid the totalization of history because of the existential structure of temporalization. Totalization is thus an operation to be negotiated, not forsaken. Debate about historical totalization is always (whether or not it knows it) effectively debate about its forms, meaning and limits, rather than its possibility *per se*. The problem with Hegelianism derives not from totalization as such, but from its specific mode: the combination of the positing of an *immanent narrative* end to history with the claim to *absolute* knowledge. Some other standpoint is needed from which to construct the idea of history as a developing whole. This is found in chapter 2 in an extension of the early Heidegger's analysis of death to the level of historical time.

Furthermore, whereas Ricoeur restricts his phenomenological exploration of narrative form to the confines of poetics, it too is extended here to embrace the ontology of historical time. There is an ontological dimension to historical temporalization which allows us to treat Heidegger's early work as a site from which the conceptual-ization of the totalizing structure of historical time might set out anew, freed from the metaphysic of an immanent narrative end. However, if Heidegger offers an ontological (more specifically, an existential) take on temporalization as a totalizing process which is nonethless *eccentric*, and thus only fleetingly resolved, his argument requires extension to history in a fundamentally different manner from that undertaken by Heidegger himself. It is here that Ricoeur's work is useful once again. For in conceptualizing history as a mediation of phenomenological and cosmological forms, it insists upon a naturalistic dimension to human existence which Heidegger's conception of human existence as *Dasein* (literally, being-there), a self-interpreting being, methodologically excludes.

Chapter 2 develops a modified Heideggerianism in order to keep the question of historical totalization alive in the wake of the collapse of Hegelianism, by reading *Being and Time* in the shadow of Hegel's philosophy of history. Chapter 3 reads Hegel's *Phenomenology* in the shadow of *Being and Time*. For if Heidegger's notion of differential temporality offers the basis for a new concept of historical time, Hegel's notion of recognition is needed to bridge the gap between Heidegger's overly individualistic definition of *Dasein* and the social space of history. Hegel's dialectic of recognition transforms Heidegger's conception of temporality in the direction of Levinas's work, questioning its inherent 'mineness' and depicting it, instead, as the product of temporalization via relations with others. Heidegger's achievement was to uncover the existential structure of temporalization in the anticipation of death. Hegel's allegorical account of the struggle for recognition socializes this picture by locating the source of death (the meaning of death), and hence of time, in the other. Chapter 3 attempts to bring these two arguments together into the coherence of a single view, from which the individual and sociohistorical aspects of the process might then be explored in tandem, on the basis of a common conceptual ground. This is attempted in the second half of chapter 3 and chapter 4, respectively: in the first case, via a consideration of the various combinations of Hegelian and Heideggerian motifs in (primarily French) psychoanalytic theory; in the second, with recourse to Walter Benjamin's historical sociology of cultural form.

Psychoanalytical metapsychology offers an account of the temporalization of time for the child by the death drive through primary identification as primary socialization. However, it is indifferent to the variety of temporal forms through which historical experience is constructed for adults through cultural practice – except insofar as they mirror the temporal patterns of unconscious desire. In this respect, psychoanalysis usurps the ancient role of philosophy as a 'practice of death'.[10] In Benjamin, on the other hand, we have the beginnings of an account of the temporalization of history by cultural form. This enables us to concretize our previous depiction of historical time (the temporalization of history by the anticipation of a timeless end, a *historical death*), in terms of a series of culturally specific representations of ends constituting history in a variety of different ways – as ethics (Levinas), tradition (Gadamer), chronology (historicism) or modernity (Heidegger and Benjamin), respectively. Furthermore, insofar as these forms are themselves the products of historically specific practices, they are possible objects of transformative practice. We are thus able to begin to give a more concrete meaning to the idea of a politics of time. A politics of time is a politics which takes the temporal structures of social practices as the specific objects of its transformative (or preservative) intent. Benjamin's and Heidegger's philosophies are themselves part of their authors' (radically conflicting) politics of time.

Modernity is a form of historical time which valorizes the new as the product of a constantly self-negating temporal dynamic. Yet its abstract temporal form remains open to a variety of competing articulations. In particular, by producing the old as remorselessly as it produces the new, and in equal measure, it provokes forms of traditionalism the temporal logic of which is quite different from that of tradition as conventionally received. Both traditionalism and reaction are distinctively modern forms. Chapter 5 extends the discussion of Benjamin's philosophical and political modernism, begun in the previous chapter, into a comparative investigation of the philosophical roots of the reactionary modernism of Heidegger's fascism. Heidegger's failure to acknowledge the social constitution of existence, identified in chapter 3, is found here to underlie the pure temporal constructivism of his construal of 'authentic historicality' as repetition. For the Heidegger of *Being and Time*, the individual can give authentic meaning to his or her existence only through the appropriation of the (mythic) destiny of a people as the choice of his or her individual fate.

One way back from such mystification to actual historical life is provided by a re-reading of 'everydayness' in *Being and Time* from the standpoint of the idea of recognition. Everydayness is also a notion which Benjamin's work requires, if the ecstatic futurity of its quasi-Messianic 'now' is to be mediated with the temporality of narrative so as to have an effect upon identity and action. The book thus closes by bringing together its readings of Ricoeur, Heidegger and Benjamin to focus on the possibilities for historical experience embedded in the apparently ahistorical everyday – a concept which is further expounded with reference to Lefebvre's reformulation of Marxism as a critique of everyday life. By concluding with a discussion of Lefebvre, the book both projects itself tentatively forward into the space of cultural analysis, and returns to the trajectory of Western Marxism at one of its most culturally productive, but theoretically fractured, points.

In setting out from a theoretical problem within cultural history (epochal periodization) with tools taken from the history of philosophy, my approach is in part reconstructive, in part diagnostic and critical, and in part constructive, throughout. The book draws its inspiration from a wide range of sources (too wide to allow anything like a comprehensive discussion of its constituent elements), to which it is heavily indebted. But for all its apparent diversity (aptly described by an early reader in terms of the danger of it turning into 'a magical mystery tour of contemporary theory'), it is nonetheless directed by a singular philosophical intent: the exploration of the idea of a politics of time. Hopefully, it offers neither an eclectic collection nor a merely syncretic combination of positions, but a movement towards theory construction through appropriative critique; hence the necessity to keep returning to Heidegger, to grapple with the complexities of adopting and extending arguments from so exclusive a thinker, whose great, early unfinished work (*Being and Time*) remains so fertile a source of both theoretical inspiration and political disquiet.

It is a sign of times, perhaps, that there is so much about Heidegger in this book, and so little about Marx. Yet this may be misleading. For if there is a single figure who stands behind its project, it is Benjamin, whose own work itself remains as radically unfinished as ever – although he would have scorned any help from Heidegger in developing its terms. In letters from the early 1930s, Benjamin outlined a way of thinking about Marxism which has considerable relevance in the current context. He distinguished between Communism (as a political tradition), historical materialism (as a theoretical project), and Marxism (as an orthodox interpretation of the latter, in which the authority of tradition constricts its development by imposing 'the unpractical, unproductive form of the credo'). Benjamin argued that the affirmation of the political tradition (Communism) left the theory (historical materialism) 'a much greater freedom than the Marxists suspect'.[11] This is a useful reminder for a period in which the crisis of the political tradition (socialism) is producing as many simple-minded ideas about the theoretically 'outmoded' as retreats to the creed, in both its 'legitimating' and 'academic' variants.[12]

One thing which Benjamin's writings demonstrate is the amount of philosophical work still to be done in developing a materialist conception of history. Another is the impossibility of doing that work consistently apart from philosophical reflection upon the forms of time-consciousness produced by the variety of historically established social practices which make up any particular present. But if there is a philosophical deficit in contemporary cultural theory (as there is, to a lesser extent, within Marxism), there is a corresponding socio-logical deficit built into the forms of universality of the philosophical tradition. Marx recognized this, but he misjudged the complexity of the problems to which it leads. One of the aims of this work is to provide some philosophical resources for rethinking the terms of a materialist cultural theory. And if, at times, its narrative takes on the frustrating appearance of a shaggy dog story, I would like to think that this has as much to do with philosophy's logic of presupposition as any resistance to theoretical completion – which is ultimately, of course, little more than a denial of death. Which brings us back to Nam June Paik and his unread pile of the most important Japanese philosophical works on the subject of time. This book is for Paik. For what if there was time to read about time? What might it tell us about the character of our times?

Earlier versions of parts of this work have been tried out as papers or published as sections of shorter texts. I would like to thank the University of Essex Symposia on 'Postmodernism and the Re-reading of Modernity' in summer 1990, for inviting me to present what turned out to be the first draft of chapter 1; an intermediate, shorter version was published as 'Modernity is a Qualitative, Not a Chronological, Category' in *New Left Review* 192, March/April 1992, and in Francis Barker et al., *Postmodernism and the Re-reading of Modernity*, Manchester University Press, Manchester, 1992. The Deutsche Haus at Columbia University, New York and the Humanities Graduate Seminar at the University of New South Wales, Australia provided me with opportunities to subject preliminary versions of my reading of Ricoeur in chapter 2 to critical scrutiny, in the spring of 1992. A summary of the general argument which follows from that reading was presented to the *Radical Philosophy* conference, 'The Politics of Experience', in London in November 1993. It subsequently appeared as 'The Politics of Time' in *Radical Philosophy* 68, Autumn 1994. The first two sections of chapter 3 were presented as a paper to the

Research Seminar of the Centre for Research in Modern European Philosophy, Middlesex University, in April 1994. Some of the material on Walter Benjamin in the second halves of chapters 4 and 5 first appeared in 'Small-scale Victories, Large-scale Defeats: Walter Benjamin's Politics of Time', in Andrew Benjamin and Peter Osborne (eds), *Walter Benjamin's Philosophy: Destruction and Experience*, Routledge, London, 1994 – the argument of which is modified here and considerably extended. The first two sections of chapter 5 develop thoughts first sketched in the concluding section of 'Tactics, Ethics or Temporality? Heidegger's Politics Reviewed', *Radical Philosophy* 70, March/April 1995. Kristin Ross induced me to think seriously about the everyday, despite initial scepticism, with an (unfulfilled) commission to reconstruct its philosophical history. The discussion of everydayness in chapter 5 benefited from presentation of a draft to the Humanities Graduate Centre Seminar, Middlesex University, in November 1994.

Andrew Benjamin, Susan Buck-Morss, Jane Chamberlain, Peter Dews, Jonathan Dollimore, Gregory Elliott, John Fletcher, John Kraniauskas, Joseph McCarney, and Jonathan Rée commented upon draft material from various chapters. I am grateful to them all for their encouragement and their criticisms. Gregory Elliott copy-edited the manuscript with his customary scrupulousness and precision. The School of Philosophy & Religious Studies and the Research Committee of the Faculty of Humanities, Middlesex University, provided me with the leave, in the form of a Faculty Research Fellowship, necessary to complete the book.

Finally, and most fundamentally, thanks are due to Lynne Segal for her loving support throughout, not to mention a certain productive scepticism about too much philosophical abstraction.

Modernity: A Different Time

*A universe in pieces, abandoned, without hope, an image of the real
. . . Everything has taken on the miraculous tint of time.*

                                                        Louis Aragon

Two fundamental assumptions underlie, and vitiate, most of the writing about 'modernity' in recent debates about historical periodization and cultural change. One is that the term can be used unproblematically to refer to some chronologically distinct span of historical time, marked out by epochal changes in the structure of European societies – whatever the precise limits of such a time-span are taken to be. The other is that the question of the forms of time-consciousness produced within European societies during this period can be separated off from the question of the temporality of periodization itself. 'Modernity' is routinely assumed to be an empirical category of historical sociology, used to register certain inaugural breaks or ruptures in the development of societies, at a number of different levels – from political, economic and legal forms, through religious and cultural organization, to the structure of the family, the relations between sexes, and the psychological constitution of the individual – within the underlying unity of a 'period'.[1] The forms of temporality with which these various domains are associated are rarely connected to the temporality implicit in, or proper to, the use of modernity as a periodizing category. Indeed, the idea of modernization, through which the sociological concept of modernity was extended beyond its original reference to European and North American societies, in the context of the processes of post-war decolonization, notoriously presumes a homogeneous continuum of historical time across which comparative judgements about social development may be made in abstraction from all qualitative temporal differences.

These assumptions served sociology well for the best part of a century, insofar as they allowed it to constitute its object as a discipline ('modern' societies) in a way which simultaneously distinguished it from history and anthropology, on the one hand, and journalism, on the other, while nonetheless retaining its links to the concerns of all three ('the past', '"other" societies' and 'the present day', respectively), in the spirit of an empirical objectivity. However, the problematic character of these assumptions comes into view as soon as the issue of *change within the present* is raised otherwise than as an extrapolation of developmental tendencies built into the relationship between pre-given structural social types ('modernity' and 'tradition'); that is to say, as soon as the present is viewed, however briefly, from the practical perspective of the radical openness of the historical process. This challenge to the sociological concept of modernity has taken two main forms: first, during the period of the formation of sociology as a discipline, from the theoretical and political alternative of Marxism; and second, more recently, through the more theoretically and politically diffuse, but no less strident, claims that have been made on behalf of the idea of postmodernity. Each disrupts the complacency of the sociological category of modernity in a different way.[2]

Marxism contests the bifurcation of history into 'traditional' and 'modern' societies through a periodization based on the idea of modes of production: historically distinct combinations of social relations and material forces of production that are understood to condition 'the general process of social, political and intellectual life'.[3] And it locates itself, practically, within this history through its identification with those social forces internal to the capitalist mode of production which it takes to represent the principle of a new system of production, in which the contradictory class dynamics of hitherto existing societies will be abolished through the abolition of economically based social classes (communism). From this perspective, the idea of modernity may be understood in two very different ways. Either it is short-hand for the most 'advanced' social forms at any particular historical moment (the forms of 'today'), judged by the criterion of their contribution to the development of the productive forces on a world-historical scale; or, in its sociological sense, it is an ideological term which masks significant differences between societies by attending only to certain superficial features they have in common.

In the first case, the term acquires a new social content by being situated within the developmental perspective of historical materialism. Marx himself often used 'modern' in this way, to refer to particular features of industrial capitalism: 'modern manufacture', for example, and 'modern industry'.[4] In the latter instance, it is more profoundly problematized. However, a crucial question remains. This is whether the relocation of the sociological concept of modernity within the developmental perspective of historical materialism affects its temporal structure as a category of historical periodization, or whether it just gives it a new, changing historical content. Is there a new conception of historical time implicit in the developmental perspective of a materialist conception of history? Or does it, like the sociology of modernity, take the homogeneous character of historical time for granted by the manner in which it makes comparative judgements between modes of production? The first position is shared by Benjamin, Sartre and Althusser; the latter is taken by Kracauer, who insists that Marx, like Comte, 'unquestioningly confide[s] in the magic of chronology'.[5] However, the difference is smaller than one might think, since all of the former agree both that the new materialist conception lacks self-consciousness, and that the Marxist tradition has tended to regress behind it in the most prevalent forms of its practical consciousness (stemming from the period of the Second International). As Sartre put it: 'Marxism caught a glimpse of true temporality when it criticised and destroyed the bourgeois notion of "progress" . . . But – without ever having said so – . . . renounced these studies and prefered to make use of "progress" again for its own benefit.'[6] Furthermore, when each of them came to develop their own version of the 'true temporality' of history, implicit in Marx's work, they turned out to be very different indeed.

The situation regarding the idea of postmodernity is rather different. It problematizes the category of modernity, neither by giving it a new content (by locating it within a different theory of history), nor by questioning its ideological function, but rather by proposing that certain societies have experienced (and are experiencing) transformations of a sufficiently radical kind to distinguish them from those social forms hitherto taken to define what is modern, to the extent of justifying their description as 'postmodern'.[7] This would seem to offer far less of a challenge to the sociological concept of modernity than Marxism, since it not only fails to contest its terms, theoretically, but actually accepts them, insofar as it defines itself through its relation to the periodizing concept of modernity, by simple temporal negation (the logic of the 'post'). Indeed, after a brief initial period in which the idea of the postmodern looked like a further, if not final, threat to a disintegrating discipline (sociology), it has since proved to be excellent cover for a return to classical sociological theorizing in a new, terminologically transformed and less empirically oriented guise. Once the 'modern' becomes 'tradition', the 'postmodern' can play the modern, and the temporal structure of the orthodox sociological concept of modernity can be redeployed across the new field. At the same time, simple slippages between usages can generate exciting new paradoxes. Thus, 'postmodernity' can appear as the product of both 'de-traditionaliza-tion' and 're-traditionalization' simultaneously, without the glimmer of a dialectic, if the reference of 'tradition' is allowed to oscillate between different uses of 'the modern'.

On closer examination, however, the idea of postmodernity turns out to have rather more subversive potential, once we set aside its relations to the *content* of the sociological concept of modernity, and reflect upon the way in which the term 'modernity' is dependent for its meaning on identification with some specific present. For if the primary, root sense of 'modernity', prior to its theoretical elaboration or the attribution to it of any particular historical content, is 'the quality or character of being modern'; and if the modern, in its primary sense, is simply that 'pertaining to the present and recent times', or 'originating in the current age or period',[8] then, paradoxi-cally, 'postmodernity' must be the name for a new modernity. Once we reflect upon this theoretically, however (as opposed to simply accepting it, and adjusting our terminology accordingly),[9] the conceptual dynamics of both terms, in their orthodox sociological usage, are thrown into crisis.[10]

There is a tension between the use of modernity as an empirical category of historical sociology and its inherent self-referentiality, whereby it necessarily denotes the time of its utterance, whenever the question of change within the present is at issue. The idea of post-modernity is constituted at the point of this tension. In this sense, it is undoubtedly part of the problematic of the modern. But this should not be taken to suggest that the new term is redundant or that, as Marshall Berman has suggested, movements which call themselves postmodern can 'only re-enact, rather than overcome, modernism's deepest troubles and impasses'.[11] For if current uses of 'postmodern' and its cognates paradoxically remain within the framework of 'modernity', they do more than just repeat its existing forms. Rather, via their paradoxical character, they both draw attention to, and further develop, its contradictory structure, which is concealed by the nominalism and empiricism of its everyday sociological construal. Examination of claims on behalf of the postmodern demand a reflexivity about the temporal structure of modernity that has hitherto been lacking. They prompt a new version of the question already raised by our brief discussion of Marxism: namely, what form of temporality is at stake in the use of 'modernity' as a category of historical periodization such that the paradox of the postmodern could arise? Or, more directly, what *kind of time* does 'modernity' | *space?* inscribe?

In addressing this question, I take as my starting point and thematic perspective Perry Anderson's critique of Marshall Berman's recovery and celebration of a phenomenological concept of modernity in his groundbreaking text *All That is Solid Melts into Air*.[12] Berman's book is, I believe, still the most immediately appealing general account of 'modernity' available, whilst Anderson's critique strikes at, but only partially hits, what I take to be both the main difficulty with the concept and the source of its enduring strength: namely, its homogenization through abstraction of a form of historical consciousness associated with a variety of socially, politically and culturally heterogeneous processes of change. Berman's book has the virtue of dealing with modernity as at once a phenomenological and a sociological category. Anderson's critique has the advantage of raising the question of whether the category is not a merely ideological one (a form of misrepresentation), in the context of a discussion of the conception of historical time required by a materialist conception of history.

This chapter focuses on three distinct but connected approaches to the concept of modernity: modernity as a *category of historical periodization*, a *quality of social experience*, and an *(incomplete) project*. Underlying and unifying its account is a concern, derived in large part from the writings of Benjamin and Koselleck, with modernity as a distinct but paradoxical form of historical temporality. Each of the three approaches discussed isolates a different temporal dimension of this underlying conception: its inscription of the *past*, the *present*, and the *future*, respectively. The key to their comprehension will thus be seen to lie in their relations to each other; that is to say, in the dialectics of a certain *temporalization of 'history'*.

Modernity as experience and misrecognition: Berman and Anderson

Berman's account of modernity as the experience of a dynamic and inherently contradictory process of constant change, a 'maelstrom of perpetual disintegration and renewal'[13] that opens up and closes down avenues of human possibility in more or less equal portions, is well known. I shall not expound it here, except to draw attention to those two of its features which bear most directly on our current concerns. One is the disjunction between the centrality to it of Berman's account of Marx (registered in the title of the book, adopted from the

Communist Manifesto) and the distance it takes from Marx's specifically political analyses. The other is its almost total disregard for the
complexities of 'modernity' as a periodizing category. Marx is not
merely celebrated as a theoretician of modernity, uncoverer of the contradictory dynamics and broader social consequences of the process of
capital accumulation; he is hailed as the herald of 'a paradigmatically
modernist *faith*'.[14] His writings are seen to combine analytic insight
into the destructive side of the process of capitalist modernization,
with an affirmation of its emancipatory potential comparable in scope
to the tragic sweep of Goethe's *Faust*. Indeed, in many respects, they
are read as a response to the challenge of *Faust*. But for all Berman's
appreciation of the dialectical structure of this picture, a crucial part of
Marx's own version of it is painted over as outmoded: the formation
of a particular class subject. However, contrary to the logic of Western
Marxism, Berman refuses to let this undermine his affirmative stance
to the processes in question. If anything, it bolsters it, replacing the
fallibility of a specific historical projection with the apparently unlimited possibilities of a radically open future. Yet a major part of the
intellectual justification for this affirmative stance has been discarded.

This cavalier approach to the elements of an integrated analysis is
mirrored in Berman's neglect of questions of periodization. Despite
its historical intent (the book aims to renew our sense of modernity
by giving us back 'a sense of our own modern roots'), no attempt is
made to trace that sense of the modern as a 'coherent whole' which is
Berman's object, back to the use of the term as a periodizing category.
What is taken to be the first phase of modernity, 'from the start of the
seventeenth century to the end of the eighteenth', is allotted a mere
six lines in a book of nearly four hundred pages. The periodization
of modernity is taken for granted, and its first phase is ignored.[15] The
reason appears to be that during this period there was no popular
vocabulary for the articulation of the emergent experience of change;
something that was not remedied until the revolutionary wave of
the 1790s. This is important to Berman because he is concerned with
a situation – his present – in which more or less all societies, world-
wide, are allegedly undergoing similar experiences of change to a
greater or lesser extent. His account thus concentrates on those forms
of cultural self-consciousness about such change (modern*ism*) that
might inform contemporary experience. Yet as Anderson shows, this
self-imposed restriction has significant theoretical effects.

Anderson's objections to Berman's account derive more or less
exclusively from his reading of Marx. They are fourfold. In the first
place, Berman is seen to have produced an egregiously one-sided

version of Marx's account of capitalist modernization, which falls prey to an uncritical, because undifferentiated, concept of historical time. This is reflected, secondly, in an abstract and 'perennial' concept of modernism, which fails to register the historical specificity of aesthetic modernism as a portmanteau concept for what is in fact a set of distinct, if conjuncturally related, movements, which are in any case now definitively over. Thirdly, his modernist ontology of unlimited self-development, although apparently derived from Marx, is actually based in an idealist form of radical liberalism which, from a materialist standpoint at least, is self-contradictory. Finally, his account of modernity as permanent revolution strips the concept of revolution of all temporal and political determinacy, robbing it, in particular, of its temporal specificity as a punctual event. 'The vocation of a socialist revolution,' Anderson concludes with a characteristic flourish, 'would be neither to prolong nor to fulfil modernity, but to abolish it.'[16]

The most striking thing about this critique is the way in which it oscillates between two different uses of 'modernity'. On the one hand, it is treated as a flawed and misleading category for the identification and analysis of historical processes which are better understood in quite different terms. On the other, it appears as the legitimate designation for an historical phenomenon, the theoretical comprehension, but not the identification, of which is contested. The difference is difficult, but crucial. Anderson equivocates. He seems, in general, to adopt the first sense: he offers a Marxist critique of the discourse of modernity. Yet his conclusion emphatically presumes the second: modernity is an historical reality, capable of 'prolongation', 'fulfilment' and 'abolition'. The connection resides in the reflexivity of historical experience itself: 'modernity' has a reality as a form of cultural self-consciousness, a lived experience of historical time, which cannot be denied, however one-sided it might be as a category of historical understanding. It is the texture of this historical experience of cultural form that Berman sets out to recreate in the name of its admittedly contradictory emancipatory potential. For Berman, in other words, modernity is in some quite basic sense an historical given, as a form of experience. For Anderson, on the other hand, whilst it might be given as an ideological form (a mode of experience produced and reproduced by the rhythm of the capitalist market), it is given in this specific, restricted and ultimately pejorative sense only. It is a misrepresentation, a form of misrecognition. In its place we are offered an alternative, Marxist account of historical development based on a periodization of modes of production, the rise and decline of classes, and the claims of 'a complex and differential temporality, in which episodes or eras

[are] discontinuous with each other, and heterogeneous within themselves'.[17] Alongside this stands the aspiration to a society that would no longer systematically generate such an illusory form of social consciousness.

The increased specificity promised by such a model of differential time gives it considerable appeal, but there are problems with its opposition to the idea of modernity. For it remains unclear what the relationship is between this model of differential temporality and the ceaseless process of temporal differentiation associated with the idea of modernity itself. In particular, it is unclear what relations there might be between the kind of discontinuity established by what Marx called 'social revolutions' and the use of modernity as an epochal category.[18] The suspicion thus arises that Anderson has seized on a deficiency in Berman's presentation of the concept of modernity (its reduction to a celebratory 'dialectic of modernisation and modernism'), rather than, as he supposes, a fundamental problem with the category itself, which he wants to replace, or at all events decode, with conjunctural analyses of the cultural consequences of capitalist development – conjunctural analyses which, in their privileging of the moment of the present, would appear to be nothing but a modification of the temporal problematic of 'modernity' itself. This uncertainty derives from the absence in both Berman's and Anderson's accounts of an independent treatment of the logic of modernity as a category of historical periodization.

Berman periodizes modernity into three fairly conventional phases – 1500–1789, 1789–1900 and 1900 onwards – of which the middle one is privileged by him as the golden age to be recovered.[19] But there is no consideration of the way in which the idea of modernity itself marks a new way of periodizing history; no consideration of the relation between the kind of historical time occupied by modernity as an epochal category and that which is internal to modernity itself and registered by Berman in terms of the temporal logic of modernism, that 'amazing variety of visions and ideas that aim to make men and women the subjects as well as the objects of modernisation'.[20] To this extent, Berman remains within the tradition of an unreflexive sociology of modernity, wherein the attempt to establish what is new about 'modern' societies fails to reflect upon the temporal co-ordinates and conceptual implications of this form of investigation itself.[21] For there *is* something decidedly new about modernity as a category of historical periodization: namely, that unlike other forms of epochal periodization (mythic, Christian or dynastic, for example), it is defined solely in terms of temporal determinants, and temporal determinants of a very specific kind. As Adorno put it: 'Modernity is a qualitative, not a chronological, category.'[22] The failure to recognize the logic of these determinants underlies naive concepts of 'post-modernity' as a new historical epoch which succeeds modernity in historical time in the same way that modernity itself might be thought to have succeeded the 'Middle' Ages.[23]

In order to get a grasp of this particular temporal logic, it is useful to refer to Koselleck's reconstruction of the semantic prehistory of *Neuzeit* (literally, 'new time'), a German term for modernity which is found in its composite form only after 1870.[24] Consideration of this history will help us to grasp the relative independence of modernity as a category of historical periodization from both the problematic of modernization, to which it is effectively assimilated by Anderson, and the idea of modernism, through which it is celebrated by Berman with such an apparent lack of social and political specificity.

From *Neue Zeit* to *Neuzeit*: Koselleck's historical semantics

The distinctive characteristic of *Neuzeit* as an epochal term is that like *der Moderne*, *les temps modernes*, or 'the modern age', which register the presentness of an epoch to the time of its classification, but even more explicitly, it 'refers only to time, characterising it as new, without, however, providing any indication of the historical content of this time or even its nature as a period'.[25] The conditions for such an abstract sense of the historical meaning of the present appear to have developed in five main stages.

1. The word *modernus*, meaning 'of today' as opposed to 'of yesterday' – what is over, finished, or historically surpassed – first came into use in the course of the fifth century AD at the time of the collapse of the Roman Empire, when the cyclical opposition of 'old and new' characteristic of pagan antiquity was replaced by the sense of an irreversible break with the past. (It derived from *modo*, meaning 'recently'.) Generational conflicts about the prestige of ancient writers had appeared in Antiquity (in Horace and Ovid, for example), but as Le Goff points out, 'they did not have a word for "modern", since they did not contrast *novus* with *antiquus*.'[26] The sense of the present as new which emerges at this time became the basis for the conflicts between Ancients and Moderns that punctuated the Middle Ages, from the second half of the twelfth century to the beginning of the Renaissance.

2. The first major semantic shift took place with the consciousness

of a new age which developed in Europe in the course of the fifteenth century. This was initially registered in three ways: by the emergence of the terms 'Renaissance' and 'Reformation' for ideas denoting the threshold of a new (unnamed) period; by the designation of the preceding epoch, now taken to be definitively over, as the Middle Ages; and by the fixing of the term 'Antiquity' to denote the pagan culture of ancient Greece and Rome. In the process, a new relationship between the antique or ancient and the modern was established at the expense of the Middle Ages, since the Renaissance gave precedence to the ancient over all other cultures. Here, modern is opposed to medieval rather than to ancient, and the modern has a right to preference only insofar as it *imitates* the ancient.

3. In the third stage, which roughly runs from the sixteenth century to the end of the seventeenth, the threshold concepts of Renaissance and Reformation through which consciousness of a new age was initially registered, were transformed into ideas descriptive of now completed historical periods. This called for a term denoting the new period as a whole which followed the Middle Ages. It is at this point that the phrase *neue Zeit* comes into use – although only in a neutral, chronological sense at first – signifying that the times are 'new' by contrast with the Middle Ages or *mittlere Zeiten*. There is no specification of a criterion of newness here. *Neue Zeit* is thus not, at this stage, a category of historical periodization in any substantive sense. Rather, it stands in for the absence of one, along with the continuing use of *modernus*. The connotations of *neue* are, however, sharper than *modernus*, since it had acquired what Le Goff describes as 'an almost sacred baptismal character'[27] in the context of medieval Christianity, for which novelty unconnected to the primordial values of the origin was sacrilegious. As Berman has recently reminded us, for the Bible it is God alone who 'makes all things new'.[28] This is, of course, also the period of the famous Quarrel of the Ancients and the Moderns, or the 'Battle of the Books' as it came to be known. If the Renaissance is to be characterized by the replacement of the authority of the Church by that of the Ancients, it was this latter form of authority which now, in turn, became the object of attack.

4. It was only during the fourth phase, the Enlightenment, that the initially neutral phrase *neue Zeit* came to acquire the sense of a qualitative claim about the newness of the times, in the sense of their being 'completely other, even better than what has gone before'.[29] The condition for this transformation of the sense of the relationship of the present (and its immediate past) to the more distant past – from being a simple addition in a linear sequence of chronological time, to

a qualitative transcendence of the past of an epochal type which is more than the mere rebirth of a more ancient spirit – was a reorientation towards the future. This reorientation could only take place once Christian eschatology had shed its constant expectation of the imminent arrival of doomsday, and once the advance of the sciences and the growing consciousness of the 'New World' and its peoples had opened up new horizons of expectation. Only at this point was a conceptual space available for an abstract temporality of qualitative newness which could be of epochal significance, because it could now be extrapolated into an otherwise empty future, without end, and hence without limit. The distinctive structure of the temporality of modernity may thus be seen to derive from a combination of the Christian conception of time as *irreversible* with criticism of its corresponding concept of eternity.[30] 'Modernity', in the subsequently consolidated sense of *Neuzeit*, may in this respect be understood as the term for an historical sublime – a point of some interest in relation to recent purportedly 'postmodern' attempts to reappropriate the concept of the sublime. It gives rise to a new, distinctively historical version of the age-old problem of legitimacy. As Blumenberg puts it: 'Modernity (*Neuzeit*) was the first and only age that understood itself as an epoch and, in so doing, simultaneously created the other epochs.' The problem of legitimacy is latent in its 'claim to carry out a radical break with tradition, and in the incongruity between this claim and the reality of history, which can never begin entirely anew'.[31] It is this problem of legitimacy that underlies the recent attraction of the term 'postmodern'.

These developments culminate at the end of the eighteenth century in the context of the acceleration of historical experience precipitated by the Industrial and French Revolutions, in the consolidation of the emergent semantic potential of *neue Zeit* in the coinage *neueste Zeit*: a phrase which definitively separates the qualitative dimension of the idea from its continuing, more 'neutral' usage. 'What could not be achieved in the concept of *neue Zeit* [because of the ambiguity produced by its continued neutral usage – PO] was effected by *neueste Zeit*. It became a concept for the contemporary epoch opening up a new period [which] did not simply retrospectively register a past epoch.' Similarly, in the decades around 1800, 'revolution', 'progress', 'development', 'crisis', 'Zeitgeist', 'epoch' and 'history' itself all acquire temporal determinations never present before:

> Time is no longer the medium in which all histories take place; it gains an historical quality ... history no longer occurs in, but through, time. Time becomes a dynamic and historical force in its own right. Presupposed by this formulation of experience is a concept of history which is

likewise new: the collective singular form of *Geschichte*, which since around 1780 can be conceived as history in and for itself in the absence of an associated subject or object.[32]

Because of the qualitative transformation in the temporal matrix of historical terms which occurs at this time, 'modernity' in the full sense of the term is generally taken to begin here. The modern is no longer simply opposed either to the ancient or to the medieval, but to 'tradition' in general.

5. It is this full sense of a 'newest time' (*neueste Zeiten*), opening up a new period by virtue of the quality of the temporality it involves, which was condensed and generalized in the second half of the nineteenth century into the ideas of *Neuzeit* and *modernité*, therewith coming to be understood as constitutive of the temporality of modernity as such. It is this, the temporality of Baudelaire's and Flaubert's, Simmel's and Benjamin's late nineteenth-century modernity, the historical force of the fundamental objects of which 'lies solely in the fact that they are new',[33] which has been the focus of recent attention to modernity as an aesthetic concept, and more broadly, as a form of social experience. The logic of the new, fashion, and aesthetic modernism as a 'rebellion against the modernity of the philistine' which nonetheless works within the same temporal structure,[34] may thus be understood as the result of an aestheticization of 'modernity' as a form of historical consciousness and its transformation into a general model of social experience. In the course of this generalization of an epochal form of historical consciousness into the temporal form of experience itself the dialectical character of the new as the 'ever-same', articulated philosophically in Nietzsche's doctrine of eternal recurrence, and deciphered economically in Marx's analysis of the logic of commodity production, is revealed for the first time.

Finally, and more tentatively, to take us up to the present, we might complete this account by adding a sixth stage, in which the peculiar and paradoxical abstractness of the temporality of the new is at once problematized and affirmed. This is the stage after the Second World War during which, as Raymond Williams has put it, '"modern" shifts its reference from "now" to "just now" or even "then", and for some time has been a designation always going into the past with which [in English] "contemporary" may be contrasted for its presentness.'[35] 'Modernity', now fixed as a discrete historical period within its own temporal scheme, as the golden age of its cultural self-consciousness, hardens into a mere name and is left stranded in the past. The Quarrel Between the Ancients and the Moderns is replaced by a Quarrel between the Moderns and the Contemporaries.[36] 'All that is left to us is to become post-moderns.'[37] However, to become post-modern, in this sense at least, is simply to remain modern, to keep in step, a companion of the times, to be con-temporary. 'What, then, is the postmodern?', Lyotard asks: 'undoubtedly part of the modern. A work can [now – PO] only be modern if it is first postmodern. Postmodernism . . . is not modernism at its end but in the nascent state, and this state is constant.'[38] It is in the irreducible doubling of a reflexive concept of modernity as something which has happened, yet continues to happen – ever new but always, in its newness, the same – that the identity and difference of the 'modern' and the 'postmodern' plays itself out at the most abstract level of the formal determinations of time.

Koselleck's semantic prehistory of *Neuzeit* shows us the lived time-consciousness of late nineteenth-century European metropolitan modernity – that 'transitoriness' which lies at the core of the 'fugitive' and the 'contingent'[39] – as an intensified social embodiment of a form of historiographic consciousness which had been developing in Europe for some considerable time. On reflection, this is not so surprising, since each seems likely to have its origin in a common source: the temporalities of capital accumulation and its social and political consequences in the formation of capitalist societies. (The latter, it should be noted, can in no way be reduced to the former.) Nonetheless, an awareness of this fact can help us to distance ourselves from the apparent immediacy of the form as an all-engulfing structure of social consciousness, in order to examine it in its own right, freed from the polemical inflections it acquires in its more familiar affirmative cultural manifestations (modern*ism*). Once we do this, it becomes possible to see Anderson's alternative analytical frame of a 'complex and differential temporality', leading to strictly 'conjunctural' analyses – derived from Althusser's 'Outline for a Concept of Historical Time'[40] – as a variation on the very temporal paradigm it sets out to oppose. At same time, the extent to which modernity is a Western concept, inextricably linked to the history of European colonialism, and as such bound up with the politics of a shifting set of *spatial* relations, becomes clear. History, in Michelet's famous phrase, 'is first of all geography'.[41]

The quality of modernity: homogenization, differentiation and abstraction

'Modernity', we have seen, plays a peculiar dual role as a category of historical periodization: it designates the contemporaneity of an epoch to the time of its classification; yet it registers this contemporaneity in terms of a qualitatively new, self-transcending temporality which has the simultaneous effect of distancing the present from even that most recent past with which it is thus identified. It is this paradoxical doubling, or inherently dialectical quality, which makes modernity both so irresistible and so problematic a category. It is achieved through the abstraction of the logical structure of the process of change from its concrete historical determinants – an abstraction which parallels that at work in the development of money as a store of value (abstract labour-time).[42] The temporal matrix which is thus produced has three main characteristics:

1. Exclusive valorization of the historical (as opposed to the merely chronological) present over the past, as its negation and transcendence, and as the standpoint from which to periodize and understand history as a whole. History, as Koselleck puts it, is 'temporalized'. It becomes possible for an event to change its identity according to its shifting status in the advance of history as a whole.[43]

2. Openness towards an indeterminate future characterized only by its prospective transcendence of the historical present and its relegation of this present to a future past.

3. A tendential elimination of the historical present itself, as the vanishing point of a perpetual transition between a constantly changing past and an as yet indeterminate future; or, to put it another way, the present as the identity of duration and eternity: that 'now' which is not so much a gap 'in' time as a gap 'of' time.[44] The dialectic of the new, Adorno argues, *represses* duration insofar as 'the new is an invariant: the desire for the new.'[45] Modernity is permanent transition.

'Modernity', then, has no fixed, objective referent. *'It has only a subject, of which it is full.'*[46] It is the product, in the instance of each utterance, of an act of historical self-definition through *differentiation*, *identification* and *projection*, which transcends the order of chronology in the construction of a meaningful present. As Meschonnic puts it: 'Each time, the subject projects the values that constitute it onto an object . . . the object varies when the subject changes.'[47] At the same time, however, *contra* Meschonnic, the object itself is not composed by projection alone. In any particular case, it is also a possible object of historical inquiry (a real, objective referent) which constrains the subject in turn, in an ongoing dialectic of the constitution of historical identities and knowledges.

Anderson's objections to Berman's affirmation of this structure of experience centre on its abstract, homogenizing tendencies and, in particular, the 'fundamentally planar' conception of development as modernization to which it can, on occasion, give rise: 'a continuous-flow process in which there is no real differentiation of one conjuncture or epoch from another save in terms of the mere chronological succession of old and new, earlier and later, categories themselves subject to unceasing permutations of positions in one direction, as time goes by and the later becomes earlier, the newer older'.[48] Anderson is right, I think, to worry about homogenizing tendencies; right, too, to be sceptical about the political potential attributed by Berman to modernism for establishing new forms of collectivity out of the common structure of experiences of disintegration and renewal – although he probably underestimates its significance in this regard. But he is wrong to reduce the idea of modernity to the homogenization of historical time; an error which is compounded when he goes on to identify this homogenization with 'the mere chronological succession of old and new'.

There are a whole series of problems here. The first concerns the differential temporality introduced into the category of 'modernity' by virtue of the distinction it involves between modern and earlier 'times'; and its negation by the idea of modernization. Secondly, there is the differential character of the temporality internal to modernity itself, which is established by its qualitative distinction between chronological and historical time. (The 'next' is not necessarily the 'new'; or, at least, the 'next as new' is never simply the chronologically next: by what scale – seconds, hours, days, months, years?) Third, associated with this, is the problem of the abstractness of the new, the way it is dealt with by empirical theories of modernity, and the consequent idea of modernity as a project. Finally, there is the question of the form of temporality at work in conjunctural analyses and the hope held out by Anderson of thereby escaping the temporal structure of modernity. The problem posed by an insufficiently differentiated concept of modernization, it will be argued, cannot be reduced to a simple opposition between 'homogeneous' and 'differential' historical times. Rather, it concerns the possibilities and pitfalls built into the dialectics of homogenization and differentiation constitutive of the temporality of modernity, and the way in which these are bound up, inextricably, with the politics of a particular set of spatial relations.

It has become commonplace to assume that whilst modernity is about new forms of experience of time, 'postmodernity' marks a revolution in spatial relations. But this is too simple. The two dimensions are inextricably bound together. Changes in the experience of space always also involve changes in the experience of time and vice versa. Spatial relations have tended to be neglected in discourses on modernity and are now increasingly the object of investigation;[49] but that is a different matter. In fact, as Benjamin points out, the shift from a Christian eschatological concept of historical time to a modern one 'secularised time into space'.[50] It is in the repressed spatial premises of the concept of modernity that its political logic is to be found. As Sakai puts it: 'The condition for the possibility of conceiving of history as a linear and evolutionary series of incidents lay in its . . . relation to other histories, other [spatially] coexisting temporalities.'[51] Modernity is a Western idea. Whether it can any longer be thought of as an *exclusively* Western concept, as Paz claims,[52] however, is doubtful. For 'there is no inherent reason why the West/non-West opposition should determine the geographic perspective of modernity except for the fact that it definitely serves to establish the unity of the West, a nebulous but commanding positivity whose existence we have tended to take for granted for so long.'[53] On the other hand, if 'the West' is not so much a geographical category as a geopolitical one, through which the historical predicate of modernity is translated into a geographical one, and vice versa, then we must accept that as the spatial relationship of the West to the non-West is transformed, through migration, tourism, communications technology, and changes in the international division of labour, new configurations of 'modernity' will emerge in both Western and non-Western places as new social subjects redefine the sites of the enunciation of the 'modern'. The prospect is opened up of a proliferation of competing modernities: 'postcolonial contra-modernities'[54] and black 'counter-cultures of modernity',[55] among others, bearing both the promise and the threat of new historicities.

Insofar as 'modernity' is understood as a periodizing category in the full sense of registering a break not only from one chronologically defined period to another, but in the quality of historical time itself, it sets up a differential between the character of its own time and that which precedes it. This differential formed the basis for the transformation in the late eighteenth century in the meaning of the concepts of 'progress' and 'development', which makes them the precursors of later, twentieth-century concepts of modernization. For the idea of the *non-contemporaneousness* of geographically diverse, but *chronologically simultaneous*, times which thus develops, in the context of colonial experience, is the foundation for 'universal histories with a cosmopolitan intent'.[56] Once the practice of such comparisons was established in anthropology, colonial discourse *par excellence*, it was easily transferable to the relations between particular social spheres and practices within different European countries themselves, and thereafter, once again, globally, in an expanding dialectic of differentiation and homogenization.[57]

Such histories are modernizing in the sense that the results of synchronic comparisons are ordered diachronically to produce a scale of development which defines 'progress' in terms of the projection of certain people's presents as other people's futures, at the level of the development of history as a whole. As such, they are indeed homogenizing. But this homogenization is premised upon a differentiation which must first be recognized in order to be negated. Furthermore, in order for this negation to occur and homogenization to be achieved, some specific criterion must be introduced to set up a further differential, within the newly homogenized time, so as to provide a content for the concept of 'progress'. Thus, when Anderson argues that the temporality of modernity knows no internal principle of variation, he is only partly right. He is right to the extent that the concept of modernity, in its basic theoretical form, itself furnishes no such principle. He is wrong, however, insofar as it must find one elsewhere, if there is to be any way of identifying the historically, as opposed to the merely chronologically, 'new'. This is the role of so-called 'theories of modernity' (as distinct from the more general theorization of modernity of the kind sketched here): to provide a content to fill the form of the modern, to give it something more than an abstract temporal determinacy.

At this point, historically, the geopolitical dimension of the concept comes into its own, providing, via the discourses of colonialism, a series of criteria of progress initially derived from the history of European nation-states, and later, in modernization theory proper, from America.[58] The failure of modernization as the paradigm of 'development' provides the starting point for that understanding of postmodernism which centres upon the construction, and deconstruction, of the idea of colonial discourse. Thus Young, for example, argues *contra* Jameson that it is 'not just the cultural effects of a new stage of "late" capitalism' which the concept of postmodernism is best thought to mark, but 'European culture's awareness that it is no longer the unquestioned and dominant centre of the world'.[59] Hence the crisis of anthropology (Lévi-Strauss's 'daughter of violence'), the disciplinary crucible for the evolutionary time-consciousness of modernization.

It was the function of anthropology to establish historical differences between different types of society within the present. Its basic temporal strategies were thus what Fabian has described as 'distancing' and the 'denial of coevalness'.[60] More recently, critical anthropology has attempted to set out from the recognition of coevalness. It has thus transformed the problem of representation from a narrowly epistemological one ('relativism'), into the more directly political form of a questioning of the social functions of the representational practices at stake; but it has not thereby solved it. Indeed, it would be more accurate to say that it has thus charted the ground of its *insolubility*, as the space of an ongoing negotiation and struggle. However, to call such anthropologies (let alone the societies about which they write) 'postmodern', in order to differentiate their activities from the colonial past, is to neglect the continuity of the basic temporal structure of historical self-definition and projection which underlies the increasing contestation of the position of enunciator of 'modernity'. It is also to court the danger of failing to differentiate their specific forms in a bland uniformity of 'difference'. Such a monolithic difference threatens to reproduce the structure of temporal distancing of the anthropological problematic in a newly prospective, rather than retrospective, mode. Non-Western societies become representatives of the future (a pure 'hybridity') within the present, just as 'primitive' ones were taken to be the representatives of the past. Postmodern ethnology is in danger of becoming anthropology in reverse.

According to Young, the value of poststructuralism as a theoretical approach to this problem is that, unlike the idea of postmodernism, 'it does not offer a critique by positioning itself outside "the West", but rather uses its own alterity and duplicity in order to effect its deconstruction.' My own approach, in line with the logic of Sakai's argument, accepts the necessity for such immanence, with one important modification: namely, that since the idea of 'the West' can no longer be understood simply geographically – even, or especially, in its intrusion as a structuring element into its 'non-Western' other – but embraces new forms found *only* within certain non-Western others (e.g. Japan), reflection upon it need not restrict itself to the pure, 'postcritical' negativity of deconstructive techniques, but may also serve as the occasion for the development of new forms of dialectical thought, grounded in the immanent development of the time-consciousness of modernity itself. In this respect, the debate about postmodernism does not just provide the occasion for a 're-reading' of modernity; such a re-reading is the essential content of the debate.[61]

Parallel to the way in which the spatial relations of modernity intrinsic to the colonial character of its Western origins produce definite political effects of their own, is the question of the gendering of modernity as a form of historical time. Kristeva has argued that 'for time, female subjectivity would seem to provide a specific measure that essentially retains repetition and eternity from among the multiple modalities of time known through the history of civilisations', in opposition to the linear temporality of a history from which women have been both symbolically and materially excluded.[62] She then points out that different generations within feminism have challenged this opposition in various ways, whilst another has affirmed it. Despite her desire to recover the differences beneath 'the apparent coherence which the term "woman" assumes in contemporary ideology', however, she nonetheless continues to use the term in such a way as to sustain its traditional symbolic unity. The problem with this strategy is that it is unable to register the disruptive symbolic significance of her 'first generation' feminism's demands for access to the 'men's time' of modernity (history). The success of such demands can thus only be thought in terms of the 'parallel existence' or 'interweaving' of different, *already established* times within women's experience; rather than as a genuinely transformative moment which would leave neither women's time nor historical time, neither 'women' nor 'history', unchanged. In opposing women's time to historical time, Kristeva explicitly associates the former with space. She thereby not only restricts the notion of historical time to a single highly specific form (linear or chronological time), but uncritically reproduces the simple opposition of historical time to space noted above. This is not to suggest that the temporality of modernity is ungendered, but only that Kristeva's pioneering essay remains both too schematic and too closely tied to traditional symbolic forms of gender representation to advance beyond identification of the issue.

Anderson's reading contains analogous problems, which can be illustrated with reference to his complaint that the temporality of modernity cannot accommodate the idea of decline.[63] Nothing could be further from the truth. Indeed, one might say that in its perpetual anxiety to transcend the present, modernity is everywhere haunted by the idea of decline. Anderson's account suppresses this increasingly palpable anxiety, because it identifies the self-transcending temporality of modernity with the blank homogeneity of chronology, on the basis of their common abstraction of purely temporal indices of periodization. But whilst the two are thus connected, they cannot, in principle, be thought of as the same. Chronology alone could never be the measure of historical progress. Modernization theory, notoriously, finds its content in a combination of quasi-spatial (geopolitical) and economic criteria. But the idea of decline is no less applicable to the system as a whole. Just as the homogeneity of modernization theory's measures of progress/decline depends upon differentials which it then

reduces to differences within a single scale, so the possibility of an
'absolute' decline derives from modernity's continual projection of a
differential into the future, which would not, in this case, be redeemed.
('Absolute' decline, in other words, is temporally relative.) The
temporal structure of the concept of modernity dictates that any
particular modernity must constantly re-establish itself in relation to
an ever expanding past. That the concept of modernity itself, in its
most general form as a kind of historical time, involves only an abstract
sense of what such a re-establishment involves (the 'new'), is no reason
to deny its reality. Rather, it is the conceptual shape to which all
'modern' theories of decline must conform, like the theories of progress
they mirror.[64]

The central problem faced by all theories of modernity, in any substantive socio-historical sense, is not that they cannot think decline,
but, rather, the reverse: the fact that modernity/modernities *grow
old*. It is to deal with this problem that, in strict accordance with the
temporal logic of modernity, the idea of the 'postmodern' has
appeared, along with (at least in its more sophisticated versions) its
own distinctive temporal paradoxes. Proponents of the idea of the
postmodern as a 'perpetual present', for example, claim to have
registered the ultimately self-defeating character of modern time-
consciousness (the new is 'an invariant' and thus the 'ever-same'),
while nonetheless using this recognition to extract one final novelty
from its seemingly exhausted repertoire (*post*-modernity).[65] Yet this
only works if we accept the familiar idealist premise that epochs may
be periodized by their structures of recognition alone. If we reject this
premise, 'postmodernity' once again regresses to being the sign for a
self-consciousness of the contradictory structure of the concept of
modernity. Naive concepts of postmodernity, one might say, register
an affirmative self-consciousness of the paradoxes and aporia of
'modernity', but fail to recognize that this is so – a truly Nietzschean
form of historical knowledge based on a wilful, active forgetting.
Fully reflexive concepts of postmodernity, on the other hand, take
us back into the paradoxes and aporia of 'modernity' at a higher
conceptual level. The 'post-' confirms the self-transcending quality of
all modernities anew, in a particular historical situation; but it cannot
substitute for a concrete historical analysis of the character of the
changes. Alternatively, substantive theories of modernity can hold
their ground, set themselves against the erosion of their historical
premises, and turn themselves into *projects*.[66]

Modernity as project: Habermas, Foucault, Enlightenment

It was noted above that it was through the temporalization of the founding geopolitical difference of colonialism that the concept of modernity first came to be universalized, and thereby, thereafter, to subordinate the differential between itself and other 'times' to differences within a single temporal scheme of 'progress', 'modernization' and 'development'. This process was accompanied at a theoretical level by the appearance of a new kind of universalizing discourse about the present: what Habermas has called the 'philosophical discourse of modernity'.[67] If it has been the function of regional theories of modernity (economic, political, religious, aesthetic, sociological, etc.) to totalize spatially across their respective domains, on the basis of specific, geopolitically determined but empirically derived criteria of the modern, it has fallen to the philosophical discourse of modernity to unify and legitimate these inquiries within the scope of a single practical definition. The question thus arises as to how this discourse has fared in the face of the inevitable but paradoxical ageing of all substantive concepts of modernity. The debate hinges on the fate of the concept of Enlightenment, or, more specifically, the Enlightenment concept of an autonomous reason. For it is through this idea that modernity first came to be conceived philosophically, not just as a new historical period or a new form of historical time, but, more substantively, as a world-historical project. Yet there is considerable space within the temporal structure of modernity for alternative conceptions of this project. This may be illustrated by the differences between Habermas and Foucault over the heritage of Kant's 1784 essay, 'An Answer to the Question: What is Enlightenment?'.[68]

Habermas and Foucault are agreed on three main points about Kant's essay. First, it inaugurates a philosophical discourse *on* modernity – a discourse which for the first time takes the character of the present in its 'present-ness' as the specific object of philosophical thought, within the horizons of a conception of history that is free from both backward-looking comparisons with the ancients and forward-looking expectations about doomsday.[69] Second, it constitutes a philosophical discourse *of* modernity, insofar as the conception of the autonomy of reason that it involves is internal to the time-consciousness of a self-transcending present which cuts itself off, in principle, from the determinations of the past. Reason, for Kant, must be able to validate its own laws to itself, within the present, without reference to history or tradition. As Habermas puts it, modernity 'has to create its normativity out of itself', through reflection.[70] Hence

Kant's famous motto of Enlightenment – '*Sapere Aude*! Have courage to use your own understanding' – and his definition of Enlightenment as 'humanity's emergence from its self-imposed immaturity', where immaturity is understood as 'the inability to use one's understanding without guidance from another'.[71] Modernity is, in this respect, an infinite task. Finally, the practical history of 'Enlightenment' in the actions of European nation-states has involved forms of domination, as well as freedom, which, furthermore, cannot be dissociated from the internal contradictions of the original Enlightenment formulation of the concept of autonomous reason. Foucault refers to the areas of scientific and technical rationality, the fate of revolutions, and colonialism. Habermas is concerned with the social application of instrumental and functionalist forms of reason, but has yet to address himself to the problems of colonial and post-colonial forms of domination. The only thing that appears as 'colonized' in his writings is the 'lifeworld' of contemporary European societies.[72]

Where Habermas and Foucault differ, quite radically, is in their respective analyses of the character and depth of the problem posed for the idea of Enlightenment by these phenomena, and its relationship to the historical present. This difference may be summed up by saying that whilst Habermas wants to 'complete' the concept of Enlightenment, by reworking its universalistic doctrine of autonomous rational individuality and free public reason so as to avoid its repressive implications (by replacing a subject-centred with an intersubjective or communicative concept of reason), Foucault remains wedded to it only in the much broader sense of what he calls its 'philosophical ethos': namely, the attitude of 'a permanent critique of our historical era'.[73] Such an attitude, Foucault argues, demands a critique of the Enlightenment as historical event which transcends the original Enlightenment model of critique: 'Two centuries later, the Enlightenment returns: but now not at all as a way for the West to take cognisance of its present possibilities and of the liberties to which it can accede, but as a way of interrogating it on its limits and the powers which it has abused. *Reason as despotic Enlightenment*.'[74] Those 'who wish us to preserve alive and intact the heritage of *Aufklärung*', Foucault insists, engage in 'the most touching of treasons'. For they suppress the very question of 'the historicity of the thought of the universal'.[75] By hanging on to Enlightenment in this way, we might say, they betray its modernity. The very existence of the post-Nietzschean challenge to Enlightenment reason undermines the latter's claim to modernity. Yet Habermas's charge against Foucault is identical. For if the temporality of modernity as a self-transcending

break with other times ties it, logically, to the ideal of rational autonomy, and Foucault's historical challenge is a challenge to this idea,
then surely it is Foucault who is the 'traitor' – purveyor of an
'irrational' anti-Enlightenment in the name of Enlightenment itself.
Either way, it would seem, 'anachronism becomes the refuge of
modernity.'[76]

Clearly, the issue cannot be settled at this level of analysis. The
maintenance of a reflexive normativity can no more be reduced to the
recovery of the 'good' side of Enlightenment reason from its alienated
other than their dialectical entanglement can be used to justify its
wholesale rejection. Rather, what the dispute would seem to demonstrate (against both Habermas and Berman) is that modernity is *not*,
as such, a project, but merely its form. It is a form of historical consciousness, an abstract temporal structure which, in totalizing history
from the standpoint of an ever-vanishing, ever-present present,
embraces a conflicting plurality of projects, of possible futures,
provided they conform to its basic logical structure. Which of these
projects will turn out to have been most truly 'modern' only time
will tell.

Differential time and conjunctural analysis: Althusser and the *Annales*

Anderson's error was to over-state the continuity of modern time-
consciousness, to reduce historical to chronological time, and
(following Berman) to confuse the idea of modernity as a structure of
historical time with the logic of modernism as its affirmative cultural
self-consciousness. What we have yet to determine is the relationship
of 'modernity' to the differential temporality of conjunctural analysis
which Anderson recommends as an alternative conception. It is here
that the limits of 'modernity', and thus the scope of its legitimate
application, come most clearly into view. At this point, it is useful to
return to Althusser to examine Anderson's notion of conjunctural
analysis at its source.

Althusser's self-proclaimed goal was to determine the specificity of
Marx's concept of history by differentiating it from both the 'everyday' (empiricist) notion and the historical logic of Hegelianism. His
method was to 'construct the Marxist concept of historical time on
the basis of the Marxist conception of the social totality'. Different
conceptions of the social whole, he argued, contain 'the secret of the
conception of history in which the "development" of this social whole

is thought'. He thus came to contrast the 'homogeneous continuity' and 'contemporaneity' of Hegelian time with the differential temporality of a Marxist conception of historical time, on the basis of the difference between Hegel's 'expressive totality' and his own distinctive interpretation of the Marxist whole as a 'complex structural unity', the level or instances of which are 'articulated with one another according to specific determinations, fixed in the last instance by the level or instance of the economy.'[77] What is of particular interest in this analysis is its critique of the category of the historical present as a critique of 'contemporaneity', and the costs it involves for thinking history as a whole.

According to Althusser, the problem with the category of the historical present is that in it, 'the structure of historical existence is such that all the elements of the whole co-exist in one and the same time, one and the same present, and are therefore contemporaneous with one another in one and the same present.'[78] In the unity of Althusser's conception of the conjuncture, on the other hand, each level or instance of the whole has its own peculiar time, 'relatively autonomous and hence relatively independent, even in its dependence, of the "times" of the other levels'. Each of these peculiar histories is 'punctuated with peculiar rhythms and can only be known on condition that we have defined the concept of the specificity of its historical temporality and its punctuations'. It is not enough, however, simply to think these various histories in their differences: 'we must also think these differences in rhythm and punctuation in their foundation, in the type of articulation, displacement and torsion which harmonises these different times with one another' in the unity of the whole.[79] It is at this point that things begin to get tricky. For since there is no essential unity to the Althusserian totality, there is no common time within which to think the articulated co-existence of its various constitutive temporalities. Taking an 'essential section' through the complex totality at any particular moment is illicit, because it reintroduces precisely that contemporaneity of a 'continuous-homogeneous time' which it was the point of the idea of differential historical times to abolish.

All we can do, it seems, is think the whole from the standpoint of a variety of different localized presents, such that the times of other levels appear within such analyses only relationally, in the form of a series of absences. The problem with this, however, is that while it may allow us to move towards a conjunctural analysis of the whole through the aggregation of the series of disjunctive analyses of its parts, each of which contains its own 'decentred' (negative) totalization from the standpoint of its specific locality, what it rules out in principle is any conception of the development of the whole as a whole, whether at the level of the social formation, mode of production or history itself. The cost of Althusser's conjunctural form of differential temporality is thus the impossibility of thinking the transition from one mode of production to another – precisely that object which it is the ultimate rationale of historical materialism to think – since, in the end, such transitions can be thought only as breaks or ruptures between different articulated sets of times. They have no time of their own.[80] Althusser's difficulty here may be illuminated by comparing his conception of time with those contained in the two very different sources out of which it was fashioned: the historiography of the *Annales* School and the structuralism of Lévi-Strauss's anthropology.

Althusser acknowledges that 'a few historians' (he refers to Febvre, Labrousse and Braudel) have begun to pose questions about the specific structure of historical time, 'and often in a very remarkable way'. But he has two major reservations about their work. In the first place,

> they simply *observe that there are* different times in history, varieties of time, long times, medium times and short times, and they are content to note their interferences as so many products of their intersection; they do not . . . relate these varieties as so many *variations* to the structure of the whole although the latter directly governs the production of those variations . . .

Second, they are consequently 'tempted to relate these varieties, as so many variants measurable by their *duration*, to ordinary time itself, to the ideological continuum'. Their questions are thus judged to be 'generally related not to the fundamental question of the concept of history, but to the ideological conception of time'.[81] Althusser, on the other hand, wants to reduce the play of temporal variations to their determination by the structure of the whole. All other attempts at an integral analysis of multiple times are associated with regression to a common-sense Hegelianism.[82]

Now, it is certaintly true that the *Annales* approach is empirically open in its treatment of multiple times, and that in its classic statement, Braudel's 'History and the Social Sciences: The *Longue Durée*' (1958), interactions between different temporal structures are treated as 'things which can be recorded only in relation to the *uniform time of historians*, which can stand as a general measure of all these phenomena, and not in relation to the multiform time of social reality, which can stand only as the individual measure of each of these phenomena separately'.[83] But could things really be otherwise? Ironically, it is Anderson who has produced the most cogent critique of Althusser on the two issues of explanatory closure and the ideological status of chronological time. It is tied up, once again, with the question of space:

> Claiming that 'it is only possible to give a content to the concept of historical time by defining historical times as the specific form of existence of the social totality under consideration', Althusser characteristically assumes that the 'social totality' in question is equivalent to a 'social formation', in other words that national ensembles form the natural boundaries of historical investigations. But in fact historical materialism above all insists on the *international* character of modes of production, and the need to integrate the times of each particular social formation into the much more complex general history of the mode of production dominant in them.[84]

Indeed, for Marx (as for the *Annales* School), these histories of modes of production must themselves be combined into an ongoing 'total' history. For Braudel, for example, 'history is the total of all possible histories'.[85] Furthermore, the dependence of historical investigation on problems defined by the present means that the openness characteristic of the present is carried over into historiography. All explanatory closures are relative to the problem at hand, not to the real object of the investigation, which remains open. Chronological time provides a *measure* for relations between different times within this ongoing history. It does not constitute this time *qua* historical time. Althusser conflates the two levels.[86] As Anderson puts it:

> Althusser's fustigation of a 'single continuous reference time' is in truth 'thoroughly misleading', because it fails to make any clear distinction between the indisputable (indeed indispensable – think of dating) existence of such time, as the medium of all history, and its lack of pertinence as a common organizing principle of the diverse scansions of historical development. The *relevant* time in which all regional histories should be convened is not an empty grid of dates, but the full movement of the social formation as a whole. At a minimum.[87]

Yet in his critique of Berman, Anderson makes precisely the same mistake himself, in failing to understand modernity as a *historical* category. Furthermore, he takes over the Althusserian, rather than the *Annales*, concept of conjuncture, in which Lenin joins hands with Lévi-Strauss to take the present outside of history altogether.

Althusser's closure of the inherent openness of empirical historical inquiry by the idea of the determination of temporal variety by the 'structure of the social whole' would seem to place him closer to Lévi-Strauss than to the *Annales* School. Yet he is as critical of the structuralist model of synchrony/diachrony as he is of the *Annales*, and oddly, for the same reason: namely, that the distinction between synchrony and diachrony is based on a conception of historical time as 'continuous and homogeneous and contemporaneous with itself':

> The synchronic is contemporaneity itself, the co-presence of the essence of its determinations, the present being readable as a structure in an 'essential section' because the present is the very existence of the essential structure. The synchronic therefore presupposes the ideological conception of a continuous-homogeneous time. It follows that the diachronic is merely the development of this present in the sequence of a temporal continuity in which the 'events' to which 'history' in the strict sense can be reduced (cf. Lévi-Strauss) are merely successive contingent presents in the time continuum. Like the synchronic, which is the primary concept, the diachronic therefore presupposes both of the very two characteristics I have isolated in the Hegelian conception of time: an ideological conception of time.[88]

This critique is fundamentally misplaced. For it confuses synchrony with the instant. In fact, synchrony corresponds much more closely to the 'no-time' of Althusser's own structural analysis. The critique of structuralism which balances the critique of the *Annales* School in Althusser's account of historical time is in this respect a mirage.

Indeed, the true critique of structuralist temporality is also a critique of Althusser. It has been summed up most succinctly by Fabian in the course of his critique of the 'allochronism' of anthropology:

> Ever since de Saussure canonised the opposition between synchrony and diachrony, it served not as a distinction *of* temporal relations (as one might expect from the presence of the component *chrony* in both terms), but a distinction *against* Time. The possibility of identifying and analysing semiological systems is unequivocally said to rest on the elimination of Time and, by implication, of such notions as process, genesis, emergence, production, and other concepts bound up with 'history'. *Diachrony does not refer to a temporal mode of existence but to the mere succession of semiological systems one upon another.* Succession, strictly speaking, presupposes Time only in the sense of an extraneous condition affecting neither their synchronic nor their diachronic constitution.[89]

Synchrony is not con-temporality, but a-temporality: a purely analytical space in which the temporality immanent to the objects of inquiry is repressed. Diachrony orders synchronic relations one 'after' the other, but it does not establish what Althusser calls temporal continuity because its sequence is not a sequence of presents at all, but only of a-temporal states. Structuralism explicitly excludes the actively constitutive phenomenological present, the durational 'now', from its framework. So too does Althusser. As a result, he is left without a temporal standpoint from which to unify his multiple social times. The concept of the conjuncture stands in for such a standpoint, but it does not, and cannot, provide one.

In the tradition of the *Annales*, the term 'conjuncture' is used to denote a level of temporality in its own right: specifically, that which comes between the relative immobility of the *longue durée* and the hectic narrative of 'events'. More precisely, in Labrousse's pioneering analyses, it refers to the periodicity of various kinds of cycle, painstakingly established by statistical correlations.[90] In Althusser, on the other hand, it is generalized to refer to the unity of all social times in the 'mode of existence of the social formation' at any particular moment. It is 'the real historical present',[91] and as such the time of *politics*. According to the Glossary appended to the English translation of *Reading Capital*, it is: 'The central concept of the Marxist science of politics (cf. Lenin's 'current moment'); it denotes the exact balance of forces, state of overdetermination of the contradictions at any given moment to which political tactics must be applied.'[92] But what is the temporality of this 'moment'? For Althusser, it cannot be chronologically specifiable, since this would return it to the measure of the continuum. It can only be constructed relationally, as a 'co-existence' of different times; yet such abstractly relational co-existence takes it out of time altogether into the purely analytical space of the synchrony it denies. Crucially, what Althusser lacks is the concept of the *coeval*, through which Fabian registers the co-existence of different temporalities, without either reducing them to a con-temporaneous present or removing them from time altogether. Times which are coeval co-exist chronologically in a way which is determined by the social dimension of their spatial relations, and is productive of further complex temporalities.[93]

For all its faults, Althusser's analysis is instructive in two main ways. In the first place, it points to the limits of modernity as a category of historical totalization, insofar as all such totalizations abstract from the concrete multiplicity of differential times co-existing in the global 'now' a single differential (however internally complex) through which to mark the time of the present. This is an inevitable effect of all forms of totalization, the cost of thinking history as a whole: that very

concept which, ironically, at the conclusion of his search for the specificity of Marx's concept of history, Althusser was unable to think
at all. This is the second lesson of Althusser's work on historical
time: the generalization of the notion of conjuncture to encompass
the 'articulation, displacement and torsion' of *all* temporalities
remains, for all its criticisms of synchrony, outside of historical time
altogether.[94] In its reduction of the idea of a totalizing present to
the idea of the 'essential section', it exchanges the difficulties and
possibilities of the (always spatially determined) 'now' for the no-time
of a disembodied 'theory'. As such, it requires the restitution of a
totalizing conception of historical time within which to move, to give
it practical significance.

It is just such a restitution that the category of modernity provides.
Born, like capitalism, out of European colonialism and the world
market, as a structure of historical consciousness 'modernity' predates
the development of capitalism proper. It operates at a different level
of analysis from the concepts of Marxist political economy, yet it is
integrally connected to them, and its shape changes with time. (Think,
for example, of the way in which recent developments in communications technology have simultaneously radically reduced the 'time of
circulation'[95] for certain goods, and intensified the time-consciousness
of historical change.) In fact, modernity is our primary secular
category of historical totalization. But what justifies this totalization
of history, theoretically, if such an operation of necessity homogenizes
and represses, reduces or forgets, certain forms of difference? And if
we are to totalize history, how are we to do it in such a way as to
preserve a sense of what is lost in the process? More fundamentally,
what is *historical time*?

2

One Time, One History?

Time is a mystery precisely in that the observations that are to be made regarding it cannot be unified.

Paul Ricoeur

In the face of the question 'why totalize history?', three kinds of response stand out as distinctively 'modern', post-theological philosophical forms. One might respond *transcendentally*, one might respond *immanently*, or one might respond in what some would consider a more philosophically fundamental manner, within the terms of some kind of *phenomenological ontology* of temporal experience. Thus, the notion of a collective singular 'history' might be defended as a limit or regulative idea implicit within the claim to objectivity of the historian's craft, as the unstated object unifying historians' activities and providing them with the horizon of their intelligibility. It might be justified as the historically emergent product of deep-seated social processes on a global scale. Or it might be expounded as a part of the existential structure of human being, as revealed by a phenomenological analysis of the constitution of experience in, through, and as time.[1]

Each approach has its adherents and its advantages and disadvantages for specific purposes. From the standpoint of a defence of historical totalization *per se*, however, it is the third one, viewed in the perspective of the second, which holds the most promise. For ultimately, if we are to justify the totalization of the historical multiplicity of differential social times into something called 'history', we will need to appeal to an idea of history situated within the terms of a totalization of time itself. After a brief discussion of the limitations of the first two approaches with respect to this task, and an extended excursus on the recently revived theme of the 'end of history', we shall thus concentrate upon the third. Each of the first two approaches places the burden of justification for totalization onto history itself, either as a form of knowledge or a real process. The third confronts it more directly as a problem in the hermeneutics of historical existence.

Conditions of possibility: the transcendental path

The first alternative – a transcendental deduction of the unity of history as the condition of possibility of historical knowledge – follows the path laid by the tradition which runs from Dilthey's prospective critique of historical reason, via Heidelberg Neo-Kantianism, to Heidegger's early essay 'The Concept of Time in the Science of History'.[2] This is the tradition through which the problem of historical time was reintroduced into German philosophy in the wake of the reaction against Hegelianism in the second half of the nineteenth century; not, as might be thought, in order to offer theoretical opposition to the positivism of contemporary historicism (Ranke), but rather as its philosophical complement.[3] What its adherents had in common, whether their enterprise took the form of a philosophy of life (Dilthey), a philosophy of values (Rickert), or an incipient philosophy of time (the early Heidegger), is a simultaneous recognition of the primacy of positive science in the production of historical knowledge and of the inadequacy of its methods to the task of the systematization of its results – the very problem, in fact, that is raised but never pursued by Marx and Engels in *The German Ideology* under the heading of the replacement of 'self-sufficient philosophy' by 'a summing-up of the most general results' of historical inquiry.[4]

It was Marx's failure to address the theoretical form and episte-mological status of this 'replacement' in any detail that opened the way for Engels's late works, and the subsequent bifurcation of Marxism, philosophically, into competing traditions.[5] As Jacoby has shown,[6] this split was at first internal to the Hegelian heritage, rather than, as it would later become, a fissure between Hegelian and anti-Hegelian Marxisms. However, whilst the Hegelian tradition, in both its phenomenological and panlogicist forms, pointed in the direction of a totalizing solution to the problem, it impeded the production of one in anything other than a clearly idealist form. In response to such perceived idealism a number of Western European Marxists turned, in the post-war period, to the anti-Hegelianism of the neo-Kantian tradition, in the then burgeoning form of post-positivist philosophy of science: in Althusser's case, to the conventionalist rationalism of Canguilhem and Bachelard, in that of Della Volpe and Colletti to the hypothetico-deductivism of a quasi-Popperian falsificationism.

Habermas's trajectory is more complicated, combining a greater diversity of critically appropriated sources with considerable theoretical
originality on specific issues, only to end up with something that is
methodologically a fairly orthodox Kantianism.[7]

Such Marxists thereby attached themselves to a tradition the beginnings of which were contemporary with, but antagonistic to the spirit
of, Marx's later work. Whether this saved them from 'idealism' is
doubtful, although the tradition had by then changed considerably
since its inception in the 1860s. What it retained was a sense of
the primacy of 'scientific' over 'philosophical' activity, and hence of
philosophy as a second-order discipline, albeit one that is no less in-
dispensable for that. What it had lost was any particular concern
for history, the discipline of the nineteenth century *par excellence*. This
was replaced by an interest in anthropological and sociological theories
which tend to abstract from the problem of historical time altogether.[8]
Thus was the ground laid for the various syncretic combinations of
Marxism and sociology that have since become the mainstream of a
philosophically ambiguous 'social theory'. In the meantime, the pursuit
of a better understanding of the idea of history was continued in
non-Marxist debates about the methodology of historiography, the
essentially transcendental form of which registers their continuity with
the project of Dilthey's critique of historical reason.[9]

However, while such discussions can help expose the presuppositions built into various pre-constituted conceptions of historical
knowledge to the scrutiny of conceptual analysis, they cannot in
themselves provide a standpoint from which to defend the idea of
history as a meaningful whole from its philosophical critics, for two
main reasons. In the first place, they beg the question of the relationship of time to history. Is history a temporally distinct domain,
qualitatively different from the temporality of nature, such that it
might be totalized independently? Or is its temporality inextricably
bound up with that of nature? If so, how? Are nature and history
all there is to time? What, for example, of eternity? Is eternity to be
understood as atemporal, or as a temporal infinite? Is there a place
in our understanding of history for a post-theological concept of
eternity? All these questions affect our understanding of the substance
of historical inquiry, and our stance towards them determines what
kind of history we believe in. Yet they remain outside the scope of
transcendental arguments which set out from descriptions of the state
of historical knowledge, since these merely serve, like transcendental
arguments everywhere, to expound the presuppositions built into the
inevitably contested descriptions in their premises.[10]

Different disciplinary practices produce and reflect different ideas about the legitimacy of historical totalization, and vice versa. Those opposed, in principle, to the totalization 'history' will simply deny the requisite practical unity of the field of historical knowledge, supporting their argument with voluminous evidence of its heterogeneity.[11] The burden of proof thus regresses from the expository form of transcendental argumentation back onto historical inquiry itself, producing the demand for an immanent demonstration of the unity in question: 'instead of the Kantian formula: "Under what conditions is historical knowledge possible?" we ... [must] ask: "Is a universally valid science of history possible? To what extent?".'[12] For if 'the full historical fact, the "integral past", is properly an Idea in the Kantian sense, that is to say, the *never attained limit* of an ever more extensive and complex effort to integrate',[13] then it is this 'effort to integrate' and its results which must be interrogated.

More fundamental still as an objection to this kind of argument is the lack, within the time-consciousness of historical studies, of an adequate sense of the future. In the constitution of historiography as a discipline, the future appears only negatively, as no more than an empty reservoir of future presents and prospective pasts for still more distant presents, waiting upon history, as the past expands into the future, to fill it with events, and hence with time. The discipline of history may be about more than just the past, insofar as it is the *relations* between past and present with which it is primarily concerned.[14] But it embraces the future only tangentially in past and present forms: *past futures* as part of its object of inquiry, *present futures* as constituents of its horizon of expectation and hence its cognitive interest in the past. It does not confront it as an independent temporal dimension which might block the very possibility of historical totalization. This is the domain of the philosophy of history. The *process* of history, on the other hand, the history that judges,[15] lies as much in the future as it does in the past, and it does so constitutively, not contingently. It is as futural as it is retrospective, and not merely in the phenomenological form of present futures, but 'objectively', in the necessary opacity of future presents. Such presents are in principle outside the scope of historical inquiry, yet they are centrally involved, if only negatively, in debates about historical totalization.

Let history judge: the immanent road

It is partly in response to this problem, this historiographic lack of futurity, that one might be tempted, following Marx (after Hegel), to try an immanent demonstration of the emergence of history in the collective singular, as world history, as itself an historical event – in the hope of breaking out of the closed circle of transcendental analysis and projecting a unity forward as part of the dynamic form of an ongoing process of self-totalization. Indeed, this is exactly the kind of argument to which an appeal has already implicitly been made in chapter 1, in our account of the spatial unification of the globe through European colonialism as the geopolitical condition for the development of the concept of modernity: the marker not just of a new historical present, but of a new temporalization of history itself. History is already totalizing itself. 'World history,' in Marx's words, 'has not always existed; history as world history [is] a result';[16] and it is a result, primarily, of capitalism. The world market established during the late feudal period in Europe became the medium for the development of capitalism as a global system, once the resolution of the social struggles internal to European feudalism had laid the ground for the development of capitalism in Europe.[17]

With capitalism came the homogenization of labour-time: the time of abstract labour (money, the universal equivalent), the time of the clock.[18] And with the rapid development of transport and communications in the course of capitalist development in the nineteenth century (the railways and the telegraph) came the beginnings of a generalized social imposition of a single standard of time.[19] Once world standard-time became established as a medium for the possible synchronization of actions on a planetary scale (and subsequent communications technology made such synchronization a reality), the idea of 'history as world history' acquired in actuality what it had previously possessed only in speculative thought: a basis for the totalization of what might otherwise be considered a series of essentially independent, if overlapping, histories.[20] Capitalism has 'universalized' history, in the sense that it has established systematic relations of social interdependence on a planetary scale (encompassing non-capitalist societies), thereby producing a single global space of temporal co-existence or coevalness, within which actions are quantifiable chronologically in terms of single standard of measurement: world standard-time. However, insofar as this measure remains a mere measure – that is to say, an abstract form of quantification, external and indifferent to the concrete multiplicity of the rhythms of different social practices – capitalism has by no means, in Vilar's phrase, 'unified' history. This, Vilar insists, will be the task of 'another mode of production'.[21]

Socialism as the unification of history – the idea has frightened a lot of people, for whom totalization and totalitarianism are but different words for the same thing (although they have worried rather less about the totalizing force holding together the de-totalized forms of capital accumulation). As Spivak has remarked of post-Marxist thought, 'if we dismiss general systemic critical perception as necessarily totalising or centralising, we merely prove once again that the subject of Capital can *in*habit its ostensible critique as well.'[22] Whether one is persuaded by Vilar's scenario or not, it is clear that the speculative projection of *some* kind of 'end' or goal is going to be required as the horizon of intelligibility for the comprehension of the past as a whole, if the constitutive incompleteness of the present is to be acknowledged, and read as a stage in the development of a broader process. 'All "new" history without totalising ambition will be a history old before its time',[23] and all immanent philosophies of history are of necessity written in the future anterior: from the standpoint of what 'will have been'. As Jameson put it, prior to his turn to postmodernism:

> Above and beyond the problem of periodisation and its categories, which are certainly in crisis today, but which would seem to be as indispensable as they are unsatisfactory for any kind of work in cultural study, the larger issue is that of *the representation of History itself*. . . . [since] individual period formulations always secretly imply or project narratives or 'stories' – narrative representations – of the historical sequence in which such periods take their place and from which they derive their significance.[24]

All such representations ultimately depend for their cognitive redemption upon the future realization of the end in question, although this is rarely understood to be a merely passive process of waiting on history. Rather, ever since the secularization of eschatology in the eighteenth century, such futures have been taken to be served by historical action based upon the very 'knowledge' that this action would, if successful, confirm.[25] Such, for example, is the experimental practical ground and fallibilistic philosophical logic of the dialectic of theory and practice in classical Marxism:

> The question whether objective truth can be attributed to human thinking is not a question of theory but is a *practical* question. Man must prove the truth, i.e., the reality and power, the this-worldliness of his [*sic*] thinking in practice. The dispute over the reality or non-reality of thinking which is isolated from practice is a purely *scholastic* question.[26]

Everything depends, firstly, upon the concrete historical content of the specific historiographic claims (imperialism as the 'highest' stage of capitalism, for example); and secondly, upon the prospects for those actions of a world-historical significance with which such claims are

associated. In general, though, from this viewpoint, '[w]hether history
has meaning, depends on whether humanity is able to constitute itself
as humanity.'[27] And this is, as yet, obviously still very much an open
question.

Methodologically, this approach has all the virtues and vices of
Hegel's dialectical resolution of the antinomy of the empirical and the
transcendental, in the phenomenological ascent of consciousness to
the standpoint of reason, from which it derives. Unlike transcendental
arguments, the ultimate fallibilism of such constructions would appear
to preserve their circularity from critique, but it throws them back
upon contingency with a jolt – albeit with nothing like the sharpness
involved in Popper's subjection of historical interpretation to the
criteria of a falsificationist philosophy of science.[28] The method-
ologist's fear of error may be, as Hegel wrote, 'the error itself', but
the alternative, immanent road is nonetheless a 'pathway of doubt, or
more precisely . . . of *despair*' on which nothing can be secured in
advance.[29] Hegel's *Phenomenology* is in this sense a gamble, albeit, as
Derrida points out, one taking the paradoxical form of a 'bet against
chance'.[30] There is an element of Pascal in Hegel's method which all
too often goes unrecognized.[31] What appears at one historical moment
to be a great philosophical strength may in another quickly be transformed into a debilitating empirical burden, threatening to undermine
the project of totalization *per se*.

For most, that day has long since arrived for all of the prospective
ends of history on offer – except, oddly enough, one that claims
to have already arrived. If, as Niethammer puts it, the philosophy of
history has 'worn itself out in the real world', it is nonetheless preserved
in negation in that 'elitist, culturally pessimistic inversion of the
optimism of progress', that 'disenchanted postscript to the nineteenth
century', which goes by the name of *posthistoire*.[32] Indeed, today, when
the speculative predetermination of the future as both ground and
result of a totalizing hermeneutic of the past is so widely discredited,
both politically and methodologically, historical 'endism' as it has
come to be known is, paradoxically, on the rise.[33] Consideration of the
status of ends within the Hegelian tradition of immanent totalizations
of history will serve to highlight the limitations of this approach.

Difference against development

Three main variants of the 'end of history' position can be discerned
within the recent literature. Each is associated with a particular

political orientation towards the historical present. Yet all three tend towards a similar *ironization* of the premises from which they set out. There is the orthodox Hegelian conception of the realization of reason within the historical present represented by Fukuyama, especially in his original article.[34] There is the pessimistic inversion of this position in the *posthistoire* literature examined by Niethammer, towards which Fukuyama's analysis is seen by some increasingly to be driven (Fukuyama the ironist), where the end of history appears as the annihilation rather than the realization of reason on a world-historical scale.[35] And there is the Marxist-Hegelian position, an extension of Left Hegelianism, for which the rationality immanent within the historical present requires the institution of a new form of society in order to be realized, but which nonetheless understands the present as itself furnishing the conditions for the transition to such a society, and hence, like Hegel himself in 1807, as 'a birth-time and a period of transition to a new order'.[36] The end of history is thus here still an unachieved goal (*telos*) or future end-state, rather than an achieved historical condition (*finis*), albeit one that is, allegedly, demonstrably immanent to the present. In the fully phenomenological version, it is an immanently produced recognition of the irrationality of the present by an agency of world-historical significance that is to lead *directly* to the transformation of that present and the realization of its rational potential. The central problem for all Marxist Hegelianisms thus becomes that of locating the appropriate agency for a philosophically predetermined historical task.[37] Marxist Hegelianism thereby distinguishes itself in principle from all kinds of Hegelian Marxism, which would subject the appropriation of Hegelian forms to the ontological discipline of a historical materialism of social being.

For Hegel, in his important early work from 1801–07, the agency was to be philosophy itself. Later, in the *Philosophy of Right* (1821), it was associated with a certain structure and ideology of the modern state. Later still, in a move which returns us in a disabused manner to the strategy of his very earliest writings, it was religion that was to undertake the mass educational task of demonstrating the rationality of the actual; although ultimately, of course, for Hegel religion was always 'the very substance' of the state. More generally, however, the question of agency is finessed by the very structure of Hegelian thought, which unites theoretical and practical reason in speculation in such a way as to restrict the relation of theory to practice to the confines of the problematic of recognition.[38]

For the early Marx, it was the German proletariat which, for conjunctural historical reasons, represented the hopes for a realization of

philosophy. Later, it was the collective worker, although the Left
Hegelian problematic of actualizing an immanent reason had by then,
to some extent, been displaced. Furthermore, the realization of the
end in question (reason as freedom, or, more strictly speaking, the
free appropriation of the historically developed potentialities of the
species) was always conceived by Marx as the conclusion of what will
at that point become *pre*-history, rather than as the end of history
tout court. Truly human history, the true realm of freedom ('that
development of human energy that is an end in itself'), the realization
of new powers and capacities, beyond – but on the basis of – the
realm of necessity, the inauguration of a truly 'historical' time, *begins*
there.[39]

In the first of our three cases of historical endism, the onus is on its
proponents to fill out the idea of an achieved historical rationality.
This requires three things: (1) evidence of a structural logic of simple
reproduction, with no immanent tendencies towards new historical
forms; (2) exposition and defence of the requisite criterion of rationality; (3) demonstration of the achievement of this criterion in the
simple, self-reproducing present. It is the fulfilment of the first two
requirements without the third that leads to the second of our three
variants: *posthistoire*. Thus, it is the combination of the apparent
strength of Fukuyama's arguments regarding the absence of systemic
alternatives to the current status quo, with the acknowledged weakness of his claim for the achievement of the required rationality
(the satisfaction of the desire for recognition), which has led some
on the Left to read his work as ultimately more conducive to a left-
wing pessimism about the present than a right-wing triumphalism.[40]
This is perhaps to pay too little attention to his affinities with what
must be considered the dominant variant of the *posthistoire* thesis:
the deep-rooted cultural pessimism of a naturalistic conservatism.
Nevertheless, either way – and Niethammer is surely right to warn
against attaching political labels to theoretical positions independently
of the national contexts in which they are propounded[41] – there can be
no doubt about the tendency of Fukuyama's Hegelianism to turn into
its opposite.

Something similar can be detected in the evolution of the last of
our three versions of this structure of argument: the Marxist-Hegelian
conception of the 'end' which projects it forward beyond historical
actuality, into a politically contingent but socially immanent future.
For once the credibility of the attribution of world-historical agency
to a particular social subject begins to be undermined empirically (the
revolutionary character of the European working classes in advanced

capitalism, for example), adherents of the position are soon faced with a *de facto* historical impasse which, while it may not be strictly incompatible with the theoretical terms of their conception of history (since they could presumably claim a temporary blindness of the historical process to itself), does unquestionably erode its plausibility. In fact, the perception of historical impasse tends to translate itself into theoretical terms quite quickly, problematizing the conception of history from which it derives. Such, for example, is a common if superficial (because too narrowly Hegelian) reading of Adorno's work. Recent events have generalized this problem to even Adorno's most orthodox critics. For while the perspective of a Marxist Hegelianism might retain its retrospective explanatory power in relation to events in Eastern Europe (we are all Mensheviks now), even its most forthright apologists acknowledge the impasse of agency. To redeem such failure methodologically, by designating the question as previously 'in principle unanswerable' (because of the state of development of the object – capitalism as a global system), while merely *assuming* it to be answerable today (contingent upon an as-yet-unwritten political economy of the world system),[42] is to make a wager on communism way beyond anything that could reasonably be thought of as demonstrably immanent to the historical process.

If the Right Hegelian position represented by Fukuyama is sustained only by the thin soup of an absence of systemic alternatives, the Left Hegelian or Marxist-Hegelian position thus currently looks similarly undernourished, since it is reduced to projecting a specific future (communism) solely on the basis of the crisis tendencies of the present system, without a demonstrably immanent principle for the construction of a new order.[43] Neither remotely fulfils the strenuous requirements of the fully-blown Hegelianism to which they aspire – hence the ironically Nietzschean conclusion to Fukuyama's attempt at a Hegelian interpretation of the present state of the world: his depiction of the 'last man'.[44] Historical experience does not just resist interpretation along the lines of any of the currently available Hegelian models; it positively mocks them, and not for the first time.

There is a range of versions of precisely which events in twentieth-century history have been the most destructive of the Hegelian perspective of an achieved, or immanently achievable, historical rationality: from the horrors of the First World War, through fascism, Auschwitz, Hiroshima and the emergent prospect of a global nuclear annihilation, the continuing exploitation of the peoples of the 'Third World' after decolonization, and the ecological crisis of the planet, to the end of historical Communism. Most decisive, perhaps, has been the cumulative impact of these events on a form of historical consciousness (historical totalization) which has been progressively eroded by the power of temporal abstraction at work in the social processes of 'modernity', to which reference was made in the last chapter. In 1946, Kojève could with some plausibility deny that 'history has refuted Hegelianism', arguing that the most one could say was that 'it has still not arbitrated between "left" and "right" interpretations of Hegel's philosophy.'[45] Today, few would disagree with Ricoeur that:

> It now seems as though Hegel, seizing a favourable moment, a *kairos*, which has been revealed for what it was to our perspective and our experience, only totalised a few leading aspects of the spiritual history of Europe and of its geographical and historical environment, ones that, since that time, have come undone. ... What has come undone is the very substance of what Hegel sought to make into a concept. Difference has turned against development, conceived as a *Stufengang* [succession of stages].[46]

Difference has turned against development conceived at the level of world history as a succession of stages. The European spirit (*Geist*) can no longer find itself in the 'absolute dismemberment' of which Hegel writes in the Preface to the *Phenomenology*, however hard it may continue to try. 'Contemplating the negative face to face', it can dwell there no longer.[47] But does this experience rule out the very possibility of historical totalization? Or does it rather, more taxingly, demand a change in our conception of its status and form? One might reverse the question: what would it mean to forego the perspective of historical totalization altogether? Is it even conceivable? To begin to get a grip on these issues, we need to look beyond the dispiriting experiences of twentieth-century history to what is implied by their reading as a 'refutation' of historical totalization and, in particular, to the structure of historical time that this involves.

Hegel's failure: end of history, end of time

One reason for the continuing importance of Hegelianism, for all its failures, is that our relation to it is considerably more than merely 'philosophical'. If Hegel failed, we may agree with Bataille that 'one cannot say that it was the result of an error.' Rather, 'it is as an authentic movement, weighty with sense, that one must speak of [such] "failure".'[48] Ricoeur writes for a generation of European intellectuals when he explains that:

for us, the loss of credibility the Hegelian philosophy of history has undergone has the significance of an event in thinking, concerning which we may say neither that we brought it about nor that it simply happened, and concerning which we do not know if it is indicative of a catastrophe that still is crippling us or a deliverance whose glory we dare not celebrate.[49]

Such a loss carries the weight of an historical experience in which, paradoxically, it is the very idea of such an experience (an experience of 'history') that is in question. There is something in 'the experience of the West' in the twentieth century – that grandiose intellectual project through which European culture traditionally constitutes itself as a reflection upon its own historical results and prospects – which generates 'incredulity' at the very thought that, as Hegel put it, 'reason governs the world' and 'history is therefore a rational process.'[50] Yet this very experience remains inseparable from such thoughts. As a result, despite 'more than a century of ruptures, and of "surpassings" with or without "overturnings"',[51] our relation to Hegel remains as problematic as ever.

But if this relation is always more than merely philosophical, there is nonetheless a philosophical side to this 'more'. There is a methodological dimension to the persistence of Hegelianism, and it concerns the question of fallibilism, or, more precisely, that peculiar combination of fallibilism and absolutism that is the dialectic of spirit as 'absolute method'. The problem, as Foucault describes it, is that:

> any real escape from Hegel presupposes that we have an accurate understanding of what it will cost us to detach ourselves from him; it presupposes that we know the extent to which Hegel, perhaps insidiously, has approached us; it presupposes that we know what is still Hegelian in that which allows us to think against Hegel; and that we can assess the extent to which our appeal against him is perhaps one more of the ruses he uses against us and at the end of which he is waiting for us, immobile and elsewhere.[52]

If the fallibilism of Hegel's phenomenological method opens up all specific Hegelianisms – all specific totalizations of history – to the test of historical experience, it also *protects* Hegelianism itself, Hegelianism as 'method', from philosophical critique. Indeed, the interpretive critique of any particular Hegelianism, any particular totalization, can always be read as a demonstration rather than a refutation of the method. But how many such demonstrations do we need before the ironizing process of so paradoxical a confirmation of rectitude begins to erode our belief in the project? Or is there no difference here from the fallibilism attendant upon all claims to knowledge, and the irony attached to all attempts to inflate such claims to the status of truth? But what, then, of the 'absoluteness' of the method? Alternatively, if we reject Hegelianism, are we to move 'beyond' it through criticism (in some presumably non-dialectical sense of 'beyond')? Or must it simply be abandoned, like a worn-out shoe?[53]

It is the great merit of Feuerbach's 1839 essay, 'Towards a Critique of Hegel's Philosophy', that, for all its apparently unmediated naturalism, it homes in on the question of time: not Hegel's presentation of the concept of time, but the time of Hegelian philosophy itself. For all its ostensible historicity, Feuerbach argues, Hegelian philosophy effectively abolishes time altogether. It has as its presupposition the 'end of the world':

> If Hegelian philosophy were the absolute reality of the idea of philosophy, then the immobility of reason in the Hegelian philosophy must necessarily result in the immobility of time; for if time still moved sadly along as if nothing had happened, then the Hegelian philosophy would unavoidably forfeit its attribute of absoluteness.[54]

Or, to put it another way, Hegel's method – dialectic as absolute method – *eternalizes the present*; not just in the sense that for Hegel the 'true present' is eternity, since 'in its concept [*Begriff*], time itself is eternal'[55] – all truth is eternal for Hegel – but in the consequent sense that Hegelian philosophy must always eternalize its *own* present, if it is to offer the possibility of an absolute knowing. However successful Hegel's method may be, hermeneutically, at any one time, in integrating historical material into the web of its supreme plot, it can only succeed by abolishing the past *as* past, and the future *as* future. The past is taken up by memory into the actuality of the present and its husk is thrown away as mere 'existence' (*Existenz*); while the future is treated as wholly immanent to the rationality of the present, the present of the interpretation. The *end of history*, the *eternalization of the present*, and the *abolition of the past as past* are the three temporal dimensions of a single method.

If the problem for transcendental justifications of historical totalization setting out from the discipline of historical studies was that they lacked futurity, immanent ones thus compound this lack by appearing bereft of any sense of the past as *loss*. The speculative projection of the future, as the basis for a totalized knowledge of past and present through which that future might be reached, acts as a form of redemption that obliterates those historical events which are not gathered up by its totalizing gaze, whilst denying the moment of absolute otherness inherent in its temporal distance from those which are recalled: that moment of otherness which ineluctably associates the passage of time with *death*. Not only does the immanent method assume that the present within which speculative projection takes place can embrace the totality of interests at play in the future (that is, in future presents) – that there will be no gap between present futures and future presents – but it assumes that the 'reality' (*Wirklichkeit*) of the past is (re)constitutable, without loss, in the speculative meaning of an interiorizing memory (*Erinnerung*). In short, Hegelianism is incapable of coming to terms with death as an *ontological* negation or *annihilation*, because it reduces thought to the reappropriative work of an essentially discursive meaning, within the constraints of demonstration, communication and self-presentation.[56] As Derrida puts it in his reading of Bataille, exploiting the economic side of the idea of speculation:

> The notion of *Aufhebung* . . . is laughable in that it signifies the *busying* of a discourse losing its breath as it reappropriates all negativity for itself, as it works the 'putting at stake' into an *investment*, as it *amortizes* absolute expenditure; and as it gives meaning to death, thereby simultaneously blinding itself to the baselessness of the nonmeaning from which the basis of meaning is drawn, and in which this basis of meaning is exhausted. . . .
>
> The blind spot of Hegelianism, *around* which can be organised the representation of meaning, is the *point* at which destruction, suppression, death and sacrifice constitute so irreversible an expenditure, so radical a negativity . . . that they can no longer be determined as negativity in a process or a system. In discourse (the unity of process and system), negativity is always the underside and accomplice of positivity. Negativity cannot be spoken of, nor has it ever been except in this fabric of meaning.[57]

We will return to the problematic yet illuminating character of Hegel's treatment of death when we come to discuss the relevance of Heidegger's work for the problem of historical totalization. For the moment, let us simply note that the problem of loss has two sides here, since those pasts that *are* lost to the present on the Hegelian model, which are denied all reality, may yet be central to future presents beyond the scope of all presently plausible futures. (On the one hand, there is not enough of a sense of loss; on the other, there is so much that it obliterates its object.) Indeed, it is only identification with such apparently obliterated pasts as 'lost' (lost not in the sense of an absence of documentation, but in the sense of their failure to establish a living relationship to the present), that can generate the will to their recovery and thereby a future for which they will no longer be lost. As Benjamin was so acutely aware, there is a politics unknown to Hegel which is 'nourished by the image of enslaved ancestors rather than that of liberated grandchildren'.[58] Once again, this is something to which we will return, below.

Thus, although at one level the constitutive role of the past in the speculative predetermination of the future in Hegelianism might be seen as part of a politics of the present, at another level it crowds out politics, philosophically, by prematurely imposing the perspective of a future which absolutizes existing relations to the past. The immanent approach, one might say, is in danger of taking the politics out of history.[59] It is what Ricoeur calls 'the finitude of the philosophical act' that is revealed here – a finitude of both loss and possibility. Its recognition forces us beyond Hegel.[60] It is connected by Feuerbach to nature.

Feuerbach's reading of Hegel in many respects anticipates Kojève's. But what is presented by Feuerbach as a critique is affirmed and defended by Kojève. The reason for this is that Feuerbach, like Hegel himself, but not Kojève, ultimately identifies historical with natural, or 'cosmic', time. Time is a category of Hegel's *Philosophy of Nature*. What appears in Kojève as the 'end of history' is thus also to Feuerbach the 'end of the world'. Focusing exclusively on the *Phenomenology of Spirit*, Kojève discusses historical time only in its independence from nature, as the product of the struggle for recognition. Indeed, Hegel's ultimate identification of cosmic and historical time is, in Kojève's view, his 'basic error'.[61] Yet in taking this position (and thereby laying the foundations for both the humanisms and anti-humanisms of postwar French thought),[62] Kojève severs the dialectic of nature and history at the heart of the Hegelian project, which constitutes its great advance over the dualism of Kantian thought. This dualism reappears in Fukuyama, Kojève's contemporary heir, as a dualism of economics and politics.[63] What looks like the crudest misunderstanding of the problematic of *posthistoire* – the conflation of the end of history as the end of a certain kind of meaning, with the end of history as the end of the world – is thus from Feuerbach's *Hegelian* standpoint the manifestation of a repressed truth. Any attempt at a post-Hegelian account of historical totalization will have to confront this unsettling thought.

Time and Narrative: phenomenological ontology

What, then, is left of the speculative totality of the immanent road, when even its fallibilism falls short of an adequate sense of its limits?

Can it be rethought in the face of the kind of critique outlined above, to preserve a sense of the whole? It is helpful at this point to turn to the phenomenological tradition in the philosophy of time, as reconstructed by Ricoeur in his major work *Time and Narrative*, from Book 11 of Augustine's *Confessions* (398) to Division Two of Heidegger's *Being and Time* (1927), via Husserl's *Lectures on the Phenomenology of Internal Time-Consciousness* (1905). For what we find there is a series of attempts to ground the understanding of historical time in an account of the temporality of human existence, explicitly contrasted with the opposing speculative tradition of thinking about time as 'cosmological fact' that takes its cue from the discussion of time as 'the number of motion with respect of "before" and "after"' in Book IV of Aristotle's *Physics*, and which finds its modern, transcendental variant in the 'Transcendental Aesthetic' of Kant's *Critique of Pure Reason*. The subjectivism of the phenomenological approach, implicit in its methodological reduction of consciousness to its eidetic core, is thus made to face up to the problem of time's objectivity as a natural condition which exceeds and precedes all constitutive activity of the self. Finally, these two philosophical accounts of time – and their aporia – are placed within the overarching context of an exploration of the temporal structures of narrative in history and fiction, which aims to demonstrate the resolution of the philosophical aporia of time in the poetics of narrative; or, at least, to show that it is within the conceptual space of historical and fictional narrative that the aporetics of temporality find their 'deepest imaginative exploration'.

In order to do this, it is necessary for Ricoeur to establish a conceptual bridge between the aporetic 'time of the philosophers' (phenomenological and cosmological) and the 'time of history', understood as narrative form. Should he have succeeded in establishing such a bridge, however, it ought to be possible to cross it back the other way – back, that is, from the analysis of historical time as narrative refiguration to the 'time of the philosophers' – in order to raise the question of the ontological status of such narrative mediation. This is the strategy that will be adopted here: a reversal in the direction of Ricoeur's analysis, back from the presentation of historical time as a 'resolution' of the aporia of the duality of philosophical perspectives, to the question of the ontological status of historical time. To anticipate my conclusion: it will be argued that, despite its ultimate self-understanding as a deepening of the *mystery* of time, Ricoeur's analysis in fact gives philosophical sustenance to the claim for the unity of time and, thereby, not merely to the possibility but to the *necessity* of historical totalization. There is only one time and this time is historical.

It is in the relations between the different forms and levels of temporalization that the key to the problem of historical totalization is to
be found, and thereby, the key to a better understanding of the
complexities of 'modernity' as a specific totalizing temporalization of
history.

The rest of this chapter falls into three main parts. It begins with a
condensed summary of Ricoeur's account of the aporetics of temporality as it develops within the philosophical tradition, from Aristotle
to Heidegger, as 'the aporia of the dual perspective' of the lived 'time
of the soul' (object of the phenomenological tradition) and the universal 'time of the world' (object of the cosmological tradition). It
moves on to Ricoeur's conception of historical time as a narrative mediation of this aporia in the form of the 'reinscription of lived time
on cosmic time', or an 'imperfect mediation' of the human and the
cosmic. This mediation gives rise to a new aporia specific to historical
time: the aporia of totality. It is this aporia, and the unexplored possibilities for the theorization of history opened up by Ricoeur's treatment
of it, with which we are primarily concerned. It is approached here by
way of an extension of the structure of Heidegger's analysis of the
anticipation of death to the problem of historical time. This raises
the question of the relationship of historical time to cosmological
time anew, as the problem of the 'independent outside' of nature – an
independent outside which is accessible to us only as the limit of its
social mediation.

Time and Narrative is a massive, complex and extraordinarily
ambitious work of synthesis that moves between literary, historical
and philosophical theory in subtle but often elusive ways. As a work
of philosophical hermeneutics, it is comparable in significance only
to Gadamer's *Truth and Method*. Yet the serial character of its
composition leads to serious ambiguities in its overall meaning.[64] In
particular, there is a gradual but definite shift in the focus of the book
between the first and third volumes, as the structural centrality of
the concept of narrative is gradually displaced by the idea of a
hermeneutics of historical consciousness which, while narrative in its
discursive form, is nonetheless implicitly ontological in orientation.
This problematizes the structure of the book, since the philosophical
status of one of its two central concepts (narrative) becomes obscure.
Consistently presented as part of poetics, in contradistinction to the
claims of the philosophical tradition, the concept of narrative nonetheless begins to play a role in relation to these claims which significantly
exceeds its formal place in the analysis. On the other hand, the 'ontological answer' to the problem of historical time, which is announced

in the first volume as forthcoming later in the book,[65] never arrives. Its position at the conclusion to the final volume is taken by an ontologically ambiguous narrative hermeneutics of historical *consciousness*. In attempting to extract what might be called an ontological concept of historical time from the book, as the basis for a critical hermeneutics of historical *existence*, I am thus in a sense merely drawing out the suppressed philosophical implications of its form.[66]

Present or instant? The time of the soul and the time of the world

Time and Narrative is structured around Ricoeur's exposition of two overlapping oppositions. On the one hand, there is the opposition internal to explicitly theoretical reflections on time between what Ricoeur calls the 'phenomenological' and 'cosmological' perspectives: the 'time of the soul' and the 'time of the world'. On the other, there is an opposition between such reflections taken as a whole (and given the name 'aporetics of temporality') and the refiguration of time through narrative in historical and fictional discourses, the exposition of which falls under the heading of a 'poetics of narrative'. The relationship which Ricoeur hopes to establish between the two is that the aporia produced by the first opposition can be shown to be resolved in the poetics of narrative which is its counterpart in the second opposition. The aporetics of temporality and the poetics of narrative come together in what we might call an 'apo(r)etics of narrative'.[67] Narrativity, or, more precisely, what in Kantian mode Ricoeur refers to as 'the narrative schemata of the productive imagination', becomes the key to the comprehension of time itself. As he puts it at the outset of the study, 'time becomes human to the extent that it is organised after the manner of a narrative; narrative, in turn, is meaningful to the extent that it portrays the features of temporal experience.'[68] It is the ultimate function of such portrayal to 'refigure' time itself. To see how this thesis bears on the question of the totalization of time as history, it is necessary to present the oppositions it articulates in a little more detail.

The opposition between phenomenological and cosmological perspectives on time, which is attributed the status of an aporia, is first located by Ricoeur internally to Augustine's discussion of time in Book 11 of his *Confessions*. Subsequently, however, it receives a more extended treatment in the form of a confrontation between Augustine's attempt at a reduction of time to a dialectic of the

intention and distension of the soul, and Aristotle's account of
the cosmological basis of time in movement in his *Physics*.[69] The
alleged irreducibility of these two times to one another – otherwise
designated as 'lived' time and 'universal' time – sets the stage for the
subsequent demonstration of the intensification of their aporetic
relation in Husserl and Heidegger, whereby 'any progress obtained by
the phenomenology of temporality has to pay for its advance in each
instance by the ever higher price of an even greater aporicity.'[70] It is
this scenario (this *narrative*) that motivates the displacement of the
problem from the domain of reflective argumentation to a narrative
poetics of temporal experience. The suspension of the 'philosophical'
in Ricoeur's account of narrative temporality is thus premised, more
or less inductively, upon the failure of reflective argumentation to
provide a theoretically unified account of time – although, as we shall
see, this 'suspension' may be read against its own methodological self-
consciousness as a form of conceptual mediation in its own right.

The aporia or impasse in question is understood as the result of an
incommensurability between two equally legitimate methodological
perspectives. On one side, we are offered accounts of the constitutive
role of the subject in the formation of temporal experience – from
Aristotle's recognition of the necessity of 'one who counts' to any
definition of time in terms of measurement, to Husserl's intentional
construction of time by consciousness, and Heidegger's location of
temporality in the self-interpreting existential structure of *Dasein*
(Heidegger's term for his particular philosophical conception of human
beings as questioning beings: literally, 'there-being').[71] On the other
side, we find an insistence on the dependence of such constructions
upon an objective 'dynamism of movement' which exceeds them in
principle, although it is only intelligible as the ontological ground of
a time which is so constructed. In Ricoeur's words, the two perspectives 'mutually occlude each other to the very extent they imply each
other'.[72] This relation of mutual occlusion is exemplified in the
allegedly 'conceptually unbridgeable gap'[73] between the Aristotelian
concept of the 'instant' and the Augustinean conception of the 'present'.
The former generates a time-scale of serial succession out of the
differentiation of two point-like instants, in relation to which it
becomes possible both to *measure* time and to speak of a 'before' and
an 'after' (but not a 'past' or a 'future'). The latter, on the other hand,
produces a dynamically differentiated past and future as the effect of
an irreducible self-referentiality.

It might be thought that the two notions simply map onto one
another, insofar as the 'now' of the present may be understood as a

specific instance of the Aristotelian instant. This would certainly seem to be how Aristotle himself saw the matter: the 'now' of the present is an instant situated by its relation to a subject at the moment of its utterance. In this respect, past, present and future would be subordinated to the instant and the more basic (objective) relation of before and after. The difficulty with this reduction, however, is that it fails to grasp the dynamism of the now as a permanent relation of simultaneous differentiation and unification, upon which the before and after depends for its sense of temporal direction. The fluid dynamism of this relation is the subject of Augustine's attention in his construction of the idea of the threefold present.

Unlike the instant, the phenomenological present contains the totality of the temporal spectrum within itself. Its elements are not differentiated by their presence as opposed to their absence from consciousness, but by the form of their presence as, respectively, objects of memory, attention and expectation.[74] (This was Augustine's elegant solution to the classical paradox of the being and non-being of time.) Furthermore, Ricoeur argues, only a threefold present of this kind can secure the essential *continuity* of time upon which Aristotle himself relies as a condition of his conception of the instant, which is produced by an operation of infinite division on a continuous spectrum. The phenomenology of the now thus asserts both its independence from the cosmology of measurable movement and its indispensability to it. It is in his efforts to clarify this phenomenological unity of time that Husserl is led, firstly, to augment Augustine's notion of the threefold present with that of an 'expanded', intentional, internally active 'present within the present' – *duration*; and secondly, to attempt the derivation of the serial succession of objective time from this newly embellished phenomenological core.

Thus, if Aristotle reduced the temporality of past, present and future to the subject's consciousness of its position within an objective time of serial succession, Husserl inverts the procedure. However, while he may thereby enrich our conception of phenomenological time, Ricoeur argues, he is ultimately no more successful than Aristotle in submitting time to a unitary conceptualization. Phenomenological and physical time, the time of the soul and the time of the world, persist in stubborn independence.

Ricoeur identifies Husserl's 'two great discoveries' as the phenomenon of retention and its futural counterpart, protention, on the one hand; and the distinction between retention (or primary remembrance) and recollection (or secondary remembrance), on the other.[75] Retention is the phenomenological basis of the expanded present.

Husserl introduces the idea with reference to the unity of the experience of a sound. Sounds do not simply occur 'in' time, but 'through' it.
Their identity is constituted over time. It is only possible to experience
the unity of a sound through the retention of phases already past
and their identification with a point-like now, such that the time of
its occurrence is constructed as a single, expanded present, or what
Gerard Granel calls 'the big now'.[76] The serial aspect of succession is
swallowed up in the continuity of a duration which flows from the
present as a perpetual source, and 'runs off' into the past, as earlier
retentions are recast by more recent ones in a process of temporal
fading which binds the present to the past (and vice versa) through an
infinity of overlapping retentions. As Heidegger puts it, even *forgetting*
is to be understood as a specific mode of retention.[77] The idea of
protention, which Husserl spends much less time discussing, extends
the analysis in the other temporal direction (the future), with reference
to the intentional modification of the present through anticipation, as
opposed to memory. It is the assumption of a fundamental symmetry
here between retention and protention that Heidegger will contest,
claiming an existential priority for the future (as Being-towards-death)
as the ground of the interpretation of *Dasein* as a whole.[78]

The idea of retention plays two main roles in Husserl's analysis.
In the first place, it definitively distinguishes the temporality of the
phenomenological now from that of the point-like instant by intro-
ducing into it a longitudinal intentionality. This stretches it out to
include what would otherwise count as aspects of the most recent past,
when measured against a serial scale of successive instants. (We have
already seen this process of identification at work at the level of
historical time, in the extended 'today' of modernity, in chapter 1.)
Secondly, it thereby establishes duration as the primary phenomenon
of a phenomenological time. It is from the unity of duration that
Husserl will subsequently attempt to derive the continuity of the series
of objective time, through a dual process of formal abstraction and
imaginary extension.[79]

Within this conception, the Aristotelian instant appears as a conceptual construction arrived at by thinking of the point-like present
which serves as the source of retentional series, independently of its
power as the source of such retentions, abstracted from the durational
continuity it establishes, through which it acquires its significance as a
'present'. Although derived, and hence in this sense only a secondary
phenomenon, the instant is, however, recognized by Husserl to be
constitutive of our sense of a *historical* past. Such a past is beyond
the reach of both retention and recollection (the recalling of faded

retentions). It can thus only be thought on the basis of the *imaginary* extension of a temporal continuum established by overlapping retentions, backwards beyond the life-span of the individual in question, to infinity. To think such a past historically – that is, as a series of past *presents* – requires the imaginative ability to take an instant from its series and represent it as the source-point of what succeeds it, as if it were a present, such that it becomes the centre of a perspective with its own retentions and protentions (protentions that may well extend as far as our own actual present). This ability is based in recollection or secondary remembrance, which has the same structure as historical thought, except for the fact that, in its case, the past which is reproduced 'coincides' with past retentions of the individual.

However, a supplementary intentionality is still required to establish the past as a *single* series. Thus, while historical consciousness, like memory, contains secondary 'intentions of expectation, the fulfilment of which lead to the present', and a sense of the present as 'the actualisation of the future of the past', not only is this past not remembered (not 'coincident with past retentions'), but it must possess a temporal structure common to *all* subjects.[80] This is achieved by disentangling the identity of temporal position (*Zeitstelle*) in recollection from the identity of the object thus remembered; or, to put it another way, by objectifying the formal aspects of temporality as succession, so as to make possible the imaginary extension (both forwards and backwards) of an endless series of quasi-presents.

Ricoeur objects to this analysis at a number of levels. Firstly, he questions whether Husserl has not borrowed determinations of objective time in his primary phenomenological descriptions of lived time. (In the same way, Heidegger sees the Aristotelian instant as being dependent for its intelligibility upon unexpressed intentional connections in his discussion of the before and after, *proteron* and *husteron*.)[81] 'Would we use the expression "sensed *at the same time*",' Ricoeur asks, 'if we knew nothing of objective simultaneity, of temporal distance, if we knew nothing of the objective equality between intervals of time?'[82] Secondly, Ricoeur points out that, ontologically, 'the perception of duration never ceases to presuppose the duration of perception', and hence a time to which the phenomenological subject is *subjected* as much as one which it constitutes.[83] Thirdly, following Heidegger, he questions the inhibitions which surround Husserl's treatment of expectation and futurity, which are effectively subordinated to the analysis of retention, while being constructed analogically as symmetrical to it, without ever being given a direct phenomenological treatment of their own. Finally, he doubts whether the continuity established by the coincidence of longitudinal intentionalities is sufficient to derive the totality of time as a unity in succession.

Each of these problems is addressed by the ontological and hermeneutical turn that the phenomenology of time-consciousness takes in Heidegger's *Being and Time*. There, we find Husserl's analysis recast within the terms of the existential analytic of *Dasein*, such that its three main stages reappear, transformed, as distinct ontological levels of temporality, ordered hierarchically according to their place in the derivation of the 'inauthentic' everyday from the ontologically 'primordial': ecstatic-horizonal temporality (*Zeitlichkeit*), historicality (*Geschichtlichkeit*) and within-timeness (*Innerzeitigkeit*). Such a transposition was designed to abolish the very framework of subject and object (subjective and objective time) which generates what Ricoeur calls the aporia of the dual perspective. However, Ricoeur argues, it does so only at the cost of its reproduction at another level: the level of the ethical. We shall come to Ricoeur's critique of the temporality of *Dasein* shortly. For the moment, let us just note, firstly, that the reason he finds the aporia of the dual perspective reproduced there is because of the failure of Heidegger's polemic against the 'ordinary concept of time', of which Aristotle is the acknowledged philosophical representative;[84] and secondly, that it is from the thus fractured hierarchy of modes of temporalization (with historicality situated *between* primordial temporality and ordinary or everyday time) that Ricoeur derives the idea of developing an independent concept of historical time as the basis for his own resolution of the aporia. However, as we have noted already, this resolution produces a new aporia of its own: the aporia of totality.

Historical time: ontology and narrative mediation

The aporia of the dual perspective (phenomenological and cosmological) that preoccupies Ricoeur throughout his discussion of the philosophy of time derives from reading the apparently irreducible duality of perspectives against the background of a fundamental metaphysical assumption: the unity of time. The argument for a distinct 'historical time' which mediates this duality is designed to overcome the aporia and re-establish the presumed unity of time at a new level: the poetics of narrative. The aporia of totality is, in this respect, simply the reappearance of the aporia of the dual perspective within a single perspective: historical time. It is the result of asking how historical time is to be understood as internally unified, if we are to avoid its reduction to the eternal present of the Hegelian absolute – and hence the accusation of the assumption of a teleological end to history. Ricoeur seeks a solution to this dilemma in two directions: in the referential constraints specific to historical (as opposed to fictional) narrative; and in the ultimate limits to human consciousness regarding the comprehension of what he calls the 'mystery' of time – a move which oscillates, symptomatically, between materialist and theological inflections.[85] So what, on this account, is 'historical' time?

For Ricoeur, historical time is the product of the '(re)inscription of lived time onto cosmic time' in the form of a threefold narrative mimesis:

mimesis 1 – a *pre*figuration of the narrative structure of historical time in the structure of human action and its everyday interpretation;

mimesis 2 – the *con*figuration of historical time through the construction of narratives that are 'overlaid' on the chronological framework of a shared cosmic time;

mimesis 3 – the *re*figuration of lived time by virtue of the effect of its narrative configuration back upon the experience of the 'reader'.

In the course of this process, 'the network of interweaving perspectives' of the expectation of the future, the reception of the past, and the experience of the present is understood to produce the 'open-ended, incomplete imperfect mediation' of a historical present open to initiative and action.[86] It is this openness to action – or time of initiative – characteristic of the fundamental futurity of phenomenological temporality, which ruptures the process of historical totalization: 'Doing means that reality is not totalizable.'[87] An essential difference is thereby maintained between 'lived' time and 'cosmic' time via the form of the connection established between them: a narrative mediation grounded, ontologically, in a temporal structure of action for which each interpretive closure opens out, simultaneously, onto the radical indeterminacy of a new beginning. It is the 'objective', cosmological time onto which lived time is inscribed which provides the basis of its totalization; and the fundamentally open structure of lived time itself, however successfully refigured, that frustrates it. The totalizations of historical narratives (mimesis 2) are fractured as they run up against the open futural time of the active reader, which they refigure (mimesis 3), but which, ultimately, they can never fully enclose. Or, to put it another way, the present is characterized by the basic autonomy of a de-totalizing 'space of experience'.

This cycle of totalization, de-totalization and re-totalization, in which historical consciousness is constantly constructed by narrative, tested in action and experience, and reconstructed but never finally sutured, looks very much like something from Sartre's later work. But Ricoeur's approach is actually rather different. Sartre is concerned to justify the intelligibility of history at the level of its content: the totality of human actions. He builds his analysis progressively out of syntheses of structures of practice: from individual praxis to the practico-inert, to groups, to history. His ultimate goal is thus similar to the Hegelian philosophy of history, although his means are different, and the second volume of the *Critique of Dialectical Reason* breaks off before the 'advent of history'.[88] Ricoeur, on the other hand, approaches the idea of history phenomenologically and hermeneutically, as the form of temporal experience. He is interested in the form of historical consciousness, rather than the structure of interaction between individuals and groups.

The connection between the two perspectives lies in the concept of action and the associated sense of history as an open process, mediation as always 'imperfect'. But there is no equivalent in Sartre of the level of analysis at which this idea is explored by Ricoeur: the level of narrative as a 'mimesis of action'. Nor is there a sense of the broader theoretical context within which the problem of historical time is posed by Ricoeur. It is this broader context (the aporia of the dual perspective) which gives ontological weight to the aporia of totality, an aporia which is negotiated or covered over, but never overcome, by the mapping of historical onto cosmological time – in much the same way as the gap between the infant and the adult is covered over, but also thereby reproduced, in the psychic process described by psychoanalytical theory as 'identification'.[89] The historical present is in this sense always 'untimely'. If universal history is to be constructed, it is always also, as Adorno insisted, to be 'denied' (*leugnen*).[90]

The problem of historical totalization, transformed now into the problem of the totalization of time as history, thus breaks up into a series of more specific issues. Totality/totalization appears at three different levels:

1. The totalization of lived time in the phenomenological unity of the process of temporalization – established in a preliminary fashion in Augustine's threefold present, and further developed in detail in Heidegger's analysis of death;

2. The establishment of objective or cosmological time as the *open-ended* totality of infinite serial succession, independent of consciousness insofar as it is dependent on movement – Aristotle;

3. The totalization of historical time as the narrative temporality of an 'imperfect mediation' of 1 and 2 – Ricoeur.

It is to this third level that the problem regresses insofar as 1 and 2 are dependent upon each other; neither can be constructed independently. What this suggests, however, is that historical time is just as 'real' as both cosmological and phenomenological time, since it is only through its mediation of the one with the other that either can be constructed at all. Indeed, might not each of these two other 'times' be merely abstractions of the individual and ideally collective elements, respectively, of a single 'historical' time, in the way that Husserl saw the Aristotelian instant as a reified abstraction from the experience of a point-like retentional source?

To put the matter methodologically: is Ricoeur's narrative construction of historical time as the imperfect mediation of an open-ended narrative totalization (a tale of three times) not *itself* a form of conceptual mediation? Only thus does it make sense to give narrative the centrality to time that Ricoeur does when he writes in conclusion: 'no thought about time without narrated time'.[91] This raises the question of the status of the totalization 'history' in a new, hermeneutical-ontological form. It also allows us to connect up Ricoeur's 'cosmological' critique of Heidegger's purely existential temporality (which we shall address shortly) to his account of historical temporality as narrative mediation. In the process, we are offered the prospect of both a new hermeneutics of historical existence and a re-entry into the conceptualization of modernity, thus reconstrued, via the question of tradition. Let us begin, however, following through the three levels at which the problem of totality now appears, with Heidegger's existential analysis of death.

Being-towards-death, being-towards-history

Heidegger's *Being and Time* marks a turning point in the history of modern philosophy which has led in two quite different directions: the ontologization of hermeneutics in Gadamer (and the restitution and reinterpretation of the category of tradition); and the rejection of all ontological thought, however fundamental, in the allegedly post-metaphysical thinking of the 'event of appropriation' (*Ereignis*) – determining both Time and Being – in Heidegger's later work and, more recently, in Derrida, albeit in a different theoretical register.[92] It is in the direction of Gadamer's thought that we will set out, although we shall ultimately have to double back to Derrida before we can make further headway with our project. We shall thus examine Heidegger's analysis of death at the beginning of Division Two of *Being and Time*, not from the standpoint of the (dubious) question of 'the meaning of Being in general' – to which it is ultimately subordinated by Heidegger – but from that for which the existential structure of *Dasein* appears as the structure of interpretation in general.

The procedure of separating out the existential analytic of *Dasein* from the question of the meaning of Being in general is, of course, fraught with dangers: most notably, the supposed humanist 'misreading' of Heidegger with which the early Sartre is associated.[93] However, insofar as it aims to draw out the repressed social and historical dimensions to Heidegger's concept of *Dasein*, rather than to individualize it further, the reading that follows works in the opposite direction from Sartre's. In this respect, it has more in common with the aspiration to a Heideggerian Marxism of Marcuse's early project for a 'concrete philosophy', sketched in a series of works between 1928 and 1932.[94] However, Marcuse's attempted synthesis, which preceded both the publication of Marx's *Paris Manuscripts* of 1844 and Heidegger's political involvement with National Socialism, was an acknowledged failure; not least because of its flattening of Heidegger's threefold temporal schema into the single dimension of an ontologically indifferent 'historicality'. In contrast, the procedure adopted here will be the methodical extension of the structure of ecstatic-horizonal temporality (*Zeitlichkeit*) to the problem of historical time.

Heidegger's analysis of death sets out from what he describes as 'the inadequacy of the hermeneutical situation' from which the preceding analysis of *Dasein*, in Division One of *Being and Time*, has taken place: namely, *Dasein*'s 'lack of totality', or failure to assure itself that 'the whole of the entity which it has taken as its theme' has been brought into what Heidegger calls the 'fore-having': that provisional understanding of the whole which is the ground of all interpretation. For while the previous analysis had considered *Dasein* as a structural whole (and defined the being of this whole as 'care', *Sorge*), it failed to consider 'the primordial unity of this structural whole'.[95] This is no mere oversight, rectifiable by a return to the previous analysis in more detail. Rather, it marks a fundamental problem, the resolution of which will take the analysis onto a new plane. For if, as Heidegger has argued earlier in the book, against all philosophies of essence, *Dasein* is '*potentiality*-for-Being', it would seem that it cannot be grasped as a whole without negating its existential structure: 'As long as *Dasein is* as an entity, it has never reached its wholeness. . . . [but] When *Dasein* reaches its wholeness in death, it simultaneously loses the Being of its "there".'[96] How are we to negotiate this impasse?

Characteristically, Heidegger's response is to seek a resolution of the dilemma in a deepening of the understanding of the question as a reflection of the existential structure of *Dasein* itself, rather than in some merely 'methodological' innovation. For:

> That which makes up the 'lack of totality' in *Dasein*, the constant 'ahead-of-itself', is neither something still outstanding in a summative together-ness, nor something which has not yet become accessible. It is a 'not-yet' which any *Dasein*, as the entity which it is, *has to be.*[97]

The incompleteness of the analysis reflects the existential structure of *Dasein*'s 'potentiality-for-Being-a-whole', the fact that it is always 'ahead-of-itself'. Its development thus lies in the further explication of this structure: the structure of a being for which its end, death, 'is' only in what Heidegger calls an 'existenti*ell*' manner – that is, as a feature of its self-understanding.[98] This is a being whose 'potentiality-for-Being-a-whole' takes the form of being-*towards*-death, since death alone is the end which, projected ahead, represents the possibility of closure. Death 'exists' as that towards which human existence is oriented as the horizon of its being. Conversely, *Dasein* 'exists' as a finite and hence *temporal* being only through the anticipation of death.

Much of Heidegger's analysis is taken up with demonstrating that 'mineness and existence are ontologically constitutive for death', that death is consequently 'a way to be, which Dasein takes over as soon as it is', and with the 'existentiell', or ethical, problem of authenticity.[99] What concerns us here, however, is less the detail of these matters than their consequences for the phenomenological unity of time as a process of temporalization, and its relations to history and nature. For what is distinctive about Heidegger's analysis is the way in which it moves beyond the subjectivism of Husserl's phenomenology, through the existential problematic of *Dasein*, without leaving its phenomeno-logical core behind, thereby transforming ontology in the direction of a hermeneutics of historical existence. The outcome in *Being and Time* itself is without doubt fractured and ambiguous. It is vitiated, ultimately, by what Adorno describes as the 'ambivalence' of the doctrine of Being, whereby ontology 'cashiers the resistance to idealism which the concept of existence used to offer'.[100] In the process, history is frozen, ontologically, by the very act that would theorize its ground, existentially, as 'historicality' (*Geschichtlichkeit*). It is into the interpretive vacuum opened up by this underdetermination of history as historicality that Heidegger's subsequent political judgements would flow, unimpeded by the discipline of mediation by social or historical theory. In this respect, the link between Heidegger's existential ontology and his personal commitment to National Socialism during the 1930s has as much to do with the theoretical arbitrariness associated with his philosophical disdain for the field of actual world history, as it does with the orientation of the terms of his ontology towards the ideology of a particular political party. Although such arbitrariness might itself be understood as emblematic of a particular kind of politics: fascism as the ontologization of nihilism.[101] In other respects, the matter is considerably more complicated.[102] What we are concerned with here, though, is whether something more productive for the understanding of history might not be teased out of the existential analysis of death, once we refuse the ontological reduction of *Dasein* to the question of the meaning of Being.

There are three main aspects of Heidegger's analysis. The first is an argument to the effect that the anticipation of death as 'the possibility of the measureless impossibility of existence'[103] constitutes *Dasein* as a totality and thereby 'temporalizes temporality' by constituting *Dasein* as a finite being or Being-towards-the-end. Without the anticipation of death as a standpoint for *Dasein*'s unification of itself as a structural whole, there would be no 'temporalization of temporality', and hence no 'experience' of time. The circularity whereby the premise of this argument appears already to contain a temporal concept (anticipation) is hermeneutical, rather than logically vicious, since the anticipation in question is existential rather than psychological. Temporality may appear as a condition of the possibility of the anticipation of death, but such anticipation is at once the very structure of the 'temporalization of temporality' for *Dasein* – the only entity to which, according to Heidegger, time 'belongs'. For Heidegger, *Dasein* is an entity 'whose *kind of Being* is anticipation itself'.[104]

Secondly, there is the character of the unity of *Dasein*, thus temporalized: namely, the manner in which, by registering the finitude of human existence, the anticipation of death simultaneously opens it up to the future as possibility, and structures that possibility through an active taking up of the past within the present into which, as a finite being, *Dasein* is 'thrown'. That is to say, for Heidegger, whilst human existence is 'essentially *futural*' (insofar as it is its freedom for death that 'temporalizes temporality' through the anticipation of its end), it is nonetheless 'equiprimordially' both *making-present* and *having-been*, since such futurity 'exists' only as the projected horizon of a present defined by the mode of its taking up of a specific past. Temporality (*Zeitlichkeit*) 'has the unity of a future which makes itself present in the process of having been'.[105] Heidegger calls this temporal unity the unity of the 'ecstases'. It is the difference, the constant differentiation, at its heart which defines temporality as something that is 'outside-of-itself'. This regulates the possible unity of all *Dasein*'s existential structures, since the 'fundamental structures of *Dasein* . . . are all to be conceived . . . as modes of the temporalizing of temporality.'[106] *Dasein* itself is thus, essentially, something 'outside-of-itself'. It is this 'being-outside-of-itself' through the unity of the temporal ecstases that opens the individual out into history.

This is the third and most ambiguous aspect of Heidegger's analysis: the dual exposition of temporality as 'historicality' and of historicality as the existential ground of history. It is the ontologization of historicality as a mode of Being (*Sein*) which, Adorno insists, 'immobilises history in the unhistorical realm, heedless of the historical conditions that govern the inner composition and constellation of subject and object'.[107] Yet it is far from clear that such ontologization (in the bad, ahistorical sense) is a necessary consequence of the analysis. The ambiguity resides in a tension between the individualism inherent in the existential analysis of death (as 'the non-relational possibility', Heidegger argues, 'death individualises'), and the Being-with-others which is a central feature of *Dasein*'s historicality insofar as it involves the bequest and repetition of a heritage ('what is historical is the entity that exists as Being-in-the-world'). This tension is concealed in *Being and Time* by Heidegger's failure to pursue what he calls 'the problem of the ontological structure of world-historical historizing', since, he claims, it would 'transgress the limits' of his theme (the question of Being). He chooses instead to focus on 'the ontological enigma of the movement of historizing *in general*' – an enigma that appears at the level of the individual *Dasein*. But is such a restriction of focus legitimate, in Heidegger's own terms? For if all 'historizing' is a historizing of history, just as all temporalizing is a temporalizing of temporality – and the former is 'just a more concrete working out' of the latter – how can 'the movement of historizing in general' be separated from 'the ontological structure of world-historical historizing'?[108] Indeed, is it not just such an artificial separation that *produces* the ontology of historicality as an 'enigma'? On the other hand, if we stick with the exposition of temporality as historicality through to its end as the 'historizing of history', we run up against the problem of totality at a new level: historical time.

On Ricoeur's analysis, it is the totalization of lived time in the phenomenological unity of the process of temporalization that provides the structure of totality on the basis of which 'history' is produced through the inscription of phenomenological onto cosmological time. Yet as we have seen, this totality (produced, on Heidegger's account, by the narrative closure of the anticipation of death) is always at the same time, and equally fundamentally, an opening onto the future. It is this openness that is captured by Ricoeur in the idea of a de-totalizing 'time of initiative'. And it is this openness, projected onto history as a whole, which renders all historical totalization not just aporetic, but antinomic. The only actual, sutured closure comes with the death *Dasein* anticipates. But this is not an event; it is a pure limit, outside of the existential structure it encloses. It is also, of course, as singular in its absolutism (the absolutism of its annihilation of the world) as the individual who is individualized by its anticipation. Yet its prospect – ceasing to be – immanent in the openness of each instant, must be sufficiently 'real', existentially, for its anticipation to carry the weight necessary to determine the structure of *Dasein* as Being-towards-death. So what does Heidegger's existential analysis of death have to offer the attempt to rethink the terms of historical totalization, ontologically, beyond the aporia of totality?

For Ricoeur, very little. For him, to pursue the ontological dimension of Heidegger's account to the level of historical narrative would be to overburden an analysis which works at the level of literary form precisely because it remains purely descriptive – descriptive of narrative as the space for the presentation of an aporia (the aporia of totality) which has no theoretical resolution. This is the paradoxical point of Ricoeur's book: it immerses us in the history of the philosophy of time in order to free us from the impulse to continue that history as theory, in order to free us from 'philosophy' for 'narrative' – albeit a highly theoretical (one might almost say, 'philosophical') version of the hermeneutics of narrative form. For all his appreciation of Heidegger, Ricoeur's phenomenological sympathies ultimately dictate agnosticism, ontologically, on matters of history. The aporia of totality is irresolvable. Time remains a mystery.[109]

It would seem that Heidegger himself has even less to offer, given the arbitrary termination of his analysis before the question of the ontological status of world history. Yet his account does perform the critical function of insisting on an ontological dimension to the problem, even if it never addresses it. And it is here that the homology

of temporal form implicit in Ricoeur's procedure of narrative inscription can be exploited. For if there can be no 'temporalization of
temporality' without the anticipation of death as index of the finitude
of existence, so, by extension, there can be no temporalization of
historical time, no historical temporality, without the anticipation
of an equivalent kind of 'end' to history: *no 'history' without the
anticipation of an 'end to history'*. If *Dasein* is being-towards-death,
and history is the product of inscriptions of phenomenological
time onto cosmological time, then we can define historical beings as
beings-toward-the-end-of-history. This is the hidden logic of Ricoeur's
reading of Heidegger.

Furthermore, just as the death which is anticipated and must
always come will never be an event in *Dasein*'s life, but exists solely
in anticipation, as the productive limit of its being, so the 'end of
history' upon which historical temporality depends, cannot be
conceived as a possible historical event, within historical time.
Rather, as the productive limit of historical beings, posited (like
death) in exteriority, it too must be given solely in anticipation. This
is its fundamental difference from the idea of the end of history as
fulfilment or reconciliation (the realization of reason) inherent in
Hegelianism, its fundamental difference from all teleology. This end
of history is not, fundamentally, a historical horizon at all, however
ultimate, but the condition of all such horizons. *Posited* as absolutely
exterior, its otherness is thereby reduced (in the phenomenological
sense of Husserl's reduction) to a constitutive moment in the intentional structure of historical beings. It is a part of the 'horizonal
schema' of historical beings, constituting us, in Merleau-Ponty's
words, as 'a process of transcendence towards the world'.[110] As
Derrida puts it in his dialectical critique of Levinas, in a rare moment
of constructive metaphysics: 'History is not the totality transcended
by eschatology, metaphysics, or speech. It is transcendence itself.
. . . history is impossible, meaningless, in the finite totality, and . . . it
is impossible, meaningless, in the positive and actual infinity . . .
history *keeps to the difference* between totality and infinity.' Indeed,
one might say that history *is* the very movement of this difference.[111]
Alternatively, with Nancy, one might thereby rethink the category
of totality, such that: 'totality is not the fastening, the completion
without remainder; it is the "having there" (*y avoir*), the taking place
(*avoir lieu*), the unlimited "coming there" (*y venir*) of the delimited
thing: which also means that totality is all, except totalitarian, and it
is obviously here a question of freedom.'[112]

But what kind of account of history is this? What kind of time is at

stake in the extension of Heidegger's analysis of death to the domain
of 'historicality'? What mediations are required to make sense of the
transition? To address these questions, we need to consider further
the relationship of what we are calling 'historical time' to the cosmological time onto which Ricoeur takes it to be inscribed, and the
existential temporality out of which he takes it to be constituted. In
particular, we need to explore the relations *within* the structure of
historical time between these two apparently different 'times' which
compose it. This requires both a broadening and a deepening of
our understanding of the main feature of Heidegger's analysis: the
anticipation of death.

Ordinary time or cosmological time? Nature and the social

Heidegger's treatment of what he calls the 'ordinary' conception of
time provides a convenient place to begin. For it is in the opposition
of the authenticity of the time-consciousness of anticipatory resoluteness (*Entschlossenheit*) in the face of death, to the inauthenticity of this
ordinary conception, that Ricoeur detects within Heidegger's work a
recurrence, at the level of the ethical, of the opposition of subjective
to objective approaches to time, which constitutes the aporia of the
dual perspective – an opposition that Heidegger explicitly tries to
avoid. Furthermore, in defending the independence of an aspect of the
ordinary conception of time against its reduction by Heidegger to a
fallen form of the existential modality of 'within-time-ness', Ricoeur
uncovers a dimension of time outside the scope of Heidegger's
existential analysis, wrecking its attempt to replace the problematic of
subject and object with a newly integral approach. This independent
outside (cosmological time) provides both the ontological backdrop
to Ricoeur's narrative inscriptions and the explanation of why they
must always finally fail to live up to the requirements of the Hegelian
idea of history as total self-mediation: the existence of a moment of
absolute exteriority in nature. It is this moment of exteriority which is
registered existentially in the anticipation of death.

However, while Ricoeur successfully establishes a connection
between the ordinary conception of time and an independent 'cosmological' time of nature – signalled by Heidegger's reading of Aristotle
in the 1927 lectures[113] – he fails to consider the social dimension
of the relation. He thus passes over the opportunity to re-establish
the ontological integrity of Heidegger's analysis of time in a newly

mediated form, using his critique, instead, to reassert the ineluctability of the aporia of the dual perspective. Yet it is precisely this ineluctability which is challenged by a reading of the ordinary conception as a social mediation of an independent time of nature, and hence as a mediating term in the inscription of phenomenological time onto it, at the level of history as a whole. This approach receives further support once we trace back the origin of existential temporality in the anticipation of death to being-with-others, via Hegel's concept of recognition, in the next chapter.

The argument that follows is thus characterized by a dual movement: affirmation of Ricoeur's critique of Heidegger's treatment of the ordinary conception of time for, like Husserl, 'forgetting nature';[114] and then the augmentation of this critique with a social dimension based on the mediating role of history in Ricoeur's own analysis – a role which may be translated into Heideggerian terms as an assertion of the constitutive significance for *Dasein*, *ontologically*, of being-with-others. For it is not only 'the interaction of the psychic and the physical' which appears in mortality in primordial form,[115] but the interaction – and mediation – of the *psychic*, the *physical* and the *social*.

Ricoeur's objections to Heidegger's downgrading of the ordinary conception of time to an 'inauthentic' form stem from his alternative reading of Aristotle. This reading has two main themes: the dependence of all time on movement, and the 'immemorial wisdom' which perceives 'a hidden collusion between change that destroys – forgetting, aging, death – and time that simply passes'.[116] This connection between cosmological time and death allows Ricoeur to suggest that Heidegger's analysis of death is the product of a 'recoil-effect' of cosmological and historical time back upon the phenomenology of individual time-consciousness. In locating different, but equally authentic, temporal registers of death at all three levels of Heidegger's hierarchy of modes of temporalization, Ricoeur thereby provides the basis for just that conceptual unification of time the possibility of which he denies.

Heidegger expounds the ordinary conception of time as a 'leveling off' and 'covering up' of primordial temporality, which has its source in the temporality of 'within-time-ness': the lowest of his three hierarchical forms of temporalization. Within-time-ness is the temporality of preoccupation or 'concern' (*Besorgen*): 'the kind of time "in which" the ready-to-hand and the present-to-hand within-the-world are encountered'.[117] It is the temporality of an 'elemental kind of behaviour', in which *Dasein* '"reckons with time"' and regulates itself *according to it*'.[118] Its main features are what Heidegger calls 'publicness' and 'averageness': 'In so far ... as everyday concern understands itself in terms of the "world" of its concern and its "time", it does *not* know "this" time *as its own*, but concernfully *utilizes* the time which "there is" [*es gibt*] – the time with which "*they*" reckon.'[119] Within-time-ness is the time of reckoning, of 'dateability' and measurement (calendars and clocks), through which 'entities which are not of the character of *Dasein*' appear to *Dasein* in the public time of 'the they'.[120] As such, it derives from a fundamental feature of human existence: its 'thrownness' into a world alongside-entities, with-others. In this sense, it is as primordial as *Dasein*'s other two temporal-existential modes (historicality and ecstatic-horizonal temporality), despite Heidegger's presentation of it, alongside historicality, as a derived form. However, whilst it may thus be existentially 'equiprimordial', its association with the everyday renders it problematic as what Heidegger calls an 'existenti*ell*' – that is, a feature of *Dasein*'s self-understanding. It is this 'existentiell' problematicity which is at issue in the ordinary conception of time.

The ordinary conception of time is taken by Heidegger to 'cover up' the character of temporality as a mode of *Dasein*'s existence, by reducing it to 'a sequence of "nows" which are constantly "present-at-hand", simultaneously passing away and coming along' in an uninterrupted flow, as if they existed externally to one another and independently of *Dasein*. As such, the ordinary conception of time is described by Heidegger as 'now-time' (*Jetztzeit*) – a usage which must be rigorously distinguished from Benjamin's subsequent and quite different use of the term, which is discussed in chapter 4. For Heidegger, it is essentially an everyday version of Aristotle's conception of time as an endless and irreversible succession of instants.[121] In presenting time as continuous (as opposed to ecstatic), and independent of *Dasein*, the ordinary conception marks itself off as the product of a 'fallen' *Dasein*, an 'inauthentic' mode of time-consciousness. What it covers up, in particular, is *Dasein*'s finitude, and hence everything that flows existentially and temporally from the recognition of that finitude. The ordinary conception of time involves a 'fleeing *in the face of* death'. It is a 'self-forgetful "representation"' through which time appears as infinite, since it is defined by the standpoint of 'the they'. For '"the they" never dies.' Indeed, 'the they' cannot die since, as we have seen, on Heidegger's analysis, 'death is in each case mine.'[122]

Ricoeur's critique links up a defence of the independence of cosmological time from phenomenological time with criticism of the 'intimism' of Heidegger's analysis of death, by reversing the direction of his reading of Aristotle. Thus, rather than reading Aristotle's conception of time as an idealization of the existential temporality of 'circumspective concern', mirroring the 'leveling' and 'forgetting' involved in the ordinary conception of time at the level of philosophical thought, Ricoeur reads the ordinary conception as an authentic apprehension of the independent infinity of cosmological time. (That cosmological time is infinite, as well as independent of human temporality, follows from the cyclical character of the astronomical motion from which it is derived by Aristotle.)

One might think that an awareness of the independent aspect of cosmological time is implicit in Heidegger's account of within-time-ness, in the concept of 'thrownness', but it is never thematized there, for methodological reasons: namely, the restriction of Heidegger's interest in time to its role as the horizon for the understanding of Being in general. Indeed, it cannot be thematized without disrupting the whole problematic of *Being and Time*. For the transformation of Husserlian phenomenology into hermeneutical ontology, from which the book sets out, ontologizes what was for Husserl the strictly epistemological method of 'reduction'. There is thus no place in *Being and Time* for the temporality of an independent nature. Indeed, in the 1927 lectures, Heidegger goes so far as to insist: 'There *is* no nature-time, since all time belongs essentially to *Dasein*.'[123] In ontologizing phenomenology, Heidegger thus reverts to that very neo-Kantian idealism about nature which Husserl had sought to avoid by the development of the phenomenological method. 'Object-domains' may become 'regional ontologies', but despite the realism of the language, they remain reducible, ontologically, to aspects of *Dasein*'s various modes of being-in-the-world. Heidegger's concept of existence (*Existenz*) is in this respect the legitimate heir to the neo-Kantian concept of facticity (*Faktizität*).[124] Despite the recognition of 'within-time-ness' as a primordial temporality (the temporality of concern), Heidegger refuses the idea of a time within which Dasein *is* when it exhibits it.

The connection of cosmological time to death is established by the fact that since the time of succession (with its basis in movement) is the time to which we must submit as natural beings, a time that 'surrounds us, envelops us, and overpowers us with its awesome strength',[125] it is the time we suffer and *because of which* we die. Existential temporality must involve some kind of relationship to this time. Indeed, what is 'the possibility of the impossibility of existence', if not a sense of the exteriority of a time to which, ultimately, we must submit? What is cosmological time, if not that which, reduced (in Husserl's sense), 'reveals' phenomenological time?[126] If, as Merleau-Ponty argued, the most important lesson which Husserl's reduction teaches is 'the impossibility of a complete reduction',[127] then the most important lesson of a phenomenological analysis of time will be the confirmation of its ultimate, irreducible exteriority.

Furthermore, since what we might call 'being-in-nature' necessarily involves being-with-others – as human beings must collectively produce their means of subsistence to ensure their biological reproduction – the relationship between cosmological time and existential temporality will always be socially mediated. Heidegger demonstrates an awareness of this in his discussion of 'everyday Being-with' (*Mitsein*).[128] However, while being-with-others thus forms part of his account of *Dasein*'s existential structure, relations *to* others are not integrated into the concept of *Dasein* at the most fundamental, ontological level, where it is the reflexive characterization of *Dasein* as an inquiring being ('a being for whom Being is in question') which takes priority. There is thus a twofold ontological deficit in the concept of *Dasein*, deriving from the constitutive exteriorities of 'nature' and 'the social', respectively.

However, there is a similar lacuna concerning the social in Ricoeur's own analysis, despite his criticism of the intimism of Heidegger's analysis of death. For he fails to make it sufficiently clear that the *form* of what he calls cosmological time – chronology as an infinite succession of identical instants – is the product of a mediation of the independent time of nature by the regulatory practices of a common social life. What we have been calling 'nature' is the *intersubjective form* of exteriority. As Husserl put it; 'the commonness of nature [is] the first thing constituted in the form of community, and the foundation for all other intersubjectively common things.'[129] This is the advantage of Heidegger's use of the expression 'the ordinary conception of time'. To the extent to which we live 'in' cosmological time, we can only ever know it in a form mediated by the temporality of lived experience; hence Ricoeur's account of the indispensability of the phenomenology of 'the now' to the cosmology of measurable movement, in his reading of Aristotle. Cosmological time is epistemologically dependent on the historical sphere of narrative inscription – action – for which it provides the temporal-ontological ground: originally, the practices of ancient Greek astronomy. This is clear from Ricoeur's own discussion of what he calls 'calendar time' or (following Benveniste) 'chronicle time', although this is not how he interprets it himself.

Three features are taken to be common to all calendars, and hence constitutive of chronicle time: (1) a founding event, axial moment, or zero-point in relation to which every other event can be dated; (2) a temporal direction defined with reference to this zero-point; and (3) a unit of measurement, derived by astronomy from the observation of cosmic intervals: most fundamentally, the day, the month, the year. Calendar time provides historical time with 'the framework of an institution based on astronomy'. As such, according to Ricoeur, it is 'the first bridge constructed by historical practice between lived time and universal time'.[130] But is it really so different in the principles of its construction from the 'universal' time of nature itself? The difference appears to hinge on the designation of a founding event. Yet this is structurally analogous to the above-mentioned dependence of cosmological time on the 'zero-point' provided by the phenomenology of the now. In this respect, calendars are socially specific versions of cosmological time. Ontologically speaking, there is no distinct 'calendar time' as such, only the *calendarization* of cosmological time. The difference is internal to social practice, not ontological as such.[131]

In fact, the very idea of cosmological time is ambiguous, insofar as it contains condensed into its construction (although not its self-understanding) *both* sides of the 'dual perspective' which produces the aporia of philosophical thinking about time. The same applies to the idea of phenomenological time, as Ricoeur's critique of Husserl demonstrated. What Heidegger calls the ordinary conception of time may thus be understood as an *existential interpretation of the social standardization of cosmological time*. We have already noted that chronological time is a relative historical novelty as the dominant form of social time-consciousness. We shall further see, in chapter 4, that it corresponds at the level of history to what Benjamin describes as the 'vulgar naturalism' of the 'empty, homogeneous time' of historicism: the bad modernity of a historiography which trades the specificity of a living remembrance for the re-establishment of continuity with an ossified past.[132]

Once we acknowledge the irreducibly social character of human life, its relations to the requirements of biological reproduction, and hence its status as a kind of 'inorganic nature' (Marx), it becomes clear that what Heidegger calls 'primordial temporalization' must have its ontological ground not only in an external nature, but also in some kind of *primal socialization* – some emergence of the human being as a social being out of its natural being. Temporalization is a product of the differentiated unity of nature and society within every human being – hence the temporal significance of death as the vanishing point of their metabolic interaction. The question thus becomes: how do cosmological time and the Other come together in the anticipation of death?

3

Death and Recognition

It still remains to be decided which death, that which is brought by life or that which brings life.

Jacques Lacan

The role of being-with-others in Heidegger's analysis of death is restricted to a consideration of the analogical significance of the death of others for 'an ontological delimitation of *Dasein*'s totality'. And its result is strictly negative. For while it might be thought that the death of others could function as a 'substitute theme' for the closure of *Dasein*'s totality, Heidegger quickly makes it clear that:

> The dying of Others is not something which we experience in a genuine sense; at most we are always just 'there alongside'. . . . When someone has died, his Being-no-longer-in-the-world . . . is still a Being . . . in the sense of the Being-just-present-at-hand-and-no-more of a corporeal Thing which we encounter. . . . The *end* of the entity *qua* Dasein is the *beginning* of the same entity *qua* something present-at-hand.

However, it is the fact that 'no one can take the Other's dying away from him [*sic*]' – that we cannot in principle experience the other's dying *qua* dying – which establishes that 'by its very essence, death is in every case mine, in so far as it "is" at all.' Demonstration of the 'mineness' of death is the reflected result of the radical 'otherness' of the other's dying.[1]

Heidegger leaves it there, moving on to consider the temporal implications of the mineness of a death *Dasein* itself can only know as the end towards which it is thrown, since for all its mineness even its own death will escape it. There is no account of where 'death' comes from. Presumably, Heidegger thinks this irrelevant to a strictly existential analysis.[2] Yet this is disputable, given the use that is subsequently made of the difference between mineness and the standpoint of 'the they' in the attribution of authenticity to different orientations towards death. It is useful at this point to turn to Hegel and his account of the role of death in the dialectic of recognition in the *Phenomenology of Spirit*. For if, as Heidegger argues, 'death individualizes', it does so only in the context of being-with-others. In Hegel, we find the resources for a social critique of the individualism of Heidegger's analysis of death, with which to supplement Ricoeur's cosmological critique of its phenomenological 'intimism'.

There is, of course, a radical disjunction between the philosophical terms of the projects at issue. Hegel sought to supersede (*aufheben*) the subject-object problematic of modern epistemology in the concept of the absolute, thereby preserving it, transfigured, in the course of its transcendence; whereas it was Heidegger's explicit intention to bypass that problematic altogether. The concept of *Dasein* registers that intention. Nonetheless, it is unclear that in defining *Dasein* as an 'inquiring' being – an entity which 'is distinguished ontically by the fact that, in its very Being, that Being is an *issue* for it'[3] – Heidegger has entirely succeeded in avoiding the structure of reflection characteristic of the concept of self-consciousness; or indeed, that such success, were it achieved, would be wholly desirable. On the other hand, in turning to Hegel's dialectic of recognition as a counter to the individualism of the analytic of *Dasein*, it is no more intended to replace the latter with the former, than vice versa. Rather, it is hoped that each problematic will work on the other, contributing to a broader rethinking of both their terms.[4]

Being-there-with-others: the dialectic of recognition

The main point of Hegel's dialectic of recognition – as opposed to Heidegger's existential analysis whereby a *Dasein* individualized by its anticipation of death is also considered, by virtue of its thrownness, to be 'with-others' – is that 'self-consciousness exists in and for itself when, and by the fact that, it so exists for another; that is, it exists only in being acknowledged. . . . A self-consciousness exists *for a self-consciousness*.'[5] If this is true, then as a self-interpreting, self-conscious being, *Dasein*'s individuality cannot be derived from its anticipation of death independently of its relations to others. Rather, *Dasein* must first, or simultaneously, be constituted as a self-conscious being through its relations with others, in a dialectic of recognition, in order that it may become the kind of being which is capable of anticipating its death as the end towards which it is thrown, and hence of constituting itself existentially as a Being-towards-death. This disrupts the whole ontological problematic of *Being and Time*. For it challenges the foundational status of Heidegger's depiction of *Dasein* – a being for whom Being is 'there' in the fundamentally inquisitive form of the question of the meaning of Being – revealing it as a dogmatic pre-supposition of Heidegger's inquiry: the result of a prior commitment to 'the question of the meaning of Being' which falls outside the scope of the inquiry's own critical procedures.

On the Hegelian model, Being can only be 'there' in Heidegger's sense of presenting itself as the object of inquiry for a fundamentally self-interpreting entity, if this entity has been previously constituted as an entity of this kind (self-conscious being) through a process of mutual recognition. Furthermore, it is only through this process of mutual recognition constitutive of *Dasein*'s consciousness of itself as a self-interpreting being that *Dasein* can acquire the sense of death in the first place. The point for Hegelians is thus not only that *Dasein* is first and foremost a being with-others, but that its being with-others is *constitutive* of a death which, while ultimately grounded ontologically in our inscription within cosmological time, nonetheless derives its existential reality from the form of our relationship to it. Heidegger's analysis may register that it is by the deaths of others that the 'mine-ness' of death is confirmed, but it provides no account of whence this thing called 'death' comes, or what its existential anticipation has to tell us, ontologically, about the character of *Dasein* as a social being. In Hegel's analysis, on the other hand, the dual priority of recognition over the anticipation of death appears explicitly in the depiction of a 'struggle for recognition' in which each must risk their life in order to be recognized by the other as a self-conscious being: the process leading up to the notorious dialectic of lordship and bondage (*Herrschaft und Knechtshaft*), or mastery and slavery, in the *Phenomenology of Spirit*. The complementarity of Hegel's and Heidegger's work here lies at the basis of the extraordinary centrality of what has become known as the 'master-slave dialectic' to French thought since the Second World War.

The key text is Kojève's *Introduction to the Reading of Hegel*, especially the appendix, 'The Idea of Death in the Philosophy of Hegel'.[6] Kojève reads Hegel not only through the lens of Nietzsche's quasi-Feuerbachian critique, but crucially 'after' Heidegger. Hence his judgement that 'the "dialectical" or anthropological philosophy of Hegel is in the final analysis a *philosophy of death*'.[7] However, while Kojève's work is thus of great intrinsic interest, this makes it extremely unreliable as an interpretation of Hegel from the standpoint of Hegel's self-conception. Of particular significance here is his translation of

Herrschaft und Knechtschaft as *maîtrise et esclavage* – equivalent to the English 'mastery and slavery', rather than 'lordship and bondage' – a usage which was followed by Hyppolite in his 1939 translation of the *Phenomenology* into French.[8] This translation replaces the feudal terms of Hegel's analysis (to which the English 'serfdom' is appropriate) with a notion of slavery resonant with both the world of ancient Greece and the heritage of European colonialism. This would prove to be a brilliant move in the years during and immediately following the Second World War, as Occupation gave way to Liberation and decolonization, revitalizing Hegel's text in hitherto unforeseen ways – as Sartre's and Fanon's appropriations of the model indicate.[9] However, precisely because of its contemporaneity, this translation has led to serious misunderstandings of both the place of this particular dialectic within Hegel's text and its relationship to Marx's work.[10]

Given this history of reception, it is as well to emphasize at the outset the role of the passage in question within the *Phenomenology* as a model for the exploration of the structure of self-consciousness, independently of either the universality of reason (*Vernunft*) or the historical forms of spirit (*Geist*) in terms of which human self-consciousness, of necessity, appears in concrete actuality.[11] In particular, it is important that this scenario is not read as an historical realism, as the depiction of an originary state of affairs through which self-consciousness came into the world. Rather, it is a conceptual model of the (contradictory) structure of self-consciousness *as such* – albeit one that is richly embellished by an illustrative social content. And it is methodologically subordinate to the broader movement of the *Phenomenology*, through which alone the analysis of recognition is completed.

Lord and bondsman (master and slave) are historically specific social roles, but that is not primarily what they signify here. Hence the justification for Kojève's translation of one pair into the other. Rather, they are allegorical forms, typifications of power relations inherent in the structure of recognition. What they mark is, on the one hand, the necessarily *social* character of all self-consciousness, and, on the other, the contradiction between *dependence* and *independence* that self-conscious beings must consequently experience outside of an association 'in which the free development of each is the condition for the free development of all';[12] or, as Hegel himself puts it in his introduction of the concept of spirit, an 'absolute substance which is the unity of the different independent self-consciousnesses which, in their opposition, enjoy perfect freedom and independence:

"I" that is "We" and "We" that is "I".[13] The fact that, in expounding the structure of self-consciousness through the dialectic of recognition, Hegel has recourse to a particular shape of spirit (the institution of serfdom) prior to the formal transition to spirit within the developmental logic of the *Phenomenology* – and the difficulties this causes for those with an independent interest in the details of his analysis – are things which need not concern us here.[14]

Hegel's argument has four main stages. The first outlines the contradictory doubling of consciousness's relationship to itself as both subject and object of knowledge as the perpetual movement of a 'return from otherness' or '*desire* in general'.[15] In the second stage, these relations are shown to be recognizable by consciousness in their unity only in a duplicated form, as relations between two different self-consciousnesses – consciousnesses which 'recognise themselves as mutually recognising one another' ('[O]nly so is it in fact self-consciousness; for only in this way does the unity of itself in its otherness become explicit for it').[16] Next, the contradictory structure of this process of mutual recognition – in which each consciousness must be at once *for-itself* and *for-another*, at once independent yet dependent for this independence on its recognition by another – is presented in the form of a 'life and death struggle', or 'trial by death', between two consciousnesses, in which 'each seeks the death of the other'.[17] Finally, this struggle is shown to achieve a preliminary resolution in the unstable, allegorical form of the relationship between lord and bondsman (master and slave), in which the opposed moments of being for-itself and for-another, inherent in all self-consciousness, appear as separate shapes of consciousness, mediated through a form of recognition that is 'one-sided and unequal':

> The lord is the consciousness that exists *for itself* . . . which is mediated with itself through another consciousness, i.e. through a consciousness whose nature is to be bound up with an existence that is independent, or thinghood in general [the bondsman].[18]

What Hegel calls 'genuine recognition' (*eigentlichen Anerkennen*) can only come about in a form of ethical life which is the practical equivalent of the standpoint of absolute knowing. Its concept is thus, strictly speaking, available only at the very end of the *Phenomenology*. It is expounded in (and as) the system of speculative philosophy.[19]

It is the second and third of these four stages that are of most interest to us here – the background to the master-slave dialectic, rather than the development of its preliminary resolution of the problem of recognition, as such: the necessity of a second self-consciousness to consciousness's recognition of itself, and the presentation of the relations between them as a 'trial by death'. It is these two arguments that cut deepest into Heidegger's presentation of *Dasein* in *Being and Time*. The former is relatively straightforward, the latter is somewhat harder to grasp. Each appears in the *Phenomenology* as part of the developmental sequence of forms of consciousness generated by the immanent dynamic of a knowing subject (natural consciousness) in search of consistency with itself.[20]

Trial by death

The duplication of self-consciousnesses in the *Phenomenology* is fuelled by consciousness's epistemic need to render its unity explicit to itself 'in its otherness' – that is, as an object of knowledge. For in order to know itself as a consciousness, consciousness must know itself as both subject and object of knowledge *at the same time*. But without another self-consciousness, this is impossible, since any relation of consciousness to itself which is modelled on its relations to objects can only oscillate between an assertion of its independence from itself as the object of its knowledge, and a supersession (*Aufhebung*) of this independence which establishes the self-certainty of the knowing subject only at the cost of demonstrating its dependence on the negated object:

> Thus self-consciousness, by its negative relation to the object, is unable to supersede it; it is really because of that relation that it produces the object again, and the desire [the desire to supersede it] as well. . . . On account of the independence of the object, therefore, it can achieve satisfaction **only when the object itself effects the negation within itself**: and it must carry out this negation of itself in itself, for it is *in itself* the negative, and must be *for* the other what it *is*. Since the object is in its own self negation, and in being so is at the same time independent, it is consciousness. . . . *Self-consciousness achieves its satisfaction* [the satisfaction of its desire to supersede itself as an object] *only in another self-consciousness*.[21]

To put it another way, since self-consciousness only exists as a knowing relationship of consciousness to itself *qua* consciousness, and this relationship eludes the structure of self-reflection (in principle), it can only exist on the model of its knowledge of another self-consciousness. Yet this other self-consciousness cannot exist either, except in the same way. The *duplication* of self-consciousnesses, their *mutual recognition*, and hence their *mutual dependence* (replacing dependence on an object, the independence of which is confirmed by our need to negate it in the satisfaction of desire), are thus all shown to be conditions of the possibility of self-consciousness, and hence, conditions of the possibility of *Dasein* as a self-interpreting being for whom Being is in question.

It is the difference between the other as 'an unessential, negatively characterised object' (an object of desire in general, 'submerged in the being of life'), and the other as another self-consciousness (pure being-for-self), which imparts to the process of recognition its peculiar character as a 'life-and-death' struggle.[22] Hegel explains it as follows. For the individual:

> The presentation of itself . . . as the pure abstraction of self-consciousness consists in showing itself as the pure negation of its objective mode, or in showing that it is not attached to any determinate being, not to the individuality common to existence as such, that it is not attached to life. This presentation is a twofold action: action on the part of the other, and action on its own part. In so far as it is the action of the *other*, each seeks the death of the other. But in so doing, the second kind of action, action on its own part, is also involved; for the former involves the staking of its own life. Thus the relation of the two self-conscious individuals is such that they confirm themselves and each other through a life-and-death struggle. . . . it is only through staking one's life that freedom is won . . . [23]

The difficulty here resides in the concepts of life and death: specifically, in Hegel's treatment of death as the negation of life. For 'life' is not used by Hegel here in the general, commonsense way which would render such equivalence unproblematic. Nor is negation so simple a relation as might be supposed. Rather, 'life' is a specific category in Hegel's phenomenological ontology, and negation comes in at least two quite different forms.

'Life' is the category which, at the beginning of chapter 4 of the *Phenomenology*, matches the reflective transition from consciousness to self-consciousness on the side of the object. In this sense, it is 'the infinite unity of the differences' between objects, the 'simple fluid substance of pure movement within itself', the 'ceaseless movement' by which the 'passive medium' of the in-itself is 'consumed'. It is 'the self-developing whole which dissolves its development and in this movement simply preserves itself'. Life is 'the *natural* setting of consciousness', or what Hegel describes as 'independence without absolute negativity'.[24] Hence, when Hegel writes that the individual's 'presentation of itself . . . as the pure abstraction of self-consciousness consists in showing . . . that it is not attached to life', what this means is that consciousness must show that it is detached from its 'natural setting', from its dependence on an independent objectivity.

The question that arises is: in what sense is this 'detachment' equivalent to death, such that to seek it in the other is to seek its 'death', while to seek it for oneself is to put one's 'life' at stake? Are we really talking about literal, *physical* death here? The rhetoric of the 'life-and-death struggle', and the historical reference to serfdom, certainly make it seem as if it were so. Yet it is clear from what follows that this is not always the case. Physical death, according to Hegel, is 'the *natural* negation of consciousness, negation without independence, which thus remains without the required significance of recognition'.[25] Now, consciousness cannot be understood to seek this for the other consciousness, since it would undercut the possibility of recognition. So how are we to make sense of Hegel's remarks? The key lies in the difference between Hegel's two senses of negation.

Death in the literal, physical sense defined above is only one way of negating 'life' in Hegel's specific sense: an abstract negation. There is also another way: a negation which 'supersedes in such a way as to preserve and maintain what is superseded, and consequently survives its own supersession'.[26] This is the kind of negation performed by consciousness on its objects in the course of its ascent through the forms of appearance to an absolute knowing. Such negation is essentially epistemological in character, but it is nonetheless of ontological signifi-cance for a subject defined as a relation of knowledge (consciousness). In the passage quoted above Hegel fails to distinguish between these two negations. He consequently fails to register sufficiently clearly the way in which they bear *differentially* on the two sides of what he presents as a single, symmetrical, twofold action: the staking of 'life' and the seeking of 'death'.

We have seen that it cannot be the achievement of the other's literal, physical death which is at issue in the seeking of death, since this would terminate the dialectic. At best, this can only generate the negative lesson for the one who survives that 'life is as essential . . . as pure self-consciousness'[27] – which takes us back to our starting point. Rather, insofar as this kind of negation of life is at issue (literal, physical death), it is present only in the 'staking of life', and it is present there only as the enactment of an *unrealized* possibility. Consciousness requires a demonstration that the other is detached from its 'natural setting' ('life') – that it is a being-for-itself – in order that it may recognize itself in it as another self-consciousness. The other's staking of its life, the free enactment of the possibility of its literal physical death, or the staging of its independence from 'life', is the only form that such a demonstration can take, since it is the only way of showing that self-consciousness is a pure being for-self, independent of objectivity. The freely embraced *possibility* of death, a life that is staked, symbolizes the freedom of consciousness from the dictates of self-preservation. Pure being-for-self manifests itself only as *freedom-for-death*. This is what one might call the existential core of the dialectic of recognition. It is in this sense that, for Kojève, humanity is 'death living a human life': in achieving self-consciousness the human being 'kills' the animal within him- or herself, supersedes his or her 'natural' being.[28] But this is already to move to Hegel's second sense of negation and, thereby, to a dialectical or metaphorical sense of death: Lacan's death which 'brings life', the life of self-consciousness. It is this second, metaphorical sense of death alone which is at issue in consciousness's seeking of the death of the other; applied in this case, not at the neutralistic level of 'life', but at the level of the independence of self-consciousness.

What consciousness seeks when it seeks the death of the other is its death *qua independent self-consciousness*, since it is the other's independence from life (not its mere 'life') which threatens the status of consciousness as a being-for-self; just as the independence of the object thwarted the satisfaction of desire in consciousness's attempt to know itself as an object. It is thus not the negation of life (in either of Hegel's two senses of negation) that is at stake in the death which is sought, but a *reduction to* 'life', in Hegel's naturalistic sense: death as the death of independence, or what we might call the *death of death*. Consciousness does not seek the supersession of the other's 'life', but the negation of its self-consciousness. Such is slavery: the contradictory refusal to recognize the humanity of the slave, the symbolic reduction of social to natural being, or the positing of social as natural being. It is in this sense that the consciousness of the slave is 'an extended act of mourning' for the loss of the slave's social being. Slavery is social death.[29]

Conversely, the life that is won by the lord or master is a life beyond mere 'life'. This is why Kojève calls the struggle one of 'pure prestige'. There is no desire at stake in the struggle beyond or beneath that of recognition. Furthermore, as Lacan argues, recognition must in fact be there from the very beginning, as 'a rule of the game'. For if, in the end, 'the loser must not perish if he is to become a slave', the pact must be 'everywhere anterior to the violence before perpetuating it'.[30] It is the 'death' of the other in slavery, and the 'life' of self-consciousness as the lord, which are the equivalent sides of a single relationship; not the life that is staked (which is literally, physically so) and the death which is sought (which is not). It is the *lack of symmetry* in this latter relationship which explains why there is in fact another option for the bondsman or slave, unacknowledged by Hegel, but amply documented elsewhere: namely, the *choice of death*, as the refusal of recognition to the master. As Gilroy puts it:

> The repeated choice of death rather than bondage [in the practice of slave suicide] articulates a principle of negativity that is opposed to the formal logic and rational calculation . . . expressed in the Hegelian slave's preference for bondage rather than death.[31]

Such self-destructive negativity both asserts the independence of consciousness on the side of the slave, as an *absolute* striving, and marks the limit of the dialectic in an underlying discontinuity between its terms ('lord' and 'bondsman', or 'master' and 'slave'). It may be realizable only in passing, as an ephemeral, transitory form, but it lives on in the memories of other slaves, as the source of a resistance which exceeds the terms of the Hegelian model of freedom through labour. Slave infanticide, as depicted by Toni Morrison in *Beloved*, for example, may be understood as a generational displacement of the same dynamic, with additional temporal complexities of its own.[32]

Hegel is unable to envisage such negativity on the part of the bondsman or slave, for methodological reasons: namely, because of his abstraction of the figure of the bondsman, as an individual, from the community of bondsmen, and his delegation of the principle of independence to the lord. As Sartre puts it in the *Critique of Dialectical Reason* (in implicit criticism of his own use of the master-slave dialectic in *Being and Nothingness*), Hegel describes 'the relations of *a* master and *his* slave through universals, without reference to their relations to other slaves or other masters'.[33] However, in fairness to Hegel, it should be pointed out that it was never his intention to apply the schema directly in historical interpretation. To the extent that his followers have done so, they have violated the methodological terms of the *Phenomenology*. This may be no bad thing, of course. But insofar as it has happened unknowingly – or, at least, unaccompanied by reflection on its conditions and consequences – it has impeded, rather than promoted, understanding of the relevance of Hegel's argument to subsequent debates. In this respect, the history of reception of the master-slave dialectic is seriously compromised, especially in France. In Hegel's own account, 'absolute negativity' or 'pure being-for-self' appears in the consciousness of the bondsman or slave only in the form of the *fear* of death.[34]

If self-consciousness is a manifestation of desire – ultimately, for Hegel, the desire for 'pure self-recognition in absolute otherness', the completion of that 'return from otherness' which is desire in general – it is also equally *fear*: a fear of death which is produced by the recognition of the independence of the other. Such recognition is a condition of the acquisition of self-consciousness, since the other must appear as pure being-for-self if it is to be a model for consciousness's relationship to itself as an independent whole. Yet this recognition thereby makes consciousness aware of its own potential nothingness for the other – a nothingness it must project onto the other in return ('seeking the death of the other'), if it is to establish itself as pure being-for-self. *Pure* self-consciousness, *pure* being-for-self, thus reveals itself to be a contradictory structure of *misrecognition* and *disavowal*, since it must repress or deny its dependence on the recognition of the other. This is the structure which is staged by Hegel in the figure of the lord or master. Pure self-consciousness is an impossible state of affairs.

Let us sum up the results of this analysis. Self-consciousness and the consciousness of death are *one*; and both come from *the other*. They are the product of *desire* and they result in *fear*: fear of death as the fear of the refusal of recognition. In both its pervasiveness and indeterminacy, such fear is equivalent to Heidegger's existential concept of *anxiety*: an anxiety in the face of 'Being-in-the-world as such' which, according to Heidegger, 'makes fear possible' (fear of any particular thing).[35] In each case, it is the consequence of a recognition of freedom. However, whereas for Heidegger it is *Dasein*'s own freedom which is at issue, its character as pure possibility – to which anxiety returns it from its absorption in the world; for Hegel, it is the freedom of the other from which fear stems, a freedom which is registered by self-consciousness as at once a threat to its identity and a condition of its existence. From the Hegelian standpoint, freedom comes, phenomenologically, from the other, and it is the ambivalence of this relationship which is the true source of existential anxiety – a suggestion which is supported by the similarity between Heidegger's concept of anxiety and Freud's.[36]

Death both appears to consciousness as, and derives its existential reality from, the possibility of an *absolute* refusal of recognition. This is why Hegel calls death the 'absolute lord'. (The lord refuses recognition of self-consciousness to the bondsman.) Death is the 'possibility of the impossibility of existence' introduced into consciousness by the recognition of its dependence on the recognition of another, who harbours within him- or herself the possibility of its denial. Anticipation of death, in Heidegger's existential sense, is to this extent a constitutive dimension of self-conscious (and therefore social) being. If temporality derives, existentially, from the anticipation of death (Heidegger's argument), and death comes from the other (Hegel's argument), so, it follows, does time. *Existential temporality comes from the other. It is recognition which 'temporalizes' time.* It is only *self*-consciousness for which death has meaning – for which death 'is', in Heidegger's sense – and self-consciousness is always socially mediated. Hegel's definition of death thus requires modification as his analysis progresses through the various stages of the *Phenomenology*. Death is not just 'the natural negation of consciousness, negation without independence', the literal, physical death with which Hegel begins. It is the natural *or unnatural* negation of a consciousness, negation without independence, which is both *for-itself* and *for-others*. For all its inherent 'mineness', which cannot be denied, what death 'is', existentially, is mediated by relations to others – in Hegel's terms, the forms of objective spirit. Its analysis will form part of an ontology of *social* being.

But what about the absolutism of Hegel's idealism, within which his account of recognition is enclosed? As we saw in the last chapter, this ends up negating both time and death, through the recuperative, transfigurative power of its interiorizing memory. What happens to Hegel's argument if we extract his dialectic of recognition from this speculative context, and pursue it outside the assumption of an '"I" that is "We" and "We" that is "I"', its ultimate presupposition and putative end? What structures of recognition are constitutive of the primordial temporality of self-interpreting *social* beings who are also part of an *exterior* nature? And what are their relations to the temporalization of 'history'?

Such questions can be approached at two different levels: the level of the psychic formation of the individual *qua* individual, as a temporal being; and the level of the social formation of individuals as historical beings. In the first case, which we shall explore in the rest of this chapter, we find ourselves on the terrain of psychoanalytical appropriations and transformations of Hegel's dialectic of self-consciousness, in the service of the development of Freud's account of the formation of the ego (*das Ich*). From this point of view, the standpoint of a psychic materialism, it would appear that 'the only way to "save Hegel" is through Lacan';[37] or, more generally, in Freud's own words, 'to transform metaphysics into metapsychology'[38] – an aspiration which, of necessity, inflects metapsychology back in the direction of metaphysics, as the continuation of ontology by other means. In the second case, which we shall take up in the course of the chapters that follow, we find a variety of competing *social modes of inscription* of phenomenological temporality onto cosmological time, among which we shall concentrate upon the two most familiar (but not necessarily the best understood): the siamese twins, modernity and tradition.

From recognition to identification: Hegel and Lacan

Allusion has already been made to the founding role played by Kojève's lectures on Hegel in postwar French thought, and the centrality to those lectures of a particular interpretation of the struggle for recognition in chapter 4 of the *Phenomenology*. Nowhere is this more apparent than in the work of the French psychoanalyst Jacques Lacan; particularly, but by no means exclusively, in its first and founding period, from the various versions of 'The Mirror Phase' (first presented in 1936) to his break with the Freudian establishment in the famous *Rome Discourse*, 'The Function and Field of Speech and Language in Psychoanalysis' (1953). The master-slave dialectic is, in Lacan's words, that from which 'at every turn, I take my bearings'.[39] Indeed, so dominant is Kojève's work in Lacan's understanding of Hegel that one commentator has remarked that 'it might be more accurate to say that Lacan is a Kojèvean rather than to suggest that he is a Hegelian.'[40]

However, although Kojève stresses the inequality of the outcome of the struggle for recognition, and hence the moment of misrecognition, the distinctiveness of his reading of Hegel ultimately lies in its relocation of this struggle to the context of the philosophy of history, and his notorious replacement of Napoleon by Stalin as 'the man of the end of history'.[41] So although he effectively halts the progress of the *Phenomenology* half way through chapter 4, Kojève still finds his way to reconciliation in the end, however tinged this end might be with Nietzscheanism. (His self-description of his position as that of a 'right-wing Marxist' neatly mirrors a certain 'left-wing' admiration for Fukuyama. Kojève was 'a Stalinist of strict observance'.) For Lacan, on the other hand, it is the systematic significance of the interruption of Hegel's analysis, and the consequent identification of recognition with *mis*recognition, which is of primary importance. For it enabled him to appropriate the mould of Hegelian thought for the reformulation of a psychoanalytical theory of the ego explicitly opposed to 'any philosophy directly issuing from the *Cogito*'.[42] If most appropriations of Hegel's master-slave dialectic violate the terms of its original context unknowingly, Lacan does so both knowingly and methodically. His work may thus be described, paradoxically, as a form of Hegelianism without reconciliation, but not thereby without the absolute: a negative or tragic Hegelianism for which the aspiration to an absolute knowing ('pure self-recognition in absolute otherness') is a paranoid but unavoidable projection of the constitutive illusion of the ego onto the plane of historical experience.

The principles of Freud's speech, Lacan claims, 'are simply the dialectic of self-consciousness, as realized from Socrates to Hegel'. What Freud does is to 'reopen the junction between truth and knowledge' by insisting on 'the opacity of the signifier that determines the I'. He thus shows that the phenomenological method 'authentically attains the subject only by *decentring* it from self-consciousness, in the axis of which the Hegelian reconstruction . . . maintained it'. Psychoanalysis provides 'Hegel's insistence on the fundamental identity of the particular and the universal . . . with its paradigm by revealing the structure in which that identity is realized as *disjunctive* of the subject, and without appeal to any tomorrow'. Freud subverts 'the question of the subject'.[43]

More specifically, in arresting the dialectic of self-consciousness at the point of misrecognition, Lacan projects the ego into the realm of the imaginary in such a way as permanently to forestall the possibility of reconciliation. 'Implicated as it is in the *méconnaissance* [misrecognition] in which the ego's identifications take root . . . the transcendental ego itself is relativised.'[44] Yet the analysis remains within the horizon of Hegelian thought, nonetheless. We are thus presented with an ambiguously Hegelian anti-Hegelianism, wherein the anti-Hegelian aspects of Lacanian thought are more the product of its displacement of Hegelian motifs than of their rejection. (This remains as true after 1953, and the introduction of a conception of the symbolic order derived from structural linguistics, as it was before, since Lacan's later innovations, however divergent in their theoretical origins, are all grafted onto the original model.) If there is a difficulty with the philosophical form of Lacan's psychoanalytical theory, it thus lies less in its Hegelian inspiration than in the character of its displacement. For in substituting the first stage of Hegel's dialectic of self-consciousness for Freud's initial (1910–1915) account of primary narcissism, to produce a new stage in the formation of the ego, Lacan introduces crucial constraints on the theorization of the social dimension of the subject. Like Sartre, he comes to reproduce the individualism of Heidegger's account of being-towards-death in the very form of his deployment of Hegelian concepts.[45]

It is only in the subsequent work of Jean Laplanche on primal seduction, the enigmatic signifier, and the temporality of human existence as the product of a constant process of translating, de-translating, and re-translating of the (often unconscious) messages inherent in all human relations, that the element of sociality intrinsic to Hegel's account is restored to the centre of the theory. At the same time, however, it is accompanied by a renewed emphasis on the asymmetrical character of the earliest forms of social relations for the infant, and the thesis of the 'fundamental passivity' of its entry into human sociality.[46] In reasserting an element of naturalism in his account of the child's earliest years, Laplanche's psychoanalytical philosophy of time thus finds itself in opposition to the future-oriented activism of existential temporality: the world of the adult. This is a contradiction which can only be mediated once we move on to another level of analysis – the level of history.

The three-stage structure of Lacan's account of the production of the subject, from the infant's original libidinal unity with the mother, through its alienating identification with the image of its body, to its entry into the symbolic order of language and the Other (*le Grand Autre*), corresponds in broad outline to the three moments of self-consciousness sketched in the introductory section of chapter 4 of Hegel's *Phenomenology*. (The more common claim – made, for example, by Forrester – that the mirror phase 'combines the essential elements of Freud's conception of narcissism with the struggle for death of the dialectic of master and slave', is quite untenable, since the bodily image in the mirror is incapable in principle of demon-strating the kind of independence from nature required by the trial by death. There is no *struggle* in the mirror phase.)[47] However, whereas for Hegel, movement between the stages takes the form of an immanent development, internal to a single consciousness's dialectical relations to its object, even when the result is the duplication of self-consciousness, in the Lacanian version it is driven by an exogenous impulse: what Lacan describes as 'a real *specific prematurity of birth*' in the human species. It is this prematurity which is 'the dynamic origin of specular capture'.[48] Thus, while the stages may map onto one another at a certain level of abstraction of their logical form (unity, differentiation/reflection, duplication/rivalry), their different contents and methodological contexts produce significantly different dynamics internal to each stage. What appears in Hegel as the internal differen-tiation of self-consciousness and its reflection into itself, followed by its duplication as a condition of mutual recognition, appears in Lacan as a process of separation and reflection in the mirror, which is only then followed by relations with others as a condition of entry into the symbolic. The relations between the relationship to self and to others is radically different in the two versions (see Figure 1).

In the Hegelian case, the movement is progressively 'outwards', from simple to ever more complex forms, whereby the later (social) stages in the progression are revealed as structural conditions of the earlier ones, within the present. (Hence the *Phenomenology*'s genealogical status: its recapitulation in thought of the structure of a history the empirical course of which has a wholly different temporality.) In the process, the various standpoints adopted by consciousness along the way are revealed to be productive of *mis*representations which the 'observing' consciousness may now transcend. This is the educative function of the *Phenomenology*. In the Lacanian case, on the other hand, the movement is from an apparently 'natural' bond (the infant-mother relationship prior to the mirror phase), 'inwards', to the production of an alienated individuality, before expanding outwards to the social, in the universal form of the symbolic order. There may be two figures involved at the first stage (mother and child),

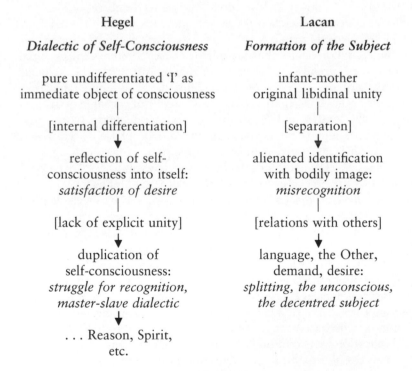

Hegel	Lacan
Dialectic of Self-Consciousness	*Formation of the Subject*
pure undifferentiated 'I' as immediate object of consciousness	infant-mother original libidinal unity
[internal differentiation]	[separation]
reflection of self-consciousness into itself: *satisfaction of desire*	alienated identification with bodily image: *misrecognition*
[lack of explicit unity]	[relations with others]
duplication of self-consciousness: *struggle for recognition, master-slave dialectic*	language, the Other, demand, desire: *splitting, the unconscious, the decentred subject*
. . . Reason, Spirit, etc.	

Figure 1

but the process is naturalized by being viewed wholly from the stand-point of the child.

Similarly, stage two abstracts from any relations of others to the child, in order to consider its constitutive relationship to itself via its bodily image. This is the stage at which a fundamental self-alienation is derived as a fixed structural element on which all future symbolization will be overlaid – what Lacan quite explicitly calls 'an ontological structure of the human world'.[49] This alienation acts as a barrier to any kind of phenomenological pedagogy, whereby the psychoanalytical reconstruction might function directly to resolve contradictions in the standpoint of the observer. For this we require that special relationship to the other (the analyst) which is enacted in the psychoanalytic session. Furthermore, the resolution at stake in this process ('the cure') is resolutely non-Hegelian in its conceptual form – unless, of course, like Žižek, we read Hegel as a Lacanian – since Freud's decentring of the subject undermines the possibility of reconciliation as the recognition of the rationality of the actual: 'The point to which analysis leads, the end point of the dialectic of existential recognition, is – *You are this*. In practice this ideal is never reached.'[50]

It is the second stage of Lacan's account – the mirror phase – that concerns us here, since it is there that the Hegelian concept of recognition merges with the Freudian concept of identification. Hegel is the inspiration for Lacan's account of the mirror phase, insofar as the early stages of Hegel's dialectic of self-consciousness offer an essentially monadic model of consciousness's relationship to itself as other. It is through this model that Lacan gives new theoretical form to the myth of Narcissus underlying Freud's early conception of primary narcissism as a developmental stage of self-love between primitive auto-eroticism and object-love.[51] In the process, however, he both deploys the concept of recognition prematurely (since it is only reached in the *Phenomenology* through the *duplication* of self-consciousnesses), and, as if to compensate, elides it with the idea of identification, to produce a distinctive new version of primary identification as self-misrecognition, thereby creating a new developmental stage between Freud's own stages of primary and secondary identification. If the slogan of Hegelianism is 'Pure Self-Recognition in Absolute Otherness', the slogan of Lacanianism might be formulated as 'Primary Identification in Absolute Self-Misrecognition'.

Lacan is explicit in understanding the mirror phase in terms of identification 'in the full sense which analysis gives to the term'. What is less certain is whether he thinks of it as 'primary' in a way which would displace the process to which the term refers in Freud – an earlier relationship to the parents – rather than augment it. To some extent, the difficulty is as much the product of the uncertain status of Freud's concept of primary identification as it is of the relation of Lacan's account of the mirror phase to earlier stages of child development. However, insofar as Lacan refers to the earlier stage as 'very curious' and 'certainly mythical', and treats the mirror phase as the sole 'source' of secondary identifications, he does appear to dispense with the earlier account.[52]

The difficulty here derives from the way in which the child's relation to the image is absolutized by being abstracted from the context of its relations to others (particularly, the mother), while being made ontologically constitutive of 'the symbolic matrix in which the *I* is precipitated in a primordial form, before it is objectified in the dialectic of identification with the other, and before language restores to it, in the universal, its function as subject'. The agency of the ego is thereby situated 'in a fictional direction, which will always remain irreducible for the individual alone, or rather, will only rejoin the coming-into-being of the subject asymptotically, whatever the success of the dialectical syntheses by which it must resolve as *I* its discordance with its own reality.' The temporal dialectic that the mirror phase enacts 'from insufficiency to anticipation' (from the existential insufficiency of the child prior to formation of the ego, to the anticipation of the self-identity of the 'I' in the grammatical function of the subject), thus terminates in 'the assumption of the armour of an alienating identity, which will *mark with its rigid structure the subject's entire mental development*'. The alienation of the mirror phase is not transcended (*aufgeheben*) in the symbolic, but carried over, transformed, in the concept of the Other (*le Grand Autre*).[53]

It is common at this point in the argument for defenders of Lacan to appeal to passages in which he 'describes the child as looking towards the mother for *confirmation* of the identification which it has just achieved – a confirmation which, of course, can never be decisive' – but which is nonetheless an essential part of the process.[54] Such a response exploits the indeterminacy inherent in the discrepancy between the temporality of Lacan's description of the child's encounter with its bodily image in the mirror as a 'stage' or 'phase' (*stade*) of psychic development, and the punctuality of his depiction of it as a scene, the dramatic point of which is restricted to the relations between two 'characters' alone: the child and its bodily image. In the latter case, confirmation of identification by the mother must either be an integral part of the scene (in which case, Lacan's celebrated paper is simply wrong, although he never repudiated it), or it must be strictly supplementary, and governed by a logic of its own. Either way, Lacan's secondary elaborations can only be read as acknowledgements of an anomaly within his original account to which he never returned, theoretically.

The permanence and rigidity of the ego's alienation is the strict result of Lacan's depiction of it as appearing in the mirror phase only as an *object*. Indeed, the child's identification with the *imago* is said to inaugurate 'objectivity' for it in general as a spatial relation: 'The object is always more or less structured as the image of the body of the subject. . . . On the libidinal level, the object is only ever apprehended through the grid of narcissistic relations.'[55] Furthermore, this idealized visuality would appear to provide the model for Lacan's conception of the phallus, in relation to which, he argues, the subject enters the symbolic. The alienating constitution of the ego in the imaginary is thus reproduced in the symbolic in the form of the Other, structuring the subject's desire, through the medium of the phallus.[56] It is this parallel which forms the point of departure for Judith Butler's attempt to unravel Lacan's distinction between the imaginary and the symbolic, by reasserting the imaginary origin of phallic identifications. The symbolic is 'unveiled' as the hegemonic imaginary.[57] The fact that the phallus is for Lacan veiled *of necessity*, and hence perpetually absent, does not undermine its purported connection to the idealized visuality of the imaginary here, so much as secure it. For it is precisely the transcendental dictat of this 'veiling' which turns the one into the other – absolutizing its ideality by cutting it off from its specular ground. Hence the contradictory status of the phallus in Lacanian theory, at the hinge of the symbolic: it is at once the penis and not the penis. It is the transcendental ground of the meaning of something from which it derives. Once this is recognized, however, its transcendental status is undermined, appearing, instead, as merely *quasi*-transcendental, sustained in its transcendental function only by the hegemony of a particular imaginary (the idealized penis).

Through the medium of the imaginary, Lacan thus reproduces in a displaced form just that idealized 'unity of the subject' which is presupposed by his main polemical opponents, ego psychology and Neo-Freudianism: 'as if the psychical had to obtain its credentials as a double of the physical organism', as he remarks sarcastically at one point.[58] Yet this is precisely what he argues is in fact the case. The unity may be imaginary, but it is still produced as 'a double of the physical organism', and its constitutive illusion lies at the existential

core of Lacan's account. As a result, the fear of death, which
was a constitutive element of self-consciousness for Hegel, just as the
anticipation of death was a constitutive aspect of *Dasein* for
Heidegger, is held by Lacan to be 'psychologically subordinate to the
narcissistic fear of damage to one's own body'.[59] How does this affect
our understanding of the relationship between existential temporality,
the anticipation of death, and recognition?

'Afterwardsness' and the death drive

The similarity of the temporal dialectic of Lacan's account of the
mirror phase ('from insufficiency to anticipation') to the existential
temporality of Heidegger's account of *Dasein* has often been noted.[60]
Indeed, in a number of writings from the 1950s, and in particular in
the *Rome Discourse*, Lacan develops his discussion of temporality
with explicit reference to Heidegger's work. At the same time, he also
maintains the Hegelian motif whereby identification with the other
(standing in, unilaterally, for the Hegelian concept of recognition)
takes place 'among the shadows of death'.[61] Lacan's work would thus
seem to offer a psychoanalytical mediation of the two accounts.
Indeed, in defining the psychoanalyst as 'a mediator between the man
of care and the subject of absolute knowledge',[62] it is explicitly
presented as such. This mediation is grounded in two main moves: a
modification of the Hegelian 'trial by death' by its relocation to the
realm of the symbolic; and an interpretation of Heidegger's Being-
towards-death in terms of Freud's concept of the death drive (*der
Todstrieb*). Both follow from the interpolation of the mirror phase
between the originary mother-child relation and relations with
others. And the second may be read as theoretical compensation for
the first.

The structure of the problem is as follows. If, following Hegel, death
comes from the other; and if, following Heidegger, it is anticipation
of death which temporalizes human existence, how can we account
for the temporality of the mirror phase, which must precede relations
with others in order to provide them with their model? How can
there be a temporality to the mirror phase at all, let alone one which
forms the temporal basis of psychical reality? Lacan's solution to
this problem is twofold. On the one hand, he argues that the 'domain
of the symbolic does not have a simple relation of succession to the
imaginary domain whose pivot is the fatal intersubjective relation. We
do not pass from one to the other in one jump from the anterior to the

posterior, once the pact and the symbol are established.' Rather, the imaginary must be conceived 'as already bounded by the register of the symbolic', albeit in a way which can only be perceived retrospectively.[63] On the other hand, Lacan is still forced to provide an independent basis for death within the subject, prior to relations with others, the symbolic significance of which can then be realized retrospectively. This is the role of the death drive, Lacan's decidedly non-Hegelian, psychoanalytical answer to the question of the onto-logical basis of Heidegger's 'anticipation of death'.

Death, which is always symbolic, has its basis in a drive which structures the imaginary, before taking on the signification of 'death'. It is the 'primitive imaginary of the specular dialectic' which introduces 'the fatal dimension of the death drive'. The way this works is that the child supposedly sees the 'image of the master' in the specular image of itself. This image then 'becomes confused with the image of death' (Hegel's 'absolute master'). The child is thus in the presence of death 'from the beginning . . . in so far as it is subjected to this image'.[64] It is the otherness of the image of the child's body in the mirror phase, an otherness with which it identifies, but which it will never fully recuperate, that underlies the consciousness of death, and hence of *time* ('from insufficiency to anticipation'). Yet this is an immanent temporality, an immanent mortality, which it can only fully experience once it accedes to the symbolic – or, to put it another way, once the 'register' of the symbolic *within* the imaginary comes into its own. This is a process which is associated by Lacan with the castration complex and the production of sexual difference.

The death drive is thus understood by Lacan to be 'constitutive of the fundamental position of the human subject . . . at the juncture between the imaginary and the symbolic'.[65] As such, it is constitutive of the subject's sense of time. When Lacan writes of the fear of death as 'psychologically subordinate to the narcissistic fear of damage to one's own body', he is thus not opposing one to the other, so much as pointing to the origin of the former (fear of death) in the latter (fear of bodily damage). Fear of bodily damage is the primal *spatial* form of what will become a temporal fear (of death), once the child accedes to the domain of the symbolic. The death drive is at work *before* there is death, or time, for the child. Lacan's mediation of Heideggerian with Hegelian motifs is achieved by virtue of a temporal lag, wherein the individualism of the Heideggerian element may be developmen-tally prior to, but is *not* thereby any more ontologically basic than, the Hegelian social dimension, since the former can only be recog-nized 'afterwards' (*nachträglich*) in the form of the latter: language.

'Afterwardsness' (*Nachträglichkeit*) – Freud's famous contribution
to the theory of time – is thus not simply one mode of temporality
among others (the temporality of the causality of the trauma), but
– on this account at least – the temporal structure which determines
the emergence of temporality itself, phenomenologically. The
temporalization of time for the child by the death drive happens
'afterwards'.

But why should the child's image of its body in the primitive
imaginary of the specular dialectic be perceived, first, as the image of
'the master', and subsequently as the image of death? What grounds
this primal 'confusion', apart from the convenient (but misplaced)
parallel with Hegel's 'master' text? It obviously has something to do
with the experience of the otherness of the image as a threat, ontologically. Yet there is nothing in Lacan's account to explain this structure.
Indeed, insofar as the mirror phase provides Lacan with his own
distinctive account of primary identification, it precedes relations with
others (except for the child's original libidinal unity with the mother),
taking the form of a *pure positing* of the *imago* as the object of
a primal ambivalence: a relationship to otherness of both fear
and recognition, grounded in loss (the loss of libidinal unity), but
not, it would seem, structured in its relation to this loss by any other
relations.

In order to *explain* this relationship, we need to take account of the
child's previous relations, prior to any object-cathexis, after the period
of auto-eroticism. We are helped here by Freud's own short outline of
primary identification as a 'direct and immediate' identification with
what he calls the father of the individual's 'own personal prehistory';[66]
and, in particular, by Kristeva's reconstruction and development of
this scenario in the first chapter of her *Tales of Love*[67] – an analysis
which shares certain features with Laplanche's account of enigmatic
signification. The importance of these works lies in their reassertion of
the social (albeit in the restricted psychoanalytical code of the familial)
at the heart of psychic formation, and thereby, at the phenomenological
core of death and time. For only thus can we do justice, psychoanalytically, to Hegel's insight into the mutual origin of self-consciousness
and the anticipation of death in the dialectic of recognition. The task
before us will then be to reconnect this analysis to our account of the
totalizing temporality of human existence as the ontological basis for
a hermeneutics of *historical* existence.

Primary identification: Kristeva's imaginary father

Freud introduces the concept of identification at the point of the child's first experience of differentiation from the mother, as a compensatory reaction to the loss of the libidinal unity of auto-eroticism. Identification is 'the earliest and most original form of emotional tie'. As such, it is the earliest stage in the process of ego-formation. In primary identification, the ego is moulded 'after the fashion of the one that has been taken as a model', in a way 'derivative of the first, *oral* phase of the organisation of the libido, in which the object that we long for and prize is assimilated by eating and is in that way annihilated'. As such, it displays an inherent ambivalence, connected to the condition of primary narcissism 'in which object-libido and ego-libido cannot [yet] be distinguished'. As the point of production of the first, fledgling (narcissistic) form of the ego, it is also taken by Freud to lie at 'the origin of the ego ideal', which substitutes for the ego as the object of satisfaction in the 'post-Oedipal' adult.[68]

There are two main things to note about this analysis: Freud's specification of the 'father of personal prehistory' as the site of primary identification and the alleged immediacy of the relation. In Freud's brief sketch, the theoretical arbitrariness of the selection of the 'father of personal prehistory' as the subject of primary identification appears, as Kristeva notes, 'undeniable', since it is derived retrospectively from the structure of the Oedipal triad, without any attempt at an immanent justification. Yet Kristeva's own account – ascertained, it is claimed, from clinical experience – ultimately fares little better, although it does contain the germ of a more adequate, if significantly different, scenario.

Kristeva's version of the story runs as follows. The auto-erotic plenitude of the child's original libidinal unity with the mother is broken up once the mother 'indicate[s] to her child that her desire is not limited to responding to her offspring's request (or simply turning it down)', but is also directed elsewhere. The child experiences this indication as a loss (loss of the mother's desire), registering the otherness of at least part of the mother. There is a psychic separation of the child from the mother, experienced as 'emptiness'. Primary identification is an attempt to recover the lost desire, 'a defense against the emptiness of separation'. It is thus directed towards the object of the mother's desire: namely, according to Kristeva, 'the Father's Phallus'. What Freud calls 'the father of the individual's personal prehistory', and Kristeva dubs 'the Imaginary Father', is thus the form in which the object of the mother's desire for another appears to the child. The child identifies with this (imaginary) object, assimilating it to itself on the oral model of incorporation. The outcome – primary narcissism – is a 'screen for emptiness' since, directed towards the other of the mother's desire, it can never overcome the separation from which it derives (separation from the mother). As in the ego-founding moment of the Lacanian mirror phase, this structural inadequacy is inherited by the ego ideal, once the subject is 'completed' in the course of its negotiation of the Oedipus complex.[69] The child's selection of the 'father of personal prehistory' as the site of primary identification is thus explained by Kristeva by the character of the mother's desire, and the relationship is conceived within the terms of the Lacanian topology as an 'imaginary' one.

However, the idea of the father of personal prehistory as the site of an imaginary identification remains problematic; and for more reasons than the one Freud himself acknowledges in a footnote to *The Ego and the Id*: namely, that since the relation precedes the child's knowledge of sexual difference, the term 'father' is misleading[70] – although this is indeed a problem. In his footnote, Freud amends his description of the site of identification from 'father' to the sexually indifferent 'parents', in the plural. (He then proceeds, however, to discuss 'only identification with the father', in order – he says – to 'simplify' his presentation.) Freud explains his amendment with the remark that: 'before a child has arrived at definite knowledge of the difference between the sexes, the lack of a penis, it does not distinguish in value between its father and its mother.' Father and mother (of personal prehistory) are thus, for Freud, apparently equivalent as potential sites of primary identification, and both are supposedly 'phallic'. However, this response to the problem of sexual indifference seriously erodes the critical potential of Freud's account.

To begin with, it replaces the recognition that primary narcissism is (in Kristeva's words) 'an already *ternary* structuration with a different articulation from the Ego-object-Other triangle that is put together in the shadow of the Oedipus complex',[71] with an indifference in 'value' between 'father' and 'mother' which is based solely on the child's ignorance of *sexual* difference. Yet it is surely the difference between the mother and father established by their different relations to the child (from the child's viewpoint) which is at issue. Secondly, in defining both unsexed parents as 'phallic', Freud retrospectively applies the coding of sexual difference from the castration complex, when there would seem to be no justification for so doing inherent in the dynamics of primary identification itself. He thus repeats the dubious theoretical logic underlying his initial description ('the father of personal prehistory') in a disguised form. On the other hand, the idea of indifference does raise the question of the child's relationship to the mother during the period of primary narcissism, which is otherwise neglected by Freud's analysis. And it suggests an answer not dissimilar to the one given by Kristeva: namely, that the mother may be the object of primary identification, but only insofar as she is 'equivalent' to the father of personal prehistory for the child – a position quite different from that developed by Klein, in which the mother is the site of primary identification in her own right.

Kristeva's emphasis on the distinctive ternary structure of the identification produces a more complex account of the unity and difference of the positions of 'mother' and 'father' in the scenario than Freud's. Yet her insistence on the role of the Father's Phallus in defining the object of the mother's desire and, subsequently, in grounding signification for the child, ultimately leads her into the same phallic dogmatism exhibited by Freud in his initial description – albeit in a hyper-linguistic, Lacanian form, and at a different level of analysis. At its simplest, the objection to Kristeva may be put like this: why restrict the mother's desire for something other than the child to 'the Father's Phallus'? Is such a restriction not as theoretically arbitrary as it is socially conventional? What reason is there to suppose that there is anything less at stake here than the totality of the mother's desire for others, and hence an investment by the child's desire of an imaginary domain corresponding to this social field *as a whole*?[72]

Kristeva's answer is that the mother passes on to the child the structure of desire fixed at the Oedipal stage of her own development. But this is to condemn the child to repeat the structure of the mother's early development, irrespective of her subsequent development, and irrespective of the fact that the 'pre-Oedipal' child cannot grasp the phallic significance of the object of its identification, since it is ignorant of sexual difference. (Here, as elsewhere, an emphasis on the 'pre-Oedipal' actually functions to reinforce the Oedipal structure, rather than to counterbalance it.) After the founding analytical instance, the argument becomes tautological: all social and historical temporality is compressed into a structure of repetition. Furthermore, we still need to explain the child's reception of the mother's desire. Or does this occur only retrospectively (*nachträglich*), after the castration complex? In which case, 'the father of personal prehistory' need not be the site of primary identification at all. It could be *any* third term.

At this point the full originality of Kristeva's account comes into view. For it is not only the role played by the mother's desire in establishing the phallus as the object of identification which is distinctive here, but the way Kristeva attempts to explain the transmission of this structure by demonstrating its ground in the structure of primary identification itself: namely, by reading the 'emptiness' that identification both implies and conceals as the ontological correlate of the gap between the signifier and signified which founds the structure of the sign. There is 'an archaic disposition of the paternal function', preceding both the symbolic and the mirror phase, which is said to ground the child's 'access' to these structures. Primary identification is for Kristeva at one and the same time *primary signification*, or the origin of what she calls *signifiance*: 'the process of formation and deformation of meaning and the subject'.[73] *This* is Kristeva's ultimate argument for the Imaginary Father as the object of primary identification, since, following Lacan, she understands the phallus as the signifier of signification. It is the dogmatism of the phallus as the transcendental signifier which necessitates that the father be the site of identification for the child – as indeed this same dogmatism necessitates that the Father's Phallus be the object of the mother's desire – necessitates it, it would seem, as a matter of *definition*, once Lacan's concept of the symbolic has been mapped onto Freud's account of the castration complex.

But the argument for the paternity of the signifying function is circular. For either it derives from the Oedipal scenario, via the mother's desire (in which case, even if we accept this formulation of the mother's desire, it is unrecognizable by the child – Freud's objection to his own initial formulation); or it derives immanently from the structure of primary identification as primary signification (in which case, it is dependent for its gendering upon the contingencies of the mother's desire). Kristeva uses each argument to support the other, in a generational loop which makes a dogma out of the identification of signification with a phallic definition of sexual difference, while ostensibly *explaining* the emergence of what was merely posited by Lacan. It is in this sense that there is a 'paternal return' in Kristeva's work, a 'race back into the arms of the law', which is not mitigated but reproduced by her valorization of the maternal as the site of the 'abject', a semiosis beyond language.[74]

Kristeva reads the alienating 'hole' at the heart of Lacan's mirror phase as merely 'the "visible" aspect' of the prior gap constitutive of primary identification/signification, the gap created by the mother's desire.[75] The *imago* thus appears as the spatial equivalent of the previously internalized otherness of the mother: namely, the Imaginary Father, or whatever we choose to call its de-phallicized equivalent: the Imaginary Other, perhaps. What is there about this Imaginary Other which might lead the child to 'confuse' its image, projected as the image of the child's own body, as the image of death? At this point Hegel's derivation of the consciousness of death from the fear of the loss of recognition, outlined above, comes into its own, psychoanalytically. For as we have seen, this fear was nothing other than the fear of the other's freedom; or, to put it in Kristeva's terms, in the child's case, it is the fear of losing the mother's desire altogether, precipitated by the indication of her desire for another. The *imago* thus bears an *insignia of death* inherited from the Imaginary Other. To understand how this insignia comes to be inscribed in the Imaginary Other in the first place, we need to remember that this Other is actually, in a fundamental sense, a part of the (Imaginary) mother for the child.

In Kristeva's terms, there is a 'coagulation' of the mother and her desire. It may only be a part of this coagulation that is the focus for the child's identification – the Imaginary Other – but it is no less a relationship to the mother herself for that. The child's relationship to the mother appears, displaced and condensed (that is to say, unconsciously), within the structure of its identification with the Imaginary Other. The key to the complexity of this fluid and ambivalent, self-negating (non-)relation lies, oddly enough, in its *immediacy*.

Freud's idea of a 'direct and immediate' identification appears to run counter to Kristeva's depiction of 'an already ternary structuration', which posits a mediating role for the mother's desire as the source of the child's Imaginary Other. On the other hand, Kristeva herself requires something like an immediate identity at this stage, if she is to develop the mirror phase out of primary identification as a moment of first reflection generated by the spatialization of the relation between its terms. This tension is alleviated, once we recall the peculiarity of identification as the continual covering over of a gap which it thereby reproduces, a self-negating 'relation' which effaces the duality of relationship – a 'being' rather than a 'having'. For as Kristeva notes, such identification is 'immediate' in the precise sense of Hegelian logic, in which the immediacy of the absolute is understood as the result of 'reflection doing away with itself'.[76] This is why, strictly speaking, the word 'object' is as inappropriate to designate the site of identification as the word 'subject' is to denote the child. As Kristeva puts it: 'A not-yet-identity (of the child) is transferred or rather displaced to the site of an Other who is not libidinally cathected as an object but remains an Ego Ideal.'[77]

This solves the problem of what kind of 'thing' the child is at the point of entry into primary identification (in Lacan's case, what 'it' could be that 'recognizes itself' in the image of its body in the mirror), which is raised by the objection that if the 'I' is formed by the relation, it cannot precede it. As Laplanche and Pontalis put it, 'it is difficult to ascribe primary identification to an absolutely undifferentiated and objectless state.'[78] But this is not the way things are, either immediately prior to or after the identification. Differentiation has already occurred. The mother is a mediating 'third' in the child's identification with the Imaginary Other, just as this Other mediates the child's relationship to the mother, reproducing the child psychically in its separation from the mother. This mediation may be 'done away with' in the moment of identification itself, but it is not thereby abolished altogether. Rather, it is 'covered over' *qua mediation*, by being condensed into the child's psychic unity with the Imaginary Other – just as the social mediation of cosmological time is 'covered over' by being condensed into the unity of phenomenological time with historical time in historical experience. Hence the ambivalence of identification.

The ambivalence inherent in primary narcissism is not merely the product of an inability to distinguish object-libido from ego-libido, as Freud suggests.[79] It is also the product of an inability to distinguish within the Imaginary Other between its status as an independent object of the mother's desire and its status as a displaced part of her. For there is a doubling of the mother's role here. She is both the site of the identification (in her 'coagulation' with the Imaginary Other) and a separate object for the child – separated from the site of identification by the structure of desire (Hegel's 'negative relation to the object' which endlessly produces both object and desire anew[80]). In identifying with the Imaginary Other, the child may be said actually (unconsciously) to be identifying with the mother. The independence of the Imaginary Other from the child, the 'gap' which identification covers over, stands in for the independence of the mother, the independence which threatens the child with 'emptiness'. We may trace the origin of 'death' within this framework back to *this* fundamental mapping or substitution.

The freedom of the other from which, in Hegel's account, the fear of death derives – via the possibility of the refusal of recognition – appears psychoanalytically as the *freedom of the mother*. Yet it presents itself to the child in primary identification as the independence of the Imaginary Other. In Hegel's dialectic of recognition, consciousness registers the independence of the other as at once a threat to its

identity and a condition of its existence. In our reworked version of
Kristeva's account of primary identification, the child registers the
independence of the mother – via the Imaginary Other – as at once a
threat to its existence and a condition of its identity. Hegel starts out
with a consciousness in search of knowledge of itself and ends up with
two self-consciousnesses, one in bondage to the other. Kristeva starts
out with a child confronted with the emptiness of separation from its
mother, and ends up with the 'not-yet-identity' of the narcissistic ego,
formed through its identification with an Imaginary Other, screening
its emptiness by finding itself everywhere in the other. The ontological
peculiarity of this fledgling 'I' reflects its transitional status as a prefigurative shadow of a function still to come. Not until the specular
dialectic of the mirror phase is its 'logical potentiality' to be actualized,
in the alienating scenario of self-(mis)recognition in which reflection
holds sway.[81]

Thus, just as for Lacan the imaginary everywhere foreshadows the
symbolic, by the register of which it is bound ('from insufficiency to
anticipation'), so for Kristeva the Imaginary Father, our Imaginary
Other, foreshadows the *imago* prior to the mirror phase: from the
insufficiency of the pre-ego of primary narcissism to the anticipation
of the otherness of the image. All three stages share a structure of
idealization, and it is this which binds them together. Yet for all its
additional complexity, is Kristeva's interpretation of this scenario
ultimately any more 'social' than the Lacanian one whose conditions
of emergence it purports to chart? Is Kristeva's 'ternary structuration'
any more interactive a scenario than the self-alienating identification
of the ego with the image of the body of the child, misdescribed
by Lacan in terms of the Hegelian concept of recognition? Or does
its restriction to the problematic of the imaginary – a discourse not
so much of internalization as of strict psychic immanence – relegate
the other, once again, to the provision of a set (familial) stock of
psychic forms with no effective productivity of its own? Might not the
practical relations of actual others to the child make a fundamental
difference to the process? But if so, how are they to be conceptualized,
since the problematic of recognition requires self-consciousness
(Lacan's symbolic) as a condition of its application? At this point the
potential and limits alike of the Hegelian model as a framework for
bringing together psychoanalytical and existential ideas of temporality
and death come most clearly into view. They are displayed in Jessica
Benjamin's attempt at a direct application of Hegel's concept of
recognition to the child's earliest interactions, in her elaboration of an
'intersubjective' view of child development in *The Bonds of Love*.[82]

In the beginning was the bond: Jessica Benjamin or Jean Laplanche?

When Kristeva writes of the 'agency' of the Imaginary Father as the 'new psychical action' to which Freud refers, when he suggests that something must be added to auto-eroticism to transform it into narcissism,[83] one might be forgiven for thinking that she is referring to the effect upon the child of a concrete interaction between it and some third party, other than the mother. This would certainly seem to be the case with Freud's own idea of the 'father of personal prehistory', however psychically mediated the result of such interaction may be. In Kristeva's case, however, this is far from clear. For although there must be some actual third party for primary identification to occur, both its specification via the mother's desire and its restriction to the terms of the Lacanian imaginary suggest that the specific actions of this third are more or less irrelevant to the structure of the process. Concentration on the immanent dynamics of the child's psychic system leads to the eradication of concrete others from the scene. How could it be otherwise?

Benjamin's answer lies in the direct application of Hegel's concept of recognition to the child's interactions, from the very beginning of its life, and the refusal to stabilize its outcome, ontologically, in any fixed form. Rather, for Benjamin, the value of the concept of recognition resides precisely in its paradoxical character, a paradox which must be sustained practically as a tension or balance between the competing principles of self-assertion and recognition of the other, if relations between selves are to be possible. It is 'the inability to sustain paradox in interaction' which, Benjamin believes, 'convert[s] the exchange of recognition into domination and submission': the master-slave relationship.[84] Such paradox finds its model in the 'direct recognition', or 'concrete intersubjective mode', which is for Benjamin as primary a state of the infant, ontologically, as the physiological dependence which forms the basis of its unity with its mother, and which is conceptualized by Freud in terms of a *non-specific* oral drive. Only later is direct or concrete recognition transformed into identification, as the result of a defensive process whereby its 'subject-to-subject' structure is replaced by the ideal of 'the symbolic phallic mode'. It is this latter mode which is the basis of self-alienation (as in Lacan and Kristeva) and, under current social conditions, of the gendering of dominant and submissive positions in the allocation of social and sexual agency. Benjamin acknowledges that identifications with the ideal are 'unavoidable'. Yet she nonetheless maintains the possibility of their transformation in such a way as to produce 'an expansion of that space where subject meets subject', through an active recovery of the complexity of the earlier structure. It is only from the standpoint of identification with the ideal that concrete recognition appears paradoxical.[85]

There are thus two main planks to Benjamin's approach: the concrete intersubjectivity of the 'first bond' and the potential for recognition free of domination which consequently persists, despite idealizing identifications, as the ontological ground of political equality. The strength of this position lies in its insistence on the significance of the concrete other for the child, and its acknowledgement that for there to be recognition at all (however unequal) there must be an element of mutuality in the relation, and hence greater social substance to the principle of freedom than is allowed by its interpretation as the mere negation of dependence upon the other. (Both of these things are missing from the Lacanian mirror phase, for example.) It is out of this element of mutuality that Benjamin builds her 'vision of recognition between equal subjects' giving rise to a new logic of paradox, 'sustaining the tension between contradictory forces'.[86] Recognition is thus conceived as an inherently fluid relationship, open to the forces of both history and politics, yet grounded in this openness by the structure of the child's earliest experiences.

The weakness of the position lies in the obscurity of the concept of recognition in its application to such a young child. Not only does the newborn baby seem to lack the capacities required to be a subject of recognition in anything like the Hegelian sense (which involves an explicitly cognitive relationship – a re-cognition of the other); the relations between this dimension of its existence, and the intrapsychic realities which are the focus of orthodox psychoanalytical theory, are left wholly unexplored, despite a formal acknowledgement of their interdependence.[87] Even if we accept the dubious early use of the concept of recognition, judgement on the feasibility and dynamics of fostering the forces of mutual recognition as a countervailing power to the 'unequal complementaries' of idealized identifications must remain suspended (suspended by the antinomy of Benjamin's method), until such time as we are offered a theoretical integration of the two approaches.

Benjamin justifies her pre-emptive use of the idea of recognition with reference to 'the new perception of the active, social infant who can respond to and differentiate others', which has arisen within recent empirical research into infancy. This leads her to 'assume that life begins with an emergent awareness of self and other', and to posit

a 'spectrum' of intersubjective development going back to the very
first days of the child's life – despite the fact that her main source
(Daniel Stern's *The First Relationship*) declines to deploy the concept
prior to the seventh month of the child's life. Yet there is a crucial
gap here between the kind of data this sort of research produces and
the language of 'the joy and urgency of discovering the external,
independent reality of *another person*' which Benjamin uses to
interpret it. For it is precisely the capacity to recognize the other as
a 'person' which, according to Hegel, is dependent upon self-
consciousness, for reasons of strict conceptual logic.[88] To render
Benjamin's position consistent with its own Hegelian categories, we
need to view the earliest phase (which Stern calls 'core relatedness')
as *unconsciously* and only *retrospectively* 'intersubjective'. But this
explodes Benjamin's whole approach, transforming it into something
not unlike that to be found in the recent work of Jean Laplanche.

Laplanche's work may be compared to Benjamin's by virtue of its
emphasis on the priority to the psychic life of the infant of its relations
to the concrete other. Just as Benjamin criticizes internalization theory
for its exclusive preoccupation with the child's intrapsychic situation,
to the neglect of its actual relations with others, so Laplanche criticizes
Lacan's Other for remaining 'a thought of the subject'. However,
whereas Benjamin responds by positing a primal relation of concrete
recognition, independent of the child's relations to its internal
representations, Laplanche interprets the priority of the other as 'the
priority of the *message* from the other on the *sexual* level' which the
child receives, but is unable to decode. He thus comes to replace
Lacan's notion of the symbolic with the idea of a signifier or message
with which the child is 'implanted' in the earliest days of its life, in
the context of a profoundly asymmetrical relationship to the adult
world. Such a message or signifier (which may be no better understood
by the adult who implants it than by the child, since it derives
at least in part from the adult's unconscious) is understood by
Laplanche as inherently 'enigmatic'. It precipitates the emergence of
the child's unconscious (repression is conceived as 'a partial "failure of
translation"'), and it may thus be thought as the 'source-object' of the
sexual drives.[89]

Clearly, there is an enormous difference between the theoretical
terms of the two approaches. Benjamin seeks to supplement the
intrapsychic perspective of orthodox psychoanalysis with the intersubjective logic of an empirical child psychology. Yet she thereby
introduces the other only at the cost of its separation from the realm
of internal representations. Laplanche, on the other hand, undertakes

a reformulation of the very foundations of psychoanalytical theory, separating off seduction from the primal fantasies with which it is associated by Freud, and understanding it, instead, as the logic of a primal 'communication situation' between adult and child: 'the implantation of the message of the other'. This reformulation is premised on a categorial distinction between the specificity of the object of psychoanalytical theory ('the human subject *in so far as* that subject is auto-hypothetical, auto-conjectural, auto-representative or auto-theorising'[90]) and the domain of a more general developmental psychology, with which it is often confused – a distinction which Benjamin's approach constantly elides.[91] Yet both are dealing with the same problem (the role of the other in the constitution and dynamics of the psyche), each draws upon Hegel, and each confronts the same difficulty in the transposition of the logic of recognition from the philosophical terrain of the concept of self-consciousness to the context of child development.

The distinctiveness of Laplanche's approach derives from its integration, within the specificity of the psychoanalytical field, of the terms which Benjamin holds apart: the action of the concrete other and the intrapsychic domain of representation. For if 'the drive originates in messages (but not, of course, solely in verbal messages), we have to conclude that there is no initial or natural opposition between the instinctual and the intersubjective, or between the instinctual and cultural'. Rather, we must understand this opposition as *produced* in the course of the child's development, as the 'seduction' of the primal situation peels a sexual layer off the 'onion' of a self-preservative function which is 'simultaneously psychical and somatic'. This sexual layer, along with the associated formation of the unconscious, provides psychoanalytical theory with its specific object. For Laplanche, its comprehension is thus inextricably bound up with the somatic dimension of the drive (*Trieb*): 'the force behind representatives which have acquired a separate status of their own: the status of the repressed and the primordial unconscious' – a concept which he insists be rigorously distinguished from the more traditional concept, also used by Freud, of instinct (*Instinkt*).[92]

Benjamin identifies herself with that post-Freudian tendency which rejects the field of drives and defences for the 'inner drama of ego and objects'. Yet it resurfaces in her work in the disguised form of a primal 'need' for recognition, and in her central contention that 'the ideal "resolution" of the paradox of recognition is for it to continue as a *constant tension*.'[93] For how else are we to interpret the idea of a constant tension other than by reference to some kind of somatic model? The idea of the 'bond' which emerges in this context is not that of recognition at all (the bond of love), but the product of the 'binding' activity of Eros in its struggle against the death drive. In place of various strictly intrapsychic versions of primary identification (Freud, Lacan, Kristeva), Laplanche returns us here to the idea of primal repression in the form of the 'primal metabolization' of a *situation* out of which the ego emerges as the unstable product of the victory of the life drive over the 'unbinding' force of the death drive. How does this affect our understanding of the phenomenological origins of temporality in the fear of death, and the source of this fear in the recognition of the freedom of the (m)other?[94]

We saw above how Lacan uses the idea of the death drive to provide the ontological ground for a death which is always symbolic, exploiting the structure of afterwardsness (*Nachträglichkeit*) to explain the 'lag' between its role in the specular dialectic of the mirror phase as the source of the child's fear of bodily damage, and the emergence of existential temporality for the child within the realm of the symbolic. The temporalization of time for the child by the death drive, we noted, happens 'afterwards'. However, we also saw that Lacan fails to explain why the image of the child's body in the mirror should come to signify death for the child, even in the purely imaginary (pre-temporal) form of bodily disintegration. It was suggested on Hegelian grounds that Kristeva's account of primary identification is preferable, since it allows us to trace back the signification of death by an Imaginary Other to the independence of the (m)other. It is the freedom of the (m)other, we argued, in the form of the possibility of the refusal of recognition, which brings death (and hence *time*) into the world of the child. But we still have the problem of explaining how the child can apprehend this possibility at such an early stage in its development.

In returning to ever earlier stages of psychic development to account for the emergence of the 'I', the application of the Hegelian concept of recognition to psychoanalysis becomes increasingly problematic, since it is premised on the existence of a knowing subject (consciousness) in search of consistency with itself, which it is the precise point of psychoanalytical theory to *derive*. It is at this point that Laplanche's conception of enigmatic signification comes into its own. For it allows him to deploy the communicative structure inherent in the concept of recognition prior to the child's development of the capacity for language (Kant's 'I think', Hegel's self-consciousness, and Lacan's symbolic) – something which Benjamin's work depends upon, but which it fails to provide with any theoretical justification. On this model, the child might be said both to 'know' and 'not know' death, insofar as it is subject to an *enigmatic signification* of the adult's fear of the death of the child; derived, perhaps, from the repressed possibilities of the adult's own freedom. What we would have, then, would be a mediated return to a Heideggerian form of anxiety (in the adult), within the framework of a modified dialectic of recognition (between adult and child), in which the adult's fear of his or her own freedom 'implants' a sense of death in the child. Such an implantation of 'death' via anxiety could then be used to explain the priority of 'drive-anxiety' (*Trieb-Angst*) over 'realistic anxiety' (*Realangst*) which, Laplanche argues, is the consequence of 'the non-existence in children of "instinctual" adaptive montage when faced with real danger'.[95]

This is not, I should stress, Laplanche's own account of the psychic origin of a sense of death, but a *direct* application of the idea of the enigmatic signifier to the problem of 'where death comes from'. It is, however, consistent with his general strategy of back-dating Lacan's scenario of 'the enigma of the adult's desire', in which the desire of the adult is apprehended by the child 'in that which does not work, in the lacks of the discourse of the Other'. For in Lacan's version of this scenario, the first object the child proposes so as to fill the lack of the other's desire is its own disappearance, *the fantasy of its own death*.[96] But where can this fantasy come from, if it has not already been implanted in the child (unconsciously) by the adult? Lacan's own answer – that it is 'a lack engendered from the previous time that serves to reply to the lack raised by the following time' (a reference to the priority of the 'real' lack of the death drive[97]) – will not do, since it reduces the content of a *fantasy* to an aspect of the *drive*. As Laplanche points out,

> Freud maintains until the end the strictest reservations concerning the developments which, almost naturally, his new conceptualisation [the death drive] would seem to invite: the occurrence of 'death anxiety' or of an originary wish to die will never be located, in analytic psychopathology, in that position of irreducible 'bedrock' which is attributed par excellence to the castration complex.[98]

Furthermore:

> The death drive implies a very specific notion of death: its model is neither the suffering and passing away [with] which we are so familiar, nor the decay of the body, and it has nothing to do with the problems that may be posed for us by our 'being towards death'. It relates to a sort of *death before life*, to the so called inanimate state of matter, to something akin to

the silence of death in Pascal's 'infinite space', or to the silence of the surface of the moon.[99]

The death drive does not seem to have anything to do with death in the existential sense, in which it is the anticipation of death that temporalizes time for human beings. In this respect, at least, 'life and death in psychoanalysis' are as different from life and death in Heidegger's *Being and Time* and Hegel's *Phenomenology* as they are from life and death in everyday life. There is a specificity to the death drive as 'the constitutive principle of libidinal circulation'[100] which allies it, not to temporalization, but to *timelessness*.

But are temporalization and timelessness as straightforwardly opposed to one another as might initially be thought? And do we really need the (empirically problematic) postulation of a *specific* enigmatic signifier of 'death' in order to utilize Laplanche's innovative reworking of psychoanalytical theory for our present purposes? It is necessary at this point to reconsider the ontology of the death drive as the background against which the temporalization of time by the child out of its relation to the (m)other takes place. For it is a distinguishing feature of Laplanche's work that it combines a reassertion of the importance of the drives with an emphasis on 'the priority of the other in the constitution of human time'. Yet it remains unclear how these two dimensions of his argument are connected. How is the apparent indifference of the death drive to time related to the constitutive role of death in temporalization?[101]

Timelessness, death, and the unconscious

Let us begin with Freud's own remarks about time. Aside from considerations of temporal aspects of the analytical process, these are restricted to registering the twofold significance of psychoanalysis for 'the Kantian theorem that time and space are "necessary forms of thought"'. This is, firstly, that 'unconscious mental processes are in themselves "timeless"' – 'they are not ordered temporally', 'time does not change them in any way', 'the idea of time cannot be applied to them'; and secondly, that 'our abstract idea of time' is 'wholly derived from the method of working of the perceptual-conscious system', and corresponds to a perception on the part of that system of its own method of working – specifically, its 'discontinuous' functioning.[102]

In the first case, Freud is registering what he rightly thinks of as an important exception to Kant's theory, which he suggests offers an approach to 'the most profound discoveries'.[103] In the second, he provides a psychological explanation for something that is treated by Kant only at the level of the transcendental, in the 'Transcendental Aesthetic' of the *Critique of Pure Reason*. (It is doubtful whether the 'abstract idea of time' Freud has in mind is sufficiently rich to encompass the constitutive role of time-determination in the 'original synthetic unity of apperception' and the activity of transcendental imagination.)[104] There is no reference in this context to the death drive. Indeed, the death drive would seem to have a privileged relationship to the unconscious, in which there is no death at all, since in the unconscious 'nothing can be brought to an end, nothing is past or forgotten' – although, according to Freud, there can be no question of restricting it to just one of 'the provinces of the mind': the death drive must 'necessarily be met with everywhere'. Freud anticipates the most 'profound discoveries' from his conception of the timelessness of the unconscious, but he acknowledges that he has not 'made any progress here' himself.[105]

The beauty of Laplanche's reformulation of the relations between these concepts is that it allows him to integrate the timelessness of the unconscious into the movement of temporalization, as 'the residue of the movement of questioning'.[106] The anticipation of death may thereby be shown not to require an enigmatic signifier of its own, but to be an integral part of the movement of enigmatic signification *per se*. The problem with Freud's account is that in confining itself to the workings of the perceptual-conscious system, it restricts itself to the level of immediate *biological* consciousness, to perceptual time: the time of 'the living being', not that of 'a historical human being'. In Laplanche's account, on the other hand, which builds on concepts 'which were neither sufficiently elaborated by Freud, nor placed in relation to each other', but exist in a practical state in his writings on the analytical process, it is always a specifically human temporality which is at issue. The drive appears as 'a symptom of the human being'.[107]

The scenario of the primal situation in which an enigmatic signifier is 'implanted' in the child by an adult leads Laplanche to treat the formation of subjectivity in the child as a conjoint process of *translation* and *temporalization*. The human infant enters into human time by means of a process of translation, in response to the *demand* of the enigmatic signifier to be translated. This demand, inherent in the enigmatic character of the message, comes from the other – who is thus the 'motor of time', 'immobile motor of the movement of temporalisation'. More specifically, it is a result of the 'imbalance' between the child and the adult world, the 'unequal development' between 'a fully developed and complex adult, with knowledge and partially unconscious sexual particularities', and 'a child in a state of helplessness', in the sense that it has 'only rudimentary means to translate the messages and excitations' presented to it. This imbalance is taken 'immediately' to give rise to the attempt to translate, and hence to the formation of 'the first rudiments of the unconscious' out of the untranslated (indeed, untranslatable) elements of the message which inevitably remain.[108]

Insofar as its subjectivity is formed through this process, the child is thus conceived as 'auto-theorising from the start': auto-theorizing *because* it has been implanted by the other. The other thus appears in Laplanche's analysis in two quite different forms: 'the inside-other (Freud's *das Andere*), that is, the other-thing in us, and the outside-other (Freud's *der Andere*), that is, the other person of our personal pre-history' – levels of analysis which are collapsed together in Kristeva's notion of the Imaginary Father. The inside-other is the unconscious. It is the product of the repression of untranslated fragments of communication, alienated from their context of origin, which consequently acquire a status of their own, at a level at which 'thoughts behave like things.' These untranslatable (or 'de-translated') fragments, are, however, endlessly *re*translated as they enter into new contexts of significance, encounter new signifiers. It is through this process of de-translation and re-translation that temporality enters the picture, as the movement of a process of translation which is 'at once a taking up and a leaving behind'. The child thus forms its subjectivity through a process of auto-translation in which it mediates its relations to outside-others through continually renewed relations to its inside-other. The temporality of this process is the temporality of a fundamental questioning, 'the movement of interrogation of the enigma', a movement in which the significance of the signifier is only ever established 'afterwards' (*nachträglich*).[109]

As we have seen in our discussion of Lacan, such temporality is constituted through a movement from the time*less* to the temporal, through which an atemporal structure acquires causal efficacy within the present. Lacan's depiction of the mirror phase deploys this structure *developmentally*, to account for the anticipation of a temporal signification ('death') within the atemporal – or, at any rate, not yet temporalized – spatiality of the imaginary. Laplanche, by contrast, deploys it *topologically*, with the implication that the child temporalizes its existence, in response to its relations to the adult world (the implantation of enigmatic signifiers), from the very beginning.

The problem with Lacan's account of the role of the death drive in the emergence of temporality for the child ('from insufficiency to anticipation') was its naturalism: the death drive functioned as the ontological ground of 'death', prior to relations with others. This is a naturalism to which Lacan's analysis is committed, despite itself, as the other side of its conception of the symbolic. It may be redeemed later, by the structure of afterwardsness, but this cannot account for the 'image of death' in 'the primitive imaginary of the specular dialectic' of the mirror phase. On Laplanche's account, on the other hand, since relations with others are constitutive of the child's subjectivity from the very beginning – indeed, constitutive of the drives themselves – death will be bound up with signification from the outset. It is the moment of exteriority or *absolute otherness* from which the movements of both translation and temporalization begin. It is the difference between this (irrecoverable) moment of otherness and 'those elements in the primal enigmatic signifiers which can be symbolised', which is taken by Laplanche to produce 'the demand for work', or the 'pressure' characteristic of a drive. It is in this sense that for Laplanche the drive is not merely somatic, but the symptom of a being which is constitutively 'with others'.[110]

But in what sense does this moment of exteriority or otherness (the enigma within the enigmatic) signify 'death'? Are we not here confronted with the same problem of attribution we encountered in Lacan's treatment of the image of the child's body in the mirror as the image of 'death'? I think not. For whereas in Lacan's account, the structure of afterwardsness is used to straddle two distinct phases of the child's development (imaginary and symbolic), and the problem of attribution occurs internally to the first phase, in Laplanche's account we are dealing with a single continuous movement of temporalization. The 'timelessness' of the moment of otherness (the inside-other, the unconscious) may thus be registered as such immediately, as soon as its difference establishes temporality, in the movement of the demand for translation. In fact, it *must* be so registered if the movement of temporalization is to continue. There is a strict conceptual logic here, linking temporality as temporalization to timelessness, and hence to death. (Time is the 'totalisation of existence';[111] death, the possibility of its impossibility.) This same logic underlies Heidegger's argument that it is the anticipation of death which temporalizes time, by constituting *Dasein* as a totality. The difference is that here the account is mediated with the modified structure of a dialectic of recognition, via the formation of the unconscious. The anticipation of death and the formation of the unconscious occur *together*, as marks of the dependence of the child upon an independent, adult other. Laplanche's primal situation takes the place of Hegel's trial by death.

It thus seems that Laplanche is wrong to separate off the death of the death drive from the death of being-towards-death (although he is right to distinguish it from the literal death of the body, with its inscription within cosmological time). The death drive may not be the 'ground' of being-towards-death in the naturalistic sense that Lacan's account suggests, but it is the same death, the same sort of 'death before life' (timelessness, Heidegger's 'impossibility of existence') which is at stake in each. Such 'timelessness', the timelessness of the unconscious, the timelessness towards which the death drive drives, appears *within* the temporal as the 'synchronic'. Hence the ease with which Lacan was able to apply the synchronic model of 'language' (*langue* as opposed to *parole*) in Saussure's structural linguistics to the interpretation of Freud's account of the unconscious.[112] However, it should not thereby be thought that the temporality to which such timelessness is opposed is 'diachronic', since (as we saw in chapter 1) the synchrony/diachrony distinction is 'not a distinction *of* temporal relations . . . but a distinction *against* Time'.[113] Ontologically, the unconscious is not synchronic. It is timeless.[114] Synchronic is how it *appears*, in its relations to the temporal. It is the concept of synchrony which produces the illusion of the possibility of repetition as the temporal reproduction of the same. How does all this fit into our argument about the temporalization of history?

Psychoanalysis, temporality, history

We have criticized the intimism of Heidegger's analysis of death, firstly, from the standpoint of the 'independent outside' of cosmological time or nature (Ricoeur), and, secondly, from the side of the social (Hegel). If temporality is tied existentially to the anticipation of death, and death comes from the other, it was argued, so too must time: it is recognition which temporalizes time out of the fear of death. In Hegel's own work, however, this dialectic is subordinated methodologically to the broader aims and movement of his philosophy – aims which tie the achievement of 'genuine recognition' ('pure self-recognition in absolute otherness') to a moment of absolute knowing which immobilizes time in identity with eternity. If we reject the possibility of this conclusion, however, in which consciousness's search for absolute identity with itself is ultimately rewarded – on materialist grounds – recognition will always also be a misrecognition: all temporalization will resist sublation in the eternal. The totalization of history as the self-recognition of a process governed by an immanent end (substance as 'the mediation of its self-othering with itself') will be wrecked by the open-endedness of the structure of misrecognition. From this point of view, if recognition is a condition of temporalization, so equally is misrecognition. The inevitability of misrecognition is the enabling opposite of the idealization inherent in thought: limit of the dialectic, product of the irrecuperable outside, it drives it on and makes it possible.

However, as we saw in the previous chapter, this does not take totalization off the agenda, so much as reorientate us towards it, philosophically, as the unity of an ongoing process of temporalization. The structure of this process as a totalization, de-totalization, and re-totalization of existence through the constant differentiation and unification of the three temporal ecstases (past, present and future) provides the model for a new concept of history as 'imperfect' narrative mediation. This involves no commitment to the objectivity of an immanent historical end, but it does (*contra* Ricoeur) contain ontological commitments of its own. Questions thus arise as to what these commitments are, and what their implications are for the understanding of historical experience.

We approached these matters via the question of which actual structures of recognition underlie the process of temporalization in the individual, figured allegorically in the 'trial by death' sketched by Hegel in the *Phenomenology*, for methodological reasons of his own. It was at this point that we turned to the appropriation of Hegel's dialectic of recognition by various psychoanalytical theorists intent on extending the terms of Freud's transformation of metaphysics into metapsychology. Psychoanalytical theory, we argued, is the continuation of phenomenological ontology by other means: a de-centred, non-Hegelian ontology of the subject which nonetheless displays a number of structures of consciousness familiar from Hegel's thought in modified forms. For a particular psychoanalytical tradition (Lacanianism), psychoanalytical metapsychology is first and foremost an ontology of misrecognition, in which the concept of identification takes the place of Hegel's concept of recognition.

However, as many difficulties arise in the transposition of the structure of Hegelian thought to the context of metapsychology as in the various attempts to apply it directly in historical analysis. In particular, these concern the individualism inherent in Freud's intrapsychic perspective (an individualism which is exacerbated, rather than mitigated, by its accompanying familialism); and the troubled ontology of his account of the relationship between the biological and psychic domains. Both bear centrally on the relationship of recognition to the anticipation of death which underlies temporalization. A brief survey of positions within the field (Lacan, Kristeva, Benjamin, and Laplanche), from the standpoint of this relationship, recommended Laplanche's work as the most promising approach to a new theoretical synthesis.

The most distinctive feature of this approach is the relocation of primary identification within a process of primal questioning, or a primal 'communication situation': the questioning by the child of an enigmatic signifier implanted in it as an effect of the adult's unconscious desire. This is essentially a psychoanalytical reworking of the Heideggerian theme whereby *Dasein* is defined as 'a being for whom Being is in question', which explains the movement of questioning with reference to the enigmatic signifier's 'demand for translation'. The child, one might say, is *a being for whom recognition is in question.* Such questioning is constitutive for the child of both the unconscious (which is timeless) and temporality, as the mutually dependent poles of a dialectic of temporalization. Timelessness, death and the unconscious become interchangeable figures of each other, fused ontologically in the restless cyclical stasis of the death drive ('principle of libidinal circulation'), which is produced in the child by its repression of the untranslatable elements of adult desire. The temporalizing effect of the anticipation of death acts through the formation of the unconscious.

It is the ambivalence inherent in the adult's recognition of the child (inherent, in fact, in the very status of childhood – Lacan's 'specific prematurity of birth'), which founds recognition as misrecognition, identification as only ever partial. However, this at least partially unconscious ambivalence thereby provides the ground of temporality as a movement of translation ('at once a taking up and a leaving behind') which is inherently, if incompletely, totalizing. The moment of misrecognition, the partiality of identification, cannot therefore be simply opposed to totalization as its contrary. Rather, it is the *motor* of totalization: the de-totalization which both makes totalization possible and necessary, but always incomplete. It is a moment in the process of temporalization without which there would be no human temporality: the functional equivalent, at the level of the individual, of Aristotle's 'unmoved mover', in fact.

The significance of all this for the concept of history is twofold. On the one hand, the psychoanalytical perspective allows us to link the phenomenological argument associating temporality with the anticipation of death to the cosmological time of nature, concretely, via the death drive. The death drive mediates the 'psychic' with the 'natural', sexuality with self-preservation. This is the place of history in Ricoeur's schema of narrative mediation. On the other hand, however, it should not be inferred that the temporality of the death drive *is* the temporality of history, since the former is conceptualized only at the level of the individual psyche, as a naturalized product of the social. As such ('principle of libidinal circulation'), it is at once both *compulsive* and *repetitious*. The death drive marks a difference between the temporal registers of nature and history within the psychic economy of the individual, at the same time that it establishes a connection between them, via the social: the sphere of that always partial identification with an (imaginary) other which temporalizes time, as the medium of misrecognition, through the difference between identity and difference.

This difference between the temporalities of the death drive and history follows from the specific function of the death drive as the natural representative (the representative at the level of 'nature') of an aspect of the social within the psychic. Repression translates the opacity of the social (the unfulfilled element of the demand for translation) into the quasi-naturalistic force of a drive. In this respect, the death drive is the by-product of those very processes of temporalization and socialization for which it provides a quasi-naturalistic ground within the individual. It is not any kind of origin of these processes, ontologically. Its temporality of repetition is the appearance within the ontological structure of the individual of the cosmological time of nature: the 'subjectification' of the serial succession of identical instants. At the same time, in its infinite circularity it *figures* the fundamental timelessness of the unconscious, which follows from its role as the psychic representative of an untranslatable exteriority – just as, from the standpoint of historical time, nature figures timelessness.

It is the symbolic equivalence here between exteriority and timelessness in the formation of the unconscious – rather than anything specifically to do with the death drive – which is of greatest significance for our understanding of the structure of historical time. For what is that 'end', the anticipation of which, it was argued, is a conceptual condition for the temporalization of history (in the same way that the anticipation of death is a condition of temporalization in general), but which cannot be construed teleologically, without contradiction, if not a standpoint beyond or exterior to history: the standpoint of a *timeless exteriority*? And how is such timelessness to be understood at the level of history, if not as the standpoint of some kind of *eternity*? The passage through psychoanalytical metapsychology returns us, methodologically, to the theological origins of the philosophy of history.

4

Modernity, Eternity, Tradition

The authentic concept of universal history is a messianic one. . . . the true conception of historical time is wholly based on the image of redemption.

Walter Benjamin

In the move from the existential origins of temporalization in identification and misrecognition to the temporalization of history, eternity joins *death*, the *unconscious*, and *nature* as a figure of timelessness, and each becomes a metaphor for the others. It is to the character and dynamics of this move – the modalities of Ricoeur's narrative inscriptions – that we will shortly turn, picking up the analysis of historical time where it was broken off, at the end of chapter 2, and carrying it forward in the direction of two specific temporalizations of history, two very different articulations of an atemporal eternity with the contents of historical experience: *modernity* and *tradition*. First, however, it is necessary to say a little more about this purely anticipatory, timeless end which, we have argued, temporalizes historical time (historizes temporality) in the same way that the anticipation of death temporalizes time in general. What is the ontological status of an end posited in exteriority and thereby paradoxically present, phenomenologically, within the very thing to which it is by definition exterior (time)? In particular, to what extent can it be understood independently of the *theological* connotations with which it is inevitably associated in the context of the Judaic-Christian tradition? After all, is not the idea of a timeless exteriority, productive of history yet in principle outside its grasp, even more unequivocally theological than the immanent end of Hegel's 'true theodicy', which we would have it displace? Does the philosophy of history not reveal itself here, once again, as an inherently theological genre, even in the new, apparently secular garb of a post-Hegelian philosophy of historical time?[1]

Unless we can counter this all-too-common charge, we remain vulnerable to the threat of a dialectical reversal which would detect in our quest for the ontological structure of historical time a relegitimation of theology on post-Hegelian grounds. This is something that Heidegger's own work came increasingly, and knowingly, to represent, albeit with respect to a mystical neo-paganism, rather than the monotheism of the Judaic or Christian traditions.[2] It is apparent in the growing appeal to Judaism 'at the end of the end of philosophy',[3] marked by the reception of Levinas's work. And it is explicit in the writings of those for whom postmodernism provides the occasion for a restoration of theology as 'post-secular' reason.[4]

Our project – the development of a post-Hegelian philosophy of historical time in the form of a critical hermeneutics of historical existence – aims to hold true to the situation and dilemmas of a secular modernity. Yet one of these dilemmas concerns the persistence of the language of religion, given the relations which obtain, historically, between philosophy and theology in Western thought. We shall approach this problem, as we shall the elaboration of the historical meaning of timeless exteriority more generally, through the work of Walter Benjamin: specifically, the concept of *messianic interruption* as reworked by Benjamin in his recasting of the mystical tradition of Jewish eschatology in the service of historical materialism. For in their conjugation of materialism with metaphysics, and their distance from all materialist metaphysics, Benjamin's later writings offer a clear alternative to the theologization of exteriority to be found in work such as Levinas's, while nonetheless employing a similar structure of thought. In particular, they insist upon treating the temporalization of history historically, through the medium of cultural form. They thereby provide us with the opportunity to return from 'the frozen waste of abstraction,'[5] on which we have struggled to articulate the concept of historical time so far, to the shore of historical experience, where we can rejoin the debates about historical periodization and cultural change (social and political theory) from which we set out.

It is important in this regard that 'modernity' is thematized in Benjamin's work not merely as a distinct form of temporal experience, produced by a range of social practices and forms (the 'quality of experience' outlined in chapter 1), but as a decisive mutation of *historical* experience, which gains its meaning from its dialectical relations to tradition. As a periodizing concept, modernity marks out the time of the dialectics of modernity and tradition as competing, yet intertwined, forms of historical consciousness, rather than that of a single temporal form, however abstract. It is here that Benjamin's work may be compared with that of Heidegger and Ricoeur, upon which we have mainly relied thus far for resources for our argument. For it is a distinctive feature of both Heidegger's and Ricoeur's work that it depends upon the category of tradition to establish that continuity with the past which is a condition of historical existence. Heidegger and Ricoeur each temporalize history as tradition (*Überlieferung*) or 'handing down'. Gadamer's hermeneutics – founded on the extension of Heidegger's analytic of *Dasein* into a general theory of hermeneutical experience – takes the form of a hermeneutics of tradition. Yet, ostensibly at least, the temporality of modernity stands opposed to that of tradition. It is not just, as Habermas has argued, that Gadamer's hermeneutics fails adequately to recognize the transcending power of reflection in modern societies;[6] more fundamentally, it fails to register the transformation which these societies have brought about in the basic form of what Gadamer calls 'effective-historical consciousness'. Neither Heidegger nor Ricoeur, Gadamer or Habermas, grasps sufficiently clearly that the question of modernity is not just, or even primarily, that of the powers and illusions of a constitutive subjectivity, but rather that of the temporalization of history itself.

Benjamin's position is far more radical. For him, modernity is in principle a *destruction* of tradition: it involves the inauguration of new forms of historical consciousness, of necessity. Its present is defined, historically, not just by its negation of the past, but by its negation of the past form of temporal negation (tradition). Yet, paradoxically, it is to the intellectual form of a 'failed' tradition (Jewish Messianism) that Benjamin turns for sustenance in his reflections 'On the Concept of History'. In the comprehension of this paradox lies the key to an understanding of the dialectical relationship of modernity to tradition which would not try to soothe the negativity of modernity with the balm of tradition, but would instead seek to produce the redemptive power associated with tradition anew, through and within the temporality of modernity itself. Benjamin's aim was to refigure the interruptive temporality of modernity as the standpoint of redemption and thereby to perform a dialectical redemption of the destruction of tradition by the new; to turn *Neuzeit* into *Jetztzeit*, new-time into now-time.

In the process, his work shifts the focus of historiography away from narrative forms of historical totalization to montage: from story to *image*. In particular, one form of narrative totalization, one kind of narrative – of progress – is read as an artificial restitution of the dead form of tradition through and as what I shall call, following Hegel, a false or 'bad' modernity.[7] What Benjamin calls 'historicism' is the functional replacement within the time-consciousness of modernity for the continuity of historical time previously established by tradition. Historicism is bad modernity. It provides the temporal framework for the problematic of modernization. Modernization is bad modernity. In the critique of historicism as blank tradition, the secularized eschatology of 'progress' appears more closely tied to the metaphysical presumptions of a religious consciousness than a historiography which is explicitly modelled, methodologically, on the structure of Jewish Messianism. New-time (*Neuzeit*) becomes the now-time (*Jetztzeit*) of a materialist messianism for which the exteriority of the messianic is found to be paradoxically immanent to the structure of temporality itself.[8]

It is in its criticisms of narrative totalizations of history and of historicism as bad modernity, respectively, that Benjamin's work engages most directly with the main themes of Ricoeur's and Heidegger's writings about time. In the first case, we may ask whether the temporalities of story and image, narrative and montage, are actually as opposed to one another as Benjamin's account supposes. In the latter, we may compare Benjamin's critique of historicism and his appeal to a quasi-Messianic 'now', with Heidegger's counterposition of what he calls 'the ordinary conception of history' to the authentic reception of a heritage in a 'moment of vision': the anticipatory time-consciousness of 'resolute decision'. This comparison reveals both the fundamental *modernism* of Heidegger's work, despite its appeal to tradition (an appeal which, as Derrida has pointed out, is 'in no way traditional'),[9] and the problematic relationship of Benjamin's work to the politics with which it is allied (Communism) – indeed, to any politics which would mediate its construction of collectivity reflectively, through discourse, rather than rely upon an impulse to action derived from a direct revelation of truth. On the other hand, the differences between the forms of temporality at stake in Benjamin's and Heidegger's work may be taken as emblematic of the extent to which modernity contains a range of possible temporalizations of history within its fundamental, most abstract temporal form. It is the idea of a competition or struggle between these different forms of temporalization, within everyday life, which leads to the idea of a *politics* of time.

First, however, let us consider the ontological status of the timeless end, the anticipation of which, we have argued, is productive of historical time, yet which nonetheless remains in principle beyond its scope. For unless we can counter the theologization of this end, any attempt to connect historical totalization with politics will be rendered problematic from the start. What exactly is it, this historizing time-lessness, external to history yet present within it, phenomenologically, as the anticipation of its end? To raise the question in this way is to place ourselves on the terrain of Levinas's thought.[10]

Exteriority and transcendence: Levinas's eschatology

It is the achievement of Levinas's work, firstly, that it offers a phenomenology of the constitutive role of the other in human temporalization;[11] secondly, that it refuses reconciliation (Hegel's 'pure self-recognition in absolute otherness'), treating relations to others in terms of *separation* and *desire*, as well as *identification* (in a phenomenological parallel to the discourse of psychoanalysis);[12] thirdly, that by treating the other as the site of an absolute exteriority, it recognizes the necessity to move beyond phenomenology to *eschatology*;[13] and finally, that in moving towards eschatology, it nonetheless continues to insist that the beyond 'not be described in a purely negative fashion ... [but be] reflected *within* the totality and history, *within* experience'.[14] In refusing Heidegger's existential reduction of *Dasein* to the 'mineness' of death, Levinas opens up another dimension to temporality besides the time of Being-towards-death: *the time of the other* as a time which includes a future after-my-death, in relation to which I constitute myself as a historical being within the present, in my orientation towards, and responsibility for, others. This future is the product of neither an extrapolation of protentions (Husserl), nor of *Dasein*'s 'stretching-along' (Heidegger), but of the 'original and concrete temporality' of 'responsiveness to the Other'.[15] It is part of a time in which there is a way of 'being *against* death' without fleeing from it; in which 'the founding of institutions ... ensures a meaningful, but impersonal world beyond death'; and in which 'I can die *as a result of someone* and *for someone*.'[16] Whether this 'empties ... [death] of the pathos that comes to it from the fact of its being my death', as Levinas suggests,[17] is doubtful. But it certainly adds a complex social dimension to the meaning of death and, with it, the temporalization of time.

It might thus seem, at first sight, that Levinas is offering us precisely what we need, philosophically, at this point in our argument: namely, a generalization of the dialectic of misrecognition into an eschatological conception of historical time. However, such a conclusion would be precipitate, if not (like much of the current enthusiasm for Levinas's work) merely wishful. For despite its affinity with the argument we have advanced so far, the trajectory of Levinas's thought diverges from it in at least two important respects. In the first place, having derived its 'phenomenology of sociality' from – albeit also against – Husserl, there is no place in Levinas's thought for a constitutive concept of recognition/misrecognition. Secondly, and consequently, in fixing the (phenomenologically paradoxical) absoluteness of the exteriority of the other in the notion of *the* 'absolutely other', Levinas brings to an abrupt halt the movement he sets in motion between phenomenology and eschatology, switching to a third, more purely theological level of discourse. From this standpoint, history is homogenized as totality in opposition to the eschatological beyond, which grounds temporality, while infinity is reserved for the description of 'the ethical'. The rapidity of this movement is instructive. For it both demonstrates the unresolved character of Levinas's relation to ontology (summed up in the word 'God'), and reveals the arbitrariness of the religious interpretation of philosophical discourse which it enacts. In Levinas's thought, religion and the ethical usurp the space of history and the social which is opened up by his idea of a time of the other. In this respect, the vogue for Levinas may be read as a symptom of a crisis in historical thought, in which the desire for ethics overwhelms the necessity of politics, with its attendant complexities of historical consciousness and action.

Yet the lessons we can learn from Levinas are by no means wholly negative. For in exploring the limits and, crucially, the point of *rupture* of a phenomenological investigation of the other, Levinas has much to contribute to the clarification of the methodology of our inquiry – a methodology which, starting out from (1) Heidegger's phenomeno-logical ontology, has subsequently had recourse to three additional ontological discourses: those of (2) the *constitutive exteriority of nature* (registered in the connection of cosmological time to death); (3) the *mediating productivity of the social* (registered by the constitutive relation to the other); and (4) the *overarching unity of history* (under-stood as the ongoing totalization of the social against the backdrop of an infinite nature). Psychoanalytical theory provides a mediating form for thinking the relations between the first three of these four perspectives, from the standpoint of the individual, in its discourse of primary identification as primary socialization. But its limitations prohibit it from thinking the fourth at all, except symptomatically, at the level of the psychic investments structuring its various representations.[18]

Levinas, on the other hand, explicitly sets out to expound the passage beyond phenomenology (and a reductive ontology of entities) as a passage from the same to the other, from totality to infinity. In thus identifying infinity with alterity, and designating their discourse as eschatology, his thought comes to occupy the place of history within our analysis, as the mediation of nature (infinity) with the social (other), at the very point at which it leaves both phenomenology and history behind. Consideration of why this move does not work (for us), and the consequences of its failure, will demonstrate the necessity, first, of historicizing our approach, by supplementing the phenomenological ontology from which we set out with the kind of immanent historical analysis to which it was initially opposed, at the start of chapter 2; and second, of situating the ontological aspect of our conception of historical time within some broader notion of natural-history. These issues are best approached via Derrida's extraordinary early critique of Levinas, to which reference has already been made in our preliminary definition of history, in chapter 2, as 'the movement of the difference between totality and infinity'.[19]

The main point of Derrida's critique concerns Levinas's opposition of history, as totality, to the infinity of the eschatological beyond, such that eschatology is understood to institute a positive relation to being 'beyond history'.[20] This opposition follows from the interpretation of the exteriority of the Other as absolutely other. Derrida's (essentially Hegelian) argument is straightforward: 'the other cannot be absolutely exterior to the same without ceasing to be other.' The absoluteness of the Other must be phenomenologically relative, must be *posited* as absolutely other, if it is to be the term of a possible relation. As Husserl recognized, absolute exteriority is part of 'the phenomenal system of nonphenomenality'. This phenomenological necessity is reinforced, ethically, by the necessity that the Other be recognized as an *ego*, if it is to be the bearer of an ethical relation, however 'other' it might otherwise be: 'If the other was not recognised as an ego, its entire alterity would collapse.' In short, Levinas's metaphysics presupposes 'the transcendental phenomenology that it seeks to put into question'.[21]

Levinas attempts to avoid this problem through the notion of the face. The face is that which, 'a thing among things, breaks through the form that nevertheless delimits it', opening us up to the infinite transcendence and ethical inviolability of the Other. The face is said to 'remain absolute within the relation'.[22] Yet as Derrida shows, the contradiction in the idea of an encounter with the absolutely other reproduces itself in the notion of the face through which Levinas tries to overcome it. On the one hand, phenomenologically, as 'the non-metaphorical unity of body, glance, speech and thought', the face must possess the essential finitude of the body, an *irreducibly spatial* exteriority. On the other hand, conceptually, as 'the corporeal metaphor of etherealised thought', it represents the positive infinity of an *absolute* (non-spatial) exteriority. The very attempt to mediate this contradiction relativizes the absoluteness of the other, phenomeno-logically, in the way we have already seen. The attempt at mediation is self-negating, returning us, as Derrida puts it, to 'the irreducibly *common* horizon of Death and the Other':

> Metaphysical transcendence cannot be at once transcendence toward the other as Death and transcendence towards the other as God. Unless God means Death . . . at once All and Nothing, Life and Death. Which means that God is or appears, *is named*, within the difference between All and Nothing, Life and Death. Within difference, and at bottom as Difference itself.

Yet, Derrida triumphantly concludes: 'This difference is what is called *History*. God [such a God] is inscribed in it.' If the face is 'neither the face of God nor the figure of man', but their 'resemblance', then there is both literally and metaphorically no place from which it can be apprehended.[23]

The lesson Derrida draws from this is, unsurprisingly, a decon-structive one. In order to comply with the logic of 'the break with phenomenology and ontology', Levinas should 'eliminate the notions of an *essence* and a *truth* of subjective existence (of the Ego, and primarily of the Ego of the Other)'. Yet he does not do so. Indeed, he 'cannot do so, without renouncing philosophical discourse'. However, according to Derrida, 'the attempt to achieve an opening toward the beyond of philosophical discourse' can *never* completely shake off the 'means of philosophical discourse'. Hence the symptomatic significance of Levinas's work. What we observe in the play of its internal contradictions is the imposition of the deconstructive necessity of 'lodging oneself *within* traditional conceptuality in order to destroy it'. Phenomenology can open a dialogue with eschatology, can '*be opened* in it', but the dialogue is interminable, since each calls the other to silence.[24]

However, one wonders whether Derrida has really done justice to Levinas's rupture of phenomenology here; indeed, whether, in his determination 'not to be enveloped by Hegel',[25] he has done justice to his own critique. What is at stake is the possibility of an expansion of the concept of experience beyond that delimited by Husserl's phenomenology, yet falling short of Hegelian speculation, in terms of which the concept of history might be understood: an eschatological conception of experience in which the ontological significance of alterity would be retained, shorn of its theological gloss, in the register of historical time. It is just such a conception which we need in order to make sense of the idea of the historization of temporality by the anticipation of a timeless end. Its structure may be sought, firstly, in the phenomenological dimension of Levinas's exposition of infinity as desire; and secondly, in Derrida's elaboration of the consequences for the category of totality of his critique of the positive infinite. The eschatological dimension of *Totality and Infinity* is barely developed by Levinas, although it provides the book with its symbolic frame.[26] Exploring it here, in the context of our inquiry into the temporalization of history, and after Derrida's critique, we will read it against the grain of its theological self-consciousness in order to open it out to the multiplicity of the social which it evokes, but cannot think. This is a multiplicity in the name of which Levinas often speaks, while fleeing its concrete forms: a multiplicity which in actuality is not merely 'anarchic',[27] but *formed* in ways which resist reduction to the Same – forms of ethical life (*Sittlichkeit*), in fact, which are the object of both political economy and the sociology of cultural form.

Notoriously, Levinas derives his notion of infinity as metaphysical exteriority from Descartes' account of the idea of God in the Third of his *Meditations*. His innovation is to expound it as the structure of the relation to the Other, and hence as the point of contact or rupture between phenomenology and what he calls 'the ethical'. The infinite is defined as 'a relation with a being that maintains its total exteriority with respect to him who thinks it', and its fundamental determination is transcendence. Indeed, 'the transcendence of the Infinite with respect to the I which is separated from it and which thinks it *measures* (so to speak) its infinitude.' Levinas is not unaware of the kind of objection Derrida will make to this construction. Indeed, his counter to it lays the ground for his 'concretisation' of this 'apparently wholly empty notion'. 'To affirm the presence in us of the idea of infinity,' Levinas argues, 'is to deem *purely abstract and formal* the contradiction the idea of metaphysics is said to harbour, which Plato brings up in the *Parmenides* – that the relation with the Absolute would render the Absolute relative.' (This is Derrida's objection.) 'The absolute exteriority of the exterior being is not purely and simply lost as a result of its manifestation; it "absolves" itself from the relation in which it presents itself.'[28] It is this process of absolution which appears, from the standpoint of the finite, as the production of desire: 'Infinity is the idea of desire. It consists, paradoxically, in thinking more than what is thought while conserving it still in its inordinateness relative to thought, entering into relationship with the ungraspable while certifying its status of being ungraspable.'[29]

Phenomenologically, then, infinity is 'not the correlate of the idea of infinity, as though this idea were an intentionality that is fulfilled in its object'. Rather, 'the marvel of infinity in the finite is the *overwhelming of intentionality*, the overwhelming of this appetite for light; unlike the saturation in which intentionality is appeased, infinity disconnects its idea.' Infinity is an *'attitude irreducible to a category'*.[30] The issue is whether we can think of this 'overwhelming of intentionality' as a special kind of experience – the experience of the limit of experience, perhaps – or whether it must not rather be conceived purely negatively, as its annihilation. Sticking to Husserl's conception of experience, as Derrida does (to avoid the spectre of Hegel), the latter option imposes itself by definition. Levinas also accepts this, as the consequence of an 'objective' conception of experience.[31] However, Levinas continues: 'if experience precisely means a relation with the absolutely other, that is, with what always overflows thought, the relation with infinity accomplishes experience in *the fullest sense of the word*.'[32] For Derrida, this is an illegitimately Hegelian sense. But is there really no third way here between Husserl and Hegel? Is it true, as Derrida maintains, that 'the only effective position to take in order not to be enveloped by Hegel' is 'to consider the false-infinity (that is, in a profound way, original finitude) irreducible'?[33] Is there not a disjunction, in fact, between original finitude and the false-infinity – that is to say, between Heidegger and Kant? Does the concept of experience associated with Heidegger's existentialism really reduce to Kant's? It seems unlikely.[34]

Derrida arrives at this position because of his hostility to all positive conceptions of transcendence: the experience of a positive infinity. But the problem with the positivity of Levinas's conception of the infinite does not derive from the structure of the 'overwhelming of intentionality'. It derives from the *supplementary* interpretation of infinity as a *being* (God). This interpretation – the enactment of an *unequivocal* (rather than, as Derrida suggests, an equivocal) 'complicity of theology and metaphysics'[35] – is, philosophically, both arbitrary and incoherent. Its logic is the *cultural* logic of identification with a particular religious tradition. *Totality and Infinity* simply announces: 'We propose to call "religion" the bond that is established between the same and the other without constituting a totality.'[36] One might do otherwise. One might call it 'the social'. Once religion becomes the ground of interpretation, the strictly philosophical coherence of the idea (hunted down so remorselessly by Derrida) becomes somewhat besides the point. Religion is very far from being a side-show when it comes to tracking the meaning and coherence of Levinas's philosophical ideas. In 'The Trace of the Other', Levinas insists:

> we will, to be sure, not succumb to the temptation and the illusion that would consist in finding again by philosophy the empirical data of positive religion, but we will disengage a movement of transcendence that is ensured like the bridgehead of the 'other shore', without which the simple coexistence of philosophy and religion in souls and even in civilizations is but an inadmissible weakness of the mind.[37]

The question is whether it is *necessary* to build this bridge in order to make philosophical sense of Levinas's ideas. Can we do without the transition to religious language? Not without certain changes in the structure and meaning of the ideas.

It is just such a transformation which I want to propose in the form of an immanent interpretation of the 'overwhelming of intentionality' as *historization* (historization of temporality/temporalization of history). From this point of view, you do not need God to play the role 'He' does in Levinas's philosophy, if you are prepared to think philosophically about history. On this model, history is immanent transcendence writ (and read) large, at the level of the species. Ultimately, its comprehension demands a dialectical reformulation of the relationship between the conventional notions of 'nature' and 'history', in the manner of something like Adorno's idea of 'natural-history' (*Naturgeschichte*).[38] This would allow us to thematize the emergence of temporality, the paradoxical idea of a nature 'before' time, and the subsequent relationship between natural and social history, within a unitary ontological discourse, thereby finally overcoming the tendency to subjectivism inherent in the phenomenological approach.[39]

Outside or end? Totality, infinity, others

The metaphysical extravagance of Levinas's conceptions of infinity and the Other has its correlate in the poverty of his construal of totality and the Same. This construal is generalized to embrace both the whole history of 'Western philosophy' and (in tautological self-demonstration) the concept of history itself as an 'identification of the same'.[40] According to Levinas,

> The judgment of history is set forth in the visible. Historical events are the visible par excellence; their truth is produced in evidence. The visible

forms, or tends to form, a totality. It excludes the apology, which undoes
the totality by inserting into it, at each instant, the unsurpassable, the
unencompassable present of its very subjectivity. The judgment at which
the subjectivity is to remain apologetically present has to be made against
the evidence of history (and against philosophy, if philosophy coincides
with the evidence of history).[41]

History is identified with judgement and the 'continuous time' of
'works', in opposition to *subjectivity*, the *instant* and the *will*, each of
which registers the infinite difference of the relation to the Other, in
one way or another. 'Each instant of historical time in which action
commences,' Levinas argues, 'is, in the last analysis, a birth, and
hence breaks with the continuous time of history, a time of works
and not wills. . . . the will seeks judgment in order to be confirmed
against death, whereas judgment taken as the judgment of history
kills the will qua will.'[42]

It is not difficult to recognize in these descriptions the 'history' of
a mundane and unreflective historiography, Heidegger's 'ordinary
understanding of history', or what Benjaman calls 'historicism'.[43]
However, while Heidegger and Benjamin approach this conception
phenomenologically, as a starting point from which to develop more
adequate alternatives, Levinas fixes the concept of history here, in
opposition to eschatology, in the realm of 'the Same'. As Derrida
remarks: 'totality, for Levinas, means a finite totality.' Yet, as we have
seen, we cannot make sense of the alterity of the 'absolute exteriority
of the other' unless it appears *within* the zone of the same. What
'other' means is 'phenomenality as disappearance'. The same cannot
be reduced to 'a totality closed in upon itself, an identity playing with
itself, having only the appearance of alterity'. It must contain the
difference between itself and the other within its difference from
itself.[44] And what else is the production of this difference but the
infinite movement of temporalization: time as infinite totalization,
temporalization as immanent transcendence (freedom)?

What of the specifically 'historical' dimension of this movement,
and its relation to eschatology? It is here that Derrida's deconstructive scepticism about the possibility of stepping outside the 'Inside-
Outside' structure of philosophical language – about the possibility of
weaning language from spatial metaphors – when combined with
Levinas's notion of the time of the other, can be put to metaphysical
use. For what Levinas cannot but think spatially through the
metaphor of exteriority (the alterity of the Other) cannot but also
appear temporally in the figure of the end: the 'absolute' horizon of
an end to time. *'Outside' and 'end' are the spatial and temporal forms*

of the intuition of otherness, respectively; as such, they are both irreducible and endlessly transcodable, one into the other. Just as absolute exteriority cannot be thought without contradiction, yet cannot not be thought if we are to acknowledge our finitude as mortal beings; so too is timelesslessness contradictory when thought as either the beginning or end point of a temporal process. Yet ultimately it too cannot be thought in any other way. In phenomenology, Derrida insists, there is never a 'constitution of horizons', but only 'horizons of constitution'.[45] Here, on the other hand, *eschatology constitutes phenomenology* temporally through the figure of the end – the death of otherness – by providing it with the 'horizonal schema' of historical time. Or, to put it another way, the anticipation of death is the manifestation within the individual (via the other) of the finitude of the species. This is the true ontological meaning of the constitutive timelessness of the end. As a result, history is at once *desire, suffering* and *utopia*.

History is desire because 'infinity is the idea of desire'[46] and history is the movement of infinitization. History is suffering because desire is never satisfied. History is the conflict of desires. ('History is what hurts'.)[47] History is utopia, not just because it contains the 'no place' of the 'not yet' (and is thus the screen for the fantasy of the end of suffering), but, more fundamentally, because it is grounded in the finitude of the species and hence the equality of death. History is a democratic utopia of death. Death is the end which structures all narrative; narrative carries with it a fatal utopian charge.

If, as we have argued, time comes from the other and (as Levinas has argued) thus always includes a time *of* the other, as a time after-my-death, our problem, methodologically, is no longer what it initially appeared to be. It is no longer that of justifying the extension of Heidegger's analysis of death beyond the temporal horizon of an individual life. For existential temporality exceeds the time of the individual's death from the outset. Temporality overwhelms intentionality. Rather, the problem becomes that of moving from an abstract and generalized notion of alterity to history; from the 'time of the other' to 'historical time'. What are the social forms through which time is temporalized as 'history' in the production of historical existence? And how do they structure or affect its temporalization? Levinas is incapable of answering these questions – indeed, he is incapable of posing them – since, as we have seen, he insists on calling 'the bond that is established between the same and the other without constituting a totality' *religion*. 'The social' appears only as a category of finite totality, wholly within the same. This short-circuits the entire analysis, catapulting us from the other person, via alterity in general, directly to God, without passing through the variety of social forms through which history is actually temporalized, in particular times and places – both at the level of action and interpretation. Yet the mediation is crucial. For as we saw in chapter 1, the idea of history in the collective singular, 'history in and for itself in the absence of an associated subject or object',[48] only emerges within European culture towards the end of the eighteenth century. If it is to provide the frame for a *critical* hermeneutics of historical existence, in tandem with the ontological discourses of 'nature' and 'the social', not only will temporality have to be 'historized', but we will need to historicize our understanding of the philosophical discourse of historization as well. (Historicize, that is, in the general sense of render historical; not in the more specific sense of historicism, of reduction to the relativity of a chronologically defined historical moment.) If they are to be truly reflexive, phenomenological accounts of the 'historization of temporality' must comprehend its forms as immanent to history itself.

There is thus no necessary incompatibility between the three methodological models of historical totalization which were intro-duced at the start of chapter 2: transcendental, immanent, and phenomenologico-ontological or existential. They need not be considered competing approaches. Rather, once the methodological priority of the existential is acknowledged, they can be seen to complement one another, as alternative ways of viewing the unity of the historical process, each with its own distinctive temporal perspective and concerns. The problems raised about the first two models in chapter 2 do not invalidate their procedures, but only the theoretical self-consciousness of their philosophical self-sufficiency or completeness as justifications of 'history'. In fact, the existential approach is more 'immanent' to temporality, ontologically speaking, than the Hegelian one which labels itself so, since it refuses a prospec-tive narrative foreclosure of the future. However, this in no way relativizes it, temporally, since its present (or 'presencing') includes all temporality, all temporal difference, within itself.

What *does* relativize historization, crucially, is the spatial perspective from which it is undertaken, in the geopolitical or social sense of existential spatiality.[49] Temporal totalization always takes place from the standpoint of specific sets of social interests and forms. It is the relationship between the epistemic productivity and constraints internal to any such standpoint, on the one hand, and those of its competitors, on the other, which is at stake in theoretical debates about historiography. At their most fundamental, these are debates about the form of historization itself: in the case in which we are interested, modernity *or* tradition? We shall approach these debates via what is probably the best-known recent account of the temporalization of history as tradition: Gadamer's hermeneutics.

The eternity of the classical: Gadamer's hermeneutics

Tradition, as commonly understood (from the Latin *tradere*, to give over), refers to the act of handing down or transmitting something from generation to generation, by practice or word of mouth, and hence to that which is thus handed down, be it a doctrine, practice or belief. Tradition shadows the biological continuity of generations at the level of social form. Anchoring ethics and politics to nature, it connects the idea of history to the life of the species.[50] Moreover, in its conventional interpretation, it is itself a quasi-natural form. Dependent in its origins upon the physical proximity of the members of a community, and kinship as a model of social power, its primary medium is not self-consciousness, but what Adorno describes as 'the pregiven, unreflected and binding existence of social forms'.[51] It is the actuality of a past in which, as Nietzsche put it, 'conquering "second nature" becomes a first'.[52] It may be that the continuity thus established is only an appearance, but as Benjamin points out, 'if this is the case, then it is precisely the persistence of this appearance of permanence that establishes continuity.'[53] In its most fundamental conceptual determination (or what we might call its 'traditional' form), tradition appears in the singular. It is taken to establish such continuity as there is in history as a whole.

As a form of temporalization, tradition is distinguished by its apparent prioritization of the past over both present and future. The future is envisaged in the image of the past, and the present appears solely in its mediating function as a link in the chain of generations. However, insofar as the continuity of this chain must be secured anew in each generation, the process of handing down is fraught with the risk of failure in the present. This is reflected in the other root meaning of *tradere*: to hand over in the sense of surrender and betrayal. Thus, as Caygill points out, within Christianity, the term 'tradition' used to refer to 'the ecclesiastical crime of surrendering sacred texts in a time of persecution – delivering them over to destruction by unbelievers'.[54] As a result, the continuity of tradition requires a constant exercise of authority to combat the threat of betrayal inherent in its temporal structure. This is a structure in which the

positions of both present and past are doubled by the simultaneous
establishment of a distance between them and a negation of that
distance, as the present presents itself as the site for the transmission of
the past into the future.[55] The future, on the other hand, appears to
offer no more than the prospect of a replication of the relationship of
'handing on' which characterizes the modality of the past within
the present: a repetition of the present in its mode as transmission of
the past. As we shall see in the next chapter, Heidegger makes much of
the temporal difference constitutive of this structure of repetition.
Here, however, we shall confine ourselves to the self-understanding of
this repetition upon which the continuity of tradition itself depends.
This is an understanding for which the difference inscribed in the
repetition is secondary to the identity of an essential content. It is
through the positing of an essential content to tradition that the
idea of eternity comes to play a role in the temporalization of history,
independently of any particular religious content.

At first sight, the concept of eternity at work in the temporalization
of history as tradition appears to be that of infinite duration, rather
than either atemporality or the perpetual or 'pure' present of
Hegelianism.[56] Tradition projects itself into the future *ad infinitum*,
with the continuity of an essential content. The transmission of this
content may not be secure, but history only has meaning within its
horizon, which includes the (catastrophic) possibility of the failure of
transmission. But how, then, can tradition temporalize history as a
whole, if (as we have argued) the temporalization of history requires
the standpoint of an *atemporal* exteriority or 'end'? The answer lies in
the illusion of permanence constitutive of the continuity of tradition
internally to any particular transmission. This illusion can be seen
at work in Gadamer's hermeneutical reconstruction of the concept
of tradition, in its treatment of the concept of the classical. For
if Gadamer opposes naturalistic misunderstandings of tradition,
deriving from Romantic opposition to the Enlightenment, he is
nonetheless ultimately obliged to reinstate its binding and monolithic
character in another way, in order to theorize the singularity of
its continuity. It is through the transcendental status of the concept
of the classical that timelessness is inscribed into Gadamer's notion of
tradition.

Truth and Method is marked, notoriously, by 'a fundamental
rehabilitation of the concept of prejudice', and the restoration of a
recognition of the fact that there are 'legitimate prejudices' to the
centre of hermeneutical understanding. Yet for Gadamer, tradition is
not 'the antithesis to the freedom of reason' and hence 'something

historically given, like nature'. Rather, on his account, 'even the most genuine and solid tradition does not persist by nature because of the inertia of what once existed. It needs to be affirmed, embraced, cultivated. It is, essentially, preservation, such as is active in all historical change. But preservation is an act of reason, though an inconspicuous one.' Indeed, it is claimed that preservation is as much a 'freely-chosen action' as 'revolution and renewal'. However, this should not be mistaken for an accommodation of tradition to the terms of the Enlightenment concept of reason. Rather, Enlightenment is reduced to the anti-tradition of a 'prejudice against prejudice, which deprives tradition of its power'. Understanding, we are told, 'is not to be thought of so much as an action of one's subjectivity, but as the placing of oneself within a process of tradition (*Überliefer-ungsgeschehen*), in which present and past are constantly fused'.[57] Reflexivity is thus introduced into the concept of tradition only within the hermeneutical bounds of the givenness of tradition itself. It is not the attribute of an autonomous subject (as it is for Habermas, for example, following Kant), but the structure of the relation into which the present must enter with the past in order for meaning to be possible – an external condition of subjectivity, rather than its self-positing ground. The self-awareness of the individual is but 'a flickering in the closed circuits of historical life'.[58] It is the absolute priority of the past within the present in this relationship which is registered by Gadamer in the concept of the classical.

Gadamer's problem is how to account for the normative significance of the classical without elevating it into a suprahistorical concept of value. His solution is to argue as follows:

It [the classical] does not refer to a quality that we assign to particular historical phenomena, but to a notable mode of 'being historical', the historical process of preservation that, through the constant proving of itself, sets before us something that is true. It is not at all the case, as the historical mode of thought would have us believe [Gadamer is polemicizing against historicism – PO], that the value judgment through which something is dubbed classical was in fact destroyed by historical reflection and its criticism of all teleological constructions of the process of history. The value judgment that is implicit in the concept of the classical gains, rather, through this criticism a new, real legitimacy. The classical is what resists historical criticism because its historical dominion, the binding power of its validity that is preserved and handed down, precedes all historical reflection and continues through it.[59]

The classical, in other words, is the substance of what is transmitted in tradition. But how can it acquire its legitimacy through historical criticism if its 'binding power' *precedes* all historical reflection? Indeed, Gadamer goes so far as to say that its significance is such that it 'cannot be lost'. It is 'independent of all the circumstances of time, in which we call something "classical" – a kind of timeless present that is contemporaneous with every other age'.[60] The eternity of the classical is *timeless*. It is the transcendental presupposition which makes the temporalization of history as tradition possible, by providing it with the guarantee of an essential content. So far, so traditional, and also so implicitly theological. For how else are we to make metaphysical sense of the timelessness of a classicism which holds history together as a meaningful whole, if not by reference to some external guarantor or standpoint of value? Yet it is precisely the idea of the classical as a suprahistorical value that Gadamer takes himself to be contesting.[61]

The timelessness of the classical is supposed to be 'timelessness as a mode of historical being',[62] not a suprahistorical value. But how can this opposition be maintained when the mode of being in question (preservation) functions as the ground of a transhistorical value which is not merely retrospective but is projected by Gadamer into the future? That it is transhistorically valuable *is* the historical value of the classical. Yet the outcome of the judgements through which the classical is supposed to be legitimated is determined in advance by a process which 'precedes historical reflection', even if it must continue to pass through it. History becomes a cipher for the confirmation of traditional values; 'criticism' the mode. Under such circumstances, it is hard to make sense of the transhistorical, except as a manifestation of the suprahistorical: the historical manifestation of a suprahistorical mode of being (preservation). In this respect, Gadamer's concept of tradition both reproduces the bad ontologization of history as historicality which we encountered in Heidegger's *Being and Time*, and parallels the mystification of the event (*Ereignis*) as the giving of Being in Heidegger's later thought. Yet if Gadamer is here true to his source, in other respects his transposition of historicality into tradition marks a retreat from the philosophical and political radicalism of *Being and Time*, in exchange for the measured pragmatism of a Burkean conservatism. (Preservation is Gadamer's primordial existential.) This is particularly clear from his abbreviated treatment of the future, exclusively in terms of the limitations imposed upon it by the past.[63]

'"To recognise what is",' Gadamer argues, 'does not mean to recognise what is just at this moment there, but to have insight into the limitations within which the future is still open to expectation and planning.'[64] These limitations constitute, for Gadamer, our primary relation to the future. They are not causal limitations, of either a naturalistic or a social kind, but hermeneutical ones: limitations of possible meaningfulness and value. Yet how can these be *known in advance*, without negating the fundamental existential openness of the future – without reducing the future to the contours of a present which is itself reduced to a reflective transmission of the past? It is at this point that Gadamer betrays the fundamental insight of *Being and Time*, from which he takes both his model of tradition as an active reception and repetition of the past, and his hermeneutical model of the anticipation of meaning: namely, the basis of temporalization in the anticipation of death, and hence the *radical futurity* of human existence. For despite his invocation of revolution as an example of 'a freely chosen action', it is hard to see how Gadamer can conceptualize fundamental historical change at all, except as a loss which, were it to occur, could no longer even be recognized as such.[65] To reject this scenario, and its homogenization of history as tradition, is not to deny that there are hermeneutical limits on the future. It is only to deny the validity of restricting such limits to the terms of the transmission of a tradition, constituted through the timelessness of the classical, in advance of history itself.

One of the problems here, as Ricoeur has seen, is that several different operations are run together by Gadamer under the single heading of tradition. Ricoeur usefully distinguishes three, which he labels *traditionality*, *traditions* and *tradition*, respectively. Traditionality is a transcendental designating the mode of transmitting received heritages. It is made up of a dialectic internal to the space of experience between 'the efficacy of the past that we undergo' and 'the reception of the past that we bring about'. For Ricoeur, it is a formal structure for the generation of historical meaning, which temporalizes history in general. It is an ineliminable dimension of *all* forms of historical experience. As soon as we move to the level of the content of this process, however, as soon as we specify a particular practice or belief, we introduce a multiplicity of traditions. As a result, it is the third conception, tradition in the singular, which is most problematic, since it functions as 'a legitimation of the claim to truth raised by *every* heritage that bears a meaning'. It is this notion of tradition in the singular which leads to the opposition between reflectivity and tradition that structures the disagreement between Habermas and Gadamer, from which, Ricoeur is careful to insist, the other two conceptions are exempt. Tradition in the singular posits 'the absolute validity of the idea of communicative truth', while the multiplicity of traditions marks 'the unavoidable finitude of all understanding'.[66]

Ricoeur attempts to overcome this contradiction by arguing that 'the truth claim of the contents of traditions merits being taken as a *presumption* of truth, so long as a stronger, that is, a better argument [derived, presumably, from another tradition – PO], has not been established.'[67] He thus aims to preserve the legitimacy of traditionality as an expression of truth through, rather than against, the principle of reflection; much as Gadamer himself tried, but failed, to do. Reflection is relegated to the secondary, but nonetheless *constitutive* role of using historiographical objectivity as 'a means for sifting through dead traditions'. Tradition in the singular is a misrepresentation of the universality of traditionality which falsely locates it at the level of the content of traditions. This goes some way towards clarifying the ambiguities and evasions of Gadamer's account of the place of reflection in hermeneutical experience;[68] but it still treats traditionality as the single, fundamental mode of 'being-affected-by-the-past'.

The defects of this position become apparent as soon as Ricoeur comes to discuss modernity. Here he follows Koselleck in separating off the futurity of the 'horizon of expectation' from the 'space of experience' in which the dialectic of traditionality constitutes the present through the reception of the past. This allows him to present the time-consciousness of modernity as a modification of a more general temporal-historical form: the transcendental status of 'traditionality' is maintained alongside the abstract futurity of modernity in such a way that the latter appears only as a disruption of historical consciousness, never a new form of it, in its own right.[69] However, the two levels of analysis (transcendental and empirical, form and content) remain unmediated. Ricoeur fails to grasp modernity ontologically, as a form of historical being. His position is thus, ultimately, not so different from Gadamer's, when the latter argues that 'we would do well not to regard historical consciousness as something radically new . . . but as a new element within that which has always made up the human relation to the past.'[70]

Yet, as Koselleck's own historical semantics shows, this disjunction between memory and expectation is itself a product of modernity. Ricoeur's allegedly transcendental traditionality is a *specifically modern form*. It acquires its transcendental status only by abstraction from (and a forgetting of) the historically specific social forms and modes of expectation through which the past is renewed. Habermas recognizes this. Indeed, in his discussion of 'Modernity's Consciousness of Time and its Need for Self-Reassurance', in *The Philosophical*

Discourse of Modernity, he uses Koselleck's semantics to derive the central philosophical problem of modernity (the need for it 'to create its normativity out of itself') from the idea of the present as a 'continuous renewal'.[71] Yet Habermas also fails to reflect upon the ontological status of this idea, taking it for granted as an external, merely empirical historical premise of his thought. He thus forgoes the opportunity for a combined – historical and philosophical – deepening of the concept of subjectivity, taking it over ready-made from Kant in its most abstract and ahistorical form.

Benjamin's approach to tradition overcomes the deficit of Gadamer's and Ricoeur's approaches in two ways. Firstly, it locates the existential core of tradition not just in preservation (understood as memory), but in the communicability of experience within the present. Secondly, it thus treats the problem of communication not just as a philosophical one, but as a problem of cultural form. This opens up tradition to a historiographic analysis in which different forms of communication appear as embodiments of different kinds of memory. Tradition appears in the guise of a cultural history of narrative forms of memorative communication. This is the decisive difference from Ricoeur's work. For whereas, for Ricoeur, the transcendental narrativity of the schema of the productive imagination underlies (and underwrites) the basic structure of historical consciousness, whatever its particular mode of narrative inscription, for Benjamin, there is only the *historically specific variety* of social forms of memorative communication. These may mainly have taken narrative forms in the past (in visual as well as literary representation), but there is no guarantee that they will continue to do so in the future. Indeed, these forms are in crisis. Narrative is in crisis as a 'living' form. It can no longer communicate historical experience. This crisis is the very meaning of modernity as a destruction of tradition. So profound is the crisis, in fact, that Benjamin can, literally, no longer conceive of the possibility of a return to tradition; nor, as we shall see, from the standpoint of his conception of history, is it something that appears desirable. This is not to say that there will be no more narrative historiography (still less that there will be no more narrative fiction). But it is to claim that historical narrative has lost its living relationship to the present, that it is no longer a genuine form of memorative communication. In the technical terms of Benveniste's linguistics, it has become narrative *as opposed* to discourse.[72]

However, just as we argued against Meschonnic in chapter 1, that the discourse of modernity cannot be wholly severed from narrative reference, so, conversely, neither can narrative ever be wholly isolated from the discursive context of its existence; although, as we shall see, it is a distinctive feature of a certain type of narrative (historicism) that it dissembles such independence, by forgetting its present. Benveniste's formalist distinction thus cannot ultimately be sustained, unless dialectically reconstrued. On the other hand, its very existence may be read as a symptom of the increasing distance between historical experience and narrative form to which Benjamin refers. In this respect, 'modernity' is to be identified less with a purely discursive form opposed to narrative (as Meschonnic would have it), than with a crisis in their relations. One way in which this is manifest is the manner in which the various discourses of modernity (philosophical, sociological, artistic, religious, etc.) distance themselves from their own performative present by narrativizing the historical conditions of their existence in such a way as to fix them in 'periods', which are then objectivistically misconstrued. An alternative response, as Rancière has shown in his reading of the *Annales*, would be to deregulate the play of the opposition by 'constructing a narrative in the system of discourse'.[73] The historiography of the *Annales* School is in this sense contemporary with Benjamin's later writings in the deepest sense of that term. In their deployment of discourse against conventional narrative, both sought a genuinely modernist historiography.[74] Benjamin's work shifts the focus of arguments about the temporalization of history away from self-sufficient philosophizing to the interpretation of the historical meaning of cultural form.

Historiography and the shattering of tradition

Benjamin's version of the death of narrative is contained in his 1934 essay, 'The Storyteller: Reflections on the Works of Nikolai Leskov'. This extraordinary essay, in which Benjamin weaves a social history of epic forms as modes of historical consciousness into his reading of Leskov's work, is paradigmatic of his practice of using occasional pieces of criticism for the elaboration of fundamental philosophical and cultural themes. It is also the closest Benjamin gets to a nostalgic reflection on modernity as loss. Influenced by both the sociological dualism of Tönnies' *Community and Society* and the Kierkegaardian Hegelianism of Lukács's *Theory of the Novel*, it needs the reflected light of its dialectical counterpart, 'The Work of Art in the Age of Mechanical Reproduction', for its own internal dialectic to become visible. Yet it contains some of Benjamin's sharpest insights, not only into modernity as a destruction of tradition, but also into the production of the idea of tradition within modernity as its inescapable dialectical other. The idea that the removal of narrative from experience makes it possible to see a 'new beauty' in what is vanishing, for example, points to the crucial role of modernity in the construction of the image of tradition to which it is opposed.[75] This helps explain the notorious ambiguity of Benjamin's attitude towards the aura, discovered at the moment of its loss, since the meaning of what is lost appears as internal to the perspective by which it is destroyed.

However, in its history of epic forms, 'The Storyteller' does not confine itself to the simple sociological dualism of modernity and tradition from which it sets out. Rather, it offers a more complex, four-stage schema: from the original unity of the epic (the unity of the one and the many narratives), through the separate appearance of its constituent elements in the multiple reminiscences (*Gedachtnis*) of the story, and the singular remembrance (*Eingedenken*) of the novel, to a present in which 'the art of storytelling is reaching its end because the epic side of truth, wisdom, is dying out' and the novel is in crisis. Those elements of the epic associated with the story crystallized into a discrete form long before the emergence of the novel, but once it evolves, the novel increasingly becomes the dominant form as the social basis of storytelling is first eroded and then collapses. Soon, however, the novel itself comes under threat as the developmental tendencies that were the basis of its existence undermine it in turn, bringing with them new forms of communication and temporal experience (*Erlebnis*).[76] The present – Benjamin's present, interwar Europe – thus comes to be defined as the site of 'a tremendous shattering of tradition', a crisis in the communication of experience (*Erfahrung*), in memory, and hence in the very possibility of historical experience.[77] Relations between generations are no longer the medium of historical continuity here, but of crisis, rupture, and misunderstanding. Youth is no longer a sign of apprenticeship, or even hope, but of an empty infinity of possibilities, disorientation and potential despair.[78]

Within this scenario, the art of the story is seen as belonging to an oral tradition grounded in the common experiences of specific communities of listeners, even when, at a certain point in its development, it begins to appear in written form. The novel, on the other hand, is essentially an alienated, written form. Directed towards the inner experience of the bourgeois individual, it is dependent on the private consumption of the book. Its totalizing standpoint was always problematic, historiographically (especially for Lukács, whose thesis of its 'transcendental homelessness' Benjamin largely endorses), since its form, reflecting 'a world gone out of joint', offers only a biographical model of closure.[79] It soon begins to fracture once the lives of individuals become increasingly dependent on the mediations of impersonal social forms, the logics of which remain opaque. (This would seem to be the fundamental social experience underlying Kafka's work, for example.) Yet the reconstitution of the original unity of the epic, the reconstitution of history as the unity of the one and the many narratives, can be no more than a forlorn hope so long as no basis can be found for it within the new forms of social experience themselves. This is the essential lesson of what Benjamin saw as Kafka's 'failure': the impossibility of communicating the experience of modernity in the language of tradition. Such failure, a sign of tradition having 'fallen ill', was for Benjamin the true meaning of Kafka's work: 'Once he was certain of eventual failure, everything worked out for him en route as in a dream.' Kafka made modernism a death-mask for tradition.[80]

Benjamin calls the new form of communication, produced in response to the heightened intensities of industrial capitalism, and 'the boundless maze of indirect relationships, complex mutual dependencies and compartmentations' of the city,[81] 'information'. In line with the new forms of social experience to which it corresponds, information serves an economy of abbreviation, both semantic and temporal: it must be readily intelligible, immediately plausible, and most important of all – corresponding to the interruptive, amnesiac temporality of shock – it 'lives' only at 'the moment in which it is new'.[82] In fact, Benjamin would soon argue, information is itself already being replaced by the experience of shock: 'the price for which the sensation of the modern age may be had: the disintegration of the aura in the experience of shock'. Consciousness shields the self from such shocks by registering them without retaining them, protecting the organism against over-stimulation by isolating them from memory. Memory becomes unconscious. At the same time, in a potentially redemptive move, shock becomes the formal principle of perception in the film; the camera, the instrument of an 'unconscious optics'.[83] Film is the paradigmatic cultural form of modernity. 'All problems of contemporary art,' Benjamin writes in the *Arcades Project*, 'find their final formulation only in relation to film.'[84] As a form for the communication of experience, its principles permeate the related literary forms of journalism, the advertisment, the placard and the pamphlet.[85]

Foremost among the forms of social experience which, for Benjamin, are constitutive of the temporality of this modernity are warfare in the age of technology, mechanized industrial labour, the jostling of the crowd in the great cities, fashion, inflation, and gambling. Each beats out a similar rhythm.[86] At the heart of his analysis, however, lies the fetish character of the commodity-form, planned centre-piece of the *Arcades Project*.[87] In the wake of the appearance for the first time in palpable form of the 'ever-always-the-same' (the commodity), the newness of the product is seen to acquire 'a hitherto unheard of significance', as a stimulus to demand. In the process, the historiographic concept of 'the modern' is radically transformed. For whereas it used to be opposed to a conception of antiquity as a stable historical referent, now 'the centuries between the present moment and that which has just been lived . . . tirelessly constitute "antiquity"' anew in the most recent past. 'Modernity' antiquates to a hitherto unheard of extent. The modern and the new become synonymous. Furthermore, as a result of the accelerating temporal rhythm, the new itself appears as the ever-always-the-same: 'the ever-always-the-same within the new'. It is the pure temporal logic of this new social form (the commodity as fetish), the modern 'measure of time', that Benjamin detects in fashion (*mode*). Hence the definition of fashion as 'the eternal recurrence of the new' (a ritual, mythic repetition), its ultimate expression as death ('the only one radical novelty, and that is always the same'), and the projected allegorical reading of modernity as Hell. For novelty is also 'the quintessence of false consciousness', of which fashion is said to be 'the tireless agent'.[88]

The temporalization of history by and as modernity appears here as its negation: the transformation of historical time back into a cyclical metaphysics of pure change. (It is in this sense that Nietzsche, the thinker of eternal return, appears as the philosopher of modernity *par excellence*.) Benjamin's reflections on the fate of tradition as the *Urform* of memorative communication seem to culminate in an aporia. The established forms of memorative communication are archaic, but the new forms of communication do not have any memorative content. At the level of social experience, modernity is a form of forgetting, or, at least, the repression of history into the cultural unconscious.[89] If 'memory creates the chain of tradition', and historiography is 'the record kept by memory',[90] the shattering of the chain, the break-down of memory, will set off a historiographic crisis. It is as a response to just such a crisis that Benjamin understands his own work. What was required was nothing less than a 'Copernican revolution of remembrance' (*Eingedenken*).[91] However, such a revolution can no more oppose itself to the time-consciousness of modernity from the outside, in the name of another, as yet unrealized socio-temporal form, than it can hope to resuscitate the dead forms of tradition.[92] Rather, it must seek its resources immanently, within the temporal forms of modernity itself. Before turning to Benjamin's attempt at a 'revolutionary' temporalization of history, based on the image of redemption, we must thus consider those other temporalizations of history, internal to modernity as a destruction of tradition, elements of which he will need to refigure to produce his historiographic equivalent to the film: historicism and the transitional classicism of Baudelaire's modernism.

Historicism as bad modernity

The term 'historicism' (*Historismus*) has been put to several, often conflicting, uses. In any particular instance, its meaning tends to be determined by the position to which it is being opposed. Apart from a relatively neutral sense in which it refers to a general belief in the historical character of knowledge, it is mainly used philosophically to designate *either* a belief in the immanent identity of truth and history of a Hegelian kind; *or* an empirical view of historical knowledge developed by the Historical School in Germany, in the latter part of the nineteenth century, in explicit opposition to Hegel's philosophy of history. In the first case, Hegel is a historicist because of his historicization of truth, relative to classical metaphysics and transcendental philosophy. In the second, he is not, because of the ultimate transcendence of time in his speculative dialectic of absolute knowing.[93]

In German philosophy, it is the second, anti-Hegelian sense of the term which is prevalent, deriving from the work of those historians – Ranke and Droysen, in particular – who opposed themselves to Hegel in the name of an 'objective' historical method. They thereby bequeathed the 'problem of historicism' to late nineteenth- and early twentieth-century philosophy, where it was taken up, first by the neo-Kantians and Dilthey, and later by Heidegger and Gadamer. This is the problem of the relationship between the historicity of knowledge and the oneness of truth, once Hegel's solution of positing their ultimate identity in the knowledge of the system has been rejected.[94] Benjamin takes over the established usage of the Historical School, for which historicism refers to an objectivism about knowledge of the past 'the way it really was' (Ranke), with one important addition. He also associates historicism with the idea of history as progress, derived from the Enlightenment philosophy of history.[95]

Critics have pointed out that this identification of historicism with progress conflates two tendencies which can be found in conflict with one another at least as often as they are discovered together, since the objectivistic time-consciousness of historicism is as amenable to relativistic interpretations as to progressivistic ones. In fact, nowadays, the term is far more likely to be associated with the former than the latter.[96] Relativistic or 'radical' historicists, such as Foucault, engage in the critique of all general criteria of progress. This has led Kittsteiner to argue that Benjamin's critique of progress displays sufficient *affinities* with what is normally called historicism to be classified as a 'materialist historicism', rather than a version of historical materialism; especially, interestingly, as regards its theological dimension.[97] However, this too is misleading. For whatever the similarities between the role of God in Ranke's and Benjamin's thought (and one might be forgiven for thinking Kittsteiner overplays them), Benjamin, like both Heidegger and Althusser, is fundamentally opposed to both progressivist *and* relativistic historicisms on the question of the nature of historical time. The affinity that Kittsteiner notes is far less significant than Benjamin's opposition to the conception of history as 'the subject of a structure whose site is homogeneous empty time', which both forms of historicism ultimately presuppose.[98] Indeed, it can only be constructed by taking one side of Benjamin's concept of history (the theological), in abstraction from the other (the materialist or immanently historical). However, since the whole point of Benjamin's work is to force these two sides together, or, at least, to map them onto one another without remainder, such a procedure does too much violence to it to be acceptable as an interpretive strategy. This aspect of Kittsteiner's critique – its presentation of Benjamin as a 'materialist historicist' – may thus be reduced to a polemical exploitation of terminological differences.

On the other hand, it is true that Benjamin (unlike Heidegger or Althusser) historicizes his analysis of historicism, treating it not merely as a theoretical position, or even an existential orientation, but as a response to a specific dilemma: the break-down of tradition. As such, its form is determined by the structure of the crisis to which it responds. It is this contextualization of historicism as a form of historical time-consciousness which leads Benjamin to associate it with the concept of progress. Historicism is read as a functional replacement within the amnestic temporality of modernity for the continuity of historical time previously established by tradition. It is a compensatory reaction, internal to the temporality of modernity, against its more disruptive effects. More specifically, historicism *regulates interruption as series* by the generalized projection of the abstract temporality of the new onto history as a whole. On

Benjamin's analysis, this creates a time in which historical events appear indifferently as 'mass-produced articles': each one new, within its own time, yet in terms of the nature of the time that it occupies, and hence its relation to the present, 'ever-always-the-same'.

This standardization of historical time has three main features. Firstly, as an 'homogeneous empty time', it allows for what we might call the 're-chronologization' or naturalization of history: historicism is a 'vulgar naturalism'.[99] This naturalism allows it to present itself as a science. Secondly, this naturalism is actually a form of forgetting, a forgetting of the constitutive role of the present in all forms of time-consciousness: that phenomenological present which alone gives direction to history, and thereby makes possible the (mis)construal of history as progress. Benjamin describes this forgetting as 'the secret magna charta for the presentation of history according to the historicist school': 'If you want to relive an epoch, forget that you know what has happened since.'[100] In reacting against the amnesia about the past inherent in the destructive force of a purely interruptive modernity, historicism falls victim to another, deeper and more deceptive amnesia of its own: amnesia about the present. This is the cost of its restoration of continuity. Historicism trades the living remembrance of a historical present for the re-establishment of an abstract continuity with the past, in a naturalized and merely chronological form.

Finally, despite its impossible attempt to remove itself from the present, historicism actually embodies a traditional definition of that present in terms of its transmission of the 'enduring values' of the past. Historicism is the form of historical consciousness within modernity which presents the phenomena of the past in terms of their 'value as heritage', or as 'cultural treasures'.[101] It is this complicity with tradition which, in Benjamin's view, places historicism in the service of barbarism:

> if one asks with whom the adherents of historicism actually empathize . . . the answer is inevitable: the victor. And all the rulers are the heirs of those who conquered before them. Hence, empathy with the victor invariably benefits the rulers. . . . Whoever has emerged victorious participates to this day in the triumphal procession in which the present rulers step over those who are lying prostrate. According to traditional practice, the spoils are carried along in the procession. They are called cultural treasures . . .[102]

On this account, historicism forgets not just the role of the present in historical memory, but, therewith, everything in the past which resists transmission as heritage: specifically, the tradition of the oppressed. This is the Benjamin with whom we are all familiar, the Benjamin of 'the image of enslaved ancestors rather than that of liberated grandchildren'. It is an avenging Benjamin, a Benjamin for whom history is an economy of violence dissembling as progress. Historicism perpetuates this illusion. In its combination of the eternity of the classical with the infinite duration of chronology (in the self-consciousness of historicism *each thing* can in principle be preserved), it functions as a radical denial of death. In this denial, historicism trades a true remembrance for its restoration of continuity with the past. Benjamin, on the other hand, is prepared to trade continuity for remembrance. History, he argues, against historicism,

> is not just a science but also a form of remembrance (*Eingedenkens*). What science has 'established', remembrance can modify. Remembrance can make the incomplete (happiness) into something complete, and the complete (suffering) into something incomplete. That is theology; but in remembrance we discover the experience that forbids us to conceive of history as thoroughly a-theological, even though we barely dare not attempt to write it according to literally theological concepts.[103]

Recognizing that a return to the original unity of the epic is no more than a forlorn hope, since there is no basis for it in the latest forms of social life (and its transmission was, in any case, based only on the authoritative imposition of the 'appearance' of permanence), Benjamin uses the remembrance (*Eingedenken*) of such a unity – the remembrance of the unity of remembrance and reminiscence (*Gedachtnis*) – as the standpoint from which to think the possibility of a new kind of historical experience.[104] The historiographic hope of the epic (totality) – renewed by Benjamin in his own novelistic narrative of its evolving forms ('The Storyteller') – provides the philosophical goal for a new kind of historiography, to be developed out of the structure of the new form of temporality itself. This goal is 'theological' in the sense that its perspective is that of the completion of history as a whole, but the method by which it is to be reached is immanently historical. In this respect, 'theology' stands for that moment of totalizing transcendence of the given which is intrinsic to the concept of history itself. It can no more be opposed to history than history can be reduced to the past. It is this determination to derive a new form of historical experience immanently, from the experience of the crisis of the old one – to redeem this crisis *as* historical experience – which explains Benjamin's growing preoccupation with both the commodity and Baudelaire's poetry, once the philosophical form of his project begins to take a more definite shape. Central to this form are the integral connection of remembrance to the promise of a redeemed future, and the ideas of *destruction* and *interruption* as the presupposition of all construction, in opposition to the 'reconstruction by means of empathy' upon which historicism depends.[105] It is in its destructive aspect that Benjamin holds out most hope for modernity, and it is in his appreciation of this aspect, and his contempt for the idea of progress, that Benjamin finds most to admire in Baudelaire.

At first sight, Baudelaire offers a radically different response to the crisis of historical continuity from the bland chronologism of historicism: namely, an explicit affirmation of the temporality of modernity as 'the ephemeral, the fugitive, the contingent'. Moder*nism*, as the affirmative cultural self-consciousness of the temporality of the new, starts here. Yet it terminates, in Baudelaire, only in the desire 'to extract from fashion whatever element it may contain of poetry within history, to *distil the eternal from the transitory*'.[106] The value of Baudelaire for Benjamin derives from his appreciation of the inestimable value of the new. Yet for all his obsession with novelty, Baudelaire is ultimately unable to 'wrest it away' from the conformism which threatens to overpower all forms of historical consciousness within modernity, returning them to the complacency of tradition. For the way in which Baudelaire registers his identification with the modern, the disruptive temporality of the new, is by making it the site of a traditional (classical) conception of the eternal. Modern poetry seeks its place in the warehouse of cultural treasures, where, as Benjamin puts it, 'the pathological aspect of the notion of "culture"' is enthroned, in the alleged independence of its entities from the production process in which they survive.[107] With Baudelaire, classicism is reborn within modernity, as a modernist metaphysics of transience.

In its 'distillation' of the eternal from the transitory, Baudelaire's modernism rejoins the indifferent, contemplative temporality of historicism as 'heritage'. What it leaves behind, however, apart from the shell of contingency, is an aspiration, a desire to embrace modernity as a *living* form, and a set of motifs to guide its comprehension, the significance of which transcend the limitations of the idea of modernism as a new classicism within which they appear. These elements, reinterpreted from the standpoint of Benjamin's present on the basis of a combination of Nietzschean and Marxist themes, provided Benjamin with the foothold he needed within modernity to relaunch historiography as a form of remembrance (*Eingedenken*) which would not be merely backward-looking, but would contain within itself the seeds of a new futurity. Most important here is the equation Baudelaire establishes between novelty and eternity, but it needs to be rethought. Baudelaire himself is seen to confront this emergent identity with 'heroic effort', in the attempt to snatch the new away from the ever-same, in the name of the eternal. Nietzsche, on the other hand, faces it with 'heroic composure', in the belief that there never will be anything new. With Blanqui, in the late cosmological work that so fascinated Benjamin, 'resignation prevails.'[108] Yet Benjamin himself adopts none of these attitudes, since for him, this is not the temporal structure of history *per se*, but merely the 'hell' of a consciousness of time from which he is seeking to escape, into a redeemed future.

What Benjamin is seeking is a fissure in this temporal structure through which to break it open onto a new form of historical experience. He finds it in the instantaneous temporality of the 'now', which marks out the 'exact repetition' of the new as the ever-same.[109] For in the experience of the repetitive succession of identical instants – abstractly projected onto history by historicism as the blank chronologism of 'homogeneous empty time' – we are returned, structurally, to the cosmological time of nature as an 'eternal and total passing away' which Benjamin had earlier declared 'Messianic' and identified with happiness.[110] The very *indifference* of the new as the ever-always-the-same that is the basis for the quantification of time in historicism, becomes, for Benjamin, the ground for a quite different, *qualitative* experience of the 'now' as an *historical* present. Eternal recurrence, he notes, is 'an attempt to link the two antinomic principles of happiness with one another: namely that of eternity and that of the yet once again'. It 'conjures out of the wretchedness of time the speculative idea (or the phantasmagoria) of happiness'.[111] It is this twofold structure which Benjamin aims to appropriate for a constructed yet concrete experience of history as new. Elements of the time-consciousness of modernism and historicism are to be refigured to produce a third, quasi-Messianic experience of historical time.

The instantaneity of the 'now', experienced for the first time within modernity as a form of historical (rather than merely 'natural') temporality, is seen to contain within its static, monadic structure the equivalent to a Messianic 'cessation of happening', *combined* with a 'recurrence', a 'yet once again', which can only be understood as a new form of remembrance. In the time of this 'now', nature and history are one, from the standpoint of an *atemporal* eternality. The past will be gathered up within the present, in the perspective of redemption, as an explosive historical 'experience' (*Erfahrung*). In opposition to the regressive, and psychologically defensive, historicist experience of the temporal order of modernity, whereby an incident is assigned a precise point in time 'at the cost of the integrity of its contents', in order to transform it into 'a moment that has been lived (*Erlebnis*)'[112] – intellectually appropriating it as a merely quantitative relation, in compensation for the failure to establish any truly living relationship to it – we are offered an alternative historico-metaphysical experience of the same temporal order: 'now-being' (*Jetztsein*).[113] But in what sense can we understand this metaphysical experience as *historical* in content, rather than just origin? And what is its active, political dimension?

Quasi-messianic interruption: images of redemption

Now-time receives a series of more or less apocalyptic descriptions in Benjamin's late work. It is 'the now of a specific recognisability' in which 'truth is loaded to the bursting-point with time'. It is 'a present which is not a transition, but in which time stands still and has come to a stop'; 'a Messianic cessation of happening' providing 'a revolutionary chance in the fight for the oppressed'. It is the 'moment of awakening' which 'rescues' history for the present, 'ignites the explosives that lie in the past', and 'blasts the epoch' out of the reified continuity of homogeneous time. It is a 'flash of lightning', in which the past is said to 'attain a higher degree of actuality than in the moment of its existence'. It 'coincides' with the birth of 'authentic (*echten*) historical time, the time of truth'. It is the site of the structure of which history is the subject.[114]

A flash of lightning, an awakening, a cessation of happening, a recognition . . . The images cohere as in the climax of a narrative, cut off, frozen, like the final frame of a film, on the threshold of a new beginning. But what of the structure of this process, this 'revolutionary' experience of stasis? What kind of time are we talking about here, exactly? Everything depends on how we understand the doubling of the now as the point of intersection of two radically different temporal perspectives, the Messianic and the immanently historical, as it opens up experience to the promise of fulfilment. Now-time is neither wholly inside nor wholly outside of history, but faces both ways at once. It is this combination of apparently contradictory temporal structures that gives Benjamin's conception both its force and complexity. It is best approached by way of negation.

In the first place, in terms of the form of its presence, now-time is neither the time of the blankly identical Aristotelian or cosmological instant, taken by historicism as the ontological ground of its chronologies and interpreted by Heidegger as the basis of the 'ordinary conception of time'; nor, even less, is it the time of the extended, durational, phenomenological present described by Husserl, of which the idea of modernity is a historical form. Rather, it aspires to condense into the punctual, one-dimensional space of the former, not just a longitudinal historical content, but the presence of history as a whole, refracted through the prism of the historical present. Neither instant nor durational present, Benjamin's now-time historicizes the structure of instantaneity, to produce it as interruption, simultaneously contracting the present into the stasis of its point-like source and expanding its historical content to infinity, in an 'enormous abridgement' of 'the entire history of humanity'.[115] Exploiting the dual, dialectical character of the present, as both durational extension and point-like source, it performs a twofold mediation: of nature (instant) with history (present), and of this historical present ('modernity') with history as a whole (eternity). Neither instant nor present, Benjamin's now-time is 'the present *as* now-time'. It is always a historically specific now.[116]

But how can this work, if history is not yet over, if the future has yet to occur? How can history present itself as a whole in the time of the now, outside the confines of the ultimately time-denying eternal present of Hegelianism? The trick lies in the monadic structure of the dialectical image, productive object of now-time. For rather than constructing a linear unidirectional series of successive instants (Aristotle's 'before/now *or* then/after'), or a three-dimensional temporal spectrum (Husserl's 'past/present/future'), Benjamin's dialectical images are constellations of the 'then' and the 'now', which, in the hermetic enclosure of their internal relations, mirror the structure of history as a whole, viewed from the standpoint of its end.[117] As such, they are not so much allegorical in their semantic structure, as of the nature of theological symbols: *images* of redemption.[118] Each image, in its totalized if temporary self-sufficiency, reflects the structure of the yet-to-be-completed whole; each image thus carries within it the *perspective* of redemption. As Adorno put it in *Minima Moralia*, effectively summarizing Benjamin's method: 'The only philosophy which can be responsibly practiced in the face of despair is the attempt to contemplate all things as they would present themselves from the standpoint of redemption. Knowledge has no light but that shed on the world by redemption: all else is re-construction, mere technique.' Furthermore, he continues, 'beside the demand thus placed on thought, the question of the reality or unreality of redemption itself (*der Wirklichkeit oder Unwirklichkeit der Erlösung selber*) hardly matters.'[119]

Redemption itself, in the strict Messianic sense, is not at stake. In this, Benjamin's later work remains steadfastly at one with his earlier writings, and with Scholem's nihilistic understanding of the Messianic idea. There is no redemption *within* historical time, only the redemption *of* history as a whole, and that is beyond human powers. The past may carry with it 'a temporal index by which it is *referred to* redemption', in the sense that 'only a redeemed mankind receives the fullness of its past' – the very idea of the past as the 'totality' of what has been, projects a historical closure – but this does not make redemption itself a *realizable* practical goal.[120] Indeed, quite the reverse, it removes it from history. It is this refusal of a direct identification of the Jewish concept of redemption with the hopes of the revolution which differentiates Benjamin's work from Ernst Bloch's Messianism[121] and aligns it with Scholem's. Like Scholem, Benjamin always insisted on the catastrophic exteriority of redemption to history, the 'nothingness of revelation' and the definition of history as infinite deferment (deferment of redemption).[122] In the words of Scholem which Benjamin quotes back to him with approval: 'The absolutely concrete cannot be fulfilled at all.'[123]

Nor did Benjamin ever give up the category of revelation, as Scholem suggests that he did once he turned to historical materialism.[124] For while his 'Messianic fixation' does indeed indicate an awareness of 'a disgrace or disorder in the relation to revelation'[125] – the shattering of tradition – Benjamin nonetheless retained an emphatic concept of truth, albeit now in an historically mediated form. It is 'an emphatic refusal of the concept of *"timeless* truth"' which characterizes the later work.[126] This is the main difference from the framework of *The Origin of German Tragic Drama*: ideas are no longer to be understood as 'timeless constellations'. The direct counterposition of history to the divine, 'characterised by pure violence or pure language', and approachable only via 'mimesis and correspondences which eschew mediation or representation',[127] is exchanged for a new concept of historical time. However, truth is not to be conceived as 'just a temporal function of knowledge'. Rather, more complexly, it is to be understood as in some way 'bound to a time kernel (*Zeitkern*)' planted in history.[128] This 'time kernel' of truth is exposed, momentarily, in the now of a *specific* recognizability: at once complete within the structure of the now, yet radically incomplete in its immediate passing (its becoming past): '"In relation to the history of organic life on earth . . . the history of civilised humanity would fill one-fifth of the last second of the last hour [of a twenty-four hour day]." Now-time . . . as a model of the Messianic . . . coincides exactly with the stature which the history of humanity has in the universe.'[129] It is this paradoxical structure of completeness/incompleteness that is the key to Benjamin's politics of the image.

Cognitively, dialectical images work metonymically, with the part (the now of a specific recognizability) imaging the whole (history as a redemptive totality). Politically, however, they work the other way around, generating their allegedly explosive practical charge from the contradiction between the transience or incompleteness of the historical present in terms of which they are constructed, and the perspective of completion inherent in their metonymic structure. The impulse to action derives from that very *partiality* of the Messianic presence which might otherwise seem to problematize the metaphysics of Benjamin's conception. The political argument implicit in Benjamin's presentation of now-time is certainly an ambitious one (too ambitious, one might think); yet it is consistent with materialism insofar as it depends upon the *impossibility*, not the imminence, of a willed redemption. Only if the Messianic remains exterior to history can it provide the perspective of a completed whole (without the predetermination of a teleological end), from which the present may appear in its essential transience, as radically incomplete. As Derrida puts it: 'Eschatology breaks teleology apart.'[130] Such exteriority figures the exteriority of a time which carries with it the inevitability of death.

Death is the material meaning of Messianic exteriority: this is the fundamental insight offered to a materialist reading of Benjamin's later writings by Heidegger's early work. History is a democratic utopia of death. That Benjamin considered these writings consistent with materialism, for all their theological terminology, is not in doubt; although few have been prepared to follow him in this.[131] For the conceptual basis of the claim has remained obscure. In Benjamin's own work the relationship between the two perspectives appears less as a theoretical issue (whereby religious thought might be read as the mystified projection of anthropological truths, for example), than as a question of the historical forms of *communicable* truth; that is, of the fate of tradition. If the theological dimension of Benjamin's writings was increasingly, if inconsistently, attenuated prior to its final appearance in what have become known as the 'Theses on the Philosophy of History', it was not because of a rejection of its theoretical structure, but because of a growing concern about its capacity to communicate as tradition. The social forms of modernity (as modes of destruction of tradition) are taken so to have undermined the social basis of religious experience that the discourse of theology has been robbed of its social meaning, appearing now only as the remnant of previous social forms: 'theology ... today, as we know, is wizened and has to keep out of sight.'[132]

Recognition of this fact did not initially affect the core structure of Benjamin's metaphysics, but it did affect his understanding of its communicable form, and thereby, ultimately, both its theoretical content and its historical meaning. Modernity renders theology esoteric. In his early work, Benjamin had prized such singularity as a sign of truth. Indeed, as late as 1926 (after his 'conversion' to Communism), he still took the perspective of Messianic exteriority to imply that, philosophically speaking, 'there are no meaningfully *political* goals.'[133] This soon changed, however, once he began to reflect upon the theoretical implications of what was initially a merely instrumental commitment to 'the value of Communist action'.[134] The result was that Benjamin came to see Communism as the social movement in which something equivalent to his early, theologically based philosophical critique of the present could be actualized in a communicable form, as politics: equivalent, but not the same. Hence the necessity for him to transpose the theological dimension of his thought into the terms of historical materialism, without remainder. As Wohlfarth puts it, if historicism, with its '"eternal" image of the past', appeared to Benjamin to be a false secularization of theology, historical materialism, with its 'unique experience with the past', was to be its true equivalent.[135]

Ironically for the theorist of the destruction of tradition, Benjamin's primary interest in Communism was as a living tradition, a collective intellectual form for the expression of the truth of historical experience. Only as such did he subsequently become interested in it as doctrine (*Lehre*). For Benjamin, 'historical materialism' was the name of the doctrine of which Communism is the tradition. However, it does not denote any particular, authoritative interpretation of this doctrine, but rather, the site of its theoretical interpretation. Benjamin deployed the hermeneutic and doctrinal resources of the Messianic tradition to reinterpret historical materialism, philosophically, in line with his conception of its political function. As such, it came to provide the standpoint from which he could both view the destruction of theology as tradition, and thereby, reflecting on this experience, reconstitute the integrity of historical experience in a new, dialectical and 'revolutionary' form. According to the terms of Benjamin's theory of translation,[136] it is no more legitimate exclusively to oppose the 'theological' to the 'materialist' text of this exchange than it is to suppose that such translation renders their contents identical.[137]

Furthermore, as not only this early theory of translation, but also the later ontology of the 'afterlife' of the object suggest,[138] both sides will be transformed by the exchange. The translator, Benjamin insists, quoting Pannwitz, 'must expand and deepen his own language by means of the foreign language'.[139] Thus did Benjamin expand and deepen the language of historical materialism, in opposition to 'Marxism', understood as the prevailing orthodoxy in its theoretical interpretation as a creed (basically, the Marxism of the Second International).[140] 'My thinking relates to theology,' Benjamin writes in a much cited passage, 'the way a blotter does to ink. It is soaked through with it. If one were to go by the blotter, though, nothing of what has been written would remain.'[141]

It is important in this respect to remember that Benjamin does not write of now-time as Messianic *per se*, but only as a 'model' (*Modell*) of the Messianic, 'shot through' with 'chips' (*Splitter*) of Messianic time, site of a *'weak'* (*schwache*) Messianic power. Redemption, the reception of the fullness of the past, does not come until Judgement Day: the end of time.[142] It is for this reason that it is an angel, not the Messiah, who watches over Benjamin's later work; an angel which is powerless to intervene.[143] However, the standpoint of this angel, Klee's Angelus Novus, to whom history appears as 'one single catastrophe',[144] is not (as is usually supposed) that of the materialist critic or historian, but that of an *inverted 'progress'*. The homogeneous empty time of historicism mirrors the indifference to all historical specificity characteristic of a purely Messianic view; an indifference which is to be found in actuality only in nature, 'by reason of its eternal and total passing away'.[145] The materialist historian, on the other hand, is always located inside a specific historical present. It is this present which is to be illuminated by the light of Benjamin's 'now'. Yet, for all its suspension of immanent temporal succession, this 'now' is ultimately as transient, and hence as incomplete, as any other. Indeed, at one point, in an apparent reduction of historical time to nature, Benjamin even suggests that what is rescued in the 'now' is already, in the very next moment, 'irretrievably' lost[146] – although he later amends this to a 'threat' suffered only by those 'images of the past' which are 'not recognised by the present as one of its own concerns'.[147]

Clearly, if now-time is to be a form of historical experience (rather than a fully Messianic intrusion, or reduction of history to nature), what it retrieves of the past must resonate in the present, beyond the timelessness of the 'now' itself, in some form or another. However, when Benjamin writes of retrieving the past in this way, he is not arguing for any kind of total recall. That is a myth of historicism:

the recovery of the past 'the way it really was'. Rather, he is pointing
to a politics of memory for which the character of the present (and
hence future) is determined by actively constructed relations to a
series of specific pasts – 'enslaved ancestors', for example, as opposed
to triumphs of nation.[148] But this does not mean that the selection
of pasts is a matter of choice. Benjamin's now is always the now of
a 'specific recognizability'. Montage may not be methodological,
but nor is it arbitrary. It is experimental. Selection is governed by a
strict cognitive criterion: the uncovering of what is 'truly new' in
the present as a sign of the possibilities it contains. In the light of the
idea of actualization, now-time uncovers the meaning of history as
concrete possibility.[149]

To put this another way, 'now-being' is a form of avant-garde
experience. For the avant-garde is not that which is most historically
advanced in the sense that (in the image of Benjamin's backward-
looking angel) it has the most history behind it – an *historicist* image
if ever there was one, even if progress is inverted into the piling up of
the wreckage of a linear catastrophism. The avant-garde is that
which, in the flash of the dialectical image, disrupts the linear time-
consciousness of progress in such a way as to enable us, like the child,
to 'discover the new anew'[150] and, along with it, the possibility of a
better future. Benjamin's philosophy of history is a critique of the
historicist concept of progress, but it is not, like Scholem's messianic
theology of hope, an historical nihilism. Its immanent critique cannot
but bring forth another, 'truer' notion of a progress which 'does not
reside in the continuity of temporal succession, but rather in its
moments of interference: where the truly new first makes itself felt, as
sober as the dawn'. As a 'fundamental historical concept', progress
may be redefined as 'the first revolutionary measures taken'.[151]
However, if the experience of the 'truly new' can only be momentary,
how is it to inform identity and action, which are inscribed within the
time of *narrative*? How are we to counter the objection that, despite
his best intentions, Benjamin has actually sketched only an ecstatic or
purely interruptive conception of now-being which (like his angel) is
powerless in the face of history; or even worse perhaps, is politically
arbitrary? The key lies in the concept of mediation.

Montage, mediation, apocalypse: towards a new narrativity

It is almost a cliché of Benjamin criticism to say, following Adorno,
that Benjamin's dialectical images lack mediation.[152] But Adorno is

surely right, insofar as what he means is that they lack the kind of immanent conceptual mediation expounded by Hegel as the structure of dialectical logic. He is wrong, however, to suggest that they lack mediation altogether; wrong to reduce the concept of mediation to a narrowly Hegelian form. After all, as we saw in chapter 2, Hegel's logic constructs precisely that 'eternal present' which would obliterate the fundamental pastness of the past and the radical futurity of the future as the yet-to-be-determined. On the other hand, what could experience be without mediation? We thus require a concept of mediation which forgoes conceptual resolution in the self-identity of some higher stage, if we are to make any headway in the elaboration and development of Benjamin's conception of historical experience. For mediation in Benjamin has more of the character of a *switch between circuits* (opening a gap in Gadamer's 'closed circuits of historical life', triggered by the metonymic structure of the image) than the production of a shared conceptual space, since the terms of its relation are located in different temporal dimensions.[153] Buck-Morss represents this diagrammatically as follows (Figure 2), with the link between temporal registers being provided by what is alternatively described as 'revolutionary' or 'political' action:

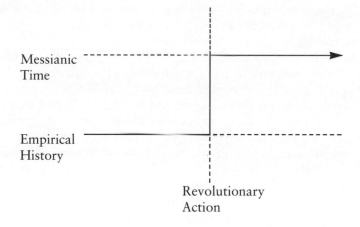

Figure 2

(From Susan Buck-Morss, *Dialectics of Seeing: Walter Benjamin and the Arcades Project*, MIT Press, Cambridge MA, 1989, p.242.)

Consideration of the problems with this diagram will help us both to clarify and develop the complex temporal structure of Benjamin's 'now'.

First, one might question whether the Messianic axis should possess a directional arrow; or indeed, whether it should be described as a form of time at all, since it is outside the temporal realm as a whole. Second, for the same reason, it seems misleading to present these two dimensions of now-time as internal to anything we might call 'historical' time, as its Messianic and empirical aspects respectively. Rather, given the exteriority of the Messianic to history, the opposition at stake seems better represented as one between the Messianic and the historical. In now-time, historical time momentarily acquires a Messianic (that is, an extra-historical) dimension, but the Messianic does not thereby become historical. That would bring history to an end. Third, however, as Buck-Morss recognizes, historical time cannot be reduced to its empirical dimension (chronology). That would be historicism. Placing the Messianic outside of historical time thus requires that we supplement the diagram with a new axis to indicate that 'empirical history' is only one dimension of an internally complex 'historical time' which *excludes* the Messianic, but which is brought into a paradoxical relationship with it in now-time. There are at least three temporal registers at play here, not two. Finally, one might question why it is revolutionary or political action which is the link between temporal registers, rather than the experience of the dialectical image itself. For political action (or, at all events, the impulse to such action) is surely the supposed effect, not the medium, of the experience.

In particular, what is missing from Buck-Morss's account (as it is from Benjamin's methodological self-consciousness, which the account reconstructs) is any consideration of the *phenomenological structure of the living present* from which the subject is ecstatically removed by the experience of the image, and to which he/she must return, enriched, if the experience is to have any practical significance. To put this another way, we need to distinguish internally to the present moment, registered by Buck-Morss on the axis of 'empirical history', between the three temporal ecstases which constitute its living, phenomenological unity: the specific past presented by the image ('then'); the extended present which is interrupted by its 'now'; and the futurity which it produces (see figure 3, below). Only thus can we explain how the experience of the image can generate any futurity at all. For unless the Messianic timelessness of the image (representative of the perspective of redemption) somehow reacts back upon the phenomenological present which it interrupts, imbricating itself into its narrative structure, we will be left with a purely interruptive conception of now-being as an exit from history into an essentially mystical space of experience.

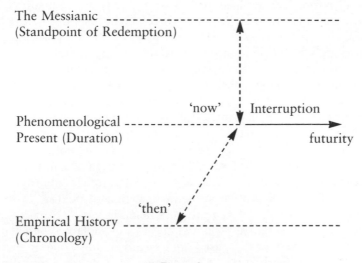

Figure 3

This is effectively Habermas's worry, albeit distorted through the prism of his misunderstanding of the relationship of now-time to the past: the act of interpretation is invested by Benjamin with 'all the insignia of praxis', but praxis itself is nowhere to be found since it is incommensurable with the temporality of the now.[154] It was Benjamin's own worry too. In his essay on Surrealism from 1929, he had identified the 'secret cargo' of art for art's sake as the 'profane illumination' of a Surrealist experience which transforms our relations to the most recent past into 'revolutionary experience, if not action'. And in 1935 he continued to proclaim Surrealism, with its 'substitution of a political for a historical view of the past', as the inspiration and model for his conception of a new kind of historical experience.[155] However, at the same time, Benjamin was always aware of the 'pernicious romantic prejudices', stressing only 'the mysterious side of the mysterious', which threatened Surrealism from within with a reduction to its 'ecstatic component'.[156] He saw his task as the *dissolution* of Aragon's 'mythology' into what he called 'the space of history'.[157] And as the 1930s progressed, he became increasingly preoccupied with the politics of the mystical misreading. By the end of 1935, an alternative and far more threatening genealogy than his own had appeared: the 'consummation' of art for art's sake in a Fascist conception of war as the provision of 'the artistic gratification of a sense perception that has been changed by technology', in which 'self-alienation has reached such a degree that . . . [humanity] can experience its own destruction as an aesthetic pleasure of the first order.' Fascism was thus read, famously, as an aestheticization of politics, to which Communism was to respond by 'politicizing art'.[158]

As an interpretation of National Socialism, the deficiencies of this formulation – simultaneously too narrow and too broad – are by now well known.[159] Yet it is equally troubling politically, since fascism itself involved a politicization of art (a political management of aesthetics) as the correlate of its aestheticization of politics. What, then, was the difference in *form* between a fascist politicization of art and the project of the Surrealists to put Surrealism 'in the service of the revolution'? In fact, did not Benjamin's appropriation of Surrealism itself involve an aestheticization of politics, in its re-definition of the political as a particular temporal mode of experience, an action-generating, as opposed to a contemplative, orientation towards the most recent past – and an involuntary one at that?[160] Such parallels clearly disturbed Benjamin. They haunted his political conscience and they dictated his literary strategy. Better, he suggested to Scholem in 1931, that he 'denature' his writings (by adopting certain formulations from orthodox historical materialism), in order to 'make them definitively and reliably unusable for the counter-revolution at the risk that no one will be able to use them', than that he should place them at its disposal.[161] In this context, the claim with which the 'Work of Art' essay opens – '[t]he concepts which are introduced into the theory of art in what follows . . . are completely useless for the purposes of fascism' – [162] must be read strategically, rather than literally: in terms of an acute awareness of the proximity of the very possibility which it denies. (It is almost a disavowal.)

The introduction of the idea of political use-values here marks an abrupt retreat on Benjamin's part from the attempt to rethink politics through temporality (a retreat from the exploration of the political legacy of Surrealism), and a return to the narrow, strictly instrumen-talist conception of his youth. There is an aporia about action in Benjamin's notion of now-time which the rise of fascism in Germany turned to stone. Yet the momentariness of Benjamin's 'now' may be less of a barrier to a development of his project in the direction of identification and action than Habermas's criticisms suggest. For while it prohibits the kind of immanent conceptual relation to practice to which the Hegelian tradition aspires, its very evanescence raises the prospect of the re-establishment of a narrative temporality, energized, enriched and thereby transformed by the disruptive after-image of the 'now'. In this respect, it is less the momentariness of the 'now' that is the problem than the insulation of Benjamin's account of now-time from a more broadly based hermeneutics of historical existence of the kind we have been working towards in this book.

To pursue this further, beyond the limits of Benjamin's self-understanding, we need only think of the way interruption functions within various modernist art practices as a determinate negation of the structures to which they are historically related, and to which they are hence inextricably linked, semantically, as the other side of a dialectical pair.[163] Once we do this, it becomes apparent that now-time is not so phenomenologically self-sufficient, so absolutely independent of the time of narrative, as Benjamin's presentation of the monadic self-sufficiency of the experience of the image might lead us to suppose. Rather, it lends itself to dialectical integration into Ricoeur's model of historical temporalization (historization) as a threefold narrative mimesis, introduced above,[164] at the intermediate level of 'mimesis 2'; albeit at the cost of certain structural modifications of the model.

There are three main things to note about Ricoeur's presentation of this model, from the standpoint of such a reintegration. The first is the doubling of narrative at the 'prefigurative' stage of level 1, as the temporal structure of human action *and* its everyday interpretation. (This is the only level at which Ricoeur is prepared to concede onto-logical significance to narrativity.) The second is Ricoeur's insistence on the narrative structure of the configuration of historical time at level 2, mediating phenomenological with cosmological time. (This is the mediation which, so we argued against Ricoeur, has history as its *ontological* condition.) Finally, there is the disjunctive role played by the time of reception as a time of initiative, at level 3, where the retroactive effect of configuration (level 2) upon its prefigurative base (level 1 reappearing as level 3) is the refiguration of an 'imperfect' mediation.

At first sight, the integration of now-time into this model at the mediating stage of level 2 looks unlikely, if not impossible, since its metonymic figuration of history through images is resolutely non-narrative – anti-narrative in fact: 'History breaks down into images, not into stories.'[165] How can now-time play a mediating role between phenomenological and cosmological time if it has been 'blasted' out of all forms of narrative continuity? The secret lies, firstly, in the Messianic character possessed by nature: that 'hidden collusion between change that destroys – forgetting, aging, death – and time that simply passes', which we noted in chapter 2 (cosmological time as absolute exteriority);[166] secondly, in the relational meaning of now-time as interruption (interruption of narrative); and thirdly, in the fact that what appears at Ricoeur's level 1 as the everyday interpretation of action already involves some form of historical consciousness – Heidegger's 'ordinary understanding of history', for example, or Benjamin's historicism as the everyday historical consciousness of modernity (modernity as tradition). If the mediating role laid down in Ricoeur's account of historical time is ontological, rather than merely poetic in significance (as we have argued), level 1 will be 'always already' historical, and Ricoeur's threefold schema will actually be a cycle in which mimesis 1 is the sedimented result of mimesis 3 from a previous circuit.[167]

Phenomenologically, historical time is not constituted from scratch, repeatedly, at every moment, as Ricoeur's quasi-Heideggerian model suggests.[168] Rather, its configuration is already a refiguration of its prefiguration in everyday life. Configuration is itself refiguration, or as Benjamin puts it: '"construction" presupposes "destruction".'[169] *Now-time configures historical time as a redemptive whole by its mode of interruption (refiguration) of the narrative continuity of its everyday form.* Disjunction is thus, in this instance (montage), already a function of configuration at level 2, prior to any disjunctive effect produced by its reintegration into the lived 'time of initiative' at level 3. So radical is this first disjunction, in fact, that we have had reason to doubt the possibility of its reintegration into the narrative continuity of experience. From the standpoint of Benjamin's now, the problem we face is thus the exact opposite of that dealt with by Ricoeur in his attempt to hold onto historical totalization without commitment to closure. We need a conceptual bridge back from now-time to a new narrativity, such that its disjunctive power might have a transformative effect on modes of identification and action. Unless we can find one, Benjamin's ecstatic 'now' will remain a *mere* 'time-lag' or 'in-between', without historical force.[170]

This bridge back to narrativity is blocked within Benjamin's own thought by the depiction of modernity in terms of the social eclipse of narrative as communicable experience ('The Storyteller'). Yet for all the insights of the sociology of modernity from which this picture derives, it is hard to think of the death of narrative as anything more than a regulative fiction since, as Ricoeur puts it: 'we have no idea what a culture would be where no one any longer knew what it meant to narrate things.'[171] Rather, what is occurring is the death of a particular form of narrativity, which Benjamin calls 'tradition'. Modernity destroys tradition, but it does not thereby destroy narrative. Indeed, as Benjamin's own analysis shows, modernity destroys tradition only in its traditional form. Tradition is replaced, not just by the time-consciousness of modernity in its pure, most abstract form, but also (and more lastingly) by a variety of rearticulations of narrative continuity within the temporal terms of modernity itself. We find an account of one such rearticulation in Benjamin's analysis of the time-consciousness of historicism as the basis for narratives of progress – that narrative form which dominates the historical consciousness of social democracy, much to Benjamin's distress. More recently, attention has been drawn to the pervasive tendency within modernity towards the 'invention' of traditions, with a hitherto unseen degree of self-consciousness, as an integral part of the formation of nations, as the destruction of tradition provokes its willed restitution, in increasingly artificial forms.[172] There is no reason to doubt the power of such inventions to articulate experience, albeit in a different sense from that conveyed by Benjamin's emphatic use of the word *Erfahrung*. In their most extreme, exclusionary, and *modernistic* form (as myth), such inventions provide an ideological basis for fascism, as we shall see in the next chapter.

It is a symptom of Benjamin's confusion here that the idea of the death of narrative is itself a narrative idea. Indeed, it is part of a particular narrative tradition, apocalyptic narrative, which has a foundational significance for Western culture. (A similar point applies to Lyotard's somewhat weaker thesis of the end of 'grand' narratives: it is itself a grand narrative; grander, in fact, than most of those it would consign to oblivion.) However, there has been a shift in emphasis within this narrative tradition in the modern period (detectable as early as Elizabethan tragedy, on Kermode's account), from the depiction of the 'last days' of mankind to that of the preceding time of crisis, as apocalyptic predictions were repeatedly invalidated, but apocalyptic narrative itself was not (interestingly enough) thereby discredited.[173] Apocalypse became a myth of crisis. It is against this generalized sense of crisis, characteristic of the time-consciousness of modernity as perpetual transition, that Benjamin wanted to restore the *finality* of the original version of apocalypse in a new form, freed from the logical constraints of having to posit a *narrative* completion of history.

It is the specific function of the metonymic structure of the dialectical image to figure temporal completion without having to establish a narrative continuity between the present and some particular end. As such, however, now-time is nonetheless still parasitic upon the temporal culture of apocalyptic narrative, since it depends upon a reading of the spatial completeness of the image in temporal terms, as a figure for the extra-historical perspective of an end to time. (The idea of the end of time must be present in advance, even if only unconsciously.) Now-time may thus be seen to have a dialectical relation to narrativity, at once outside and within, in a way which is analogous to the place of the unconscious in the human psyche. It is, one might say, an historically produced experience of our constitutive outside (nature) as the productivity of the limit of experience itself (the anticipation of death). As we saw in our discussion of Heidegger in chapter 2, this limit produces time as an open-ended but tensely structured narrativity. By intensifying the interruptive element of this narrativity, now-time draws attention to its utopian core: a pair of ideals (fulfilment and equality) which derive their meaning from the level of history as whole.

Something similar to this shift in the form of narrative has occurred internally to the structure of the novel, as the narrativity of tradition has given way to the more complex and fractured temporalities of modernity. These developments (essentially, a structural refusal of narrative completion) are frequently understood as anti-narrative tendencies. Yet as Ricoeur has shown, they are more properly conceived as modifications in narrative form, since the criterion of narrative completeness can be abandoned without giving up the idea of closure, essential to narrative unity. Today, we are more likely to view a well-closed fiction as one which 'opens an abyss . . . in our symbolic apprehension of the world', rather than trying to complete the realization of a particular mode of symbolization.[174] Closure, as opposed to completeness, can function as a form of interruption in its own right. In fact, narrative closure figures completion, without having to project a determinate historical content, in the same way that the spatial self-sufficiency of the dialectical image figures the completion of history as a whole.

There is thus no reason to fear that a mediating return from now-time to narrativity need reintroduce the requirement of narrative completion into history – although we may continue to project completion at the level of *fantasy*, in order to take part in debates about the historical meaning of the present which pass beyond registering its lack (lack of fulfilment and equality), to pose concrete alternatives for the future. Rather, within this mediated return, the memory or after-image of the now might be thought to provide a measure of temporal fulfilment, doubling the disruptive futurity of Ricoeur's time of initiative by providing a more emphatic sense of the present as lack, and hence of the need for completion. (The basic principle of historical materialism 'is not progress, but actualisation'.[175]) Benjamin's 'now' can thus be conceived as an integral moment within a new, non-traditional, future-oriented and internally disrupted form of narrativity.

What might the politics of such a new narrativity be? At this point, it is useful to return to Heidegger and his horizonal notion of the ecstatic, to ponder the political dangers inherent in Benjamin's refiguration of the temporality of modernity into a metonymic experience of history as a whole: the hijacking of its interruptive futurity by the conservative revolution of a *reactionary* modernism (fascism as reactionary modernism). For there are certain similarities between Benjamin's and Heidegger's views about time which contrast sharply with the differences between their political commitments to Communism and fascism, respectively. Consideration of these affinities in the context of their accompanying differences will provide us with the opportunity to establish a more nuanced relationship to both bodies of work, before bringing our inquiry to a close. It will also return us, at a different level, to the topic from which we set out: the extraordinary complexity of modernity as the historical temporality of the new.

5

Avant-Garde and Everyday

Everyday life has until now resisted the historical.

Guy Debord

That Heidegger was a National Socialist is well known. That there is a connection between this political commitment and his philosophical thought is increasingly acknowledged. What the precise character of this connection is, however, remains highly contested. Much of the dispute is internal to the interpretation of Heidegger's philosophical writings: the meaning of 'resoluteness' in *Being and Time*, for example, or the dating and significance of the 'turn' in his thought, away from the existential analytic of *Dasein* toward an epochal account of the history of Being dominated by the relationship between metaphysics and technology. The complexity of the textual issues here is often daunting. However, there is also a broader context from which these matters ultimately cannot be disengaged, involving debates about fascism itself. For as an object of reflection and inquiry, 'fascism' is notoriously resistant to conventional forms of political and ideological analysis. Herein, in part, lies its significance: fascism problematizes 'the political', while presenting itself as its truth.[1] As such, it opens itself up to philosophical forms of interpretation and analysis which, while based on its history as a political movement, nonetheless of necessity exceed its bounds. From this perspective, fascism is no *merely* political form – one among a series of alternatives to be listed in the catalogues of comparative politics as competing forms of organization or rule – but a manifestation of deep-rooted historical, or even metaphysical, tendencies or possibilities of the age.

This was certainly how both Benjamin and Heidegger conceived it in the 1930s. For Benjamin, fascism was an 'aestheticization of politics', a political management of aesthetics which exploited the technological and cultural potential of modernity for reactionary and destructive ends. As such, it is a permanent possibility inherent in the social forms of modernity itself.[2] For Heidegger, on the other hand, for a time at least, National Socialism was the political representative of a force for national renewal which corresponded to the deepest practical impulses of his own thought.[3] Later, in a displacement of his disappointment with it onto its ideologues, it would be judged to have betrayed its 'inner truth and greatness' by misunderstanding its historical task.[4] In the end, it came to be seen as an exemplary expression of the very forces to which Heidegger had initially hoped it was the antidote.

I shall not pursue Heidegger's belated interpretation of National Socialism as a manifestation of planetary technology here, although I am considerably less impressed by it than some.[5] Nor shall I consider Benjamin's futurist-inspired analysis of fascism as a political manipulation of the need for expression. Rather, I shall take the notion of aestheticization more literally as the cue for an inquiry into the politics of Heidegger's analysis of temporality in *Being and Time*: the politics of what is effectively an *aestheticization of ontology* or ontologization of transcendental aesthetics.[6]

Any appeal to the notion of fascism in a philosophical analysis of temporality is fraught with dangers. Name-calling, political reductionism, guilt by association – all threaten to trivialize, travesty or otherwise compromise the seriousness of the inquiry. In this case, there is also the danger of anachronism, since the publication of *Being and Time* predates Heidegger's apparently sudden conversion to the cause of National Socialism in the spring of 1933 by a full six years.[7] Yet there can be no doubt that the politics of nations is at stake in the analysis of 'co-historizing' as 'destiny' in *Being and Time*; or that, as Wolin puts it, following Löwith, 'Heidegger intended his political involvements of the 1930s as *the existentielle consummation of the categorial framework of his 1927 book*; more specifically, . . . the philosopher viewed his entry into the Nazi party as a concrete historical manifestation of authentic resolute existence.'[8]

Being and Time is remarkable for its attempt to derive its account of authentic existence directly from its analysis of time. However, this does not make it a 'fascist' text or Heidegger's existentialism a fascistic philosophy. The 'consistency' which Löwith notes between Heidegger's political involvement and the 'fundamental thesis' of *Being and Time*[9] is too weak a basis upon which to build a political reading of that text. In fact, it encourages a biographical one, insofar as it makes Heidegger's political commitment an exemplary instance of an existential choice. After all, why should Heidegger have chosen

fascism as opposed to, for example, Communism? (The conversion of
Lukács to Communism in the aftermath of the First World War, in
the context of a similarly Kierkegaardian philosophical background,
springs to mind as an alternative instance of such a choice.) A
conceptual connection between the argument of *Being and Time* and
the *content* of Heidegger's political choice must be established,
if the book is to submit to a properly political reading. Here both
the specificity of Heidegger's understanding of fascism (his 'private
National Socialism'[10]) and the prematurity of *Being and Time* in
relation to his political choice must be taken into account. For each
suggests that the key to Heidegger's politics is to be found not in the
concept of fascism as such, but in a specification of the broader yet
related notion of conservative revolution.

Conservative revolution: fascism as reactionary modernism

'Conservative revolution' is a phrase coined by Hugo von
Hofmannsthal in 1927 to refer to the politics of radical reaction
which prospered in Germany in the period immediately after the First
World War. It marks a distinctive adaptation of the Romantic tradition of counter-revolution against the Enlightenment to the changed
circumstances of the twentieth century. The distinguishing feature of
this politics was its combination of an aggressive rejection of social,
cultural and political modernity with an *embrace of technology*,
which it detached from the semantic context of 'civilization' and
symbolically recoded in terms of an irrationalist and nationalistic
conception of 'culture' (*Kultur*). Pioneers of the search for a 'third
way' between capitalism and Communism, conservative revolutionaries such as Spengler and Jünger (both of whom Heidegger referred
to frequently in his early Freiburg lectures) are generally held to have
laid the intellectual foundations for the success of National Socialism.
As the first organization fully to exploit modern technology for
political ends, the Nazis directly appropriated many of their themes.
However, ideologically, German fascism is nonetheless a distinct
form, insofar as it developed its own racial mythology. How central
such mythologies are to the concept of fascism in general – as
opposed to its specific German variant, Hitlerism – is one of the issues
at stake in the debate over Heidegger's politics. Few of either Hitler's
allies or opponents in the early 1930s envisaged the extent to which
his personal ideology would become a decisive political fact in the
development of the Nazi regime.[11]

Heidegger no more shared the conservative revolutionaries' unrestrained enthusiasm for technology than he did the Nazis' biologistic racial version of nationalism; although he did believe that the Germans had a special mission to combine *Technik* and *Kultur*.[12] What he did share with both of them, however, was a diagnosis of the world-historical situation as one of crisis and decline, a nationalist definition of its political shape (conservative revolution as *national* revolution), and a hope for the future grounded in a quite particular revolutionary temporality of renewal. Like the conservative revolutionaries' affirmative but mystical relation to technology, this sense of crisis had its origins in the First World War and its immediate aftermath in the turbulence of the Weimar Republic. It came to a head in the trauma of the Great Slump (1929–32), which provided the Nazis with their opportunity for power. For the German Right as a whole, the postwar years were fundamentally defined by the experience of war, as the 'afterwar' (*Nachkriege*). This experience was, first, that of the extraordinary (destructive) power of modern technology; and second, one of extreme national humiliation and loss. Out of this dual experience sprang a mystical theory of war (exemplified by the writings of Ernst Jünger) which was simultaneously *nationalistic*, *technological* and *cultic*. Germany was to be reborn through a new symbolic dimension, manifest most fully in war, in which '*the natural* reaches through the plaster layers of the modern cities and fills the operation of machines and cleaned-up marionettes with a deeper life, one superior to the purposeful life and whose essence cannot be grasped with mathematics.'[13]

Heidegger's appropriation of aspects of Jünger's thought is well known.[14] However, it is less the mystical-technological aspect of what Herf has dubbed 'reactionary modernism' with which I am concerned – although it undoubtedly helps to explain Heidegger's mistake about the Nazis' relation to technology – than the paradoxical temporality of the ideas of conservative revolution and reactionary modernism themselves. For like all fundamental political categories of modernity (such as crisis, to which it was a response), conservative revolution is an essentially temporal notion. It is also, of course, a central term in Habermas's critique of Benjamin's thought.[15] We can interpret Herf's notion of reactionary modernism in strictly temporal terms. The problem with Herf's own more restricted definition (the conjunction of a backward-looking politics with an affirmation of technology) is that its modernism is identified with technology, rather than with the temporal structure of the combination itself. The latter consequently appears as the paradoxical product of a mere aggregate of contradictory tendencies, rather than a novel, complex, but *integral* form of modernism in its own right.

This leads Wolin, for example, to conflate the ideology of conservative revolution with 'the entrenched *anti*modernism of the German mandarin intelligentsia'.[16] On the other hand, Herf opposes Heidegger's position to reactionary modernism, on the grounds of his views about technology, despite their common temporal structure.[17] Yet, as a counter-*revolutionary* ideology, conservative revolution is modernist in the full temporal sense (outlined in chapter 1) of affirming the temporality of the new. Its image of the future may derive from the mythology of some lost origin or suppressed national essence, but its temporal dynamic is rigorously futural. In this respect, it is the term 'conservative' which is the misnomer, rather than 'revolution'. Conservative revolution is a form of revolutionary *reaction*. It understands that what it would 'conserve' is already lost (if indeed it ever existed, which is doubtful), and hence must be created anew. It recognizes that under such circumstances the chance presents itself fully to realize this 'past' *for the first time*. The fact that the past in question is primarily imaginary is thus no impediment to its political force, but rather its very condition (myth). Hence the conduciveness of Herf's label to a strictly temporal reading, despite his own more restricted definition.

What Herf calls reactionary modernism is not a hybrid form (modernism + reaction). Rather, it draws our attention to the modernistic temporality of reaction *per se*, once the destruction of traditional forms of social authority has gone beyond a certain point. This point appears to have been reached in the leading European societies around the time of the First World War; hence the tremendous contemporary upsurge of revolutionary ideologies of both 'reactionary' and 'progressive' types. Moreover, this should not be conceived as a merely transitional phenomenon – in the way, for example, that a certain historical revisionism would now see the whole period from 1914–45 as *merely* a transitional, if exceptionally troubled, phase between stages of capitalist development. For both may be regarded as temporally integral political forms of capitalist societies, alternative political articulations of the revolutionary temporality of the social form of capital accumulation itself: that 'constant revolutionising of production, uninterrupted disturbance of all social conditions, everlasting uncertainty and agitation', which Marx and Engels identified as the distinguishing feature of the present epoch nearly one hundred and fifty years ago.[18]

Marx and Engels's error was to see in this process an ultimately linear tendency towards the elimination of every social bond 'other than naked self-interest . . . callous "cash payment"': a drowning of 'the heavenly ecstasies of religious fervour, of chivalrous enthusiasm, of philistine sentimentalism, in the icy waters of egotistical calculation'.[19] To the contrary, it has turned out to involve, not their elimination, but their *transformation* and *contradictory reintegration* into the fabric of social relations in capitalist societies. As Balibar has argued, the history of capitalist societies is best viewed as 'a history of the *reactions* of the complex of "non-economic" social relations, which are the binding agent of a historical collectivity of individuals, to the de-structuring with which the expansion of the value form threatens them.'[20] This applies as much to those Marx cites (religion, occupational status, family, nation, age and sex) as to those he omits (race, ethnicity). Indeed, one might go so far as to say that it is the contested articulation of these relations with those of the production and circulation of capital which constitutes the political process in capitalist societies. The historical articulation of temporal form is one of the main things at stake in such struggles.[21]

There are at least three 'revolutionary' temporalities at play, quite apart from the various rearticulations of temporalities of tradition: the hegemonic temporality of the self-revolutionizing process of capitalist production; the revolutionary temporality of the oppositional practice of social transformation in the name of a new, post-capitalist (traditionally, socialist) economic form; and the counter-revolutionary temporality of a variety of reactionary modernisms. Both the second and third of these present themselves at the cultural level as avant-garde (by virtue of their explicit political identifications with radically new futures); while the first could be said to correspond, culturally, to modernism in its regulated, post-World War Two sense as 'the tradition of the new'.[22]

The hypothesis guiding what follows is that Heidegger did not become a National Socialist because of what we now identify as the distinctive ideological traits of Nazism (anti-Semitism and biologistic racism – Heidegger always rejected the latter), but because the Nazis appeared to him as the authentic representatives of conservative revolution in Germany. From the standpoint of the temporal structure of its project, fascism is a particularly radical form of conservative revolution. National Socialism was a reactionary avant-garde. It is here that its pertinence to the understanding of modernity as a temporalization of history lies (along with the pertinence of a political reading of Heidegger's philosophy): in the temporality of what Lacoue-Labarthe and Nancy have called the 'Nazi myth'.[23]

On this analysis, a myth is a narrative symbolizing a distant origin which posits the present as the site of its 'total self-fulfilment'. National Socialism was based upon a mythical construction of the German people (*Volk*) as an organic, racial-spiritual whole. In instituting a struggle over the 'means of identification' in the name of this myth, it posited the realization within and against the present of the truth of its originary meaning. However, this meaning, represented by the Nazis as inherent in the biological constitution of the German people as the 'soul' of the race (essentially, its 'culture-bearing' ability to found civilizations), was actually, of course, an extremely recent invention. Indeed, as Hobsbawm points out, 'the race destined through Hitler to dominate the world did not even have a name until 1898 when an anthropologist coined the term "Nordic".'[24] Its very existence, historically, was contingent upon the speculations of the new science of genetics; while its future (the realization of the myth) depended on the application of the new 'knowledge' as eugenics. As such, the Nazis' 'German people' was less the symbolic reflection of any kind of historical continuity, of culture or descent, than the expression of the will to power of a purely constructive present, the nationalism of a pure modernity – that *will to will* which Heidegger would later identify (in his 1940 essay on Nietzsche's metaphysics) as part of the essence of nihilism.[25]

Thus, contrary to received opinion, although fascism may involve the social mobilization of residual or even archaic forces resistant to modernity – the attempt 'to make the rebellion of suppressed nature against domination directly useful to domination'[26] – it should not thereby itself be judged archaic or even 'noncontemporaneous'[27] as a political form. Rather, like the rise of various neo-nationalisms, religious 'fundamentalisms' and racisms today,[28] it is neither a relic nor an archaism, but a form of *political modernism*; just as Heidegger's existentialism is a form of *philosophical modernism*. What the two have in common is a quite particular (reactionary) articulation or inflection of the temporality of modernity. Fascism is a reactionary political modernism; Heidegger's existentialism is a reactionary philosophical modernism – in the literal sense of 'reaction' as a movement towards the reversal of an existing tendency or state of affairs. Italian futurism, the poetry of Eliot and Pound, and the novels of Wyndham Lewis have long been recognized as examples of politically reactionary artistic modernisms;[29] although some have found the conjunction hard to swallow. What I am suggesting is that the temporal structure of such phenomena contains the key to a broader understanding of the politics of reaction more generally.

Furthermore, just as we may read historicism as a 'bad' modernity (in Hegel's sense of the bad infinity),[30] so reactionary modernism may be understood as a bad modernism; not (or not primarily) in a moral or political sense, but in terms of the contradiction internal to its temporal structure. This structure – the structure of radical reaction within and against modernity – is of necessity contradictory, since one of the things it aims to reverse is the production of the very temporality to which it is itself subject. Radical reaction cannot but reproduce, and thereby performatively affirm, the temporal form of the very thing against which it is pitted (modernity). Hence the necessity for it to misrepresent its temporal structure to itself as some kind of 'recovery' or 'return'. As we shall see, this is also one of the effects of Heidegger's discourse on 'Being', as it is of the historical dimension of most religious discourses.[31]

National Socialism radicalized the nationalist dimension of conservative revolution both ideologically and organizationally: ideologically, by turning it into an 'anti-Jewish revolution';[32] organizationally, by providing it with a new kind of political party at the head of a mass movement. (The ideologues of conservative revolution, in the restricted historical sense in which it predates National Socialism, had retained a certain attachment to traditional political élites.)[33] In the process, the Nazis also radicalized the mythic dimension of its temporal structure. It was *this* radicalization with which Heidegger identified in the fantasy of his 'private National Socialism', despite his rejection of the Nazis' biologistic racial coding of the myth, in favour of a more abstruse philosophical version deriving from eighteenth-century Hellenism.[34] Heidegger's politics in the 1930s were those of a 'heroico-tragic' national-revolutionism of the Right,[35] for which his philosophy provided both the inspiration and the interpretive frame. All that was needed for their union was for the Nazis to recognize this philosophy as the truth of their project and Heidegger himself as their spiritual-intellectual leader. Heidegger appears to have clung onto this hope, despite its relatively swift disappointment by the Nazi establishment, for some considerable time.[36] The roots of this kind of identification and aspiration in the thematics and political history of nineteenth-century German philosophy have been expounded elsewhere.[37] Here it is the philosophical specificity of Heidegger's fantasy, rather than its discursive conditions, which is at issue.

What is the relationship between the ecstatic-horizonal temporality of *Dasein*, as lived in the moment of vision and resolute decision (outlined in *Being and Time*), and the temporal structure of conservative

revolution as a reactionary political modernism? How is each related
to the ecstatic dimension of the totality which structures Benjamin's
conception of historical experience? And what, if any, are the political
implications of our extension of Heidegger's argument about death to
history? These are the questions which must be addressed if Benjamin's
conception of historical time is to be uprooted from its original context
and put to work critically in the present, in the way that was suggested
at the end of the previous chapter.

Vision and decision: existence as repetition (against decisionism)

Being and Time is remarkable for its attempt to derive an account
of authentic existence directly from its analysis of time as temporalization. The main stages of this argument concern: (1) the origin of
temporality in the anticipation of death and the determination of
existence as finite transcendence; (2) the exposition of authenticity
(*Eigentlichkeit*: literally, ownness or propriety) as the 'existentiell'
appropriation (*Aneignung*: literally, making one's own) by *Dasein* of
its existential structure; (3) the elaboration of such appropriation
as anticipatory resoluteness in the face of death, or the choice of
fate; and (4) the characterization of this choice in terms of the idea
of destiny as the 'historizing' of a people (*Volk*). Stage one is the
founding philosophical gesture and unique achievement of Heidegger's
existentialism. Stage two adopts and existentially reworks the structure of reflection constitutive of the metaphysical definition of the
subject, to provide *Dasein* with an immanent factical ideal.[38] At
the third stage, this ontological structure of possible propriety
acquires a more definite (ontical) orientation, via the categories of
situation and *heritage* (*Erbschaft*). Finally, the account is completed
by the addition of a social dimension, giving its complex practical
structure a determinate political meaning. Only at this fourth stage
does it become possible for Heidegger to think history as the product
of the 'co-historizing' of *Dasein* or 'historizing of peoples'. The
authentic temporality of anticipatory resoluteness appears here as
'authentic historicality': the repetition (*Wiederholung*) of a heritage of
possibilities, through a process of 'communication and struggle' in
which, it is said, 'the power of destiny becomes free.'[39]

Such repetition is described by Heidegger as occurring in a
'moment of vision' (*Augenblick*: literally, a glance of an eye) which
'*deprives* the "today" of its character *as present*'. In the temporal

difference constitutive of repetition in the moment of vision, history appears as 'the "recurrence" of the possible'. This is contrasted with a situation in which 'one's existence . . . is loaded down with the legacy of a 'past' which has become unrecognisable, and . . . seeks the modern (*das Moderne*).'[40] Heidegger is thus explicitly opposed to the interpretation of his work in terms of the category of the modern. Yet in the concrete futurity of vision and decision, and the underlying existential priority of possibility over actuality, that is precisely what it is revealed to be. The difficulty consists less in understanding Heidegger as a distinctively 'modern' thinker than in comprehending the way in which he turns the temporality of modernity against itself, by combining a sense of futurity as the essence of existence (finite transcendence) with the idea of destiny, to produce a radically reactionary point of view. The key lies in the novelty of his conception of repetition. For it is here, it will be argued, rather than in any kind of 'decisionism', that the politics of Heidegger's temporalization of history is to be found.

To see how this works, we need to attend to what we might call the 'double coding' of *Being and Time*, whereby its strictly existential or deconstructive aspect is underwritten by a prior and unstated conception of history, associated with a correspondingly unexamined set of sociological assumptions. These unexamined assumptions are the source of the interpretive determinacy which gives the book its phenomenological force or living meaning. This double coding is marked within the text itself in the definition of *Dasein* as a being which is 'ontically distinctive in that it *is* ontological': a being whose understanding of Being is a 'definite characteristic' of its own being.[41] However, as we shall see, this ontical-ontological factor plays a far greater role in the book than that which is formally prescribed for it. There is an *overdetermination of the ontological by the ontical* in *Being and Time* which structures the book as a whole. In this respect, it is quite impossible to 'extract ourselves from all gestures of valorisation and from their prejudices or presuppositions' – as Nancy, for example, hopes[42] – in order to be true to the purely deconstructive, or more strictly existential, side of Heidegger's argument. Or, at any rate, it is impossible to do this without liquidating the book's practical side, by accepting 'the impossibility of a practical philosophy drawn from the "thought of being"' of *whatever* kind – a position to which the deconstructive strategy (derived from Heidegger's later writings) appears inevitably to lead.[43] To do this, however, is to obliterate the site of greatest interest in Heidegger's early work: the relationship of time to politics. On the other hand, one must acknowledge that it is the (failed) attempt to read *Being and Time* purely deconstructively, in defensive response to the debates over Heidegger's politics, which has brought its dual structure most clearly to the fore.[44] In the process, it has also served to highlight the inadequacies of the prevailing 'left' interpretation of the politics of *Being and Time* in terms of the idea of decisionism.

It would not be too much of an exaggeration to say that Heidegger's existentialism is a philosophy of freedom which lacks a concept of action, and deliberately so. Its fundamental impulse is practical (the search for a 'proper' or 'authentic' existence), yet its theoretical terms subvert the very idea of practice as traditionally construed, as an object of deductions from principles. In the order of systematic philosophy since Aristotle, ethics and politics follow from metaphysics as first philosophy. Yet it is precisely this conception of philosophy as metaphysics ('the traditional content of ancient ontology') which Heidegger sets out in *Being and Time* to 'destroy'.[45] We must thus seek the practical meaning of the book elsewhere, in the terms of this destruction itself.

This is, in fact, the first move in the decisionist reading. It acknowledges the undermining of the traditional conception of action by the existential understanding of the self, and the replacement of the notion of the will by the existential determination of 'resoluteness'. However, in rejecting all normative principles which might function as regulative measures of resoluteness (as constraints on *Dasein*'s essential existential openness), *Being and Time* is taken to open up a theoretical vacuum around action – '[i]n the moment of vision nothing can occur'[46] – into which a positive but arbitrary notion of the will inevitably flows, as the actual determinant of resolute existence. Existentialism is thus understood politically to lead to decisionism, despite the contradiction between the (subjectivistic) philosophical terms of this notion of the will and Heidegger's concept of existence. An 'energetic but empty' sense of possibility collapses into the positivism of an identification with authority.[47] This regression is marked within Heidegger's text in the 'secular mystical fatalism' according to which individual decisions are only authentic if they repeat the 'destiny of the people' to which *Dasein* belongs. Destiny is thus interpreted here as an authoritarian political category through which individualistic and organic-collectivist perspectives are fused, to produce a situation in which subordination to a *völkisch* authority masquerades as radical freedom. Authentic existence is a constantly reiterated leap into communal identification, wherein the content of action is externally determined by the authority best able to promote itself, at any particular moment, as the embodiment of the destiny of the people. At best, 'the logic of *Being and Time* oscillates indecisively pro and contra the heritage of philosophical subjectivism'; at worst, it is *'nakedly opportunistic'*.[48]

This reading fits well with the subsequent development of Heidegger's thought, insofar as the latter was motivated by the attempt to eliminate the remnants of metaphysical subjectivism implicit in earlier formulations. In fact, it is arguable that Heidegger's political involvement during the period of his rectorship functioned experimentally, as a test of the activist side of his thought. The acknowledged 'failure' of the rectorship (Heidegger's own description) may then be seen to register the failure of *Being and Time* itself, leading Heidegger to rethink its terms.[49] This is borne out by the lectures on Nietzsche (1936–40), albeit with 1938 rather than 1934 appearing as the turning point, theoretically speaking.[50] The engagement with Nazism appears as the key to the later writings, in which the idea of 'releasement' or 'letting-be' (*Gelassenheit*), as a 'will not to will', replaces the wilful resoluteness of the decision of existence, as Heidegger retreats from the technologically dominated world of action into a supposedly more deeply historical 'thinking at the end of philosophy' in preparation for a new epoch of Being. With the termination of the attempt to find an existential equivalent to practical reason, world history is reduced to a mere aspect of a self-sufficient, philosophically defined, 'history of Being'.[51]

However, there are problems with this approach which go beyond its reduction of the specificity of existential analysis to an unstable combination of previously established positions: 'voluntarism', 'fatalism', 'decisionism', etc.;[52] beyond the problem of the will, and the question of whether resoluteness does or does not imply 'the deliberate action of a subject', whatever Heidegger may have intended.[53] They concern its neglect of the temporal logic of 'authentic historicality', its neglect of repetition. Decisionist interpretations of resoluteness attribute its determinacy in practice to its indeterminacy in theory; an indeterminacy which exalts the pathos of decision, while capitulating to power.[54] Yet for all the absence of regulative *principles*, Heidegger's resoluteness is far from being as lacking in determinacy as this reading suggests. It is true that it is the situation, and the situation alone, which is always decisive, in the sense of giving concrete factical content to the constantly reiterated 'decision to exist'. But if it is to be authentic, the character of this resolution must nonetheless be shaped by *Dasein's* appropriation of its historicality as repetition.[55] There is a temporal structure of meaning to Heidegger's concept of resoluteness, ignored in its decisionist interpretation, which gives it a measure of determinacy by providing the framework for the process of 'communication and struggle' which is taken by Heidegger to be constitutive of resolution itself.[56]

Indeed, we might go so far as to say that Heidegger's notion of historicality *narrativizes resoluteness as repetition*: the repetition of the heritage of a people. It thereby provides *Dasein* with a form of historical identification with a definite political meaning. In *authentic* historicality, the possible always (and only) recurs as the possibility of repeating the past. Furthermore, despite the existential formality of Heidegger's discourse on repetition as a consequence of thrownness, it is accompanied in *Being and Time* by a conception of history of a quite different (epochal) order, whereby (in a founding instance of the overdetermination of the ontological by the ontical, referred to above) the logic of Heidegger's personal philosophical development is projected as the structure of historicality itself. Within this conception, the present is narrated as crisis and decline (loss of living meaning), while the future appears within the horizon of a 'return to a new beginning' through a recovery of the hitherto concealed meaning of metaphysics, via the interrogation of its Greek origin: that 'raising anew' of the 'forgotten' question of the meaning of Being which institutes the discourse of *Being and Time* as fundamental ontology.[57]

It is a mistake, in this respect, to think of *Being and Time* as a purely existential text, and the movement of Heidegger's thought away from it as one of increasing historicization (from 'existence' to the 'history of Being'). *Being and Time* already embodies a form of historical consciousness, immanently, in its founding philosophical act. This consciousness reappears later, condensed, in Heidegger's concept of repetition. It sums up the experience of Heidegger's prior intellectual trajectory: from (1) his initial acceptance of the system of Catholicism (with its roots in the medieval reception of Aristotle), via (2) a critique of this system from the standpoint of Husserl's phenomenology (understood as philosophical modernity, the intellectual representative of the 'living present'), to (3) an ontological critique of phenomenology (using the phenomenological *recovery* of Aristotle's ontology to explode the structure of phenomenology itself, from within).[58]

It is this final move which is crucial to Heidegger's sense of repetition, since it brings together the *radical futurity* associated with his reception of the phenomenological concept of the 'stream of life', with his *backward-looking* interest in Aristotle as the origin or source of the system of Catholicism, into a new conception of historical experience.[59] The depth and continuity of Heidegger's theological concerns is, in this regard, central to the historical dimension of his philosophy, since it sustained his interest in Aristotle, whose work he wanted to liberate from the dead hand of tradition (scholasticism). This led to what Kisiel describes as the 'peculiar backflow' of ancient ontology into Heidegger's attempt to radicalize Husserl's critique of neo-Kantian objectivism. Its outcome, *Being and Time*, is a peculiarly 'neo-Hellenic' form of phenomenology.[60] Heidegger's existentialism is neo-Hellenic phenomenology. Hence his reluctance to associate it with Kierkegaard, despite a series of both terminological and conceptual parallels.[61] Nonetheless, it is also Christian theology, due to the character of its interest in ontology. Heidegger's acknowledgement of the 'fundamental atheism of philosophy' (1922) modified, but did not contradict, his sense of himself as a 'Christian theo*logian*', working on a project he described to Bultmann in the wake of the publication of *Being and Time* as 'an ontological founding of Christian theology as a science'.[62] Indeed, only his relation to Catholicism can explain how Heidegger could have viewed the destruction of Greek ontology as a 'critique of the *present*' – a phrase which recurs in his manuscripts from the early 1920s, anticipating Foucault's reflections on the ethos of Enlightenment.[63] Furthermore, this theological dimension underpins the transformation which takes place in the meaning of temporality in the passage from 'possibility' (death) to 'repetition' (history), since it fosters the sense of authentic existence as a '*return* to a new beginning' – a paradoxical temporal dynamic which is incomprehensible without a sense of Being as the originating source of historicity itself, and hence as having once been in some sense 'prior' to, or 'outside' of, time. In the process, the existential openness of *Dasein* to the future is reduced to a mere formality in the face of the people's 'appointed task' of entering into its endowment.[64] In the case of the German people, for Heidegger, this was (somewhat abstrusely) the philosophical endowment of Greek thought: the question of the meaning of Being.

It is here, in the mapping of a specific national (and nationalistic) narrative of originary meaning onto the existential structure of resoluteness, via repetition, that the politics of *Being and Time* is to be found; rather than in the ecstatic dimension of its temporal structure as such. Indeed, this ecstatic structure has to be overridden by Heidegger – or reduced to an empty formalism, at least – in order that historicality may be given a political meaning through repetition. The problem with Heidegger's work is thus actually the reverse of that suggested by the decisionist reading: the ecstatic dimension, the

moment of interruption, is insufficiently maintained to sustain a genuine futurity in the face of the reassurance afforded by the myth of
nation in giving a determinate social content to temporal experience,
however formally voluntaristic its embrace. Decisionism is about
the relationship of authority to power; Heidegger's politics is about
originary meaning. The 'struggle' so frequently evoked by Heidegger
in his political writings is understood by him, philosophically, as a
struggle over meaning.

What is most striking about this struggle is that even at the level of
its most abstract philosophical description in *Being and Time*, it is conceived exclusively as internal to the interpretation and appropriation
of 'the heritage of a people'. 'The people' (*Volk*), in the nationalistic
rather than the radical-democratic sense, is the sole philosophically
recognized form of social existence, and its 'heritage' is rigorously
singular, albeit contested. Hegel's 'struggle for recognition' appears
in the restricted, exclusivistic form of a *struggle for repetition*. This
crushing sociological simplification is offered without defence, or even
comment, and there is no indication of the possibility of alternative
conceptions. Thus was Heidegger able to link up his philosophy to a
worldly power (National Socialism), despite his inability to think the
concept of power in anything but the other-worldly form of Being itself.
There is a capitulation of philosophical questioning to what Nancy
describes as 'an *existentiell* prejudice (quite *banal* itself, moreover,
and typical of an attachment to the representations and values of
the exceptional, greatness, heroism, even the originary and ownness
themselves), which the text does not acknowledge, and whose
mediocre character it does not perceive'.[65] As Lacoue-Labarthe admits,
'Heidegger never ceased to connect the possibility of History (historicality) with the possibility of a people or of the people', and 'his analysis
of historicality has no meaning if it is not seen against this horizon.'[66]
In everyday political terms, given the historically established institutions of bourgeois democracy and liberal property rights, this meant
that he never repudiated his commitment to the idea of a national
revolution. The 'repetition' which he sought was actually the *creation*
of the organic unity of the German people. Hence the modernism of
his project, despite itself. The revolutionary character of Heidegger's
nationalism derived from its radical difference from existing insti-
tutional forms, rather than any penchant for revolution *per se*. Quite
the reverse, in fact: like other reactionary modernists, politically,
Heidegger was a modernist only under historical duress. As we have
already noted, as a reactionary avant-garde, fascism pitted itself against
the historical temporality of its own project.

Heidegger's philosophical commitment to conservative revolution as a manifestation of the temporality of 'authentic historicality' was made on the pre-philosophical ground of a commitment to 'people' and 'nation' which *Being and Time* furnishes few resources to question, since (as we noted in chapter 3) it fails to integrate Being-with-others into its definition of *Dasein* at a sufficiently fundamental level for social forms to acquire a genuinely ontological significance. It is the mythic (as opposed to properly historical) status of 'the people' within this discourse which grounds the temporality of repetition, by providing a pseudo-historical cipher for the temporalizing movement of Being, as disclosed through the existential structure of *Dasein*, site of its self-concealing unconcealment.[67] For it is a distinctive property of myth that its elements exist at once both inside and outside of historical time – hence its suitability for the synchronic form of structural analysis practised by Lévi-Strauss in *The Savage Mind*. Synchrony is no-time.[68] In terms of its temporal ontology, Heidegger's 'people' mimics time's giving of Being, which is thereby revealed as itself a quintessentially mythic notion. In Heidegger's political writings, the myth of the people and the myth of Being function as political and ontological translations of one another, constantly transcoded through the middle term of 'German *Dasein*'.[69]

Repetition is the temporality of myth, the naturalization of history, and the registration of cosmological time within the psyche (the temporality of the unconscious as 'the other within'). It is the temporality of both historicism and the death drive.[70] How does this essentially mythic notion of existence as repetition compare with the moment of remembrance in Benjamin's work?

Repetition or remembrance?

There is an uncanny convergence between Benjamin's and Heidegger's views on historical time. Both are critics of historicism, and for broadly similiar reasons. More importantly, their respective alter-natives each relies upon the interruptive force of some notion of the ecstatic to disrupt any straightforward narrative continuity to experience, and impart to it an inherent qualitative dynamism. Both are modernists in their affirmation of the temporality of modernity as the ground for the refiguration of experience (whatever Heidegger may say about 'the modern', and however reactionary his modernism may be). And each locates his conception of historical experience within the terms of a rethinking of the political as a particular existential-temporal mode: Benjamin, on the basis of Surrealism; Heidegger, by imbibing his own personal cocktail of Heraclitus, Nietzsche and Jünger. Yet Benjamin was consistently scathing about Heidegger's work, long before the latter became a Nazi; long before *Being and Time*, in fact.[71] Indeed, one commentator has gone so far as to claim that Benjamin's entire intellectual project emerged from his critique of Heidegger in the early programmatic sketch for *The Origin of German Tragic Drama*, and developed in opposition to his thought thereafter.[72]

From this perspective, for all the intriguing similarities between their problem-situations and their common intellectual opponents, there is a fundamental distinction to be drawn between Benjamin's sense of historical time as in principle unfulfilled and Heidegger's search for an authentic relationship to time within history – whether through Dilthey's neo-Hegelian concept of the creation of culture (*Kulturschaffen*), his own notion of resoluteness, or his later (anti-) practical philosophy of letting-be (*Gelassenheit*). As Caygill puts it, summarizing Benjamin's 1916 fragment '*Trauerspiel* and Tragedy': 'Benjamin identifies Heidegger's understanding of historical time as tragic, one in which past, present and future can be gathered in time, whereas for him fulfilled time is Messianic, a gathering *of* time which is not *in* time.'[73] This corresponds to the difference between what we might call the 'vertical' exteriority of Benjamin's constitutive outside, and the horizontal or 'horizonal' status of the anticipation of death in *Being and Time*, offering, in Heidegger's words, 'ecstatic entry into the unconcealment of Being . . . the opening up of human being, out of its captivity in beings, to the openness of Being . . . *out-standing standing-within the essential sunderance of the clearing of beings*'.[74]

However, clear as this distinction may be in relation to Benjamin's early writings, when his practical philosophy was that of a 'theocratic anarchism' or 'programmatic anti-politics',[75] it soon breaks down once his work enters its political phase, and the Messianic framework of the earlier work is transformed into a conceptual model for a new kind of immanent materialist historicism, which explodes the temporality of historicism in the conventional sense of the term. At this point, just as Heidegger gives over the site of tradition to the 'agonal and tragic struggle' of the existential subject with his or her destiny (Derrida's 'appeal to tradition which is in no way traditional'), so Benjamin makes history the site for those momentary glimpses of the truth of time which are condensed into the experience of his 'now'.[76] In viewing the moment of death as 'but one of a series of insignificant moments', *The Origin of German Tragic Drama* has more in common with the vulgar naturalism of historicism than anything in Benjamin's later work.[77]

It is true that the experience of Benjamin's 'now' is one of futurity, rather than fulfilment. But there is no fulfilment in Heidegger either; at least, not in the Christian-Hegelian sense to which the exteriority of Benjamin's materialist messianism is opposed. In fact, there is arguably less even of a *perspective* of fulfilment in Heidegger than Benjamin, since Heidegger fails to extend his argument about the temporally constitutive role of the anticipation of death to the level of history. Consequently, as we have seen, there is a purely formal futurity to authentic historicality. On the other hand, however, at a more concrete level, this space is filled by the backward-looking futurity of the temporal self-fulfilment of myth: the destiny of the German people not merely to repeat, but thereby to *appropriate*, its heritage. The disruptive force of the ecstatic (death) is transformed into a moment within a national narrative of repetition through struggle (the creation of the space of experience), the end of which is historically given by the concept of destiny.

In attempting a materialist translation of the truth of Jewish Messianism, Benjamin effectively performs the extension of Heidegger's argument about death to the level of history which Heidegger himself was unable (or unwilling) to conceive. The anticipation of historical death, the death of the species, is the material meaning of Messianic exteriority. Recently, with the development of nuclear technologies, it has acquired the tangible social reality of a possible historical event. (Nuclear weaponry revives apocalyptic narrative in its original, pre-modern form, laying the ground for its displacement back onto nature in the catastrophic narratives of radical environmentalism; narratives which thereby converge with the various 'fundamentalist' forms of religious revivalism.) Unlike Heidegger, Benjamin extends the futurity of existential temporality to the level of history, where it appears as part of the culture of modernity: the historical temporality of the new. However, he therewith faces a similar difficulty to that encountered by Heidegger at the level of the individual *Dasein*: namely, the radical indeterminacy of freedom as pure possibility, or what Kant called 'the power of freedom to pass beyond any and every specified limit'.[78] It is the principled indeterminacy of this transcendental discourse on futurity (however existentially 'concrete') which allows Heidegger to fall back upon the notions of fate and destiny, in order to give a determinate practical meaning to authentic existence. Is there not a danger that Benjamin's conception of historical experience will be subject to a similar regression? Indeed, have we not increased this likelihood by insisting upon the reintegration of now-time as interruption into a more dialectically complex narrativity than the one to be found in Benjamin's own identification of narrative with tradition? Or, to put the matter another way: might not this new, internally disrupted narrativity turn out to have the temporal structure of Heidegger's concept of repetition?

This is effectively what one commentator has argued in proposing that 'repetition, though more significantly, the anorginally present *divisions within* repetition ... be taken as central to any understanding of Benjamin's construal of the task of the present'.[79] On this reading, Benjamin's explicit rejection of the idea of repetition, according to which even 'the appearance of repetition doesn't exist for ... [the materialist historian] in history',[80] must be understood as opposition to a far simpler and more literal notion of repetition than Heidegger's – that tied to 'the persistence of the appearance of permanence' which establishes the continuity of tradition, perhaps.[81] On the other hand, Heidegger is seen to have suppressed the full potential of his own conception of repetition by his privileging of 'original propriety' over the effects of iteration. In its historical or epochal sense, for Heidegger, the present is 'always already given by the history of Being'.[82] (This is that ontologization of historicality which we identified as the philosophical counterpart to the self-fulfilling temporal logic of myth.) We are thus offered a distinctive combination of Benjamin's and Heidegger's positions in the form of a reading of Benjamin's 'potential'. The combination is fused by the addition of a third element, Freud's concept of *Nachträglichkeit* ('afterwardsness'), interpreted here as 'reiterative reworking'. The present, it is argued, is 'partial and intense' because it is 'continually structured by repetition as a working through, iterative reworking, and thus as the potential site of its disruptive continuity. ... The "without" [Benjamin's quasi-messianic exteriority – PO] ... founders, yielding its place to the inevitability and ineliminability of the other repetition, as that which works the present.'[83]

It is instructive to consider the way in which this reworking of Benjamin's notion of remembrance as a form of repetition distorts, rather than develops, its philosophical trajectory, reducing its narrative potential (our 'new narrativity') to a more sophisticated version of the narrativity of tradition. The issue is ontological: namely, whether the concept of repetition can, in fact, be disengaged from Heidegger's discourse on Being, as the above account supposes, and hence from the temporalization of history as tradition. (Heidegger's discourse on Being is the ontology of a fundamental traditionality.)

This is extremely doubtful, since the idea of repetition does not seem to make sense outside of *some* connection to the indifference of Being, however much we emphasize its character as a differential. For without such indifference, there would be no 'again', however different. This is what ties repetition to naturalism, historicism, and the death drive, for all Heidegger's attempts to give it an alternative ('existentiell') characterization, as the appropriation of possibility itself. Yet if it really were the latter, there would be scant grounds for calling it repetition, since the temporal differential thereby reproduced would not carry with it any particular historical content. On the contrary, it would be an inscription of the new. Existentially, it is 'the possible' which recurs as history *per se*, not some particular heritage. The latter idea is wholly the result of the arbitrary restriction of co-historizing to an organic social ontology of 'the people'. Without this restriction, there would not be anything sufficiently in common for the citizens of a particular nation-state to repeat. (This is that reduction of traditionality to tradition which Ricoeur diagnosed.)[84]

In Benjamin, on the other hand, the after-life of the object in remembrance has a quite different ontological significance from that conveyed by the idea of repetition, since the 'after' is precisely *not* the 'again'. Rather, the 'after' is constitutive of the ontology of the object in a way which reduces the 'again' to an *illusion* of retrospection. Unlike the trauma, or the temporalization of time for the child by the death drive, *history* does not have the temporal structure of Freud's concept of 'afterwardsness'.[85] The 'after' of the after-life marks a temporal difference across which the object must be produced *anew* in the present, through the *destruction* of the illusion of its continuity with the past, on the basis of the present itself. Only thus can the past be 'put to work' in the present as remembrance. Benjamin's remembrance, like the present in which it is produced, is a constructive one. History needs to be *constructed*, not made through repetition. This is why Benjamin insists that 'real political experience' is 'absolutely free' from 'the appearance of things always being the same'.[86]

The disrupted narrativity of the paradoxical 'present as now-time' is more radically differential, more radically futural, than the concept of repetition will allow, however differentially construed. In this respect, it is Benjamin, rather than Heidegger, whose work would be in danger of decisionism, were it not for the measure of the 'truly new' (interference) which regulates its sense of possibility. This is the concrete, immanently historical side of Benjamin's thought. The 'without' (exteriority) neither founders nor yields to the other (Heideggerian) repetition. Instead, it appears *within* historical temporality as a founding interruption (now-time), ground of a futurity which cannot otherwise be thought, except in terms of a narrative completion to history. What, though, of the forms of social experience (narrativity and communication) out of which this futurity erupts, and within which it must reverberate if it is to have a practical effect? This leads to our final point of comparison between Benjamin and Heidegger, at which the difference between the politics of their respective conceptions of time stands out most clearly: the idea of the everyday.

From Marxism to Surrealism: 'the mystery in the everyday'

Everyday life flows through the whole of Benjamin's later writings. Worked and reworked exhaustively by a series of interpretive models, it is their principal theme or topic, yet it is rarely to be found reflectively, as the object of an explicit theorization. Multiple and contradictory, ubiquitous and diffuse, it eludes direct analysis, appearing only through historically concrete figures and forms: the arcades and dioramas, world exhibitions and interiors, the streets and barricades of nineteenth-century Paris, for example; or the *bohème* and the *flâneur*, the man in the crowd, the gambler, the big city dweller, the whore.[87] This is Benjamin the sociologist of modern city life, Benjamin the micrologist, prefiguring more recent forms of cultural analysis, Benjamin the writer of memoir as much as Benjamin the critic.[88] However, if he forgoes a directly conceptual approach in favour of the construction of images, Benjamin's orientation towards the everyday is nonetheless clear and consistent, at least in outline – from his early programmatic expansion of the concept of experience in 'On the Programme of the Coming Philosophy' (1917–18), through the essay on Surrealism (1929), to the dialectics of lived and weighed experience (*Erlebnis* and *Erfahrung*) in 'On some Motifs in Baudelaire' (1939). The everyday is to be treated with the utmost seriousness as an object – it will become the privileged object – of an expanded, metaphysical conception of historical experience.

'In epistemology,' Benjamin writes,

> every metaphysical element is the germ of a disease that expresses itself in the separation of knowledge from the realm of experience in its full freedom and depth. The development of philosophy is to be expected because

each annihilation of these metaphysical elements in an epistemology simultaneously refers it to a deeper, more metaphysically fulfilled experience.[89]

Benjamin conceived his work as part of this process of deepening the concept of experience, by which he understood 'the uniform and continuous *multiplicity* of knowledge'. There is a unity of experience, he insisted,

> that can by no means be understood as a sum of experiences, to which the concept of knowledge as theory is *immediately* related in its continuous development. [. . .] To say that knowledge is metaphysical means in the strict sense: it is related via . . . [this] original concept of knowledge to the concrete totality of experience, i.e. *existence*.[90]

To begin with, in what we might call his esoteric phase, up to 1924, Benjamin identified this concrete totality of experience with religion. The everyday appears as the site of possible revelations of spiritual powers; as in the notorious remark recorded by Scholem, that 'a philosophy that does not include the possibility of sooth-saying from *coffee grounds* cannot be a true philosophy.'[91] Benjamin poses three demands: 'first, the virtual unity of religion and philosophy, second, the incorporation of the knowledge of religion into philosophy, third, the integrity of the tripartite division of the system'.[92] Subsequently, however, from the collage of Weimar city life of 'One-Way Street' (1925–6) onwards, we could replace the word 'religion' in the above quotation with 'the everyday'. It is the 'construction of life', as the opening line of that text has it, which becomes Benjamin's object: the construction of life 'in the power of facts . . . as have scarcely ever become the basis of convictions'.[93] Surrealism was the inspiration for this construction (behind which stands Freud's *Psychopathology of Everyday Life* [1901], among other things); and it is in the essay on Surrealism, while distancing himself from what I have called the 'mystical misreading', that Benjamin provides the most direct statement of his relationship to the everyday:

> Any serious exploration of occult, surrealistic, phantasmagoric gifts and phenomena presupposes a dialectical intertwinement to which a romantic turn of mind is impervious. For histrionic or fanatical stress on the mysterious side of the mysterious takes us no further: we penetrate the mystery only to the degree that we *recognise it in the everyday world*, by virtue of a dialectical optic that perceives the everyday as impenetrable, the impenetrable as everyday.[94]

The main mystery in the everyday world of modern capitalism is, of course, the commodity. 'The wealth of societies in which the capitalist mode of production prevails appears as "an immense accumulation of commodities".' In the increasingly common sense of Marxism (whatever the fate of Communism as a political movement), commodity fetishism replaces popular religion. With commodities, Marx writes, 'a definite social relation betwen men . . . assumes . . . for them, the fantastic form of a relation between things.' The life-process of society is shrouded in a 'mystical veil'. 'Magic and necromancy' abound. Yet for Marx, 'religious reflections of the real world' will not vanish until 'the practical relations of everyday life' present themselves in 'a transparent and rational form'; until, that is, the advent of a society of freely associated producers, regulating their collective practices 'under their conscious and planned control'. In the meantime, value 'transforms every product of labour into a social hieroglyphic'.[95]

Marx deciphered these hieroglyphs in terms of 'the peculiar social character of the labour that produces them' ('abstract' or 'simple average' labour).[96] But he was interested in them only insofar as they were misrepresentations of the economic process: the production of value. Surrealism, on the other hand, exploiting both the psychic dynamics of fetishism (outlined contemporaneously by Freud),[97] and the anthropological reference of a burgeoning ethnology (which Marx rationalistically relegates to the status of a mere 'analogy'),[98] *rewrote* them in the detritus of the everyday, not merely interpreting them, but working on them, in their twofold character as symptoms of alienation (disavowal) and figures of possibility (desire).[99] In so doing, it mapped the conflicted psychic structure of fetishism onto the social contradiction of the commodity.[100] The historical ambivalence of the commodity becomes charged with both the anthropological universality of ritual and the sexual ambivalence of the fetishistic image. As Foster puts it:

> ambivalence regarding both machine and commodity is figured . . . in terms of feminine allure *and* threat, of the woman as erotic *and* castrative, even deathly. In this regard as in so many others, the surrealists presuppose a heterosexist subject, whose fetishisms they exacerbate. And yet they also exploit the anxieties of this subject vis-a-vis the machine and the commodity.[101]

'In *Nadja*', Benjamin writes:

> Breton and Nadja are the lovers who convert everything that we have experienced on mournful railway journeys . . . on Godforsaken Sunday

afternoons in the proletarian quarters of the great cities, in the first glance through the rain-blurred windows of a new apartment, into revolutionary experience, if not action. They bring the immense force of 'atmosphere' concealed in these things to the point of explosion.[102]

In this respect, Breton may be read as the first psychoanalytically informed Marxist in France, while Benjamin appears in his wake as a gothic Marxist, preoccupied with historical questions about fantasy, representation and dreams.[103]

It is the depth of these psychic investments which underlies the Surrealists' transformation of everyday objects into the site of what Benjamin called 'revolutionary' experience; just as it is the directness with which such essentially sexual anxieties are staged that has rendered Surrealism so fertile a source for a certain feminist theory and art practice, despite (or rather, precisely because of) its heterosexist erotic display.[104] However, it is the temporal logic of this experience with which Benjamin was primarily concerned, and this derives from its relation to the commodity form. The Freudian concept of the unconscious may have provided Surrealism with its distinctive version of revelation, whereby reality appears as a dreamwork, open to interpretation,[105] but there was nothing in Surrealism's formation to aid the comprehension of the historical dimension of this process; nothing to help it understand the 'residues of the dream-world' of nineteenth-century Paris as the 'ruins of the bourgeoisie'.[106] It is here that Benjamin's contribution lies: not as a historian of Surrealism, but as the theorist of Surrealist experience *as* historical experience.

Surrealism liberated the pent-up psychic energy trapped in the autonomous work of art, freeing the consciousness of the 'aesthetic' as a domain for the experience of truth to roam over the entire world of cultural experience. Benjamin theorized this liberation as a liberation of historical energy, trapped in the commodity form, the social form of autonomous art. Marxism and Surrealism converge in Benjamin's approach to the everyday. Together, they offer the possibility of the refiguration of its experience into a new form of historical life. Breton's most 'extraordinary discovery', according to Benjamin, was 'the revolutionary energies that appear in the "outmoded"', the perception that 'destitution . . . can be suddenly transformed into revolutionary nihilism';[107] but it was an essentially practical discovery, or, at least, a theoretical discovery in a 'practical state'. Breton grasped these energies only under the ultimately mystical heading of 'surreality'; Benjamin interpreted them historically, as metaphysical effects of the temporal dialectics of the commodity form.

As objects of fetishization, commodities destined for everyday consumption display two closely related features: one is an apparent self-sufficiency or independence from their processes of production; the other is the appearance of novelty, required to make them attractive in the face of competing products. The first is theorized by Marx, the second by Benjamin. In the first case, it is the constitutive power of labour, and hence the social relations of mutual dependence, which is the object of fetishistic disavowal. In the second case, it is both the standardization of the commodity and the corrosive effects of time (ageing, death) which are acknowledged only through their negation. In its fetishization of novelty, Benjamin argued, fashion 'tirelessly constitutes "antiquity" anew out of the most recent past'.[108] It thus constantly leaves its objects behind as 'outmoded', reinforcing their independence, and thus their quality as fetishes, *before they have been exhausted by experience*. In their fetishized but outmoded independence, these objects thus come to subsist, their novelty sealed up inside them, like time capsules. Signifiers of socialized desire (the desire for the new), they are resistant to the self-negating side of novelty (its invariance), by virtue of their very redundancy. In an extraordinary dialectical reversal, the outmoded becomes the privileged site for the experience of novelty, and hence futurity itself. It thus came to be fetishized by the Surrealists, as the site for the enactment (and displacement) of their revolutionary desires. The politics of the fetish is itself fetishistic.

However, once we place this structure of experience in the context of the ethnographic dimension of fetishism, as the Surrealists repeatedly did (by pairing their own fetishes with those from other cultures), there is an additional, anthropological effect, crucial to the historicity of the experience. The objects are reduced to the same historical time. From the standpoint of the fetishization of novelty which takes place under capitalism, and the self-presentation of capitalism as new (its identification with modernity against tradition), the commodity form itself suddenly appears outmoded, by virtue of its very fetishistic structure. It is in this move – the reintroduction of historical time into the conceptualization of Surrealist experience – against the mythological side of Aragon's thought,[109] that the originality of the approach to the everyday in Benjamin's work lies. Benjamin himself associated it with what he called Breton's 'trick' of substituting a 'political' for a 'historical' view of the past. 'The substitution of a political for a historical view of the past':[110] this is the phrase that links the 'Theological-Political Fragment' (1920–1) to the theses 'On the Concept of History' (1940); the 'old' to the 'new'.

This is the phrase which, in the context of the attempt to read Surrealist experience simultaneously as political experience and as an historically specific form of cultural experience, redefines political experience *as* historical experience, historical experience (in its full metaphysical sense) as 'political'. The site of this experience is the refiguration of the everyday through interruption.[111]

Surrealism generalized and transformed aspects of religious and aesthetic experience into a model of the avant-garde experience of the everyday. Benjamin critically appropriated this model in the service of his 'Copernican revolution of remembrance'. One of the main things at stake in Benjamin's work is thus the political legacy of Surrealism, as it is (in different ways) in both deconstruction and cultural studies. As Spivak has pointed out, there is a 'free-playing, smaller surrealist' side to a certain kind of deconstruction.[112] Deconstruction is linguistic existentialism. It is practised, by some, as small Surrealism (small in its metaphysical ambitions, that is). Benjamin, on the other hand, was a big surrealist. Materialist messianism is big Surrealism. (How big a surrealist Derrida is, remains obscure.) In cultural studies, the connection to Surrealism has more to do with the intensity of its investment in the everyday (in politics as a politics of the everyday) than with any particular theoretical or practical orientation towards it. This is both the mark of its greatest potential – as a continuation of Western Marxism by other means – and the site of its greatest disappointments. Nonetheless, however this relationship is inflected, most cultural theory in postwar Europe and North America shares with Benjamin, not merely a theoretical interest in the everyday, but a broadly affirmative attitude towards its political potential. It thereby takes its distance from Heidegger and the inauthenticity attributed to everydayness, in principle, by the terms of his analysis. On the other hand, by treating the idea of everydayness existentially, Heidegger opens up the prospect of a more systematic approach to its methodological function of unifying what Benjamin called 'the concrete totality of experience, i.e. *existence*.'

The verso of modernity: from everydayness to historical life

We have seen how, while Heidegger may formally acknowledge the importance of 'Being-with' as one of a series of primordial modes of existence, he fails to register its constitutive role in the anticipation of death, through which *Dasein* is individualized. *Being and Time* lacks concepts of identification and recognition (or their equivalents) through which the social constitution of existence might become an object of philosophical inquiry, and ontological and historical discourses might be brought together, in acknowledgement of their mutually constitutive relations. In their place, we find, on the one hand, a dogmatic historiography of 'peoples', giving social content to historization; on the other, a phenomenology of the everyday through which the commonplaces of a right-wing sociology of élites are served up as ontology, impervious to both their own historicity and the evidence and arguments of competing historical and social-scientific positions – a secret sociological supplement to the organic nationalism of Heidegger's view of history, for which it provides the inauthentic backdrop, the ground against which the authentic temporality of resolute decision (repetition) may stand out.[113]

However, this is not the only function of everydayness within Heidegger's analysis. It also plays a more general methodological role, which follows directly from the connection between the three component parts of Heidegger's method: ontology, phenomenology, and hermeneutics. *Being and Time* is ontology (*fundamental* ontology), insofar as it takes the forgotten question of the meaning of Being as both its starting point and ultimate goal. It is phenomenology insofar as phenomenology is the method by which the Being of beings (entities) is understood to be revealed: 'a let[ting] that which shows itself be seen from itself in the very way in which it shows itself from itself'. (This follows from Heidegger's ontological or 'Greek' redefinition of 'phenomenon'; from his neo-Hellenic reorientation of Husserl's approach.) Finally, *Being and Time* is hermeneutical, a hermeneutic of *Dasein*, insofar as it proceeds from the fact that the question of Being is 'obscure', and yet we do nevertheless have some 'vague, average understanding' of Being. Its clarification takes the form of an inquiry into the character of the being that asks the question (*Dasein*), a being which is ontologically defined by Heidegger by this very questioning of Being.

These three elements come together in Heidegger's redefinition of philosophy as 'universal phenomenological ontology', which 'takes its departure from the hermeneutic of Dasein, which, as an analytic of *existence*, has made fast the guiding line for all philosophical inquiry at the point where it *arises* and to which it *returns*.'[114] The existential conception of everydayness follows directly from this definition. Everydayness is that mode of *Dasein*'s Being (ontology) through which the question of the character of its Being (hermeneutics) is best approached, since it is the (phenomenologically) first or most familiar (*every*day) mode in which *Dasein* shows itself to itself, 'in itself and from itself'.[115] In particular, as *Dasein*'s most familiar mode of Being, everydayness is the least differentiated. However, it is not thereby indeterminate: 'This undifferentiated character of Dasein's every-dayness is *not nothing*, but a positive phenomenal characteristic of this entity. Out of this kind of Being – and back into it again – is all existing, such as it is.'[116]

This *determinate lack of differentiation* is central to all conceptions of the everyday, yet it is rarely thematized as such, as it is here by Heidegger. It is what makes the everyday at once so uniquely elusive yet unavoidable a category. (Think of the analogous role of the in-determinate 'ordinary' in ordinary language philosophy, for example.) It is this positive lack of differentiation which makes everydayness the starting point for all phenomenological reflection. (The justification for Hegel starting the *Phenomenology* with sense-certainty, insofar as there is one, can only be that it is the epistemological everyday: the way the object presents itself 'first', prior to the subject's reflection – a claim which has only to be stated as such to be doubted, since it is the construct of a *philosophical* empiricism.) Yet everydayness is only the starting point, epistemologically, since, as Heidegger puts it (following Hegel): 'That which is ontically closest and well known, is ontologically farthest and not known at all; and its ontological signifi-cation is constantly overlooked.'[117] Philosophy has always, at least since Plato, opposed itself to *doxa* (opinion) as *episteme* (knowledge).

However, everydayness is also, according to Heidegger, the end point of this process: the kind of Being 'back into which' all existing goes. It is this latter, *terminal* quality of everydayness which gives it its practical significance. Philosophical insights have existential power only insofar as they are capable of flowing back into, informing and transforming, everydayness. It is because of this that, despite having judged everydayness to be inauthentic, Heidegger will argue that authentic Being-one's-self is not 'an exceptional condition of the subject', detached from the everyday, but rather its 'existentiell modification' (its modification by *Dasein*'s interpretive self-relation). In the moment of vision, existence may 'gain the mastery over the "everyday"; but it can never extinguish it.'[118] Everydayness is an '*essential* existentiale'; or, in Benjamin's terms, 'a unity of experience that can by no means be understood as a sum of experiences, to which the concept of knowledge as theory is *immediately* related in its continuous development'.[119] Difficulties arise in *Being and Time* when Heidegger moves on to characterize the positive lack of differ-entiation in everydayness as 'averageness' (*Durchschmittlichkeit*) and to conceive averageness as the standpoint of 'the they' (*das Mann*).

Everydayness becomes Being-in-the-world as a they-self, and the they-self, despite its status as an existentiale, is deemed inauthentic (*uneigentlich*), since it is not, as a matter of definition, *Dasein*'s 'own' (*eigentum*).[120]

This is the point at which Heidegger's existential discourse becomes sociologically overdetermined, *without any indication of the change in the level of analysis*, and hence without suitable methodological safeguards. The problem occurs at two different levels. On the one hand, there is the specific sociological content of Heidegger's phenomenology of everydayness as a 'dictatorship of the "they"'.[121] On the other, there is the underlying ontological determination of *Dasein*'s 'mineness' against which all non-organic forms of sociality will be judged inauthentic. The former is sketched, rather than expounded, but its hostility to democratic forms is clear; nowhere more so than in its treatment of publicity (*Offentlichkeit* – the German word most commonly translated into English as 'public sphere'). For Habermas, for example, the public sphere is a positive democratic category, albeit one which is restricted by the social forms of its bourgeois origins and threatened by the development of the media.[122] For Heidegger, by contrast, it is constituted by 'the "levelling down" (*Einebnung*) of all possibilities of Being'.[123] 'In utilising public means of transport and in making use of information services such as newspapers,' Heidegger insists, 'every Other is like the next. This Being-with-one-another *dissolves one's own Dasein completely* into the kind of Being of "the Others", in such a way, indeed, that the Others, as distinguishable and explicit, vanish more and more.'[124] The contrast with Hegel's appreciation of the newspaper as 'a kind of realistic morning prayer' could hardly be greater.[125] What appears within Marxism as an effect of the commodity form (alienation) reappears here in the familiar reactionary guise of a result of modernity *per se*. Critique of 'the they' in the name of the 'I' is the everyday of a right-wing sociology of élites.[126]

However, the sociological content of this account could be changed without undermining the phenomenological structure of the preceding argumentation. Indeed, in his initial treatment of everydayness, in his 1924 lecture to the Marburg Theological Society, 'The Concept of Time', Heidegger himself thematized it quite differently. There, everydayness stands for 'what one traditionally says about Dasein and human life ... the "One", tradition (*Tradition*)'.[127] Only later is the transition made from tradition to the sociology of modernity, via questions of temporality: specifically, the everydayness of what Heidegger calls 'the ordinary conception of time'. Benjamin's positioning of historicism as a functional replacement within modernity for the continuity of the temporality of tradition is borne out here, by the logic of Heidegger's development. In fact, it is only in the second half of *Being and Time*, when the initial analysis of everydayness is replayed from the standpoint of temporality, that the argument concerning its inauthenticity is philosophically (as opposed to merely etymologically) secured, by its characterization as a fleeing from the authentic temporality of the 'mineness' of death.[128]

This is the precise point in Heidegger's argument which we have questioned: the exclusion of the other from *Dasein*'s relation to death, and hence the exclusion of a 'time of the other' from existential consideration. Once this barrier is removed, the ecstatic-horizonal structure of existential temporality, and hence *Dasein*'s character as a being 'outside of itself', appears as the temporal register of a fundamental and ultimately irrecoverable *sociality*, marked within the individual by the existence of the unconscious (Laplanche's 'other within'), and outside, by the existence of history. The existential modality of everydayness as the register of our most familiar and least differentiated relations to others must, then, be rethought in the terms of the historically specific forms of recognition and misrecognition, historically specific '*we*-selves', out of which and back into which existing goes, at particular times in particular places. However, at this point, we might wonder whether there is not something both specifically *modern* and intrinsically *dialectical* about the very concept of everydayness, whatever its precise sociological content, through which it might be connected to historical experience.

This is what Henri Lefebvre believed. It is to Lefebvre that we owe the project of systematically combining a philosophical concept of the everyday with a sociological analysis of its evolving forms, a project which is conceivable only within the horizon of its transformation, as the practice of a reciprocal critique. 'The limitations of philosophy – truth without reality – always and ever counterbalance the limitations of everyday life – reality without truth.'[129] For Lefebvre, the everyday is 'a philosophical concept that cannot be understood outside philosophy'. It designates 'for and by philosophy the non-philosophical'. It is a concept that 'neither belongs to nor reflects everyday life, but rather expresses its possible transfiguration in philosophical terms'. Yet it is no more the product of a pure philosophy than it is of the everyday itself: '[It] comes of philosophical thought directed towards the non-philosophical, and its major achievement is in this self-surpassing.'[130] 'To study philosophy as an indirect criticism of life is to perceive (everyday) life as a direct critique of philosophy.'[131] In

Lefebvre's work, the Marxist discourse of the supersession of philosophy lives on as the critique of everyday life, a critique which is to be grounded, in part, within everyday life itself. 'Man must be everyday or he [sic] will not be at all.'[132]

Critique of everyday life was a project pursued by Lefebvre for over fifty years: from his 1933 essay with Guterman, 'Mystification: Notes towards a Critique of Everyday Life', through the three volumes of *Critique of Everyday Life – Introduction* (1947; 1958), *Foundation of a Sociology of Everydayness* (1962), and *From Modernity to Modernism (Towards a Metaphilosophy of the Everyday)* (1981) – until his death in 1991, stopping off along the way for a series of regional investigations, polemical interventions, and the like.[133] It stands at the crossroads of four intellectual movements central to the formation of the present: Marxism, Surrealism, Existentialism, and Cultural Studies (in the sense in which, as Jameson has pointed out, Cultural Studies is the name for a particular *desire*).[134] Lefebvre was a critic of Surrealism and existentialism, a tireless proponent of Marxism, and a forerunner of cultural studies. He was concerned to distance himself from the first two: from Surrealism, because of its 'pseudo-dialectic of the real and the dream, the physical and the image, the everyday and the marvellous', ending up with those 'particular forms of alienation: the *image-thing*, magic and the occult, semi-morbid states of mind' (a critique which evokes the 'pernicious romantic prejudices' of Benjamin's reading);[135] and from existentialism, for having 'drawn closer to everyday life . . . only to discredit it, under the pretext of giving it a new resonance', devaluing it in favour of 'pure or tragic moments – criticism of life through anguish or death – artificial criteria of authenticity, etc.'.[136] But if he was concerned to distance himself from these two movements, he was nonetheless influenced by them, and profoundly so. And despite phases of orthodoxy, dictated by his tactical relations to the French Communist Party, his Marxism was suitably heterodox as a result.[137]

After the war, and following on from his critique of existentialism (*L'Existentialisme*, 1946), Lefebvre sought to redefine Marxism on the basis of the early Marx's concept of alienation as 'critical knowledge of everyday life'.[138] In thus concretizing the concept of alienation, he simultaneously prepared the ground for what we now call 'cultural studies', as a sociology of the everyday, and anticipated the New Left's attempt to expand the definition of socialism beyond political economy to encompass the totality of human relations. Socialism, he argued, 'can only be defined *concretely* on the level of everyday life, as a system of changes in what can be called lived experience'.[139] In this dual analytical and political role, 'everyday life' plays a similar part in Lefebvre's work to that played by the term 'culture' in Raymond Williams's – comparison with which has much to tell us about the different historical and political sensibilities of the two (French and British) traditions of cultural analysis.[140]

Marx's concept of alienation, and the anthropology of species-being with which it is associated, fell out of favour, philosophically, long before Marxism entered its current crisis of intellectual faith. Yet their role within Lefebvre's work is primarily transitional, as the pathway from a Marxism of citation to the open-ended exploration of a dialectical sociology of the everyday.[141] There are good reasons for believing that the project they initiated can survive without them (at least in their objectionable, ahistorical forms), especially if we are prepared to accept some methodological help from Heidegger, along the lines of our previous critique. For it is the function of these concepts within Lefebvre's work to provide the element of universality in terms of which the everyday may be conceived, sociologically, as a unification of experience. There is the 'good', but unrealized universality of an historically produced species-being and the 'bad', abstract but realized, universality of its alienated forms (money, the commodity, the state, etc.). Lefebvre's innovation was to concretize the former as *partially* realized in the practices of everyday life. He thus changed the character of its universality from that of a merely implicit, historically speculative anthropology, to that of an existential phenomenology or hermeneutics of historical existence. And he thereby rendered it historical in a way which appears to side-step the critique of its essentialism, placing it on a par, ontologically, with the universality of its alienated forms.

On Lefebvre's best-known definition, everyday life is not merely that which is phenomenologically most familiar and hence least differentiated, but that which is sociologically 'residual' too. It is '"what is left over" after all distinct, superior, specialised, structured activities have been singled out by analysis . . . *defined as a totality*'.[142] It is thus not so much a positive *lack* of differentiation (as it is in Heidegger) as an underlying phenomenological unity which *accompanies* all differentiation, providing it with its social meaning. 'Considered in their specialization and their technicality,' Lefebvre argues,

superior activities leave a 'technical vacuum' between one another which is filled up by everyday life. Everyday life is profoundly related to *all* activities, and encompasses them *with all their differences* and their conflicts; it is their meeting place, their bond, their common ground. And

it is in everyday life that the sum total of relations which make the human
– and every human being – a whole takes its shape and its form. In it are
expressed and fulfilled those relations which bring into play the totality of
the real, albeit in a certain manner which is *always partial and incomplete*:
friendship, comradeship, love, the need to communicate, play, etc.[143]

It is the dual character of this totality, at once real (phenomenologically and practically), yet radically incomplete (in its actual social
content), which is the key to its critical function. As Debord puts it,
despite its status as a residue, everyday life is a concept

> some people are averse to confronting because it at the same time repre-
> sents the *standpoint* of totality; it would imply the necessity of an integral
> political judgement. . . . Everyday life is the measure of all things: of the
> fulfilment or rather the nonfulfilment of human relations; of the use of
> lived time; of artistic experimentation; of revolutionary politics.[144]

As the foundational category of a dialectical sociology, 'everyday life'
is thus at once *empirical* and *utopian*. It is empirical in the multiplicity
and variety of its concrete forms (unities of work, leisure, and family/
'private' life); it is utopian in its harbouring of the promise of a
concrete universality of relations at the level of society as a whole, in
the fullness of its complex sociality. It is in the disjunction between
these two moments or aspects of the concept – what we might call
its chronotopical specificity and its figuration of a philosophical
universality – that its power lies.

Yet this is still to treat it too formally. For while it is possible to
generalize its application sociologically, across time and space, on
the basis of its phenomenological universality ('Everyday life has
always existed, even if in ways vastly different from our own'),[145]
in Lefebvre's specific dialectical sense 'everyday life' is primarily a
category of capitalism, of modernity, and of postwar 'consumer'
capitalism – capitalism *as* modernity, in particular. The reasons
for this are complex. One is that it is only in the context of the generalized proliferation of 'distinct, specialised, structured activities'
– an intensification in the social division of labour – that what Lefebvre
calls the 'residue' of such activities achieves a distinct social reality,
experienced as such, which is capable of investment with utopian
force. This is part of the problematic of romantic anti-capitalism,
bound up with the historical co-ordinates of classical sociological
theory, of which Marx's early writings may be considered a part. The
disruption of previous life-forms leads to the retrospective construction
of images of the integrity of the past: the 'inherence of productive

activity in . . . life in its entirety', for example, in Lefebvre's description of peasant life.[146] These images of integrity become criteria for a critique of the present at the same time as they remain associated with the remnants of the life-forms in question. A romantic critique of the present is thus able to present itself as immanent to the historical process, despite its appeal to transcendent principles constructed from a retrospective idealization of the past. This is reflected in Lefebvre's occasional quasi-vitalist use of the expression 'everyday *life*' (*la vie quotidienne*), in contrast to Heidegger's adverbial everyday*ness* (*Alltäglichkeit*), and in his identification of the 'secret of the everyday' with *dissatisfaction* (dissatisfaction with life).[147]

However, crucially, in Lefebvre's case (as opposed to, for example, Bakhtin's apparently similar affirmation of the everyday as the site of democratic resistance to authority and of popular creativity), the attribution of a concrete universality to everyday life derives, less from a backward-looking historiography, than from a praxis-based phenomenology of social life for which it is the alienated universality of modern social forms that provides the model of universality to which the disalienating impulse of the everyday corresponds; although the connotations of the former, constantly transcoded, are never far from hand.[148] Furthermore, it is only once the development of productivity within capitalism permits a shortening of the working day, and the market for consumer goods expands to include the working class, that Lefebvre's 'residue' comes, increasingly, to reproduce the alienation with which it was initially contrasted, internally, as an unavoidable dimension of itself, in the commodification of 'leisure'. In the past, in Lefebvre's peasant societies, in which productive activity inheres in 'life in its entirety', the everyday was off-set by the interruptive break of the religious holiday, the festival, or the carnival. In capitalist societies, on the other hand, the break from work becomes increasingly routinized within the everyday: 'Saturdays and Sundays are given over to leisure as regularly as day-to-day work.' Thus, while it continues to bear the promise of release, since it has 'only one meaning: to get away from work', in its everyday form leisure loses its ruptural force. It comes to function both economically (as a site for the realization of value), and politically (as a moment in the reproduction of the relations of production) within the the terms of the established order – functions which increasingly converge in the demand-managed capitalist democracies of the West in the postwar period. As a result, leisure becomes inherently ambiguous, 'the non-everyday in the everyday'.[149] Only at this point does the idea of every-day life become genuinely dialectical. Disalienation must take place, at least in part, through alienated forms: '*the increasing fulfilment of man* – and also an *increasing alienation* . . . The one in the other. The one via the other.' The two sides of everyday life, 'the bourgeois and the human', are fused in its contradictory actuality.[150]

Yet the more everyday life is colonized by the commodity form in what, by the 1960s, Lefebvre had come to call 'the bureaucratic society of controlled consumption', the more attenuated its utopian practical core becomes: that 'substance of everyday life – "human raw material" in its simplicity and richness', which 'pierces through alienation and establishes "disalienation"' within the everyday.[151] This is accompanied, on the one hand, by an intensification of the utopian charge associated with its remaining sites; and on the other, by a growing consciousness of the need actively to intervene within the everyday, to *produce* – as well as to draw attention to – its utopian side. It is this utopian dimension of Lefebvre's work which feeds first and foremost into Situationism, and then, secondly, into the compensatory development of a philosophy of desire (Deleuze and Guattari), only to be consummated, in an inverted form, in Baudrillard's cynical celebration of the aesthetics of the commodity as the hyperreal.[152] In his later work, Lefebvre registers this split within everydayness terminologically, as that between a positive 'everyday life' and a negative, degraded 'everyday'. What concerns us here is the temporality of the dialectic associated with the division, its connection to modernity, and the possibilities for historical experience which it contains.

The connection of the everyday to modernity can be established in a number of different ways. Two have already been suggested, insofar as modernity may be understood as a general term for the experience of capitalism. However, both concern the everyday as a distinctive kind of social space, which is defined (phenomenologically) and produced (practically) by the way it is lived.[153] Neither draws upon the temporal connotations of the two terms. Yet both 'modernity' and 'the everyday' are primarily temporal terms and each derives its broader significations from its temporal form. Thus, as Heidegger acknowledges, although what he intended to convey by the expression 'everydayness' in *Being and Time* was 'a definite "how" of existence' ('the comfortableness of the accustomed', for example) and, he insists, his 'every day' is not to be understood 'calendrically', there is nonetheless 'still an overtone of some such temporal character': 'That which will come tomorrow (and this is what everyday concern keeps awaiting) is "eternally yesterday's". In everydayness everything is all one and the same, but whatever the day may bring is taken as diversification.'[154]

Heidegger seems genuinely perplexed by the relation between these two sides of his own analysis (the 'how' of everydayness and its temporality), and he consequently postpones an 'adequate conceptual delimitation' of the temporality of everydayness until he has established 'a framework in which the meaning of Being in general and its possible variations' can be discussed in principle – something which never happens, since the third division of Part One of *Being and Time* was never published.[155] Perhaps he saw that the two sides of his analysis were in conflict, since an existential account of the temporality of everydayness would, by its very nature, undermine the inauthenticity of publicness, which it purported to ground. (The *temporality* of everydayness, it should be noted, is a very different matter from the 'ordinary conception of time', that 'self-forgetful *"representation"* of the "infinity" of public time',[156] to which Heidegger eventually reduces it, via the temporality of within-time-ness, in the final chapter of the book. Everydayness is a temporal mode of existence, an existential, not a 'representation' as such at all.) We, however, are confronted by no such problem, since we have rejected Heidegger's phenomenology of 'the they' as a philosophically individualistic, sociologically shallow and politically reactionary form. We are thus free to trace back the existential quality of everydayness to its mode of temporalization as a distinctive combination of *presentness* and *repetition*.

It is ironic that Heidegger should have chosen to mark his conception of authentic historicality as resolute decision with the very term best suited to describe the (missing) temporality of his inauthentic everyday (*Wiederholung*). For how else are we to conceive 'that of which all the parts follow each other in such a regular, unvarying succession that those concerned have no call to question their sequence', the 'undated and (apparently) insignificant' which, 'though it occupies and preoccupies', is 'practically untellable' – Lefebvre's description of the Heideggerian world of everydayness[157] – except as something structured by repetition? And how are we to conceive this repetition except as the lived experience of what Benjamin called historicism, that *naturalization* of modernity through which the new appears in its most abstract structural form as the ever-always-the-same? As Lefebvre puts it:

> The everyday is situated at the intersection of two modes of repetition: the cyclical, which dominates in nature, and the linear, which dominates in processes known as 'rational'. The everyday implies on the one hand cycles, nights and days, seasons and harvests, activity and rest, hunger and

satisfaction, desire and fulfilment, life and death, and it implies on the other hand the repetitive gestures of work and consumption.

In modern life the repetitive gestures tend to mask and to crush the cycles. The everyday imposes its monotony. It is the invariable constant of the variations it envelops. The days follow one another and resemble one another, and yet – and here lies the contradiction at the heart of everydayness – *everything changes. But the change is programmed*: obsolescence is planned. Production anticipates reproduction; production produces change in such a way as to superimpose the impression of speed on that of monotony. Some people cry out against the acceleration of time, others cry out against stagnation. They're both right.[158]

As such, for Lefebvre, everyday life both 'responds and corresponds' to modernity. It is 'the meeting place of all repetitions', 'the verso of modernity, the spirit of our times'.[159] The temporality of capital accumulation (expanded reproduction), ideologically misrepresented as modernity (the new), imposes itself upon the incompleteness of the present as repetition, in a mimesis of the cyclical temporality of nature (the day, the month, the season, the year). It is in this sense that, for Lefebvre, the everyday and the modern 'mark and mask, legitimate and counterbalance each other', 'the one crowning and concealing the other, revealing and veiling it'.[160] And it is in this dialectic that Benjamin's hopes lay for a *refiguration* of the everyday, a recovery of history, whereby the negation of historical time by the logic of repetition might be reversed via the transformation of the empty chronology of the 'instant' into the fullness of the historical 'now'.

For since, phenomenologically, everydayness is constituted as a living, extended or durational present, in principle incomplete, it cannot be structured by repetition alone. Rather, it is the place where 'the riddle of recurrence intercepts the theory of becoming.'[161] The inherent incompleteness of the present, which 'demands continuation',[162] is turned back upon itself, but it can never be fully contained. It is as such – an always incomplete *de*historicization – that the everyday derives its potential as a site for the *re*historicization of experience. Benjamin, we might say, reworking his description of Surrealism, sought to recognize the avant-garde in the everyday, the everyday in the avant-garde, as forms of historical experience.

Epilogue

Everyday life is lived in the medium of cultural form. Its phenomenological immediacy is the sedimented result of myriad repetitive
practices, yet it is constantly open to the randomness of the chance
occurrence, the unexpected encounter, the surprising event, as well as
to the refiguration of its meanings by more explicit forms of social
intervention. The novel is 'a culture of everyday life',[1] as are television
and video, the various forms of print journalism and a multiplicity of
other, more informal modes of communication. And if, as Bakhtin
argued, all literary genres have increasingly been subject to noveliza-
tion as a process of linguistic familiarization and the creation of a
certain semantic open-endedness, so, we might argue, all genres of
communication (including the novel) have subsequently been subject
to cinematization, the logic of montage and the image, and an intensification of that 'revolution in the hierarchy of times' whereby 'the
present becomes the center of human orientation in time and in the
world', which Bakhtin associated with the novel.[2]

It is easy to see this process, at one with commodification, in which
the present itself shrinks successively towards the instantaneity of
what Husserl idealistically (mis)described as its retentional source,
as a tendential dehistoricization of life, within which events are consumed as images, independently of each other, and without narrative
connection.[3] Yet this is to ignore both the narrative unification of
experience inherent in the totalizing structure of temporalization,
however internally disjunctive and incomplete (chapter 2), and the
potential for new historizations, new temporalizations of history,
created by new cultural forms (chapter 4). Schizophrenia can no more
provide a plausible theoretical model for the structure of subjectivity
associated with these forms than it can for theory itself, since it would
render even the most rudimentary modes of social reproduction
impossible; let alone that 'genuinely dialectical attempt to think our

197

present of time in History' which is the self-conception of Jameson's postmodernism.[4]

It is important in this respect to distinguish the repetition of the everyday, in even its most commodified forms, from that of both the death drive, Laplanche's 'principle of libidinal circulation' (chapter 3), and Heidegger's resolute decision (chapter 5). Ontologically constitutive of the individual as a simultaneously social and natural being, by its internalization of the exteriority of the social as a quasi-natural force (the unconscious), the death drive is indifferent to all specificities of social and historical temporalization. As an existential act, or 'decision of existence', on the other hand, appropriating the past through an act of pure possibility, the repetition of Heideggerian resolution is indifferent to nature. It is part of a purely constructive presencing; hence both its status as an extreme form of avant-garde experience (not so much negating as dissolving the present in a process of pure presencing) and its amenability to the self-fulfilling temporal logic of myth.

Unlike either of these forms, the temporality of the everyday is both internally complex and inherently contradictory, since it must mediate a variety of repetitive cycles (both social and natural) with the inherent directionality of the phenomenologically extended, incomplete present of primordial temporalization. It is the consciousness of these contradictions which allows us to grasp the dehistoricization of life by the commodification of the everyday as the historical process it is, in which the immanent historicity of existential temporalization is turned back upon itself, but can never be fully contained. In the process, the question of possibility – and therefore of politics – is shifted from the structure of primordial anticipation (Being-towards-death) to the *social production of possibility* through the temporalization of historical time. Ontologically, the everyday is no more opposed to history than history can be reduced to war.[5]

To think 'our present of time in history', it was argued in chapter 1, requires not the confusing novelty of the concept of the postmodern, but a rethinking of the dialectics of modernity as a structure of temporalization (the *historically* new) which inscribes the spatial logic of social differences into a totalization of historical time. Modernity, as Bhabha has put it, is about 'the historical construction of a specific position of historical enunciation and address', a specific 'we' that 'defines the prerogative of my present'. It involves 'a continual questioning of the conditions of existence; making problematic its own discourse not simply "as ideas" but as the position and status of the locus of social utterance.'[6] This is a conflicted social process of identification, interrogation and disavowal – recognition and misrecognition – of extraordinary complexity, which requires the constant production of new pasts to maintain its rhythm of temporal negation and projection, as urgently as new images of the future.

Bhabha has drawn attention to a particular aspect of this process: the importance of colonialism to the historical constitution of its disjunctive form, and the displaced repetition of the structure of colonial difference within the postcolonial, across a series of new racial and ethnic forms.[7] Yet there is not *necessarily* anything specifically 'postcolonial' about the reproduction of the more general structure – Bhabha's bid on behalf of the hegemony of the concept notwithstanding[8] – although the repetition of colonial differences is undoubtedly currently one of its most important, and hence most heavily contested, sites. As Spivak points out, the stories of the post-colonial world 'are not necessarily the same as the stories coming from "internal colonization", the way the metropolitan countries discriminate against the disenfranchised groups in their midst.'[9] Nor should they be restricted to the code of displaced repetition, given the plurality of forms of social difference (especially class and gender) making up the world they represent. Indeed, as we have seen in Heidegger's work, the trope of displaced repetition is liable to a formalist reading which reinstates original difference across its supposed temporal rupture in a more purely constructed form. In this instance, the affirmation of 'postcoloniality' is in danger of being transformed into its disavowal, as an ethnicist culturalism becomes the legitimating ground of 'the very thing it claims to combat' (neo-colonial structures within the ex-colonial states).[10]

'Modernity' can be (and is) produced out of any of the full range of differential social forms; and its representations will only ultimately be adequate to the degree to which they are able to articulate all those which are most important in practice. To this extent, they require an even more 'interstitial' perspective than Bhabha himself allows. Furthermore, insofar as it is the name for both an existential and a social process, as well as a project of theoretical elaboration, 'modernity' must be understood to embrace dimensions of temporalization beyond the purely *enunciative* present of the sign – material processes of socialization and 'real abstraction' which, whilst necessarily coded, cannot be reduced to the temporal logic of the sign. There are (changing) limits to the temporalization of history by and as 'modernity', the exploration of which must constitute an ineliminable part of any materialist politics of time.

There is a widespread tendency to counterpose the categories of 'capitalism' (Marx) and 'modernity' (Durkheim and Weber) as competing alternatives for the theoretical interpretation of the same historical object. Yet there is no obligation to continue to use terms in the way in which they have been most consistently abused. For if structural categories of historical analysis, like 'capital', are to be rendered effective at the level of experience, they will have to be mediated by the phenomenological forms through which history is lived as the ongoing temporalization of existence. 'Modernity' is one such form; 'progress', 'reaction', 'revolution', 'crisis', 'conservation', 'stagnation' and 'the new' are others – to name only the most obvious. These are not the products of competing totalizations of historical material across a common temporal frame. They are not just based on different selections of which practices and events are most historically significant. They represent alternative temporal structures, alternative temporalizations of 'history', which articulate the relations between 'past', 'present' and 'future' in politically significantly different ways.

It is in this sense that I write of a 'politics of time'; indeed, of all politics as centrally involving struggles over the experience of time. How do the practices in which we engage structure and produce, enable or distort, different senses of time and possibility? What kinds of experience of history do they make possible or impede? Whose futures do they ensure? These are the questions to which a politics of time would attend, interrogating temporal structures about the possibilities they encode or foreclose, in specific temporal modes. Think, for example, about the way in which the political significance of unemployment in capitalist democracies is determined by the horizon of expectation within which it is received; and of how that horizon is related to broader forms of historical consciousness and social practice. Think, in particular, about the problems posed for a politics of emancipation by a horizon of expectation within which the replacement of capitalism within any current lifetime is no longer a feasible prospect; and the social forces traditionally assigned to the job can no longer be looked upon with any confidence to 'grow into' their allotted political role.

Walter Benjamin wrote that it was the experience of his generation that 'capitalism will die no natural death'.[11] It has been the experience of succeeding generations that it will not die at their hands either. What does 'anti-capitalism' mean, concretely, in this context? This poses a genuinely new political problem for the radical left, inextricably bound up with questions about historical time. For radical politics depends upon the social production of possibility at the level of historical time. 'Possibility' is produced by and as the temporal structure of particular types of action; it is sustained by others, and eroded and undermined by others still. And it is produced in a variety of temporal forms. It is in this deep structural sense that there is a crucial political significance to culture – culture as formation, not culture as value – and a need for a left cultural politics which would engage in the willed transformation of the social forms of subjectivity at their deepest structural levels. (Cultural politics is subject production.) For it is these forms, including the form of 'the political' itself, which determine (and ration) that 'simple possibility that things might proceed otherwise', which Bourdieu detects in the probabilistic logic of social laws[12] – a possibility that must nonetheless be produced as experience if the otherwise is to proceed. Under these conditions (the conditions of existence), those with an interest in social change have no option but to rethink 'modernity' as the transformation of *its* conditions of existence gather pace with time.

Notes

Preface

1. Wulf Herzogenrath, 'The Anti-technological Technology of Nam June Paik's Robots', in *Nam June Paik: Video Works 1963–88*, Hayward Gallery, London, 1988, p. 16.

2. See, for example, Stephen W. Melville, *Philosophy Beside Itself: On Deconstruction and Modernism*, University of Minnesota Press, Minneapolis, 1986, ch. 2, and Peter Dews, *Logics of Disintegration: Post-Structuralist Thought and the Claims of Critical Theory*, Verso, London and New York, 1987, ch. 1 – a book which was originally to have been entitled *A Critique of French Philosophical Modernism*.

3. It is recognition of this fact which places Fredric Jameson's work on the subject so far ahead of its competitors, however inconsistent or ultimately contradictory its presentation of postmodernism as a 'cultural logic' may be. For a reflection on some of these contradictions, via a critique of Jameson's appropriation of Adorno, see my 'A Marxism for the Postmodern? Jameson's Adorno', *New German Critique* 56, Spring/Summer 1992.

4. Marshall Berman, *All That Is Solid Melts into Air: The Experience of Modernity*, Verso, London, 1983, p. 33. Habermas's lectures were given in 1983–4 and published in Germany in 1985. They are translated by Frederick Lawrence as Jürgen Habermas, *The Philosophical Discourse of Modernity: Twelve Lectures*, Polity Press, Cambridge, 1987.

5. See Friedrich Engels, *Ludwig Feuerbach and the End of Classical German Philosophy* (1888), Progress Publishers, Moscow, 1946. Engels's title is more accurately translated as '*Ludwig Feuerbach and the Way Out of (or Exit from) [der Ausgang] Classical German Philosophy*'. The distinction is important, since if the way out is blocked, one must either turn back or remain on the threshold until such time as the way is clear: 'Philosophy, which once seemed obsolete, lives on because the moment to realize it was missed.' Theodor W. Adorno, *Negative Dialectics* (1966), trans. E.B.Ashton, Routledge and Kegan Paul, London, 1973, p. 3.

6. Jean-François Lyotard, *The Postmodern Condition: A Report on Knowledge* (1979), trans. Geoff Bennington and Brian Massumi, University of Minnesota Press, Minneapolis, 1984, p. xiv.

7. This paradox was avoided by earlier purely semiotic or literary analyses of historiographic form, since they were agnostic about epistemological issues. See, in particular, Roland Barthes, 'Historical Discourse' (1967), in Michael Lane (ed.), *Structuralism: A Reader*, Jonathan Cape, London, 1970 and Hayden White, *Metahistory: The Historical Imagination in Nineteenth Century Europe*, Johns Hopkins University Press, Baltimore and London, 1973. Ricoeur's *Time and Narrative* (three volumes, 1983–5, trans. Kathleen McLaughlin and David Pellauer, Chicago University

Press, Chicago, 1984–8; hereafter *TN* 1–3) only partly belongs to this tendency, since it takes the more theoretically ambiguous form of a *dialectical negation* of both philosophy and positive science by poetics; thereby inscribing the conceptual logic of one of its superseded moments into the heart of its result – a dilemma faced by all attempts to go 'beyond' Hegel, or philosophy more generally.

8. Charles Baudelaire, 'My Heart Laid Bare', CXI, in his *Intimate Journals*, trans. Christopher Isherwood, Black Spring Press, London, 1989, p. 56.

9. For a synoptic overview of the intensification of time-consciousness during a particularly important phase of this process, see Stephen Kern, *The Culture of Time and Space, 1880–1918*, Harvard University Press, Cambridge MA, 1983.

10. See Plato, 'Phaedo' (67e), in *The Dialogues of Plato*, trans. Benjamin Jowett, Clarendon Press, Oxford, 1953, Volume 1, p. 418, and Sigmund Freud, 'Thoughts for the Times on War and Death' (1915), in *Civilisation, Society, Religion: Group Psychology, Civilisation and its Discontents and Other Works*, trans. James Strachey, Penguin Freud Library, Volume 12, Harmondsworth, 1985, p. 89: 'We recall the old saying: *Si vis pacem, para bellum*. If you want to preserve peace, arm for war. It would be in keeping with the times to alter it: *Si vis vitam, para mortem*. If you want to endure life, prepare yourself for death.'

11. Benjamin to Scholem, 6 May 1934, in *The Correspondence of Walter Benjamin, 1910–1940*, ed. by Gershom Scholem and Theodor W. Adorno, trans. Manfred R. Jacobson and Evelyn M. Jacobson, University of Chicago Press, Chicago, 1994, p. 439. See also the earlier letter to Scholem of 17 April 1931, *ibid.*, pp. 376–8.

12. See Raymond Williams, 'Notes on Marxism in Britain since 1945', in his *Problems in Materialism and Culture*, Verso, London, 1980, p. 237.

1. Modernity: A Different Time

1. See, for example, the four volumes in the recent Open University series edited by Stuart Hall that go under the general heading of *Understanding Modern Societies: An Introduction*, Polity Press/Open University, Oxford, 1992.

2. For an excellent account of the 'ahistorical historicism' of sociology's reliance on 'logically ordered contrasts between structural types', see Philip Abrams, 'The Sense of the Past and the Origins of Sociology', *Past and Present* 55, 1972, pp. 18–32. A similar disruption of temporal complacency occurs in anthropology as soon as the social relations of fieldwork become the object of an explicitly political theoretical interest. See Talal Asad, *Anthropology and the Colonial Encounter*, Ithaca Press, London, 1973; Johannes Fabian, *Time and the Other: How Anthropology Makes its Object*, Columbia University Press, New York, 1983; James Clifford, 'On Ethnographic Authority' (1983), in *The Predicament of Culture: Twentieth Century Ethnography, Literature, and Art*, Harvard University Press, Cambridge MA, 1988, pp. 21–54; James Clifford and George E. Marcus (eds), *Writing Culture: The Poetics and Politics of Ethnography*, California University Press, Berkeley, 1986.

3. Karl Marx, *Contribution to a Critique of Political Economy* (1859), Progress Publishers, Moscow, 1970, pp. 20–1.

4. Karl Marx, *Capital: A Critique of Political Economy*, Volume 1, (1867) trans. Ben Fowkes, Penguin, Harmondsworth, 1976, ch. 15.

5. Siegfried Kracauer, *History: The Last Things Before the Last*, Oxford University Press, New York, 1969, p. 38.

6. Jean-Paul Sartre, *Search for a Method* (1960), trans. Hazel Barnes, Vintage Books, New York, 1968, p. 92. Cf. Walter Benjamin, 'Theses on the Philosophy of History' (1940), in his *Illuminations*, ed. Hannah Arendt, trans. Harry Zohn, Fontana, London, 1973, Theses XI–XII, pp. 260–3; Louis Althusser, 'Marxism is not a Historicism' (1968), in Louis Althusser and Étienne Balibar, *Reading Capital*, trans. Ben Brewster, Verso, London, 1979, Pt II, ch. 5.

7. See, for example, Scott Lash, *The Sociology of Postmodernism*, Routledge, London and New York, 1990; Zygmunt Bauman, *Intimations of Postmodernity*, Routledge, London and New York, 1992.

8. *The Shorter Oxford English Dictionary*, Clarendon Press, Oxford, 1973, p. 1342.

9. See, for example, Ulrich Beck, *Risk Society: Towards a New Modernity* (1986), trans. Mark Ritter, Sage Publications, London, Thousand Oaks and New Delhi, 1992.

10. It is ironic, in this respect, that Beck's updating of the classical sociology of modernity should sail under the flag of 'reflexive modernization', since it is the very reflexivity of modernity which undermines the temporality of modernization. Oddly, there is no theoretical discussion of time or temporality in *Risk Society*. See also Ulrich Beck, Anthony Giddens, Scott Lash, *Reflexive Modernisation: Politics, Tradition and Aesthetics in the Modern Social Order*, Polity Press, Cambridge, 1994.

11. Marshall Berman, 'Why Modernism Still Matters', in Scott Lash and Jonathan Friedman (eds), *Modernity and Identity*, Blackwell, Oxford, 1992, p. 34.

12. Marshall Berman, *All That is Solid Melts into Air*; Perry Anderson, 'Modernity and Revolution', *New Left Review* 144, March/April 1984, pp. 96–113. See also Berman's reply to Anderson, 'The Signs in the Street: A Response to Perry Anderson', *New Left Review* 144, pp. 114–23. Anderson's essay is reprinted in his *A Zone of Engagement*, Verso, London and New York, 1992, pp. 25–45, with the addition of a Postscript from 1985, pp. 46–55. References below are to the original place of publication.

13. *All That is Solid*, p. 15.

14. Ibid., p. 20; emphasis added.

15. Ibid., pp. 35, 88, 16–17.

16. Anderson, 'Modernity and Revolution', p. 113.

17. Ibid., p. 101.

18. In his discussion of the concept of revolution ('Modernity and Revolution', p. 112; 'Postscript', pp. 46–7), Anderson focuses exclusively on its political rather than its social form, despite the occurrence in his description of the modernist conjuncture of 'the imaginative proximity of social revolution' ('Modernity and Revolution', p. 104). An earlier piece, 'The Notion of Bourgeois Revolution' (1976), suffers from a similar restriction of scope, while nonetheless offering some interesting reflections which bear directly on the question of the relationship between the two forms. Perry Anderson, *English Questions*, Verso, London and New York, 1992, pp. 105–18.

19. *All That is Solid*, pp. 16–17. In 'Why Modernism Still Matters', the 'classic age' contracts, to run 'from the 1840s to the aftermath of the First World War' (p. 34); but this is now the age of modernism, not modernity. 'Modernity' more or less drops out of the picture altogether, confirming the culturalism of the earlier analysis.

20. *All That is Solid*, p. 16.

21. The self-fulfilling character of theories of modernism which remain unreflexively bound to the perspective of their objects is a preoccupation of Raymond Williams's late work on modernism. See Williams, *The Politics of Modernism: Against the New Conformists*, ed. Tony Pinkney, Verso, London, 1989, chs 1 and 2. But the problem is equally if not more acute in sociological theories of modernity. 'Modernity' is not just the privileged object of classical sociological theory; the concept constituted its standpoint as an academic discipline at the time of its foundation in the closing decades of the nineteenth century. David Frisby, *Fragments of Modernity: Theories of Modernity in the Work of Simmel, Kracauer and Benjamin*, Polity Press, Cambridge, 1985, p. 2.

22. Theodor W. Adorno, *Minima Moralia: Reflections From Damaged Life* (1951), trans. E.F.N. Jephcott, Verso, London, 1978, p. 218.

23. The term 'postmodern' first appears in the 1930s in discussions of Latin American poetry (*postmodernismo*), but its meaning there lacks its current epochal dimension. An often cited early occurrence of the latter sense is the 1947 edition of Arnold Toynbee's *A Study of History*. The word first began to gain a general currency

in American literary theory in the early 1960s, particularly through the work of Leslie Fielder. It was only in the 1970s and early 1980s, however, that it came to acquire the critical prominence which was the basis for its more recent wholesale circulation as a general label for the character of the times. Central to this process of popularization were Charles Jencks, *The Language of Postmodern Architecture*, Academy Editions, London, 1977; Jean-François Lyotard, *The Postmodern Condition: A Report on Knowledge*; and Fredric Jameson, 'Postmodernism, or the Cultural Logic of Late Capitalism', *New Left Review* 146, July/August 1984, pp. 53–92. For a discussion of the history of the term, see Ihab Hassan, *The Postmodern Turn: Essays in Postmodern Theory and Culture*, Ohio State University Press, 1987, pp. 84–96. The recent attempt to trump the postmodern with the idea of the 'post-contemporary' (as in the series of 'Post-Contemporary Interventions', edited by Stanley Fish and Fredric Jameson for Duke University Press) looks like another, if more desperate, variant of the same self-defeating temporal logic.

24. Reinhart Koselleck, '"*Neuzeit*": Remarks on the Semantics of the Modern Concept of Movement', in his *Futures Past: On the Semantics of Historical Time*, trans. Keith Tribe, MIT Press, Cambridge, MA, 1985, pp. 231–66. For other, more wide-ranging surveys of the semantic prehistory of 'modernity', see Hans Blumenberg, *The Legitimacy of the Modern Age* (*Die Legitimität der Neuzeit*, 1966–76), trans. Robert M. Wallace, MIT Press, Cambridge MA, 1983; Matei Calinescu, *Five Faces of Modernity: Modernism, Avant-Garde, Decadence, Kitsch, Postmodernism*, Duke University Press, Durham, NC, 1987, pp. 11–92; Hans Robert Jauss, 'Literarische Tradition und gegenwartiges Bewusstein der Modernitat', in *Literaturgeschichte als Provokation*, Suhrkamp, Frankfurt, 1970; and Jacques Le Goff, 'Antique (Ancient)/ Modern', in *Memory and History*, trans. Steven Rendall and Elizabeth Claman, Columbia University Press, New York, 1992, pp. 21–50. I have drawn liberally from each of these sources in what follows, abstracting from the differential register in which the new temporal logic is to be found in different European languages, which is bound up with the different forms and rates of economic, political and cultural development in European nation states. However, it is important to distinguish this complexity, internal to European development, from differences in the meaning of the modern in 'non-Western' cultures, produced by their exposure to European ideas and social forms in the context of colonial and post-colonial relations of military and economic domination.

25. Koselleck, *Futures Past*, p. 233.

26. Le Goff, *Memory and History*, p. 27.

27. Ibid., p. 26.

28. Berman, 'Why Modernism Still Matters', p. 33.

29. Koselleck, *Futures Past*, p. 238.

30. Octavio Paz, *Children of the Mire*, trans. Rachel Phillips, Harvard University Press, Cambridge MA, 1974, p. 23. For further discussion of the multiplicity of relations between the concepts of modernity and eternity, see ch. 4.

31. Blumenberg, *The Legitimacy of the Modern Age*, p. 116; translation amended.

32. Koselleck, *Futures Past*, pp. 249, 246. See also Blumenberg, 'The Epochs of the Concept of an Epoch', in *The Legitimacy of the Modern Age*, pp. 457–82.

33. Walter Benjamin, *Gesammelte Schriften* [GS] I, 3, Suhrkamp Verlag, Frankfurt M. 1980, p. 1152; quoted in translation in Frisby, *Fragments of Modernity*, p. 15.

34. Calinescu, *Five Faces*, p. 45.

35. Williams, *The Politics of Modernism*, p. 32.

36. Calinescu, *Five Faces*, p. 92.

37. Williams, *The Politics of Modernism*, p. 32.

38. Lyotard, 'Answering the Question: What is Postmodernism?', in *The Postmodern Condition*, p. 79.

39. Baudelaire, 'The Painter of Modern Life' (1863), in Charles Baudelaire, *The Painter of Modern Life and Other Essays*, trans. and ed. Jonathan Mayne, de Capo Press, New York, n.d. (reprint of Phaidon Press ed., 1964) pp. 12–13.

40. Althusser and Balibar, *Reading Capital*, Pt II, ch. 4.

41. Jules Michelet, *Histoire de France*, Volume II, Paris, 1885, p. 161.

42. For an account of money as the 'first form of appearance of capital' (self-expanding value), see Marx, *Capital*, Volume 1, chs 3–6. The major work of Georg Simmel, the first sociologist of 'modernity', was of course *The Philosophy of Money* (1900), ed. David Frisby, trans. Tom Bottomore and David Frisby, Routledge, London, 1990.

43. Koselleck, *Futures Past*, p. 250.

44. Hannah Arendt, *Between Past and Future: Eight Exercises in Political Thought*, Penguin, Harmondsworth, 1977, p. 13.

45. Theodor W. Adorno, *Aesthetic Theory* (1970), trans. C. Lenhardt, Routledge and Kegan Paul, London, 1984, p. 41. Cf. Benjamin's definition of fashion as 'the eternal recurrence of the new', in 'Central Park', trans. Lloyd Spencer, *New German Critique* 34, Winter 1985, p. 46.

46. Henri Meschonnic, 'Modernity, Modernity', *New Literary History*, Vol. 23, 1992, p. 419.

47. Ibid.

48. Anderson, 'Modernity and Revolution', p. 101.

49. See, for example, Edward W. Soja, *Postmodern Geographies: The Reassertion of Space in Critical Social Theory*, Verso, London, 1989; David Harvey, *The Condition of Postmodernity: An Inquiry into the Origins of Cultural Change*, Blackwell, Oxford, 1989, pp. 201–323; and, for a critique, Doreen Massey, 'Politics and Space/Time', *New Left Review* 196, November/December 1992.

50. Walter Benjamin, 'N [Re the Theory of Knowledge, Theory of Progress]' – Konvolut N from the 'Notes and Materials' which make up the Arcades Project – trans. Leigh Hafrey and Richard Sieburth in Gary Smith (ed.), *Benjamin: Philosophy, Aesthetics, History*, Chicago University Press, Chicago, 1989, p. 62.

51. Naoki Sakai, 'Modernity and its Critique: The Problem of Universalism and Particularism', in Miyoshi, Masao and Harootunian, H.D. (eds), *Postmodernism and Japan*, Duke University Press, Durham, NC, 1989, p. 106.

52. Paz, *Children of the Mire*, p. 23.

53. Sakai, 'Modernity and its Critique', p. 94.

54. Homi Bhabha, '"Race", Time and the Revision of Modernity', in his *The Location of Culture*, Routledge, London and New York, 1994, ch. 12.

55. Paul Gilroy, *The Black Atlantic: Modernity and Double Consciousness*, Verso, London, 1993, ch. 1.

56. Immanuel Kant, 'Idea for a Universal History with Cosmopolitan Intent' (1784), in Kant, *Perpetual Peace and Other Essays*, trans. Ted Humpreys, Hackett Publishing Co, Indianapolis and Cambridge, 1983, ch. 1.

57. See, for example, Ernst Bloch's analysis of fascism in 'Non-contemporaneity and Obligation to its Dialectic' (1932), in his *Heritage of our Times*, trans. Neville and Stephen Plaice, Polity Press, Cambridge, 1991, pp. 97–148. As Bloch puts it: 'We do not all live in the same now.' Bloch's dialectics raises his work well above the conceptual level of modernization theory, especially in his analyses of the 'hollow' and contradictory time of montage. Nonetheless, its neglect or derogation of the geo-political determination of differences in historical time restricts it to a struggle at the limits of the paradigm. See, for example, his remark that montage is one form 'of making sure of the old culture perceived from the perspective of *travel and consternation*, no longer of *learning*'. Ibid., p. 208; emphasis added. On the other hand, one might detect here the prefiguration of a critique of postmodern anthropology.

58. For an overview of theories of development, see Jorge Larrain, *Theories of Development: Capitalism, Colonialism and Dependency*, Polity Press, Cambridge, 1989; especially the historical map on p. 4.

59. Robert Young, *White Mythologies: Writing History and the West*, Routledge, London and New York, 1990, pp. 19–20.

60. Fabian, *Time and the Other*, chs 1–3. Fabian's book is fundamental as a critique

of the form of temporality constitutive of anthropology as a discipline, which separated off its object, in principle, from both history and sociology.

61. See Francis Barker et al. (eds), *Postmodernism and the Re-Reading of Modernity*, Manchester University Press, Manchester, 1992, in which an earlier version of this chapter appeared.

62. Julia Kristeva, 'Women's Time', in *The Kristeva Reader*, ed. by Toril Moi, Blackwell, Oxford, 1986, p. 191.

63. 'Modernity and Revolution', pp. 101–3.

64. My objections to Anderson here are not to his critique of Berman, so much as to his *acceptance* of Berman's characterization of 'modernity' as a dialectic of modernism and modernization. By accepting Berman's account of modernity, Anderson unwittingly becomes complicit in the object of his own critique. His real complaint is against the generic modern*ism* of Berman's version of modernization: his affirmation of the temporal logic of modernity in abstraction from its underlying social dynamics and specific cultural forms. When he extends this critique to aesthetic modernism, however, Anderson is less persuasive. Modernism is indeed a 'perennial' concept, but that is its point. In its deepest and most theoretically productive sense, it is neither a stylistic nor a movement concept – part of an empiricist art history – but a term identifying the immanent historical logic of a particular dynamic of artistic development. It provides a temporal frame for the historical interpretation of works; not that interpretation itself. See Peter Osborne, 'Adorno and the Metaphysics of Modernism: The Problem of a "Postmodern" Art', in Andrew Benjamin (ed.), *The Problems of Modernity: Adorno and Benjamin*, Routledge, London and New York 1989, pp. 23–48.

It was Benjamin who took as his explicit goal the construction of a form of historical experience 'beyond' the categories of progress and decline. Benjamin, 'N [Re the Theory of Knowledge]', in Smith (ed.), *Benjamin*, pp. 44, 48. In so doing, however, he was explicitly opposing himself to precisely that homogeneous continuum of modern time-consciousness which Anderson accuses of *lacking* a concept of decline.

65. See, for example, Fredric Jameson, 'Nostalgia for the Present', in his *Postmodernism, or, The Cultural Logic of Late Capitalism*, Verso, London, 1991, ch. 9.

66. See Jürgen Habermas, 'Modernity – An Incomplete Project', trans. Seyla Benhabib, in Hal Foster (ed.), *Postmodern Culture*, Pluto, London, 1985, pp. 3–15.

67. Jürgen Habermas, *The Philosophical Discourse of Modernity: Twelve Lectures*.

68. Immanuel Kant, 'An Answer to the Question: What is Enlightenment?', in Kant, *Perpetual Peace and Other Essays*, pp. 41–8. See also Michel Foucault, 'Georges Canguilhem: Philosopher of Error', trans. Graham Burchell, *Ideology and Consciousness* 7, Autumn 1980, pp. 51–62; 'Kant on Enlightenment and Revolution', trans. Colin Gordon, *Economy and Society*, Vol. 15, no.1, pp. 88–96; 'What is Enlightenment?', trans. Catherine Porter, in Paul Rabinow (ed.), *The Foucault Reader*, Penguin, Harmondsworth, 1986, pp. 32–50; Jürgen Habermas, 'Taking Aim at the Heart of the Present: On Foucault's Lecture on Kant's What is Enlightenment?', in his *The New Conservatism: Cultural Criticism and the Historians' Debate*, ed. and trans. Shierry Weber Nicholson, Polity Press, Cambridge, 1989, ch. 7. For an example of the way in which this dispute has been taken up by a younger generation of academics in America, see the exchange between John Rajchman and Richard Wolin: Rajchman, 'Habermas's Complaint', *New German Critique* 45, Fall 1988, p. 163–91; Wolin, 'On Misunderstanding Habermas: A Response to Rajchman', *New German Critique* 49, Winter 1990, pp. 139–54; Rajchman, 'Rejoinder to Richard Wolin', *New German Critique* 49, pp. 155–61.

69. In *The Philosophical Discourse of Modernity*, it is initially Hegel who is credited with being 'the first to raise to the level of a philosophical problem the process of detaching modernity from the suggestion of norms lying outside of itself in the past' (p. 16). Later in the same volume (p. 295), however, following the remarks in his 1984 memorial address for Foucault ('Taking Aim at the Heart of the Present'), Habermas

concedes Foucault's identification of Kant as the initiator of the discourse. The absence of a discussion of Kant in *The Philosophical Discourse*, where there is no reference to Kant's essay, despite the fact that it is essentially Kant's project that Habermas is defending, is thus extremely unfortunate.

70. Habermas, *The Philosophical Discourse*, p. 7.

71. Kant, 'An Answer to the Question: What is Enlightenment?', p. 41.

72. Foucault, 'Georges Canguilhem', p. 54; Jürgen Habermas, *Theory of Communicative Action* (1981), Volume 1, *Reason and the Rationalisation of Society*, trans. Thomas McCarthy, Heinemann, London, 1985; Volume 2, *Lifeworld and System: A Critique of Functionalist Reason*, trans. Thomas McCarthy, Polity Press, Cambridge, 1987. See also Theodor W. Adorno and Max Horkheimer, *Dialectic of Enlightenment*, (1944), trans. John Cumming, Verso, London, 1979.

73. Foucault, 'What is Enlightenment?', p. 42.

74. Foucault, 'Georges Canguilhem', p. 54. Note: 'Reason as despotic Enlightenment'; not 'Enlightenment as despotic reason' – a formulation that would commit Foucault to the elaboration of an alternative model of practical reason. For critiques of Foucault along the lines that he is, in any case, so commited, but unable in principle to produce such an alternative, see Peter Dews, 'Power and Subjectivity in Foucault', *New Left Review* 144, March/April 1984, pp. 72–95 and Nancy Fraser, 'Foucault on Modern Power: Empirical Insights and Normative Confusions', *Praxis International* 1, 1981. This is also Habermas's line in *The Philosophical Discourse*, pp. 266–93, where he accuses Foucault of 'cryptonormativism'.

75. Foucault, 'Kant on Enlightenment and Revolution', p. 95.

76. Adorno, *Minima Moralia*, p. 221.

77. Althusser and Balibar, *Reading Capital*, p. 97. Cf. the important early essays, 'Contradiction and Overdetermination' (1962) and 'On the Materialist Dialectic' (1963), in Louis Althusser, *For Marx*, trans. Ben Brewster, New Left Books, London, 1977, pp. 87–128, 161–218.

78. *Reading Capital*, p. 94.

79. Ibid., pp. 99–100.

80. The inability of Althusser's Marxism to think historical change is notorious. It was the rock on which the whole project foundered. It is ironic that it was precisely because of its supposed political value that Althusser focused on the notion of conjunctural analysis, derived from Lenin, in the first place. Althusser's main objection to the temporality of Hegelianism is that its ontologization of the present 'prevents any anticipation of historical time, any conscious anticipation of the future . . . any knowledge of the future'. Consequently, he argued, there can be for it no 'science of politics': 'no Hegelian politics is possible strictly speaking' (*Reading Capital*, p. 95; cf. *For Marx*, p. 204). In fact, of course, there are at least two types of Hegelian politics: the notorious 'left' and 'right' Hegelianisms. Their error is actually the reverse of that attributed to Hegel by Althusser: namely, their *over*-anticipation of the future, closing it off from what we might call 'unconscious anticipations'. In seeking *knowledge* of the future, Althusser was more of a Hegelian than he realized. Cf. Derrida's remark that anti-Hegelian thinkers tend to come closest to Hegel 'at the very moment when . . . [they are] apparently opposed to Hegel in the most radical fashion'. 'Violence and Metaphysics', in *Writing and Difference* (1967), trans. Alan Bass, University of Chicago Press, Chicago, 1978, p. 99.

81. *Reading Capital*, pp. 96–7.

82. The identification of Hegelianism with an everyday or 'ordinary' form of homogeneous time-consciousness derives from $82 of Heidegger's *Being and Time* (1927), trans. John Macquarrie and Edward Robinson, Blackwell, Oxford, 1962. However, as we shall see in the next chapter, this identification, mediated by a mutual relation to Aristotle, fails to grasp the temporal specificity of Hegelianism, which has problems of its own. For an extended 'deconstruction' of the relevant passage in Heidegger, see Jacques Derrida, '*Ousia* and *Gramme*: Note on a Note from *Being and Time*', in *Margins of Philosophy*, trans. Alan Bass, Harvester Wheatsheaf, Hemel Hempstead,

1982, pp. 29–67. For a discussion of Heidegger's account of the 'ordinary conception of time', see pp. 62–8 above.

83. Fernand Braudel, *On History*, trans. Sarah Matthews, Weidenfeld and Nicolson, London, 1980, p. 49; emphasis added.

84. Perry Anderson, *Arguments within English Marxism*, Verso, London, 1980, pp. 75–6. I am grateful to Gregory Elliott for drawing my attention to this passage.

85. *On History*, p. 34. Braudel describes Marx as 'the first to construct true social models, on the basis of the historical *longue durée*'. Ibid., p. 51.

86. For an alternative account of Althusser's relations to the *Annales* School, emphasizing the convergence between Althusser's distinction between the 'real object' and the 'object of knowledge', and the *Annales*' conception of history as a 'history of problems', see Peter Schöttler, 'Althusser and Annales Historiography – An Impossible Dialogue?', trans. Gregory Elliot, in Michael Sprinker and E. Ann Kaplan (eds), *The Althusserian Legacy*, Verso, London, 1992, pp. 81–98.

87. *Arguments*, p. 75.

88. *Reading Capital*, p. 96.

89. Fabian, *Time and the Other*, pp. 55–6; final empahsis added.

90. See Anderson, *Arguments*, p. 74.

91. *Reading Capital*, p. 106.

92. Ibid., p. 311.

93. Fabian, *Time and the Other*, pp. 156–65.

94. The knowledge of history, according to one of Althusser's more notorious formulations, 'is no more historical than the knowledge of sugar is sweet'. *Reading Capital*, p. 106.

95. See Marx, *Capital: A Critique of Political Economy*, Volume 2 (1885), trans. David Fernbach, Penguin, Harmondsworth, 1978, chs 5, 7, 12–15.

2. One Time, One History?

1. Jameson's view that '[h]istory as ground and untranscendable horizon needs no particular theoretical justification' (Fredric Jameson, *The Political Unconscious: Narrative as a Socially Symbolic Act*, Methuen, London, 1981, p. 102), whilst appealing, contradicts itself in the act of its articulation, by using just such a phenomenological category – 'untranscendable horizon' – which consequently remains unexamined.

2. Wilhelm Dilthey, 'The Construction of the Historical World in the Human Studies', in *Selected Writings*, trans. and ed. H.P. Rickman, Cambridge University Press, Cambridge, 1976; Heinrich Rickert, *Science and History: A Critique of Positivist Epistemology*, trans. George Reisman, ed. Arthur Godard, D. Ven Nostrand, Princeton, 1962; Martin Heidegger, 'The Concept of Time in the Science of History' (1916), trans. H.S. Taylor and H.W. Ufflemann, *Journal of the British Society of Phenomenology*, Vol. 9, no. 1, 1978, pp. 3–10.

3. Herbert Schnadelbach, *Philosophy in Germany 1831–1933*, Cambridge University Press, Cambridge, 1984, ch. 2. See also Lukács's remarks in the introduction to his *The Young Hegel* (1948), trans. Rodney Livingstone, Merlin Press, London, 1975, p. xvi, concerning 'the victory in neo-Kantianism of the Schopenhauerian line of the history of philosophy' and the subsequent attempt 'to press Hegel's philosophy into the service of an imperialist, reactionary restructuring of neo-Kantianism'. Dilthey is subjected to particular scorn.

4. Karl Marx and Frederick Engels, 'The German Ideology' (1845), in their *Collected Works* Lawrence and Wishart, London, 1975–89 – Volume 5, p. 37. Cf. Raymond Aron's definition of the object of the philosophy of history as 'synthesis (choice, interpretation, the organisation of the material)', rather than the merely methodological critique of its scientific preliminaries, in his *Introduction to the*

Philosophy of History: An Essay on the Limits of Historical Objectivity (1938; 1948), trans. George J. Irwin Weidenfeld and Nicolson, London, 1961, p. 9.

5. Engels, *Anti-Dühring: Herr Dühring's Revolution in Science* (1878), trans. Emile Burns, Progress Publishers, Moscow, 1947, Pt I and *Dialectics of Nature*, trans. Clemens Dutt, Progress Publishers, Moscow, 1934. The latter was never published in Engels's lifetime. It first appeared in full only in 1925, in a Soviet edition, one year after the publication of Stalin's *The Foundations of Leninism*.

6. Russell Jacoby, *Dialectic of Defeat: Contours of Western Marxism*, Cambridge University Press, Cambridge, 1981.

7. See, for example, 'Towards a Reconstruction of Historical Materialism', in Jürgen Habermas, *Communication and the Evolution of Society*, trans. Thomas McCarthy, Heinemann, London, 1979. In her brief discussion of neo-Kantian Marxism (*Hegel Contra Sociology*, Athlone Press, London, 1981, pp. 24–38), Gillian Rose back-dates this tendency to include both Lukács and Adorno, extending Lukács's idea of a neo-Kantian neo-Hegelianism to envelop Lukács himself.

8. See n. 2 to ch. 1, above.

9. Paul Ricoeur, *The Contribution of French Historiography to the Theory of History*, Clarendon Press, Oxford, 1980, and 'History and Narrative', Pt II of *TN* 1. For the Anglo-American literature, see Patrick Gardiner (ed.), *Theories of History*, Free Press, New York, 1959. Althusser's brief engagement with the *Annales* School is a rare example of an exchange between Marxism and this tradition. A belated Soviet engagement with the analytical literature is Eeero Loone, *Soviet Marxism and the Analytical Philosophies of Histories* (1980), trans. Brian Pearce, Verso, London, 1992.

10. As Aron puts it (*Introduction*, p. 44): 'There exists no science of history whose validity would impose acceptance as inevitably as did the Newtonian physics in the case of Kant.' This is even more so today than at the time of Aron's book (the 1930s).

11. For a brilliant example of this, see Michel de Certeau, *The Writing of History* (1975), trans. Tom Conley, Columbia University Press, New York, 1988, especially Pt I.

12. Aron, *Introduction*, p. 10.

13. Paul Ricoeur, 'Objectivity and Subjectivity in History' (1952), in *History and Truth*, trans. Charles A. Kelbley, Northwestern University Press, Evanston, Illinois, 1965, p. 24.

14. Marc Bloch, 'History, Men, and Time', in *The Historian's Craft*, trans. Peter Putnam, Manchester University Press, Manchester, 1954, pp. 20–47. Note the title of the influential British journal founded in 1952 in the spirit of the *Annales* School: *Past and Present*.

15. See for example, Fidel Castro, *History Will Absolve Me*, Book Institute, Havana, 1963.

16. Karl Marx, *Grundrisse: Foundations of the Critique of Political Economy (Rough Draft)*, trans. Martin Nicolaus, Penguin, Harmondsworth, 1973, p. 109.

17. See Fernand Braudel, *The Wheels of Commerce: Civilisation and Capitalism, 15th–18th Century*, Volume 2, trans. Sian Reynolds, Collins, London, 1982; Immanuel Wallerstein, *The Modern World-System: Capitalist Agriculture and the Origins of the European World-Economy in the Sixteenth Century*, Academic Press, London, 1974; T.H. Aston and C.H.E. Philpin (eds), *The Brenner Debate: Agrarian Class Structure and Economic Development in Pre-Industrial Europe*, Cambridge University Press, Cambridge, 1985.

18. Jacques Le Goff, 'Labour-Time in the "Crisis" of the Fourteenth Century: From Medieval Time to Modern Time' (1963), in his *Time, Work, and Culture in the Middle Ages*, trans. Arthur Goldhammer, Chicago University Press, Chicago, 1989, pp. 43–57; E.P. Thompson, 'Time, Work-Discipline, and Industrial Capitalism', *Past and Present* 38, 1967, pp. 56–97; Frederick Cooper, 'Colonising Time: Work Rhythms and Labour Conflict in Colonial Mombasa', in Nicholas B. Dirks (ed.),

Colonialism and Culture, University of Michigan Press, Ann Arbor, 1992, pp. 209–46.

19. Eviatar Zerubavel, 'The Standardisation of Time: A Sociohistorical Perspective', *American Journal of Sociology*, Vol. 88, no. 1, 1982, pp. 1–23. Important background conditions to the imposition of the quantifiable continuum of a homogeneous clock-time in early capitalism include the development of the schedule as a way of regulating life in Benedictine Monasteries, and the increasing autonomy established by merchants' time from church time during the course of the fourteenth century. See Eviatar Zerubavel, 'The Benedictine Ethic and the Modern Spirit of Scheduling: On Schedules and Social Life', *Sociological Inquiry* 50, pp. 157–69, and Le Goff, 'Merchant's Time and Church's Time in the Middle Ages' (1960), in *Time, Work, and Culture in the Middle Ages*, pp. 29–42.

20. The theoretical basis for the application of an abstractly chronological conception of time to history was laid by the discovery of geological time, which destroyed the restricted theological time-scales of creationism. See Stephen Jay Gould, *Time's Arrow, Time's Cycle: Myth and Metaphor in the Discovery of Geological Time*, Penguin, Harmondsworth, 1988.

21. Pierre Vilar, 'Marxist History, A History in the Making: Towards a Dialogue with Althusser', *New Left Review* 80, July/August 1973, p. 105. It is important to distinguish here between the idea of 'history as world history', in the fully global sense, and Wallerstein's idea of a 'world system', which is both relative to the state of the social unification of the globe at any one time and essentially structural (that is, synchronic/diachronic) in its conception of time. See, for example, the account of an earlier 'world system', prior to the establishment of relations between the Americas and other continents, in Janet Abu-Lughod, *Before Europe's Hegemony: The World System, A.D. 1250–1350*, Oxford University Press, New York and Oxford, 1989.

22. Gayatri Chakravorty Spivak, 'Scattered Speculations on the Question of Culture Studies', in her *Outside in the Teaching Machine*, Routledge, New York and London, 1993, p. 256.

23. Vilar, 'Marxist History', p. 106.

24. *The Political Unconscious*, p. 28; emphasis added.

25. See, for example, the account of the dialectic of projection and planning in the secret societies of the masons in eighteenth-century Germany, in Reinhart Koselleck, *Critique and Crisis: Enlightenment and the Pathogenesis of Modern Society* (1959), Berg, New York, 1988, ch. 9.

26. Karl Marx, 'Theses on Feuerbach', in Marx and Engels, *Collected Works*, Volume 5, p. 3.

27. Theodor W. Adorno, '*Geschichte-Philosophie*', unpublished lecture series, p. 19, quoted in Robert Hullot-Kentor, 'Back to Adorno', *Telos* 81, Fall 1989, p. 13.

28. Karl Popper, *The Poverty of Historicism* (1957), Routledge, London, 1960.

29. G.W.F. Hegel, *Phenomenology of Spirit*, trans. A.V. Miller, Clarendon Press, Oxford, 1977, pp. 47, 49.

30. Jacques Derrida, 'From Restricted to General Economy: A Hegelianism Without Reserve', in *Writing and Difference*, p. 260.

31. Cf. Agnes Heller, *A Philosophy of History in Fragments*, Blackwell, Oxford, 1993, chs 1 and 6.

32. Lutz Niethammer, *Posthistoire: Has History Come to an End?*, trans. Patrick Camiller, Verso, London and New York, 1992, pp. 137, 144, 149.

33. The stimulus has, of course, been Francis Fukuyama, 'The End of History?', *The National Interest*, Summer 1989, pp. 3–18, later expanded into *The End of History and the Last Man*, Penguin, Harmondsworth, 1992.

34. It is the structure of Hegel's conception of the rationality of the historical present that I am concerned with here, not his own account of its content, as represented by the politics of his *Philosophy of Right*.

35. See Joseph McCarney, 'Endgame', *Radical Philosophy* 62, Autumn 1992, pp. 35–8.

36. Hegel, *Phenomenology*, p. 6.

37. See, for example, Joseph McCarney, 'What Makes Critical Theory Critical?', *Radical Philosophy* 42, Winter/Spring 1986, pp. 11–23, and 'The True Realm of Freedom: Marxist Philosophy After Communism', *New Left Review* 189, September/October 1991, pp. 19–38.

38. Compare 'Religion ist Eine' (1793), trans. H.S. Harris as the Appendix to his *Hegel's Development Volume 1: Towards the Sunlight, 1770–1801*, Clarendon Press, Oxford, 1972, with the later *Lectures on the Philosophy of Religion*, trans. E.S. Haldane, Routledge and Kegan Paul, London, 1952. See also *Hegel's Philosophy of Mind*, trans. William Wallace, Clarendon Press, Oxford, 1971, p. 282.

39. Karl Marx, 'Contribution to the Critique of Hegel's Philosophy of Law. Introduction' (1843), in Marx and Engels, *Collected Works*, Volume 3; *Capital: A Critique of Political Economy*, Volume 3, (1894) Lawrence and Wishart, London, 1959, p. 820. I provide a reconstruction of the relations between theoretical and practical reason in German philosophy from Kant's *Critique of Practical Reason* to Marx and Engels, *The Communist Manifesto* in my doctoral thesis, 'The Carnival of Philosophy: Philosophy, Politics, and Science in Hegel and Marx', unpublished D.Phil thesis, University of Sussex, 1989.

40. Perry Anderson, 'Ends of History', in his *A Zone of Engagement*, pp. 331–57; McCarney, 'Endgame', pp. 37–8; Fred Halliday, 'An Encounter with Fukuyama', *New Left Review* 193, May/June 1993, pp. 89–95; Gregory Elliott, 'The Cards of Confusion: Historical Communism and the "End of History"', *Radical Philosophy* 64, Summer 1993, pp. 3–12; Joseph McCarney, 'Shaping Ends: Reflections on Fukuyama', *New Left Review* 202, November/December 1993, pp. 37–53. This literature is almost sufficiently profuse to constitute a left school of Fukuyama interpretation.

41. *Posthistoire*, p. 28.

42. McCarney, 'The True Realm of Freedom', pp. 31–2. See also Joseph McCarney, *Social Theory and the Crisis of Marxism*, Verso, London, 1990, Pt III.

43. See here István Mészáros, 'The Cunning of History in Reverse Gear', *Radical Philosophy* 42, Winter/Spring 1986, pp. 2–10 and 'Marx's "Social Revolution" and the Division of Labour', *Radical Philosophy* 44, Autumn 1986, pp. 14–23. Mészáros's reading of 'what is living and what is dead' in Marx is the basis for McCarney's reconstruction of the hopes of a Marxist Hegelianism.

44. Fukuyama, *The End of History*, Pt V.

45. Quoted by Anderson, 'The Ends of History', p. 322.

46. *TN* 3, pp. 204–5.

47. Georg Wilhelm Friedrich Hegel, *Phänomenologie des Geistes*, Ullstein, Frankfurt/M., 1970, p. 29; *Phenomenology of Spirit*, p. 19 (translation altered).

48. Georges Bataille, 'Hegel, Death and Sacrifice' (1955), trans. Jonathan Strauss, in Allan Stoekl (ed.), *Yale French Studies 78: On Bataille*, Yale University Press, New Haven, 1990, p. 27.

49. *TN* 3, p. 202.

50. Ibid.; G.W.F. Hegel, *Reason in History: A General Introduction to the Philosophy of History*, trans. Robert S. Hartman, Bobbs-Merrill, Indianapolis, 1953, p. 11 (translation amended).

51. Derrida, 'From Restricted to General Economy', *Writing and Difference*, p. 253.

52. Michel Foucault, *L'Ordre du Discours*, Gallimard, Paris, 1971, pp. 74–5; quoted in his own translation by David Macey, *The Lives of Michel Foucault*, Hutchinson, London, 1993, p. 243. Cf. the remark by Derrida quoted in note 80 to Ch. 1, above.

53. Ricoeur reads Gadamer as abandoning Hegel, 'rather than conquering him through criticism.' *TN* 3, p. 324, n. 14. Derrida reads Bataille as having stayed too close to him because he saw the dialectical trap inherent in both alternatives so clearly. Yet ironically, when Derrida tries to 'sharpen' Bataille's displacement of Hegelian discourse by accentuating the absolutism of his critique, he merely *returns* him to Hegel at another level. Count the absolutes in Derrida's reading of Bataille: absolute difference, absolute

risk, absolute failure, absolute erasure, absolute unknowledge, absolute excess, absolute non-discourse, absolute adventure . . . 'From a Restricted to a General Economy', *Writing and Difference*, pp. 251–77.

54. Ludwig Feuerbach, 'Towards a Critique of Hegel's Philosophy', in *The Fiery Brook: Selected Writings of Ludwig Feuerbach*, trans. Zawar Hanfi, Anchor Books, Garden City NY, 1972, pp. 53–96, (pp. 57–8).

55. *Hegel's Philosophy of Nature*, trans. William Wallace, Oxford University Press, Oxford, 1970, pp. 39, 36.

56. Feuerbach, 'Towards a Critique of Hegel's Philosophy', pp. 62–73. '[T]otality or the absoluteness of a particular historical phenomenon or existence,' Feuerbach writes, 'is vindicated as predicate, thus reducing the stages of development as independent entities to a merely historical meaning; although living, they continue to exist as nothing more than shadows or moments, nothing more than homeopathic drops on the level of the absolute' (p. 55). The ultimate mark of their independence is, of course, the absoluteness of their death. See also Bataille, 'Hegel, Death and Sacrifice', where representation is presented as at once the condition for the knowledge of the constitutive role of death in human life and the barrier to a true knowing of death.

57. 'From a General to a Restricted Economy', pp. 257, 259. Cf. Georg Lukács, *The Ontology of Social Being. 1. Hegel's False and his Genuine Ontology*, trans. David Fernbach, Merlin Press, London, 1978.

58. Walter Benjamin, 'Theses on the Philosophy of History', in *Illuminations*, p. 262. Consider the centrality of the recovery of working-class, women's and ethnic histories to the political movements of the last forty years.

59. This is probably what Althusser was getting at when he said that 'no Hegelian politics is possible strictly speaking', although he misidentifies the character of the problem. See ch 1, n. 80.

60. *TN* 3, p. 206. Cf. Hans-Georg Gadamer, *Truth and Method* (1961; 1965), Sheed and Ward, London, 1979, pp. 305–10, 317–25.

61. Alexandre Kojève, *An Introduction to the Reading of Hegel*, ed. Allan Bloom, trans. James H. Nichols Jr., Basic Books, New York and London, 1969, p. 133, n. 20.

62. See Vincent Descombes, *Modern French Philosophy*, trans. L. Scott-Fox and J.M. Harding Cambridge University Press, Cambridge, 1980, ch. 1; Kate Soper, *Humanism and Anti-Humanism*, Hutchinson, London, 1986.

63. Note the lack of mediation between Pts II & III of Fukuyama's *The End of History*. A similar problem notoriously bedevils Georg Lukács, *History and Class Consciousness: Studies in Marxist Dialectics* (1923), trans. Rodney Livingstone, Merlin Press, London, 1971.

64. Its three volumes were first published in French in 1983, 1984 and 1985, respectively.

65. *TN* 1, pp. 85, 92–3, 227.

66. As the phrase 'hermeneutics of historical existence' is intended to convey, I do not mean the term 'ontological' here to denote anything opposed to history or temporality, in the traditional sense of an ontological 'ground'. Rather, I use it only in its most general descriptive sense, to denote the domain of problems about being and existence, however these problems might be construed philosophically in relation to time. Adversion to 'ontology' as a realm of philosophical reification is increasingly extended beyond the restricted sense of the term to all questions about being and existence, reinforcing the epistemological subjectivism of modern thought at the very moment of its most radical critique – a trait of which neither negative dialectics nor deconstruction can be said to be completely free. In Ricoeur's *Time and Narrative* this tension is played out between the different volumes.

67. I owe this ingenious formulation to Jane Chamberlain.

68. *TN* 1, p. 3. Cf. Jameson, *The Political Unconscious*, p. 13, where narrative is referred to as 'the central function or *instance* of the human mind'.

69. *TN* 3, pp. 12–22. Heidegger, by contrast, locates the contradiction internally to Aristotle's account, and privileges the phenomenological moment in his reading of it,

thereby cutting off the threat of ontological objectivism at its source. See Martin Heidegger, *The Basic Problems of Phenomenology*, trans. Albert Hofstader, Indiana University Press, Bloomington, 1988, pp. 237–56.

70. *TN* 3, p. 11.

71. *TN* 3, pp. 23–44, 61–85; Heidegger, *Being and Time*, pp. 32–49. Ricoeur expounds this side of Aristotle's analysis only with reference to the way it is taken up by Augustine, where, as Heidegger notes, it occurs 'in a much more emphatic sense' (*Basic Problems*, p. 256).

72. *TN* 3, pp. 17, 15.

73. Ibid., p. 19.

74. *TN* 1, p. 8.

75. *TN* 3, pp. 25–6.

76. Quoted by Ricoeur, ibid., p. 28.

77. Heidegger, *Basic Problems*, p. 260.

78. See in particular, Heidegger, *History of the Concept of Time: Prolegomena*, trans. Theodore Kisiel, Indiana University Press, Bloomington, 1992, pp. 305–20: 'death is always already *impending* [*bevorstehend*]. As such, death belongs to Dasein itself even when it is not yet whole and not yet finished, even when it is not dying. Death is not a missing part of a whole taken as a composite. Rather it *constitutes the totality of Dasein from the start*, so that it is only on the basis of this totality that Dasein has the being of temporally particular parts, that is, of possible ways to be. [. . .] Dasein is essentially its death' (p. 313).

79. The *locus classicus* for the philosophical interpretation of duration is Bergson's *Time and Free Will: Essay on the Immediate Data of Consciousness* (1889), trans. F.L. Pogson, George Allen and Unwin, London, 1910. Heidegger had intended to devote the first section of the main part of his lectures on the 'History of the Concept of Time' in the summer semester at the University of Marburg in 1925 to Bergson's theory. But, as so often, he only completed the first part of his three-part plan. His position, as stated in the outline, was that Bergson is important because of his explicit attempt to go beyond the traditional concept of time to a 'more original' one; but that he fails and so remains traditional (*History of the Concept of Time*, p. 9). The substance of this analysis is hinted at in a note to *Being and Time* (pp. 500–01, n. xxx), in which Heidegger claims that Bergson's view 'has obviously arisen from an interpretation of the Aristotelian essay on time' by way of a 'counter-orientation'. The idea of time as quantitative succession is countered by that of duration as qualitative succession. Bergson's analysis of duration is thus going in the right direction (towards 'the way time is grasped ... our "consciousness of time"'), but its theorization as 'qualitative succession' marks it out as still dependent upon the old view.

A further aspect of this reading is revealed in Heidegger's lectures from the summer of 1927 on 'The Basic Problems of Phenomenology', which include a section entitled 'Interpretive exposition of Aristotle's concept of time' that presumably fulfills the plan for the third section of the central part of the 1925 lectures. In a brief preamble to the exposition of Aristotle (*Basic Problems*, pp. 231–2), Heidegger locates the untenability of Bergson's counter-concept of duration in 'a misunderstanding of Aristotle's way of understanding time'. Characteristically, Heidegger generates his own 'counter-concept' (the temporality of *Dasein*) out of a reading of Aristotle that deepens, rather than avoids, the aporias of this thought. However, although it does not refer to it, this reading actually rests upon the conceptual structure of Husserl's 1905 analysis. There is a common source to Husserl's and Bergson's thought in Brentano's descriptive psychology (cf. Heidegger, *History of the Concept of Time*, p. 23).

Interestingly, there is no reference to Bergson in Heidegger's original 1924 lecture to the Marburg Theological Society, from which all his subsequent analyses flow (Martin Heidegger, *The Concept of Time*, trans. William McNeill, Blackwell, Oxford, 1992). However, the reference there to Einstein (p. 3), when placed beside the reference to Bergson's critical examination of Einstein's theory of relativity in the second edition of his *Duration and Simultaneity* (1923) in *Basic Problems* (p. 232), suggests that it was in response to this work of Bergson's that Heidegger's thinking about time began.

80. *TN* 3, p. 35.

81. Heidegger, *Basic Problems*, pp. 240–56.

82. *TN* 3, p. 24.

83. Ibid., p. 25.

84. *TN* 3, p. 85.

85. For an account of the methodological role of the category of mystery in the philosophy of history, see Ricoeur's earlier 'Christianity and the Meaning of History' (1951), in his *History and Truth*, pp. 81–97. The general structure of Ricoeur's concept of history is already in place in the essays which make up this early work. For a contemporary critique, see Louis Althusser, 'Sur l'objectivité de l'histoire (Lettre à Paul Ricoeur)', *Revue de l'Enseignement Philosophique*, Vol. 5, no. 4, 1955, pp. 3–15. Ricoeur's response to Althusser's later work can be found in his 'Althusser's Theory of Ideology' (1975), in Gregory Elliott (ed.), *Althusser: A Critical Reader*, Blackwell, Oxford, 1994, pp. 44–72.

86. *TN* 3, p. 207.

87. Ibid., p. 231.

88. Jean-Paul Sartre, *Critique of Dialectical Reason I: Theory of Practical Ensembles*, trans. Alan Sheridan-Smith, New Left Books, London, 1976, pp. 42–76; *Critique of Dialectical Reason II: The Intelligibility of History*, trans. Quintin Hoare, Verso, London, 1991, Bk III, Pt III & Appendix.

89. See ch. 3 pp. 91–7, above.

90. Theodor W. Adorno, *Negative Dialektik* (1966), Suhrkamp, Frankfurt M., 1982, p. 314; *Negative Dialectics*, p. 320.

91. *TN* 3, p. 241.

92. Hans-Georg Gadamer, *Truth and Method*; Martin Heidegger, 'Time and Being' (1962), in *On Time and Being*, trans. Joan Stambaugh, Harper Torchbooks, New York, 1972, pp. 1–24; Jacques Derrida, 'Différence' (1968), *Margins of Philosophy*, pp. 1–27.

93. Jean-Paul Sartre, *Existentialism and Humanism* (1946), trans. Philip Mairet, Methuen, London, 1973; and for Heidegger's effective reply, the 'Letter on Humanism' (1947), in *Basic Writings*, ed. David Farrell Krell, Routledge, London, 1993, pp. 213–65. For Ricoeur's defence of separating out the analytic of *Dasein* from the question of Being, see *TN* 3, pp. 60–1.

94. See Barry Katz, *Herbert Marcuse and the Art of Liberation*, Verso, London, 1982, pp. 58–86, and Douglas Kellner, *Herbert Marcuse and the Crisis of Marxism*, Macmillan, London, 1984, pp. 38–68. Marcuse's first book-length work, a study of Hegel, opens with the declaration: 'Any contribution this work may make to the development and clarification of problems is indebted to the philosophical work of Martin Heidegger.' Herbert Marcuse, *Hegel's Ontology and the Theory of Historicity* (1931), trans. Seyla Benhabib, MIT Press, Cambridge MA, 1987, p. 5.

95. *Being and Time*, pp. 279, 275, 188–95. Cf. Gadamer, *Truth and Method*, pp. 235–41, 258–67.

96. *Being and Time*, pp. 280, 281.

97. Ibid., p. 288, emphasis added.

98. Ibid., p. 277.

99. Ibid., pp. 284, 289, 312–48.

100. *Negative Dialectics*, p. 129.

101. Peter Osborne, 'Overcoming Philosophy as Metaphysics: Rorty and Heidegger', *Oxford Literary Review*, Vol. 11, 1989, p. 94.

102. See ch. 5.

103. *Being and Time*, p. 307.

104. Ibid., p. 424; *Basic Problems*, p. 262; *Being and Time*, p. 307 (emphasis added).

105. Ibid., p. 427, 374.

106. Ibid., pp. 377, 401–2, 352.

107. *Negative Dialectics*, p. 129.

108. *Being and Time*, pp. 309, 440, 441 (emphasis added), 434.

109. As one of his translators has put it, Ricoeur wants 'to undertake the philosophy of history without engaging in the philosophy of history.' *History and Truth*, p. xiii. This ambivalence is the source of both the subtlety and the ultimate limitation of Ricoeur's work.

110. *Being and Time*, p. 416; Maurice Merleau-Ponty, *Phenomenology of Perception* (1946), trans. Colin Smith, Routledge and Kegan Paul, London, 1962, p. xv. After *Being and Time*, as part of the move from the temporality of *Dasein* to the temporality of Being, the idea of 'horizonal schemas' disappears from Heidegger's work. The return to it here marks our rejection of Heidegger's 'turn' in favour of a critical extension of the analytic of *Dasein*, through its confrontation with the alternative ontological problematics of 'nature' and 'the other'.

111. 'Violence and Metaphysics', in Derrida, *Writing and Difference*, pp. 117, 123; emphasis added. I use the term 'critique' advisedly. For an alternative, but in my view unconvincing, reading of Derrida's essay on Levinas as a proto-deconstructive 'double reading', see Simon Critchley, *The Ethics of Deconstruction: Derrida and Levinas*, Blackwell, Oxford, 1992, pp. 94–7. See also Derrida's discussion of the three modes of ending in Heidegger's *Being and Time* – perishing (*Verenden*), demising (*Ableben*) and dying (*Sterben*) – in his *Aporias*, trans. Thomas Dutoit, Stanford University Press, Stanford, 1993, pp. 35–40. *Dasein* 'is', as a temporal being, in that movement between totality and infinity which is the anticipation of death (*Tod*): recognition of possibility as the possibility of the impossibility of existence. Dying itself (*Sterben*) is simply impossible.

112. Jean-Luc Nancy, *The Experience of Freedom* (1988), trans. Bridget McDonald, Stanford University Press, Stanford, 1993, pp. 158–9.

113. *Basic Problems*, pp. 231–56. See also *Being and Time*, p. 473.

114. *TN* 3, p. 59.

115. Emmanuel Levinas, *Totality and Infinity: An Essay on Exteriority* (1961), trans. Alphonso Lingis, Duquesne University Press, Pittsburgh, 1969, p. 235.

116. *TN* 3, p. 18.

117. *Being and Time*, p. 465.

118. Ibid., p. 456.

119. Ibid., p. 464.

120. Ibid., p. 465.

121. Cf. Althusser's identification of Hegel's idea of time with 'the empiricism of the false obviousness of everyday practice', 'the ideological conception of a continuous-homogeneous time', in *Reading Capital*, p. 96. Heidegger treats Hegel's idea of time as essentially Aristotelian (*Being and Time*, pp. 480–6). As far as I am aware, the Heideggerian roots of Althusser's critique of the temporality of Hegelianism, nourished by the soil of a common anti-humanism, have yet to be examined in any detail.

122. Ibid., pp. 474–7. For a reading which links this problematic of 'the they' to a Marxist theory of ideology via Lukács's concept of reification, see Lucien Goldman, *Lukács and Heidegger: Towards a New Philosophy*, trans. William Q. Boelhower, Routledge and Kegan Paul, London, 1977.

123. *Basic Problems*, p. 262; emphasis added.

124. For a genealogy of the conceptual framework of *Being and Time*, see Theodore Kisiel, *The Genesis of Heidegger's 'Being and Time'*, University of California Press, Berkeley and London, 1993. The terminological aspect of Kisiel's work is summarized in a useful 'Genealogical Glossary of Heidegger's Basic Terms, 1916–1927', ibid., pp. 490–511.

125. *TN* 3, p. 17.

126. Ricoeur, 'Husserl and the Sense of History' (1949), trans. in Paul Ricoeur, *Husserl: An Analysis of his Phenomenology*, Northwestern University Press, Evanston, 1967, p. 149. The issues to which *Time and Narrative* is addressed are already formulated here, as problems internal to the development of Husserl's work.

127. *Phenomenology of Perception*, p. xiv.

128. *Being and Time*, pp. 153–63.

129. Edmund Husserl, *Cartesian Meditations* (1929), trans. Dorion Cairns, Kluwer, Dordrecht, 1993, p. 120.

130. *TN* 3, pp. 106–7, 229, 105.

131. The social (and hence political) dimension of the calendar is most apparent from its early history. As guardians of the state calendar in Republican Rome, the college of priests is said to have been amenable to inducements from interested groups to hasten or delay its announcement of a new year. The word 'calendar', from *calendare*, to call out or announce, retains the connection to these times. An official would parade through the streets announcing when the new moon had been officially sighted and thus a new month begun. See Norbert Elias, *Time: An Essay*, trans. Edmund Jephcott, Blackwell, Oxford, 1992, pp. 192–9.

132. See Walter Benjamin, 'N [Re the Theory of Knowledge, Theory of Progress]' (N 2, 6), trans. in Smith (ed.), *Benjamin: Philosophy, Aesthetics, History*, p. 48, and the 'Theses on the Philosophy of History', *Illuminations*, p. 263.

3. Death and Recognition

1. *Being and Time*, pp. 281–5.

2. $49 of *Being and Time* is dedicated to distinguishing existential from 'biographical or historiological, ethnological or psychological' approaches.

3. Ibid., p. 32.

4. It was Marcuse's failure to see just how radically Hegel's *Phenomenology* challenges the terms of Heidegger's ontology which vitiated his attempt to use Hegel as the common source on which to base his transformation of Heidegger's early thought into a Marxist philosophy of revolution, in *Hegel's Ontology and the Theory of Historicity*. The attempt by Levinas to use Husserl, instead of Hegel, as the basis from which to develop an ethical ontology of the Other, beyond Heidegger's existentialism, in *Totality and Infinity*, is similarly misplaced, since it is in the methodology of Husserlian phenomenology that the individualism of Heidegger's analysis has its roots. Levinas is also, of course, a critic of Husserl, charging him with a failure to grasp the infinite alterity of the other. Yet his notion of infinite alterity is the inverted product of the very individualism it seeks to counter. Interestingly, Derrida's attempt to defend Husserl against Levinas (by reinterpreting the account of intersubjectivity in the Fifth of the *Cartesian Mediations* in a way which is more amenable to Levinas's analysis) only works to the extent that it produces an Hegelian reading of Husserl. See Derrida, 'Violence and Metaphysics', *Writing and Difference*, pp. 123–33. For further critical discussion of Levinas, see ch. 4, above, pp. 117–27.

5. *Phenomenology of Spirit*, pp. 111, 110.

6. Kojève, *Introduction à la lecture de Hegel*, Gallimard, Paris, 1980. This appendix is unfortunately omitted from the English translation. Bataille's important 'Hegel, Death and Sacrifice' is an excerpt from an unfinished study of Kojève's thought, centred on this appendix.

7. Ibid., p. 539; quoted by Bataille, 'Hegel, Death and Sacrifice', p. 10.

8. G.W.F. Hegel, *La Phenoménologie de l'Esprit*, trans. Jean Hyppolite, 2 volumes, Paris, 1939. I am grateful to Jonathan Rée for pointing out the significance of this translation to me.

9. Jean-Paul Sartre, *Being and Nothingness: An Essay on Phenomenological Ontology* (1943), trans. Hazel Barnes, Methuen, London, 1958, pp. 361–430; Frantz Fanon, *Black Skin, White Mask* (1952), trans. Charles Lam Markmann, Paladin, London, 1970. See also Sartre's Preface to Frantz Fanon, *The Wretched of the Earth* (1961), trans. Constance Farrington, Penguin, Harmondsworth, 1967.

10. See Chris Arthur, 'Hegel's Master-Slave Dialectic and a Myth of Marxology',

New Left Review 142, November/December 1983, pp. 67–75. For the broader picture, see Judith Butler, *Subjects of Desire: Hegelian Reflections in Twentieth Century France*, Columbia University Press, New York, 1987.

11. These are the topics of the chapters which follow (5 and 6) in Hegel's pedagogic reconstruction of the path of natural consciousness from the immediacy of sense-certainty to the standpoint of an absolute knowing.

12. Karl Marx and Frederick Engels, 'Manifesto of the Communist Party' (1848), *Collected Works*, Volume 6, Lawrence and Wishart, London, 1976, p. 506.

13. *Phenomenology*, p. 110.

14. Hegel's conception of the relationship of the historical to the philosophical content of the *Phenomenology* is to be found at the beginning and end of the work, pp. 21–34, 493. He distinguishes *history*, as the standpoint of the contingency of events, from *phenomenology of spirit*, as the comprehension of the organization of these events from the standpoint of 'the antithesis of being and knowing' (appearance), and *speculative philosophy*, as the exposition of the movement of spirit in-and-for-itself. Hence the ambiguous status of the *Phenomenology* between empirical history and its philosophical comprehension. The *Phenomenology* is a *genealogy* of philosophical consciousness – something which tends to go unrecognized by those who engage in historicist critiques of something called 'the Hegelian subject'.

15. Ibid., p. 105.

16. Ibid., pp. 112, 110.

17. Ibid., pp. 113–14.

18. Ibid., pp. 116, 115.

19. Ibid., p. 116. '*Pure* self-recognition in absolute otherness,' Hegel argues, 'is 'the ground and soil of Science or *knowledge in general*. The beginning of philosophy presupposes or requires that consciousness should dwell in this *element*.' As the intro-duction to and beginning of science, it is the function of the *Phenomenology* to 'show ... [the individual] this standpoint within himself'. Ibid., pp. 14–15. The problem with Kojève's reading is that it halts the dialectic of recognition at the first stage (the master-slave dialectic), effectively ending the *Phenomenology* at the close of ch. 4.

20. The *Phenomenology*'s methodological self-consciousness as a genealogy of philosophical consciousness is outlined in its Introduction, pp. 45–57.

21. Ibid., pp. 109–10; bold emphasis added.

22. Ibid., p. 113.

23. Ibid., pp. 113–14 (translation altered); *Phänomenologie*, p. 116.

24. *Phenomenology*, pp. 106–8, 114. For Marcuse's alternative 'ontological' read-ing of this passage, see *Hegel's Ontology*, pp. 228–63.

25. *Phenomenology*, p. 114.

26. Ibid., pp. 114–15.

27. Ibid., p. 115.

28. Bataille, 'Hegel, Death and Sacrifice', pp. 10–13.

29. Paul Gilroy, *The Black Atlantic: Modernity and Double Consciousness*, Verso, London, 1993, p. 63; Orlando Patterson, *Slavery and Social Death*, Harvard University Press, Cambridge MA, 1982. In this regard, the institution of slavery appears to correspond more closely to Hegel's allegorical intent than the serfdom to which he actually refers.

30. Jacques Lacan, *The Seminar of Jacques Lacan, 1: Freud's Papers of Techniques, 1953–1954*, trans. John Forrester, Cambridge University Press, Cambridge, 1988, p. 223; 'The Subversion of the Subject and the Dialectic of Desire in the Freudian Unconscious' (1960), in his *Écrits: A Selection* [henceforth *ES*], trans. Alan Sheridan, Tavistock, London, 1977, p. 308.

31. *The Black Atlantic*, p. 68.

32. Ibid., pp. 68–71, 187–223; Gayatri Spivak, 'Remembering the Limits: Difference, Identity and Practice', in Peter Osborne (ed.), *Socialism and the Limits of Liberalism*, Verso, London, 1991, pp. 227–39; Homi K. Bhabha, *The Location of Culture*, Routledge, London and New York, 1994, pp. 16–17. The limit to the dialectic

here is set by an emphatic sense of 'cultural difference'. This is not a difference internal to a universal conception of human culture, but one marked by what Bhabha describes as a 'momentous, if momentary, *extinction* of the recognised object of culture in the disturbed artifice of its signification'. Ibid., p. 126; emphasis added. This extinction is matched, on the side of the slave, by the extinctions of suicide, infanticide, or murder of the master, respectively. There would thus seem to be a dialectic even to the termination of the dialectic of recognition here.

33. *Critique of Dialectical Reason*, Volume 1, p. 158 n. Cf. Sartre, *Being and Nothingness*, pp. 235–44, 361–430. The early Sartre acknowledged a 'multiplicity of "Others"', but argued that despite the fact that this multiplicity is 'not a *collection* but a *totality*', it is nonetheless 'on principle impossible for us to adopt "the point of view of the whole"'. Ibid., p. 252. He thus came to combine a *serial* application of Hegel's master-slave dialectic to relations between individuals, with a Heideggerian approach to the social as a whole, using Hegel to embellish, rather than to counter, the individualism of Heidegger's approach – an individualism which had already been bolstered by Sartre's rewriting of the structure of *Dasein* within the terms of the Cartesian *Cogito* as a tragic dialectic of the for-itself and the in-itself.

34. *Phenomenology*, p. 117.

35. *Being and Time*, p. 230.

36. For an interesting comparison of Heidegger's concept of anxiety with Freud's, see Richard Boothby, *Death and Desire: Psychoanalytic Theory in Lacan's Return to Freud*, Routledge, New York and London, 1991, pp. 208–9.

37. Slavoj Žižek, *The Sublime Object of Ideology*, Verso, London and New York, 1989, p. 7.

38. Sigmund Freud, *The Psychopathology of Everyday Life* (1901), Penguin Freud Library Volume 5 Penguin, Harmondsworth, 1975, p. 322.

39. *Seminar* 1, p. 222. Cf. Lacan's distinctively Kojèvean claim that Hegel 'deduced the entire subjective and objective process of our history' from the master-slave dialectic. Jacques Lacan, 'Aggressivity in Psychoanalysis' (1948), *ES*, p. 26. Elsewhere Lacan is a little more vague, referring to 'in the first place the master slave dialectic, or the dialectic of the *belle âme* and of the law of the heart' – three quite *different* dialectical forms in the *Phenomenology*, albeit ones which were all important to Kojève. Jacques Lacan, 'The Function and Field of Speech and Language in Psychoanalysis' (1953), *ES*, p. 80.

40. David Macey, *Lacan in Contexts*, Verso, London, 1988, p. 98.

41. Denis Hollier (ed.), *The College of Sociology (1937–1939)*, trans. Betsy Wing, University of Minnesota Press, Minneapolis, 1988, p. 86. The reference is to Roger Callois' account of Kojève's lecture to the College of Sociology on 4 December 1937.

42. Jacques Lacan, 'The Mirror Phase as Formative of the Function of the I' (1949), *ES*, p. 1.

43. *ES*, pp. 79–80, 301, 307, 80, 293; emphases added.

44. Ibid., p. 307.

45. Confusion over the philosophical form of Lacan's thought has been fostered by two directly opposed, and equally mistaken, tendencies. One, on the model of Althusserian structuralism, would see the recourse to structural linguistics as inherently incompatible with any form of Hegelianism. The other, represented by Jean Wahl, would see Lacan's reading of psychoanalysis as a displaced Hegelianism, as itself a nostalgia for Hegel – a reading which is dialectically recuperated by Lacan in his psychoanalytical reading of philosophy as paranoia.

For Lacan's denial that he has been 'lured by a purely dialectical exhaustion of being', see *ES*, p. 302. For a broadly Lacanian reading of Hegel's *Phenomenology*, see Jean Hyppolite, 'Hegel's Phenomenology and Psychoanalysis' (1955), in W. Steinkraus (ed.), *New Studies in the Philosophy of Hegel*, Holt, Rinehart and Wilson, New York, 1971, pp. 57–70. See also Jean Hyppolite, 'A Spoken Commentary on Freud's *Verneinung*' (1954), translated as the Appendix to Lacan's *Seminar* 1, pp. 289–97. Lacan comments on Hyppolite's text in 'Introduction and Reply to Jean Hyppolite's

Presentation of Freud's *Verneinung*', ibid., pp. 52–61. For a more detailed Lacanian reading of Hegel, see Slavoj Žižek, 'Why Should a Dialectician Learn to Count to Four?', *Radical Philosophy* 58, Summer 1991, pp. 3–9.

Lacan's account was, of course, developed gradually over a considerable period of time, with significant modifications and shifts of emphasis – not just between the early and the later periods, but especially within the latter. However, for the purposes of expository clarity and argumentative strategy, I present a simplified, composite picture here.

46. Jean Laplanche, 'Psychoanalysis, Time and Translation' (1990), in John Fletcher and Martin Stanton (eds), *Jean Laplanche: Seduction, Translation, Drives*, Institute of Contemporary Arts, London, 1992, p. 177. I am grateful to John Fletcher for impressing on me the philosophical significance of Laplanche's recent work.

47. John Forrester, *The Seductions of Psychoanalysis: Freud, Lacan and Derrida*, Cambridge University Press, Cambridge, 1990, p. 104.

48. *ES*, pp. 4, 308.

49. Ibid., p. 2.

50. Lacan, *Seminar 1*, p. 3. In understanding reconciliation as reconciliation to the inevitable failure of reconciliation, Žižek's Lacanian Hegelianism is, effectively, a lively and eccentric modification of Right Hegelianism. For a critique, see Peter Dews 'Hegel in Analysis: Slavoj Žižek's Lacanian Dialectics', *Bulletin of the Hegel Society of Great Britain*, Nos 21/22, 1990, pp. 1–18. If Žižek's reading of Hegel is too Lacanian, his reading of Lacan is nonetheless still too Hegelian.

51. Freud later projected its reference backwards, to the first state of life, epitomized by life in the womb. For an exposition of the difference between Freud's two accounts, see J. Laplanche and J.-B. Pontalis, *The Language of Psycholoanalysis* (1967), trans. Donald Nicholson-Smith, Karnac Books, London, 1988, pp. 337–8. Lacan remarks that the term primary narcissism 'reveals in those who invented it the most profound awareness of semantic latencies'. *ES*, p. 6.

52. *ES*, p. 2; Jacques Lacan, *The Four Fundamental Concepts of Psychoanalysis*, trans. Alan Sheridan, Penguin, Harmondsworth, 1979, p. 256; *ES*, p. 2.

53. *ES*, pp. 2, 4; translation amended by adopting 'it' rather than 'he' for the ego (emphasis added).

54. Peter Dews, personal communication, 4 March, 1994. See, for example, *The Four Fundamental Concepts*, p. 257, where Lacan alludes to the 'reference-point' of the parent's look as he or she holds the child up in front of the mirror as the site for the later transformation of the ego ideal into the ideal ego.

55. Lacan, *The Seminar of Jacques Lacan, 2: The Ego in Freud's Theory and in the Technique of Psychoanalysis, 1954–5*, trans. Sylvanna Tomaselli, Cambridge University Press, Cambridge, 1988, pp. 166, 167.

56. 'The Signification of the Phallus' (1958), *ES*, pp. 281–91.

57. Judith Butler, 'The Lesbian Phallus and the Morphological Imaginary', in *Bodies that Matter: On the Discursive Limits of "Sex"*, Routledge, London and New York, 1993, pp. 57–91.

58. *ES*, p. 294.

59. *ES*, p. 28.

60. Peter Dews, *Logics of Disintegration: Post-Structuralist Thought and the Claims of Critical Theory*, pp. 66–7; Macey, *Lacan in Contexts*, pp. 104–6. Hyppolite finds a similar structure in Hegel's *Phenomenology*, when he reads natural consciousness as 'the unconsciousness of consciousness', or 'an anticipation of knowledge'. Hyppolite, 'Hegel's Phenomenology and Psychoanalysis', pp. 58–61.

61. *ES*, p. 105.

62. Ibid.

63. *Seminar 1*, p. 223.

64. Ibid., pp. 148–9.

65. Ibid., p. 172.

66. Sigmund Freud, 'The Ego and the Id' (1923), in *On Metapsychology*, Penguin Freud Library, Volume 11, Penguin, Harmondsworth, 1984, p. 370.

67. Julia Kristeva, *Tales of Love* (1983), trans. Leon S. Roudiez, Columbia University Press, New York, 1987.

68. Sigmund Freud, 'Group Psychology and the Analysis of the Ego' (1921), in *Civilisation, Society and Religion*, pp. 134–40 ; 'On Narcissism: An Introduction' (1914), *On Metapsychology*, p. 95; 'The Ego and the Id', *On Metapsychology*, p. 370.

69. Kristeva, *Tales of Love*, pp. 40, 42, 22, 21, 45; Lacan, *ES*, pp. 306–7.

70. *On Metapsychology*, p. 370.

71. *Tales of Love*, p. 23, emphasis added.

72. Gilles Deleuze and Felix Guattari, *Anti-Oedipus: Capitalism and Schizophrenia* (1972), trans. Robert Hurley, Mark Seem and Helen R. Lane, University of Minnesota Press, Minneapolis, 1983, pp. 42–68. One does not need to accept Deleuze and Guattari's account of the positivity of desire to recognize the force of their criticisms of the 'familialism' of Freudian psychoanalysis.

73. *Tales of Love*, pp. 22, 44, 23.

74. Jacqueline Rose, 'Kristeva – Take Two', in her *Sexuality in the Field of Vision*, Verso, London, 1986, pp. 161, 151; Julia Kristeva, *Powers of Horror: An Essay on Abjection* (1980), trans. Leon Roudiez, Columbia University Press, New York, 1982.

75. *Tales of Love*, p. 23.

76. Ibid., p. 39.

77. *Tales of Love*, p. 41.

78. *The Language of Psychoanalysis*, p. 336. For a critique of Freud's theory of narcissism as a whole along similar lines, see Mikkel Borsch-Jacobsen, *The Freudian Subject*, trans. Catherine Porter, Macmillan, London, 1989, pp. 113–26.

79. 'On Narcissism', in *On Metapsychology*, p. 95.

80. See n. 17 above.

81. *Tales of Love* p. 22.

82. Jessica Benjamin, *The Bonds of Love: Psychoanalysis, Feminism, and the Problem of Domination*, Virago, London, 1990.

83. *Tales of Love*, pp. 45, 22.

84. *Bonds of Love*, p. 12.

85. Ibid., pp. 131–2. It is important to distinguish Benjamin's ideal of paradoxical subject-subject relations from the possibilities for the transformation of gender identities consequent upon changes in the differential relations of boys and girls to the idealizing identifications of early infancy, with which much of the book is taken up. This latter, Chodorovian theme is internal to a concept of identification to which the concept of recognition is counterposed. However, Benjamin's exposition sometimes elides the two in an ambiguous way.

86. Ibid., p. 221.

87. Ibid., p. 21n.

88. Ibid., pp. 19, 36, 29–30, 44; emphasis added. Oddly, despite her explicit use of Hegel to demonstrate it, Benjamin attributes the concept of intersubjectivity to Habermas.

89. Jean Laplanche, 'Interview', in Fletcher and Stanton (eds), *Jean Laplanche*, pp. 5–12 (emphasis added); Jean Laplanche, *New Foundations for Psychoanalysis* (1987), trans. David Macey, Blackwell, Oxford, 1989, ch. 3.

90. *New Foundations*, p. 84.

91. Ibid., pp. 54–88.

92. Ibid., pp. 137, 145, 144, 142; Laplanche and Pontalis, *Language of Psychoanalysis*, pp. 214–17. The elaboration of the specificity of the drive vis-à-vis the instinct (a distinction which is concealed by the Standard English translation of Freud's *Trieb* as 'instinct') is one of the main insights adopted by Laplanche from Lacan's reading of Freud.

93. *Bonds of Love*, pp. 12, 36; emphasis added.

94. Unlike Kristeva, who accepts the familial terms of orthodox psychoanalysis, Laplanche insists that 'the fact that a child is brought up by *parents*, or even by *its* parents, is, ultimately, a *contingency*, even if it is rooted in biology and human history, and not a universal fact which is necessary in itself.' He thus uses the neutral term

'adult' to designate the child's other in the primal situation. The adulthood of this other is, however, crucial, since what the other offers to the child is signifiers 'pregnant with unconscious sexual significations'. *New Foundations*, pp. 124, 126. Laplanche's own example is, however, conventional: the unconscious sexual cathexis of the woman's breast. In order to convey this combination of principled neutrality with a practical recognition of the force of convention, I shall henceforth refer to the adult in the primal situation as the '(m)other'. This also indicates the fact that Laplanche maintains the theoretical convention of treating the child's 'other' in the primal situation as a *singular* 'adult', thereby exposing his position to the general social dimension of the Deleuze-Guattarian critique of psychoanalytical familialism. Laplanche is, however, aware of the problem, self-consciously describing the dyad of adult and child as a 'prototype'. *Jean Laplanche*, p. 175.

95. Jean Laplanche, 'A Metapsychology Put to the Test of Anxiety', *International Journal of Psycho-Analysis*, Vol. 62, 1981, p. 83. Laplanche here inverts Freud's position in 'Inhibitions, Symptoms and Anxiety' (1926) (in *On Psychopathology: Inhibitions, Symptoms and Other Works*, Penguin Freud Library, Volume 10, Penguin, Harmondsworth, 1979, pp. 237–315) on the priority of 'adaption'.

96. Lacan, *The Four Fundamental Concepts of Psychoanalysis*, 1979, p. 214.

97. Ibid., pp. 215, 204–5.

98. Jean Laplanche, *Life and Death in Psychoanalysis* (1970), trans. Jeffrey Mehlman, Johns Hopkins University Press, 1976, p. 6.

99. *New Foundations*, p. 50.

100. *Life and Death in Psychoanalysis*, p. 124.

101. *Jean Laplanche*, p. 17. It should be noted that Laplanche's work on a 'psychoanalytical philosophy of time' remains in progress. The account of his position which follows is constructed on the basis of papers, lectures and interviews setting out its preliminary results, read in the context of the summary of his theoretical approach in *New Foundations*.

102. Sigmund Freud, 'Beyond the Pleasure Principle' (1920), *On Metapsychology*, pp. 299–300; 'The Unconscious' (1915), ibid., p. 191; *New Introductory Lectures on Psychoanalysis* (1933), Penguin Freud Library, Volume 2, Penguin, Harmondsworth, 1973, p. 106; 'A Note upon the 'Mystic Writing-Pad'' (1924), *On Metapsychology*, p. 434.

103. *New Introductory Lectures*, p. 107.

104. See Immanuel Kant, *Critique of Pure Reason* (1781, 1787), trans. Norman Kemp-Smith, 2nd ed., Macmillan, London and Basingstoke, 1933, pp. 120–75.

105. Sigmund Freud, *The Interpretation of Dreams* (1900), Penguin Freud Library, Volume 4, Penguin, London, 1976, p. 733; 'An Outline of Psychoanalysis' (1940), quoted in Laplanche and Pontalis, *The Language of Psychoanalysis*, p. 102; *New Introductory Lectures*, p. 107.

106. *Jean Laplanche*, p. 17.

107. Ibid., pp. 166, 168, 39.

108. Ibid., pp. 17, 175–6.

109. Ibid., pp. 176, 174; *New Foundations*, p. 51; *Jean Laplanche*, pp. 176, 17. Laplanche sketches his relation to the history of Freud's concept of *Nachträglichkeit* in 'Notes on Afterwardsness', ibid., pp. 217–23.

110. *New Foundations*, pp. 143, 39.

111. Ricoeur *TN* 3, p. 66.

112. This move is replicated in Andrew Benjamin's reading of Laplanche, in 'The Unconscious: Structuring as a Translation', *Jean Laplanche*, p. 147.

113. See chapter 1, n. 89.

114. For Laplanche's realist view of the unconscious, see Jean Laplanche and Serge Leclaire, 'The Unconscious: A Psychoanalytic Study' (1960), *Yale French Studies* 48, 1972, pp. 118–78. In 'The ICA Seminar' (1990), Laplanche acknowledges that his discussion of temporalization operates 'on the same level' as Heidegger's, although his ontological position is different. *Jean Laplanche*, p. 69.

4. Modernity, Eternity, Tradition

1. This has been the prevailing opinion in both European and Anglo-American philosophy in the postwar period, across the political spectrum. See, in particular, Karl Löwith, *Meaning in History: The Theological Presuppositions of the Philosophy of History*, University of Chicago Press, Chicago, 1949.

2. See John D. Caputo, 'Heidegger's Gods: From Demythologising to Remythologising', *Demythologising Heidegger*, Indiana University Press, Bloomington, 1993, ch. 10.

3. Gillian Rose, *Judaism and Modernity: Philosophical Essays*, Blackwell, Oxford, 1993, p. 13.

4. John Milbank, *Theology and Social Theory: Beyond Secular Reason*, Blackwell, Oxford, 1990, and 'Problematizing the Secular: The Post-Postmodern Agenda', in Philippa Berry and Andrew Wernick (eds), *Shadow of Spirit: Postmodernism and Religion*, Routledge, London and New York, 1992, pp. 30–44.

5. Adorno, *Negative Dialectics*, p. xix.

6. Jürgen Habermas, 'A Review of Gadamer's Truth and Method', trans. in Fred R. Dallmayr and Thomas A. McCarthy (eds), *Understanding and Social Inquiry*, University of Notre Dame Press, Notre Dame, 1977, p. 359.

7. Cf. Hegel's discussion of 'bad infinity' in his *Science of Logic*, Bk1, Section I, ch. 2, C. I follow the felicitous translation by Johnston and Struthers, George Allen and Unwin, London, 1929, Volume 1, p. 164. The 'ordinary' or 'bad' sense of the infinite, 'its simple determination, the affirmative as negation of the finite' (p. 150) is, according to Hegel, 'the expression of a contradiction, which pretends to be the solution' (p. 164). In simple opposition to, or as an abstract negation of, the finite, the infinite is itself finite. Similarly, in its ordinary or 'bad' sense – its affirmation as an abstract negation of tradition – modernity itself appears as a tradition: the tradition of the new. It is this 'ordinary' or 'bad' (reflective or non-speculative) sense of modernity which in turn gives rise to the idea of postmodernity as the affirmation of *its* abstract negation.

8. It should be noted that Benjamin's objection is not to the concept of progress *per se*, but only to the 'uncritical hypostatization' which results 'as soon as it becomes the signature for the course of history *in its totality*'. As 'a measure of *specific* historical changes', the idea of progress is seen to perform 'a critical placing into question' of history as a whole. Benjamin, 'N' (13, 1), in Smith (ed.), *Benjamin*, p. 70. Secularization is one such category of progress which is usually (mis)applied to the course of history as a whole.

9. Derrida, 'Metaphysics and Violence', *Writing and Difference*, p. 81.

10. Once again, for reasons of expository clarity, I shall treat the body of work at issue here as a developing whole, referring to differences between its phases only where they bear directly on the point at issue. What follows is not intended as an overview of Levinas's thought. It engages with it only insofar as it impinges most directly upon our present concerns.

11. Emmanuel Levinas, 'Time and the Other' (1947), in *Time and the Other and Other Essays*, trans. Richard A. Cohen, Duquesne University Press, Pittsburgh, 1987.

12. *Totality and Infinity*, Sections I, B and D, and II, A: 'Separation and Discourse', Separation and the Absolute', 'Separation as Life'.

13. Ibid., Preface.

14. Ibid., p. 23.

15. Emmanuel Levinas, 'The Trace of the Other' (1963), trans. Adolfo Lingis in Mark C. Taylor (ed.), *Deconstruction in Context: Literature and Philosophy*, Chicago University Press, Chicago, 1986, p. 349; Levinas, 'Diachrony and Representation' (1982), in *Time and the Other*, pp. 116, 104–5. Levinas distinguishes between *l'autrui*, the personal other, the other person, and *l'autre*, otherness in general, or alterity. This distinction is usually rendered by his English translators as that between the Other (capital 'O') and the other (small 'o'). The former is the privileged term. There is a

danger of confusion here with the capitalization of 'the Other' in psychoanalytical discourse, adopted in the previous chapter, to mark the representation of otherness within the symbolic (Lacan's *le grand autre*), as opposed to its supposedly purely specular existence within the imaginary. Distinct from Lacan's, Levinas's Other is the site of a concrete relation defined *prior to signification* by the 'face to face': 'the alterity of the other person to an ego is first – and I dare say, "positively" – the face of the other person obligating the ego, which, from the first – without deliberation – is responsive to the Other. *From the first,* that is, the ego answers "gratuitously", without worrying about reciprocity.' 'Diachrony and Representation', pp. 105–6.

16. *Totality and Infinity*, pp. 224, 236, 239. First emphasis added.

17. Ibid., p. 239.

18. See, for the example, Michel de Certeau, *The Writing of History*, Pt IV, 'Freudian Writing'.

19. See p. 61, above. To the extent that it diverges from the position outlined in *Totality and Infinity*, Levinas's later work, especially *Otherwise than Being or Beyond Essence* (1974) (trans. Adolfo Lingis, Kluwer Academic Publishers, Dordrecht, 1991), may be largely considered a response to Derrida's critique. Levinas responds explicitly to Derrida's work in 'Wholly Otherwise' (1973), trans. Simon Critchley, in R. Bernasconi and S. Critchley (eds), *Re-Reading Levinas*, Athlone Press, London, 1991. However, insofar as the aspect of Derrida's critique to which Levinas responds primarily concerns problems of expression produced by the inescapability of the connotations of a certain philosophical *language* – rather than anything to do with his treatment of history – most of the substance of the earlier critique continues to apply. Essentially, Levinas responds by dropping the terminology of infinity in favour of the more neutral 'otherwise than being', replacing the distinction between infinity and totality with that between 'the saying' and 'the said', and rethinking alterity, which originally appeared as the relation to the face of the Other, in terms of the idea of substitution. The emphasis shifts from exteriority to transcendence. Indeed, *Otherwise than Being* might well have been subtitled 'An Essay on Transcendence'.

Meanwhile, as if overwhelmed by the generosity of Levinas's response, Derrida's second piece on Levinas, 'At this Very Moment in this Work Here I am' (1980) (trans. Ruben Berezdivin, in *Re-Reading Levinas*), is closer to an appreciation than a critique – for all its rhetoric of 'radical ingratitude'. Derrida's recent work is profoundly marked by Levinas's later thought, to the point of eliding the implications of his own earlier critique.

20. *Totality and Infinity*, p. 22.

21. 'Violence and Metaphysics', pp. 126, 125, 133.

22. *Totality and Infinity*, pp. 198, 195.

23. 'Violence and Metaphysics', pp. 115, 109.

24. Ibid., pp. 110–11, 133.

25. Ibid., p. 119.

26. It is the enigmatic subject only of the Preface and the final chapter, prior to the 'Conclusions': 'The Infinity of Time'.

27. *Totality and Infinity*, p. 294.

28. Ibid., pp. 49–50, emphases added.

29. 'The Trace of the Other', pp. 353–4.

30. Ibid., p. 354, first emphasis added.

31. 'The relation with infinity cannot, to be sure, be stated in terms of experience, for infinity overflows the thought that thinks. Its very infinition is produced precisely in this overflowing. The relation with infinity will have to be stated in terms other than those of objective experience. . . . ' *Totality and Infinity*, p. 25.

32. Ibid., emphasis added.

33. 'Violence and Metaphysics', p. 119.

34. See ch. 5, n. 59.

35. Derrida, 'Violence and Metaphysics', pp. 108–9.

36. *Totality and Infinity*, p. 40.

37. 'The Trace of the Other', p. 348.

38. Theodor W. Adorno, 'The Idea of Natural History' (1932), trans. Bob Hullot-Kentor, *Telos* 60, Summer 1984, pp. 111–24; *Negative Dialectics*, pp. 354–60. The analysis derives from a reading of Walter Benjamin's *Origin of German Tragic Drama* (1928) (trans. John Osborne, New Left Books, London, 1977) in the context of a critique of Heidegger's concept of historicality.

39. It is not possible to address these matters adequately here. They are the issues at stake in the 'primal history of subjectivity' sketched by Adorno and Horkheimer in *Dialectic of Enlightenment*. The central ontological category at work there is *mimesis* – not representation (narrative) as the 'mimesis of action', as in Ricoeur, but action itself as *primary mimesis*. I plan to return to this issue in a subsequent work.

40. 'The Trace of the Other', p. 364; *Totality and Infinity*, p. 40.

41. *Totality and Infinity*, p. 243.

42. Ibid., pp. 58, 240–1.

43. Heidegger, *Being and Time*, pp. 429–33; Benjamin, *Illuminations*, pp. 255–66. Compare the following statement by Levinas with the sixth of Benjamin's 'Theses on the Philosophy of History' (ibid., p. 257): 'Historiography recounts the way the survivors appropriate the work of dead wills to themselves; it rests on the usurpation carried out by the conquerors, that is, by the survivors; it recounts enslavement, forgetting the life that struggles against slavery.' *Totality and Infinity*, p. 228. For Benjamin's concept of historicism, see above, pp. 138–44.

44. Derrida, 'Violence and Metaphysics', pp. 107, 129, 126.

45. Ibid., p. 120.

46. See n. 29.

47. Jameson, *The Political Unconscious*, p. 102. As Levinas puts it, the 'supreme ordeal' of both freedom and the will is 'not death, but suffering'. *Totality and Infinity*, p. 239.

48. See ch. 1, n. 33, above.

49. See pp. 15–18 above. The important idea of existential spatiality remains theoretically underdeveloped. Heidegger's treatment of it in *Being and Time* (pp. 134–48) is brief and unsatisfactory. Merleau-Ponty improves upon it considerably in his discussion of the body in *Phenomenology of Perception* (Pt I), but he fails to extend his analysis to the wider social spaces of historical existence. Recent work in social geography could be said to operate with the concept in a practical state, but it lacks the philosophical resources to theorize it, and the precise character of its analyses are often unclear as a result. However, whatever its philosophical terms, the social forms of existential spatiality are undoubtedly being revolutionized at present, through the operationalization of the new information technologies. (Cf. Heidegger's remark about the radio in ibid., p. 140.) The consequences of this process for possible new forms of historical consciousness are as yet unclear, although there will undoubtedly be important consequences. One thing it will *not* entail, however, is the 'end of history'; the tendential elimination of certain specific forms of historical consciousness, perhaps, but the generation of new ones, without doubt.

50. Ricoeur, *TN* 3, p. 110.

51. Theodor W. Adorno, 'On Tradition' (1966), *Telos* 94, Winter 1992–3, p. 75.

52. Friedrich Nietzsche, *Uses and Abuses of History*, trans. Adrian Collins, Bobbs-Merrill, Indianapolis, 1957, p. 22.

53. Benjamin, 'N [Re the Theory of Knowledge, Theory of Progress]', in Smith (ed.), *Benjamin*, p. 81.

54. Howard Caygill, 'Benjamin, Heidegger and the Destruction of Tradition', in Benjamin and Osborne (eds), *Walter Benjamin's Philosophy: Destruction and Experience*, Routledge, London and New York, 1944, p. 12. 'One guilty of the crime of "tradition" was a "traditor" or, in later usage, a "traitor".' Ibid.

55. Cf. Heidegger's description of the 'remarkable double meaning' of the past in *Being and Time*, p. 478.

56. For the distinction between these three philosophical concepts of eternity, see

Michael Theunissen, 'Metaphysics' Forgetfulness of Time: On the Controversy Over Parmenides, Frag. 8, 5', in Axel Honneth et al. (eds), *Philosophical Interventions in the Unfinished Project of Enlightenment*, MIT Press, Cambridge MA, 1992, pp. 3–28.

57. *Truth and Method*, pp. 246, 249, 250, 240, 258. The German term *Überlieferungsgeschehen* is central to Gadamer's construal of tradition. It may be translated, alternatively, as 'occurrence of transmission' or 'happening of tradition', giving it an empirical or more ontological inflection, respectively.

58. Ibid., p. 245. It is interesting that Gadamer's prose should light up on the rare occasion of his use of a televisual image, such that the historicity of the image works in direct opposition to the idea it is being used to convey.

59. Ibid., p. 255.

60. Ibid., p. 256.

61. The idea that history is held together by tradition is connected, historically, to the use of the term in both Judaism and Christianity to refer to the authoritative transmission of divinely sanctioned beliefs within a temporal order to which the ultimate sanction for such beliefs is external.

62. *Truth and Method*, p. 257.

63. For a more extended comparison of Gadamer's and Heidegger's hermeneutics, see Theodore Kisiel, 'The Happening of Tradition: The Hermeneutics of Gadamer and Heidegger' (1969), in Robert Hollinger (ed.), *Hermeneutics and Praxis*, Notre Dame University Press, Notre Dame, 1985, pp. 3–31.

64. *Truth and Method*, p. 321.

65. Cf. Blumenberg's paradox of secularization. Secularization is 'something that would not even exist for us if we were not still in a position to understand what had preceded it, what the hope of salvation, what the next world, transcendence, divine judgment, refraining from involvement in the world and falling under the influence of the world once meant.' Its final stage would thus be 'a situation in which no remains of these elements were left in existence, but at that point one would cease to be able to understand the term "secularisation" at all.' *Legitimacy of the Modern Age*, pp. 3–4.

66. *TN* 3, pp. 219–29, emphasis added.

67. Ibid., p. 227, emphasis added.

68. Despite its title, the section devoted to 'The Limitations of Reflective Philosophy' in *Truth and Method* (pp. 305–10) is actually more of a hymn to its 'compulsive power' than an account of its limits, in stark contradiction to certain passages elsewhere in the book.

69. *TN* 3, pp. 210–16.

70. *Truth and Method*, p. 251.

71. *Philosophical Discourse of Modernity*, p. 7.

72. Émile Benveniste, *Problems in General Linguistics*, trans. Mary Elizabeth Meek, University of Miami Press, Coral Gables, 1971, pp. 195–215. For Benveniste, *discourse* is a linguistic form marked by the temporal proximity of its object to the present of its utterance. It uses all the personal pronouns, and all the verb tenses, but essentially the present, perfect and future, which are related to the moment of its utterance. *Narrative*, on the other hand, cultivates temporal distance and objectivity, through the preferential use of the third person, along with aorist, imperfect and pluperfect tenses, avoiding the present, perfect and future. Cf. Meschonnic's purely discursive concept of modernity, to which reference was made in chapter 1 above, p. 14.

73. Jacques Rancière, *The Names of History: On the Poetics of Knowledge* (1992), trans. Hassan Melehy, Minnesota University Press, Minneapolis, 1994, p. 14.

74. For Rancière, it is Michelet who is the pioneer of this movement, with his perfection of the absolute 'nominal phrase', abolishing temporal markers in order to absolutize the meaning of the event. Ibid., pp. 42–75.

75. *Illuminations*, p. 87. Cf. Marx's remarks on the allegedly enduring 'charm' of ancient Greek art, within which he explicitly includes the epic, in the *Grundrisse*, p. 111. Benjamin's analysis is markedly more historical.

76. Benjamin, 'The Storyteller' (1934), *Illuminations*, pp. 83–108; 87–8. The

picture is further embellished by reference to such sub-genres as the chronicle, the fairy-tale and the proverb, which persist into the present, despite their 'archaic' status, in new but socially marginal forms.

77. Benjamin, 'The Work of Art in the Age of Mechanical Reproduction' (1936), *Illuminations*, p. 223; 'The Storyteller', ibid., pp. 83–5. Cf. 'Some Motifs in Baudelaire' (1939): 'Experience is indeed a matter of tradition, in collective existence as well as private life'. *Charles Baudelaire: A Lyric Poet in the Era of High Capitalism*, trans. Harry Zohn, Verso, London and New York 1983, p. 110.

/8. In European culture in the nineteenth century, youth, as represented in the *Bildungsroman* or novel of formation, was the symbolic figure of the new age, the very 'essence' of modernity. Franco Moretti, *The Way of the World: The* Bildungsroman *in European Culture*, Verso, London, 1987, p. 5. By the time of the First World War, however, the *Bildungsroman* had become impossible – except in the negative form of Musil's *The Man Without Qualities*. Youth had become a self-enclosed social category, a movement of its own, alienated from society to a hitherto unknown extent. It is significant that Benjamin's earlier works were written in the febrile context of the Free Youth Movement in Freiburg in the years immediately preceding the First World War. As in so many instances of high modernist culture in Europe (Heidegger's existentialism is another example), it is the First World War which provides the traumatic background to Benjamin's cultural theory, fascism its ultimate context. See John McCole, 'Benjamin and the Idea of Youth', in his *Walter Benjamin and the Antinomies of Tradition*, Cornell University Press, Ithaca and London, 1993, ch. 1.

79. *Illuminations*, p. 89; Georg Lukács, *Theory of the Novel*, trans. Anna Bostock, Merlin Press, London, 1971, pp. 41, 17. This analysis of the novel may be disputed. See, in particular, Mikhail Bakhtin, 'Epic and Novel' (1940), in his *The Dialogic Imagination: Four Essays*, trans. Carly Emerson and Michael Holquist, Texas University Press, Austin, 1981, pp. 3–40. Bakhtin's analysis has certain affinities with Lukacs's, but breaks with it decisively in other respects.

80. Benjamin, letter to Scholem, 12 June 1938, in Gershom Scholem (ed.), *The Correspondence of Walter Benjamin and Gershom Scholem, 1932–1940*, trans. Gary Smith and Andre Lefevere, Schocken Books, New York, 1989, pp. 225–6. For an analysis of the significance of Benjamin's reading of Kafka (which develops during the period of composition of 'The Storyteller') to both the avant-garde and theological dimension of his project, see the section on 'Kafka's Failure' in my 'Small-scale Victories, Large-scale Defeats: Walter Benjamin's Politics of Time', Benjamin and Osborne (eds), *Walter Benjamin's Philosophy*, pp. 69–81.

81. 'Conversations with Brecht', in Walter Benjamin, *Understanding Brecht*, trans. Stanley Mitchell, New Left Books, London, 1973, p. 111.

82. *Illuminations*, p. 90.

83. 'Some Motifs in Baudelaire' (1939), in *Baudelaire*, pp. 112–17, 154, 132; 'The Work of Art', *Illuminations*, p. 239; 'A Small History of Photography', *One-Way Street and Other Writings*, trans. Edmund Jephcott and Kingsley Shorter, New Left Books, London, 1979, p. 243. For a development of this 'neurological' side of Benjamin's understanding of modernity, see Susan Buck-Morss, 'Aesthetics and Anaesthetics: Walter Benjamin's Artwork Essay Reconsidered', *October* 62, Fall 1992, pp. 3–41. In modernity, Buck-Morss argues, 'the cognitive system of synaesthetics has become, rather, one of anaesthetics.' Such anaesthetics is 'the ground from which fascism can again push forth' (pp. 18, 41).

84. *GS* V, p. 498 (K 3,3). Cf. 'One-Way Street', *One-Way Street*, pp. 45, 61–2; 'The Work of Art', *Illuminations*, p. 239; 'A Small History of Photography', *One-Way Street*, p. 243.

85. Cf. Benjamin's reading of Dada as the attempt 'to create by pictorial – and literary – means the effects which the public today seeks in the film'. 'The Work of Art' essay, *Illuminations*, p. 239.

86. See, in particular, 'Some Motifs', where the temporal correspondences between the various different experiences are most explicit: 'The shock experience which the

passer-by has in the crowd corresponds to what the worker "experiences" at his machine'; '[t]hat which determines the rhythm of production on a conveyor belt is the basis of the rhythm of reception in film'; '[t]he jolt in the movement of a machine is like the so-called *coup* in a game of chance'. *Baudelaire*, pp. 133–4.

87. Benjamin to Scholem, 20 May 1935, *Benjamin/Scholem Correspondence*, p. 159.

88. 'Central Park', pp. 48, 36, 35, 49, 43, 46, 40; Susan Buck-Morss, *Dialectics of Seeing: and the Arcades Project*, MIT Press, Cambridge MA, 1989, pp. 97, 195. For a reading of the corresponding material in the *Passagen-Werk*, see *Dialectics of Seeing*, pp. 96–109. It was the reading of modernity as Hell, in what he referred to as the 'glorious first draft' of the *Passagen-Werk* (1929), to which Adorno was especially attracted. Ibid., p. 57.

89. See, for example, John Kraniauskas, 'Beware Mexican Ruins!: *One-Way Street* and the Colonial Unconscious', in Benjamin and Osborne (eds), *Walter Benjamin's Philosophy*.

90. 'The Storyteller', *Illuminations*, pp. 98, 97.

91. *GS* V, pp. 490–1 (K1, 1–3).

92. As Irving Wohlfarth points out, it is in the exceptional figure of Proust alone that Benjamin finds a restoration of the story in his generation: 'On the Messianic Structure of Walter Benjamin's Last Reflections', *Glyph* 3, 1978, p. 155. However, the length of Proust's novel is taken by Benjamin as an index of the effort such a restoration required, and Proust's moment is in any case itself already past. Proust's novelistic restoration of the story 'is part of the inventory of the individual who is isolated in many ways', whereas Benjamin aspires to reunite 'contents of the individual past' with 'material of the collective past'. Benjamin, *Charles Baudelaire*, p. 113. Furthermore, Proust's model of memory is *involuntary*, whereas Benjamin seeks to recombine involuntary with voluntary memory, actively to produce the past which has been involuntarily forgotten. Hence his turn to film and avant-garde literary production in search of formal methods. Nonetheless, Proust's involuntary memory does become a model for Benjamin of the fullness of the moment in which, in the conjunction of a specific present with a specific past, history as a whole becomes 'legible'. Like now-time, the time of involuntary memory is interruptive: 'Each situation in which the chronicler is touched by the breath of lost time is thereby rendered incomparable and removed from the sequence of the days.' Ibid, pp. 143, 147.

93. A similar ambiguity obtains in the application of the term to Marxism. Thus Gramsci, for example, (following Croce) maintained that 'Hegelian immanentism becomes historicism', but he reserved the term 'absolute historicism' for what he calls 'the philosophy of praxis', i.e. Marxism. Antonio Gramsci, *Selections from the Prison Notebooks*, ed. and trans. Quintin Hoare and Geoffrey Nowell Smith, Lawrence and Wishart, London, 1971, p. 417. Althusser, however, insisted that 'Marxism is not a historicism', on the grounds that all historicisms employ a Hegelian conception of historical time, with which Marx broke definitively (*Reading Capital*, ch. 5). For Althusser, Hegel and his later nineteenth-century 'historicist' opponents ultimately share a single conception of historical time – much as they do for Heidegger. See ch. 2, n. 121, above. ('The emergence of the problem of "historicism",' Heidegger argues, 'is the clearest symptom that historiology endeavours to alienate Dasein from its authentic historicality'. *Being and Time*, p. 448.) The identification is misleading. Nonetheless, both historicism and Hegelianism are equally opposed to the conceptions with which they are contrasted here: Althusser's 'differential historical time' and Heidegger's 'historicality', respectively.

94. In this respect (*pace* Gramsci), the term 'absolute historicism' is more suited to Hegel's than to Marx's work, on a parallel with his description of the dialectic as 'absolute method', in which form and content are one. As with his relationship to so many other -isms, so here, Hegel is really only an historicist insofar as historicism 'completes itself' in advance in his work, dialectically turning into its opposite, while preserving itself along the way. See, for example, Gadamer's account of the 'antithesis'

between the Historical School and Hegel, in which the mediated return to Hegel in Dilthey's work – 'from relativity to totality' – is read as a gradual recognition of the superiority of the Hegelian philosophy of history, against which the Historical School had rebelled. *Truth and Method*, pp. 173–214.

95. The terminological situation is further confused in the English-language literature by the influence of Karl Popper's *Poverty of Historicism* (1957), in which the term 'historicism' is used to refer to the attempt to predict the future course of history by the application of general laws – an idiosyncratic variant of the first, Hegelian sense, stemming from a scientistic misreading of Hegel. However, insofar as Popper's usage is an aberration in the critical literature, with no direct bearing on the issues in which we are interested here, there is no need for us to consider it further. A similar point applies to the more recent coinage 'new historicism' to denote a movement in US literary criticism opposed to the formalism of New Criticism and deconstruction. (See for example, Marjorie Levinson et al., *Rethinking Historicism: Critical Readings in Romantic History*, Blackwell, Oxford, 1989.) This 'historicism' has no more theoretical unity than that provided by a generalized appeal to the (diverse range of) most recent historiographic methods. Supposedly influenced by Marx, it is usually more Foucauldian in inspiration. Either way, it leads away from, rather than towards, the ontological problem of historical time, in which the 'old' historicism terminated and with which we are concerned.

96. See, for example, Robert D'Amico, *Historicism and Knowledge*, Routledge, London, 1989.

97. H.D. Kittsteiner, 'Walter Benjamin's Historicism', *New German Critique* 39, Fall 1986, pp. 179–215.

98. Benjamin, 'Theses on the Philosophy of History', *Illuminations*, p. 263. The proponent of historical relativism needs to assume Ranke's God's-eye perspective in order to be able to fix the various incommensurable periods within the discriminating unity of a single gaze.

99. Benjamin, 'N' (2, 6), in Smith (ed.), *Benjamin*, p. 48.

100. 'N' (8a, 3), ibid., p. 62. Benjamin is quoting Fustel de Coulanges, as cited by Julien Benda.

101. 'N' (9, 4), ibid., p. 63.

102. 'Theses on the Philosophy of History', *Illuminations*, p. 258.

103. Benjamin, 'N' (8, 1), in Smith (ed.), *Benjamin*, p. 61; translation amended.

104. Cf. Wohlfarth, 'On the Messianic Structure of Walter Benjamin's Last Reflections', p. 198, n. 5.

105. Benjamin, 'N' (7, 6), in Smith (ed.), *Benjamin*, p. 60.

106. Baudelaire, *The Painter of Modern Life*, p. 12; emphasis added.

107. Benjamin, 'N' (19, 3), in Smith (ed.), *Benjamin*, p. 81; and 'Eduard Fuchs, Collector and Historian', *One-Way Street*, p. 360.

108. 'Central Park', p. 43.

109. *Baudelaire*, p. 134. Benjamin takes this model of an 'exact' repetition, without difference, from the chapter on 'Machinary and Modern Industry' in Marx's *Capital*, Volume 1.

110. 'Theologico-Political Fragment (1920–1), *One-Way Street*, p. 156.

111. 'Central Park', p. 50.

112. *Baudelaire*, p. 117.

113. *GS* V, p. 495 (K 2, 3).

114. *GS* V, pp. 578, 608, 591–2, 495, 592, 576, 495, 578 (N3,1; N18,4; N9,7; K2,3; N9a,6; N2a,3; K2,3; N3,1); *GS* I, pp. 701–3 (Theses XVI, XVII, XIV). Translations: Smith (ed.), *Benjamin*, pp. 50, 80, 64, 65, 49, 50; *Illuminations*, pp. 263–5.

115. *GS* I, p. 703 (Thesis XVIII); *Illuminations*, p. 265; translation altered.

116. *GS* I, p. 704 (Theses, Appendix A); *Illuminations*, p. 265 (emphasis added). Habermas is wrong to characterize this experience as a 'leap into past *Jetztzeiten*' ('Walter Benjamin: Consciousness-Raising or Rescuing Critique', in Smith (ed.), *On Walter Benjamin*, p. 118). *Jetztzeit* is a mediation between different temporalities

within the present. 'Past *Jetztzeiten*' are not accessible as *Jetztzeiten*, but only as part of the past in the present *Jetztzeit*. As Augustine emphasized, the past is a part of the present. There is no need to 'leap' anywhere to reach it. If there is a leap, it is into a wholly new and more complex temporal space. The temporality of Benjamin's 'now' is quite different from all three of the traditional philosophical concepts of eternity – perpetual duration, atemporality and the 'pure' present – although it depends upon its relation to an atemporal dimension for its ruptural force. Habermas's reading leads to the 'magical' Benjamin, intent on the mystical task of establishing communicative relationships with the dead, to be found in Axel Honneth, 'A Communicative Disclosure of the Past: On the Relationship between Anthropology and Philosophy of History in Walter Benjamin', *New Formations* 20, Summer 1993, pp. 83–94. For a critique of Habermas's identification of the redemptive with the conservative in his essay on Benjamin, see Peter Bürger, 'Walter Benjamin's "Redemptive Critique": Some Preliminary Reflections on the Project of a Critical Hermeneutics' (1979), in Peter Bürger, *The Decline of Modernism*, trans. Nicholas Walker Polity Press, Cambridge, 1992, pp. 19–31.

117. Benjamin, 'N' (2a,3), in Smith (ed.), *Benjamin*, p. 49.

118. For an acute account of the relationship between the dialectical image, the allegorical image, and the theological symbol, see Buck-Morss, *Dialectics of Seeing*, pp. 221–45.

119. *Minima Moralia*, p. 247; Theodor W. Adorno, *Gesammelte Schriften*, Volume 4, Suhrkamp, Frankfurt/M., 1980, p. 281.

120. Theses II and III, *Illuminations*, p. 25; emphasis added.

121. See Anson Rabinbach, 'Between Enlightenment and Apocalypse: Benjamin, Bloch and Modern German Messianism', *New German Critique* 34, Winter 1985.

122. See, in particular, the 'Idea for an Arcanum' which Benjamin sent to Scholem along with his letter of the end of November 1927, trans. in Gershom Scholem, *Walter Benjamin: The Story of a Friendship* (1975), Faber and Faber, London, 1982, pp. 144–5.

123. Benjamin, letter to Scholem of 28 February 1933, *The Correspondence of Walter Benjamin and Gershom Scholem*, p. 28.

124. *Story of a Friendship*, p. 194. Cf. Gillian Rose, 'Walter Benjamin – Out of the Sources of Modern Judaism', *Judaism and Modernity*, p. 181, where Scholem's reading is extended backwards to Benjamin's earliest works.

125. Rose, *Judaism and Modernity*, p. 181.

126. Benjamin, 'N' (3, 2), in Smith (ed.), *Benjamin*, p. 51; emphasis added.

127. Rose, *Judaism and Modernity*, p. 182.

128. Benjamin, 'N' (3,2), in Smith (ed.), *Benjamin*, p. 51.

129. *GS* I, p. 703 (Thesis XVIII); *Illuminations*, p. 265; translation altered.

130. 'The Deconstruction of Actuality: An Interview with Jacques Derrida', trans. Jonathan Rée, *Radical Philosophy* 68, Autumn 1994, p. 32.

131. See for example, Richard Wolin, *Walter Benjamin: An Aesthetic of Redemption*, Columbia University Press, New York, 1982, p. 154; Scholem, 'Walter Benjamin and his Angel', in Smith (ed.), *On Walter Benjamin*, p. 82. Wolin chooses the 'materialist' Benjamin, while Scholem plumps for the 'theological' one. However, like so many who took part in the polemics over Benjamin's work in the late 1960s and 1970s, they are in agreement that the two tendencies are incompatible.

132. Thesis I, *Illuminations*, p. 255.

133. Benjamin to Scholem, 29 May 1926, in *The Correspondence of Walter Benjamin, 1910–1940*, p. 301.

134. Ibid. For a more detailed discussion of Benjamin's route to Marxism, and his instrumentalist conception of politics, see Sandor Randoti, 'Benjamin's Politics', *Telos* 37, Fall 1978.

135. Benjamin, Thesis XVI, *Illuminations*, p. 265; Irving Wohlfarth, 'Re-fusing Theology: Some First Responses to Walter Benjamin's Arcades Project', *New German Critique* 39, Fall 1986, p. 14. However, the concept of secularization is more

problematic than this formulation of Wohlfarth's allows, since it is dependent upon the temporalization of history as tradition. 'True' secularization must thus be understood against the grain of the conventional use of the idea, in an emphatic sense: that is, as a secularization of the category of secularization itself, which would replace the continuity of some essential content (be it substantial or functional) with a sense of the merely retrospective construction of continuity through translation. See n. 65 above. Ultimately, for Benjamin, the incommunicability of Messianic theology became a sign that it was no longer a bearer of truth.

136. Benjamin, 'The Task of the Translator' (1923), *Illuminations*, pp. 69–82.

137. Wohlfarth verges upon the latter error (of identity) when he argues that theology and materialism are *'nowhere . . . ultimately at odds with one another'* in Benjamin's work. Irving Wohlfarth, 'On Some Jewish Motifs in Walter Benjamin', in Andrew Benjamin (ed.), *Problems of Modernity: Adorno and Benjamin*, Routledge, London and New York, 1989, p. 202; emphasis added.

138. Benjamin, 'Eduard Fuchs, Collector and Historian', in *One-Way Street*, pp. 349–86; 'N' (2,3), in Smith (ed.), *Benjamin*, p. 47.

139. 'Task of the Translator', *Illuminations*, p. 81.

140. See Benjamin, letter to Scholem of 6 May 1934, *Correspondence*, pp. 438–41. Cf. Kittsteiner: 'Benjamin did not misunderstand Marxian theory. Nor did he want to interpret it differently; he wanted to change it.' 'Walter Benjamin's Historicism', *New German Critique* 39, p. 202. I would rather say: he interpreted it differently and *thereby* changed it.

141. 'N' (7a, 7), in Smith (ed.), *Benjamin*, p. 61.

142. GS I, pp. 703, 704, 694 (Thesis XVIII, Appendix A, Theses II and III); *Illuminations*, pp. 265, 256.

143. See Gershom Scholem, 'Walter Benjamin and his Angel' (1972), trans. Werner Dannhauser, in Smith (ed.), *Walter Benjamin*. In medieval theology, angels occupied a 'third order of duration, distinct from time and eternity'. Frank Kermode, *The Sense of an Ending: Studies in the Theory of Fiction*, Oxford University Press, New York, 1967, p. 70.

144. Benjamin, Thesis IX, *Illuminations*, 259–60.

145. See n. 109 above.

146. GS V p. 592; 'N', (9,7), in Smith (ed.), *Benjamin*, p. 64.

147. Ibid., p. 695 (Thesis V); *Illuminations*, p. 257. The instability of the formulation is symptomatic of Benjamin's lack of clarity, theoretically, about the relationship of his 'now' to the present, in its phenomenological, durational sense. Indeed, at times, he seems to lack this latter conception altogether, moving between now-time and chronology as if they were the only temporal forms at issue, after the destruction of tradition.

148. Ibid., p. 700 (Thesis XII); *Illuminations*, p. 262.

149. 'N' (2, 2), in Smith (ed.), *Benjamin*, p. 47. There is one textual exception to this reading of a specific series of pasts: namely, the 'minor methodological recommendation' in 'N' (1a, 3), that an infinite series of divisions of historical material be instituted, into historically 'positive' (forward-looking) and 'negative' (backward-looking') parts, 'until *all* of the past has been brought into the present in an historic apocatastasis'. Smith (ed.), *Benjamin*, p. 46; emphasis added. This passage is, in my view, an anomaly, inconsistent with the rest of Benjamin's methodological remarks. Nothing equivalent appears in any of the texts published during his lifetime. Unfortunately, it is this very passage which Andrew Benjamin has taken as the basis for his reconstruction of his namesake's conception of now-time, in 'Time and Task: Benjamin and Heidegger Showing the Present', in Benjamin and Osborne, *Walter Benjamin's Philosophy*, pp. 234–9. His extremely interesting reading of the relationship of this passage to the temporality of Leibniz's monads must thus be taken as the basis for an *alternative* conception of historical time to Walter Benjamin's. See pp. 178–80 above.

150. '*das Neue wiedererkennen*', GS V, p. 493 (K 1a, 3). The translation follows Buck-Morss, *Dialectics of Seeing*, p. 274.

151. 'N' (11, 4; 9a, 7; 10, 2), in Smith (ed.), *Benjamin*, pp. 67, 65, 66.
152. Adorno, letters to Benjamin of 10 November 1938 and 18 March 1936, trans. in Ernst Bloch et al., *Aesthetics and Politics*, New Left Books, London, 1977, pp. 128–9, 114; 'A Portrait of Walter Benjamin', in Adorno, *Prisms*, trans. Samuel and Shierry Weber, Neville Spearman, London, 1967, pp. 227–41.
153. See Buck-Morss, *Dialectics of Seeing*, pp. 240–52.
154. Habermas, 'Consciousness-Raising or Rescuing Critique', p. 118. See n. 115 above.
155. Benjamin, *One-Way Street*, pp. 229–30; Benjamin to Scholem, 9 August 1935, *Correspondence*, p. 165. Cf. his earlier remark, from 1927, that his work on the Paris arcades was 'a philosophical Fortinbras, who will claim the legacy of Surrealism'. Quoted in Bernd Witte, *Walter Benjamin: An Intellectual Biography*, trans. James Rolleston, Wayne State University Press, 1991, p. 110.
156. *One-Way Street*, pp. 236–7.
157. 'N' (1, 9), in Smith (ed.) *Benjamin*, p. 45.
158. Benjamin, 'The Work of Art' essay, *GS* I, p. 508; *Illuminations*, p. 244.
159. Russell A. Berman, 'The Aestheticisation of Politics: Walter Benjamin on Fascism and the Avant-Garde', in his *Modern Culture and Critical Theory: Art, Politics and the Legacy of the Frankfurt School*, University of Wisconsin Press, Madison, 1989, p. 41.
160. Both the Surrealist and Proustian models of experience from which Benjamin drew so much inspiration have an involuntary character which places them, subjectively, in the domain of chance. Their compelling force depends upon it. Yet as Benjamin himself shows, in his discussion of gambling as the transformation of time into a narcotic, to embrace chance is to surrender to the temporality of modernity as forgetting: intellectual mastery through practical submission. Benjamin, *Baudelaire*, p. 174. See also ibid., pp. 134–8. In the *Passagen-werk*, Benjamin refers to historicism as 'the strongest narcotic of the century'. 'N' (3, 4), in Smith (ed.), *Benjamin*, p. 51.
161. Letter to Scholem of 17 April, 1931, translated in Scholem, *Story of a Friendship*, pp. 232–3.
162. *Illuminations*, p. 220.
163. See Osborne, 'Adorno and the Metaphysics of Modernism', pp. 35–9. This is confirmed, rather than refuted, by the 'postmodern' attempt to escape the modernist narrative of negation. See n. 7 above. It is ironic that resources to enable Benjamin's theory of experience to escape its aporia about action should be found in Adorno's determinedly 'resigned' reflections on art. Cf. Theodor W. Adorno, 'Resignation' (1969), *Telos* 35, Spring 1978.
164. See ch. 2, p. 53.
165. Benjamin, 'N' (11, 4), in Smith (ed.), *Benjamin*, p. 67.
166. See ch. 2, n. 116.
167. Ricoeur is blinkered by his use of Aristotle for his paradigm of action here, despite his impressive extension of the terms of Aristotle's poetics in *TN* 2, pp. 7–29. A similar problem occurs in Heidegger, despite his awareness of historicity, since his use of Husserl's phenomenological method relegates historicity to a secondary position, methodologically, which the subsequent course of the analysis fails to reverse, despite its intent.
168. See the discussion of existence as repetition in ch. 5, pp. 168–80.
169. 'N' (7, 6), in Smith (ed.), *Benjamin*, p. 60. Cf. Marx's discussion of the relationship between production and consumption in the introduction to the *Grundrisse*, pp. 90–4.
170. For the concepts of the time-lag and the in-between, see Homi Bhabha, *The Location of Culture*, chs 8, 9 and 12.
171. *TN* 2, p. 28.
172. Eric Hobsbawm and Terence Ranger (eds), *The Invention of Tradition*, Cambridge University Press, Cambridge, 1983; Benedict Anderson, *Imagined*

Communities: Reflections on the Origin and Spread of Nationalism, Verso, London, 1983; Raphael Samuel, *Theatres of Memory. Volume 1: Past and Present in Contemporary Culture*, Verso, London and New York, 1994.

173. Kermode, *The Sense of an Ending*, ch. 4, 'The Modern Apocalypse'. Cf. Ricoeur, *TN* 2, pp. 19–28, and Kracauer, *The Last Things Before the Last*. An analogous, if inverse, logic can be seen to have been at work in the founding moment of Jewish apocalyptics out of the failure of prophecy, insofar as it compensates for the failure of nation by projecting fulfilment beyond history, without giving up its basic idea – in its case, fulfilment; in our case, the 'end of time'. See Rudolf Bultmann, *History and Eschatology. The Gifford Lectures 1955*, The University Press, Edinburgh, 1957, chs 1 and 2.

174. *TN* 2, p. 21.

175. See n. 149 above.

5. Avant-Garde and Everyday

1. Cf. Philippe Lacoue-Labarthe, *Heidegger, Art and Politics: The Fiction of the Political* (1987), trans. Chris Turner, Blackwell, Oxford, 1990, p. 77.

2. Benjamin, 'The Work of Art' essay, *Illuminations*, pp. 219–53. See also Buck-Morss, 'Aesthetics and Anaesthetics'.

3. See the texts by Heidegger translated in the first part of Richard Wolin (ed.), *The Heidegger Controversy: A Critical Reader*, MIT Press, Cambridge MA, 1993.

4. Martin Heidegger, *An Introduction to Metaphysics* (1953), trans. Ralph Manheim, Yale University Press, New Haven and London, 1959, p. 199. These lectures were delivered in 1935. The differences between the spoken and (later), 'fully reworked', written form have been the occasion of much debate. The series of exchanges set off by Habermas's review of the book in the *Frankfurter Allgemeine Zeitung* (translated as ch. 11 of Wolin's *The Heidegger Controversy*) is generally taken to constitute the first German 'Heidegger controversy'. It is important to note that even in the published text of 1953, it is not Nazi politicians whom Heidegger berates for failing to recognize 'the inner truth and greatness' of their movement, but only 'the works that are being peddled about nowadays as the *philosophy* of National Socialism'. Ibid.; emphasis added.

5. Such as Lacoue-Labarthe, who regards Heidegger as having 'taught us to think philosophically, what fascism, plain and simple, is about'. 'Who in our age,' he asks, 'has said so much and so much of such "profundity" on fascism – and, consequently, of our "world"?' *Heidegger, Art and Politics*, p. 110.

6. The Kantian dimension to *Being and Time* is clear from the title of its only published part, 'The Interpretation of *Dasein* in Terms of Temporality and the Explication of Time as the Transcendental Horizon for the Question of Being', along with its two-part organization into an 'analytic' and a second division treating the possibility of *Dasein* 'being-a-whole'. It is rendered explicit in Heidegger's *Kant and the Problem of Metaphysics* (1929; 1973), trans. Richard Taft, Indiana University Press, Bloomington and Indianapolis, 1990. The originality of the *Critique of Pure Reason* is seen there to lie in its establishment of the transcendental imagination as the origin of pure sensible intuition. Retrospectively, *Being and Time* may be read as an exploration of the ontological consequences of this argument. Cf. *Being and Time*, p. 45.

7. Marcuse claims that Heidegger's public declaration of support for National Socialism came as a 'complete surprise' to his students: 'from personal experience I can tell you that neither in his lectures, nor in his seminars, nor personally, was there ever any hint of his sympathies for Nazism.' 'Heidegger's Politics: An Interview with Herbert Marcuse', in Robert Pippin et al. (eds), *Herbert Marcuse, Critical Theory and the Promise of Utopia*, Bergin and Garvey, South Hadley MA, 1988, p. 99. Other evidence suggests otherwise. Pöggeler, for example, claims that Heidegger's 'opting for

Hitler' predated 1933. Otto Pöggeler, 'Heidegger's Political Self-Understanding', in Wolin (ed.), *The Heidegger Controversy*, p. 214. Günther Stern reports that Elfride Heidegger (Heidegger's wife) was already 'openly anti-semitic and openly Nazi' in 1925, actively recruiting Heidegger's students to the National Socialist student group in Marburg, cited in Klaus Theweleit, *Object-Choice (All you need is love . . .)*, trans. Malcolm R. Green, Verso, London, 1994, p. 28. Farias notoriously traces Heidegger's politics back to his social, religious and educational origins, suggesting an unbroken allegiance to a 'tradition of authoritarianism, antisemitism and ultra-nationalism'. Victor Farias, *Heidegger and Nazism* (1987), trans. Paul Burrell and Gabriel Ricci, Temple University Press, Philadelphia, 1989, p. 4. See also Hugo Ott, *Heidegger: A Political Life* (1989), trans. Allan Bluden, Harper-Collins, London and New York, 1993. There would seem to be an element of retrospective self-justification in Marcuse's generalization of his 'surprise'.

8. Wolin, *The Politics of Being: The Political Thought of Martin Heidegger*, Columbia University Press, New York, 1990, pp. 34–5. Cf. Karl Löwith, 'The Political Implications of Heidegger's Existentialism' (1946), in Wolin (ed.), *The Heidegger Controversy*.

9. 'Only an essentially futural being . . . that is free for its death and can let itself be thrown back upon its factical "there" by shattering itself against death . . . can, by handing down to itself the possibility it has inherited, take over its own thrownness and be in the *moment of vision* for "its time".' *Being and Time*, p. 437; cited in this (slightly different) translation by Löwith in 'The Political Implications of Heidegger's Existentialism', in Wolin (ed.), *The Heidegger Controversy*, pp. 169–70.

10. The phrase originates in a National Socialist Minister's remarks about Heidegger's 1933 Rectoral Address. The idea that Heidegger had invented a distinct 'Freiburg National Socialism' also apparently circulated among students at Freiburg at the time. See Pöggeler, 'Heidegger's Political Self-Understanding', in ibid., pp. 214, 205.

11. Jeffrey Herf, *Reactionary Modernism: Technology, Culture, and Politics in Weimar and the Third Reich*, Cambridge University Press, Cambridge, 1984, p. 3. For the concept of conservative revolution, see Herf, ch. 2 and George L. Mosse, *The Crisis of German Ideology: Intellectual Origins of the Third Reich* (1964), Schocken Books, New York, 1981, chs 16 and 17. For an account of the specificity of German fascism in relation to other contemporary forms of reactionary politics, see Eric Hobsbawm, *Age of Extremes: The Short Twentieth Century, 1914–1991*, Michael Joseph, London, 1994, ch. 4. For the distinction between *Zivilisation* and *Kultur*, see Norbert Elias, *The Civilising Process. Volume One. The History of Manners*, trans. Edmund Jephcott, Blackwell, Oxford, 1978, ch. 1.

12. Herf, *Reactionary Modernism*, p. 109.

13. Ernst Jünger, 'Nationalism and Modern Life' (1927), as quoted in Herf, *Reactionary Modernism*, p. 82. In the words of Benjamin (whose own work shows the marked influence of Jünger's phenomenology of modernity as shock): 'the new nationalists' metaphysical abstraction of war signifies nothing other than a mystical and unmediated application of technology to solve the mystery of an idealistically perceived nature. . . . In the parallelogram of forces formed by . . . nature and nation – war is the diagonal.' Walter Benjamin, 'Theories of German Fascism: On the Collection of Essays *War and Warrior*, edited by Ernst Jünger' (1930), trans. Jerolf Wikoff, *New German Critique* 17, Spring 1979, pp. 126–7. For more on Jünger, whose reflections on his wartime experience, *The Storm of Steel* (1920), shaped the views of a generation, see *New German Critique* 59, Spring/Summer 1993, *Special Issue on Ernst Jünger*.

14. See Michael E. Zimmerman, *Heidegger's Confrontation with Modernity: Technology, Politics, Art*, Indiana University Press, Bloomington and Indianapolis, 1990, chs 3–6. Heidegger discussed Jünger's *The Worker* (1932) twice with small groups of his closest associates: once on its publication and then again in 1939–40. Pöggeler, 'Heidegger's Political Self-Understanding', *The Heidegger Controversy*, pp. 211, 213. Wolin includes a translation of Jünger's 'Total Mobilisation' – which

first appeared in the collection reviewed by Benjamin in his 'Theories of German Fascism' – in *The Heidegger Controversy*.

15. See ch.4, n. 116, above.

16. Wolin, *Politics of Being*, p. 23; emphasis added.

17. Herf, *Reactionary Modernism*, pp. 110–15.

18. Marx and Engels, *Manifesto of the Communist Party* (1948), Progress Publishers, Moscow, 1952 p. 45.

19. Ibid., p. 44.

20. Étienne Balibar and Immanuel Wallerstein, *Race, Class, Nation: Ambiguous Identities*, trans. Chris Turner, Verso, London and New York, 1991, p. 8.

21. Apart from his much-cited remarks on the imitative, backward-looking character of the historical self-consciousness of the French Revolution (in the *Eighteenth Brumaire*), and the enduring charm of Greek art (in the Introduction to the *Grundrisse*), the treatment of temporality in Marx's later writings is restricted to its quantitative role in the production and circulation of capital, and the effect of the former on the intensity of labour and the length of the working day. (See Marx *Capital*, Volume 1, ch. X, 'The Working Day', ch. XV, section 3, 'The Proximate Effects of Machinery on the Workman', ch. XX, 'Time-Wages'; Volume 2, ch. V, 'The Time of Circulation', ch. VII, 'The Turnover Time and the Number of Turnovers', chs XII & XIII, 'The Time of Production' & 'The Time of Circulation'.) The scale of Marx's systematic project, combined with his methodology of 'ascending' from the abstract to the concrete, made a lifetime too short to complete the analysis of 'the process of capitalist production as a whole' (the subtitle to *Capital*, Volume 3); let alone the transition to the analysis of capitalist societies or social formations.

22. Harold Rosenberg, *The Tradition of the New* (1959), University of Chicago Press, Chicago and London, 1982.

23. Philippe Lacoue-Labarthe and Jean-Luc Nancy, 'The Nazi Myth', trans. Brian Holmes, *Critical Inquiry* 16, Winter 1990, pp. 291–312. Cf. the attempt at a generic definition of fascist ideology as 'a palingenetic form of populist ultra-nationalism', in Roger Griffen, *The Nature of Fascism*, Routledge, London and New York, 1993, ch. 2. (Palingenesis is a process of rebirth or regeneration.) I am grateful to Mark Neocleous for bringing this text to my attention.

24. *Age of Extremes*, p. 118.

25. Martin Heidegger, *Nietzsche. Volume Three: The Will to Power as Knowledge and as Metaphysics* (1939–40), trans. Joan Stambaugh, David Farrell Krell and Frank Capuzzi, Harper, San Francisco, 1987, p. 196: 'Only will for willing is will, namely, will to power in the sense of power for power.' The discussion of nihilism follows directly from this account of the will to power. In his 1966 interview with *Der Spiegel*, Heidegger identifies his Nietzsche lectures as the principal site of his doctrinal confrontation with National Socialism – although he remained a party member at this time; indeed, until the very end of the war. Wolin (ed.), *The Heidegger Controversy*, p. 103.

26. Adorno and Horkheimer, *Dialectic of Enlightenment*, p. 185.

27. Ernst Bloch, *Heritage of Our Times*, Pt II.

28. See, Balibar and Wallerstein, *Race, Class, Nation*, Pt I.

29. See, for example, Marjorie Perloff, *The Futurist Moment: Avant-Garde, Avant Guerre, and the Language of Rupture*, Chicago University Press, 1986; Andrew Hewitt, *Fascist Modernism: Aesthetics, Politics, and the Avant-Garde*, Stanford University Press, Stanford, 1993; Fredric Jameson, *Fables of Aggression: Wyndham Lewis, the Modernist as Fascist*, University of California Press, Berkeley, 1979.

30. See ch. 4, note 7, above.

31. The analogous positions of 'people', 'Being' and 'God' within the three discourses is instructive. As we shall see, for all its sophisticated conceptual innovations, the theological and political presuppositions of Heidegger's analysis ultimately dominate its temporal form.

32. Mosse, *The Crisis of German Ideology*, ch. 17.

33. See Mihaly Vajda, *Fascism as a Mass Movement*, Alison and Busby, London, 1976, p. 14. For the mass democratic context of the National Socialist conception of the people, see George L. Mosse, 'Fascism and the French Revolution', *Journal of Contemporary History*, Vol. 24, no. 1, January 1989.

34. For some reflections on Western philosophy as an invented 'Hellenomanic' tradition, see Simon Critchley, 'Black Socrates? Questioning the Philosophical Tradition', *Radical Philosophy* 69, January/February 1995, pp. 17-26. Hellenism was also part of Rosenberg's version of the Nazi myth, but only as a subsidiary figure. Thus, while in his version Aryan blood could be traced back to Atlantis, the Greeks were nonetheless the great Aryans of antiquity since, as Lacoue-Labarthe and Nancy put it, they 'produced myth as *art*. The Greeks put their soul (their blood) [the identification is crucial to this version – PO] into form.' 'The Nazi Myth', p. 309.

35. Cf. Lacoue-Labarthe, *Heidegger, Art and Politics*, pp. 109, 115.

36. See Ott, *Heidegger: A Political Life*, Pt 3.

37. See in particular, Hans Sluga, *Heidegger's Crisis: Philosophy and Politics in Nazi Germany*, Harvard University Press, Cambridge MA and London, 1993.

38. Cf. ch. 3, p. 70, above. *Dasein* carries the possibility of authenticity within itself insofar as it is, firstly, characterized by 'mineness' (*Jemeinigkeit*; See *Being and Time*, p. 68) and thus, secondly, subject to the logic of propriety, which is taken by Heidegger to govern the hermeneutics of questioning as a mode of Being.

39. *Being and Time*, p. 436.

40. Ibid., pp. 442-4; (*Sein und Zeit*, p. 391).

41. Ibid., p. 32.

42. Jean-Luc Nancy, 'The Decision of Existence', in his *The Birth of Presence*, trans. Brian Holmes et al., Stanford University Press, Stanford, 1993, pp. 405-6, n. 45. See also his *The Experience of Freedom* (1988), trans. Bridget McDonald, Stanford University Press, Stanford, 1993, chs 3-5, 12-14.

43. Reiner Schürmann, *Heidegger on Being and Acting: From Principles to Anarchy* (1982), trans. Christine-Marie Gross, Indiana University Press, Bloomington, 1987, p. 7. Schürmann insists that Heidegger must be 'read backwards' if the implications of his thought for practice are to be fully appreciated. Ibid., p. 15.

44. Cf. the Postface to Christopher Fynsk, *Heidegger: Thought and Historicity*, Cornell University Press, Ithaca, 1993, 'The Legibility of the Political'.

45. *Being and Time*, §6, pp. 41-9, 'The Task of Destroying the History of Ontology'; cf. Schürmann, *Heidegger on Being and Acting*, pp. 2-11.

46. *Being and Time*, p. 388.

47. Schürmann, *Heidegger on Being and Acting*, p. 245; Löwith, in Wolin (ed.), *The Heidegger Controversy*, p. 173. Decisionism is opposed to 'normativism' in legal theory. It is associated in German philosophy with the work of the fascist legal theorist Carl Schmidt, who first used the term in the Preface to the 1928 edition of his book *The Dictator* (1921). It is generally traced back to Hobbes' formula '*Auctoritas, non veritas, facit legem*': Authority, not truth, makes right. However, it is the notion of a 'pure' or 'absolute' decision that is distinctive of Schmidt's work, which dissolves legitimacy into dictatorship. See, for example, his *Political Theology: Four Chapters on the Concept of Sovereignty* (1922), trans. George Schwab, MIT Press, Cambridge MA, 1985, pp. 66-7. Löwith pioneered the decisionist reading of Heidegger, which has been taken up more recently by Wolin.

48. Wolin, *The Politics of Being*, pp. 43, 37, 65.

49. In a process of reworking dating back to the 1922 introduction to his unpublished book on Aristotle, it was only in the final 'Kantian' draft of *Being and Time* that Heidegger turned to an existential terminology which, with one brief exception, he had previously conscientiously shunned. The activist side of the book was thus introduced at the very last moment and its terms are correspondingly underdeveloped. Heidegger was unable to finish the book within these terms (only the first two divisions of Part One were ever published). See Kisiel, *The Genesis of Heidegger's Being and*

Time, Pts II and III. In this regard, the famous first sentence of the 'Letter on Humanism' (1947) – 'We are still far from pondering the essence of action decisively enough' – may be read self-referentially, as well in the wider epochal sense of the 'we'. Martin Heidegger, *Basic Writings*, Routledge, London, 1993, p. 217. See also the 1956 'Addendum' to 'The Origin of the Work of Art' (1935–6), in which the 'distressing difficulty which has been clear to me since *Being and Time*' of 'the relation of Being and human being' is raised once again. *Basic Writings*, p. 211.

50. This was the year Heidegger withdrew his co-operation from the commission preparing a new edition of Nietzsche's work, after the intensification of interference by the Party establishment. It also registers a turn in Heidegger's stance towards Nietzsche within the lectures themselves. See David Farrell Krell, 'Introduction to the Paperback Edition: Heidegger Nietzsche Nazism', in Martin Heidegger, *Nietzsche. Volumes I & II: The Will to Power as Art & The Eternal Recurrence of the Same*, Harper, San Francisco, 1991, pp. ix–xxvi; and the section on 'Contexts' in his 'Analysis', which follows the text in Martin Heidegger, *Nietzsche. Volume IV: Nihilism*, Harper, San Francisco, 1987; 1991, pp. 262–76.

51. See, for example, Heidegger's epochal definition of 'today' at the end of his lectures on Nietzsche (1940) as 'the metaphysical determination of historical mankind in the age of Nietzsche's metaphysics'. *Nietzsche*, Volume 4, p. 195. The difference from the acute conjunctural consciousness of 1933–4 could hardly be greater.

52. For a critique of which, see Schürmann, 'The Problem of the Will', in *Heidegger on Being and Acting*, pp. 245–50. Unfortunately, Wolin fails to grasp the logic of Schürmann's reading of Heidegger, in which the concept of anarchy is used outside of the oppositions of subject and object, theory and practice, to mean 'without first principles' (an-archy). He thus reduces Schürmann's position to a version of the very 'radical individualism' to which it is explicitly opposed. Wolin, *The Politics of Being*, pp. 53–5.

53. See Heidegger, 'The Origin of the Work of Art', *Basic Writings*, p. 192.

54. See the passage by Löwith quoted by Schürmann, *Heidegger on Being and Acting*, p. 376, n. 40. Cf. Wolin, *Politics of Being*, pp. 64–5.

55. As Heidegger puts it: '*The existentiell indefiniteness* of resoluteness never makes itself definite except in a resolution; yet it has, all the same, its *existential definiteness*.' *Being and Time*, p. 345.

56. This struggle is essentially an interpretive one, a conflict over meaning (the meaning of a heritage) rather than a clash between pure wills, since for Heidegger 'resoluteness' is a mode of disclosure, just as 'understanding' is a form of projection. Existentially, knowing and willing are always united. See *Being and Time*, pp. 384–5; 'The Origin of the Work of Art', *Basic Writings*, p. 192. In this respect, Heidegger's 'appreciation' of Schmidt's quotation of a passage from Heraclitus, in a note accompanying his gift to Heidegger of a copy of the third edition of his *The Concept of the Political* (Heidegger to Schmidt, 22 August 1933, trans. in *Telos* 72, 1987, p. 132), should not be taken to indicate agreement over its meaning. Rather, it is more likely to have been Heidegger's way of opening a dialogue with Schmidt about it, in order to convince him of his own view. Heidegger was seeking Schmidt's 'decisive cooperation' in reconstituting the Law Faculty at Freiburg at this time.

57. *Being and Time*, pp. 19–35.

58. See Kisiel, *The Genesis of 'Being and Time'*, chs 2–6.

59. Like Benjamin, Heidegger uses the German word *Erfahrung* to designate an emphatic sense of experience, in distinction from *Erlebnis*. However, unlike Benjamin, for Heidegger this is essentially another word for the Being of *Dasein*. See Martin Heidegger, *Hegel's Concept of Experience*, Harper and Row, New York, 1970, p. 113. For a discussion of the way in which Heidegger's concept of experience reflects the structure of the development of his own thought, see Robert Bernasconi, *The Question of Language in Heidegger's History of Being*, Humanities Press International, Atlantic Highlands, ch. 6. Bernasconi is concerned with the experience of the 'turn' (*Kehre*) in Heidegger's thought, from metaphysics to the thinking of the event (*Ereignis*). What I

am arguing, however, is that this process is at work much earlier, in the founding phase of Heidegger's development as a philosopher.

60. Kisiel, *The Genesis of Being and Time*, pp. 269, 369.

61. As Heidegger put it: 'Kierkegaard explicitly seized upon the problem of existence as an existentiell problem, and thought it through in a penetrating fashion. But the existential problematic was so alien to him that, as regards his ontology, he remained completely dominated by Hegel and by *ancient philosophy as Hegel saw it.*' *Being and Time*, p. 494, Division Two, section 45, n. vi; emphasis added.

62. Kisiel, *Genesis of 'Being and Time'*, pp. 113, 7, 452.

63. Ibid., pp. 254, 260, 261, 356. For Foucault's notion of an 'ontology of the present', see ch. 1, pp. 21–2, above.

64. Heidegger, 'The Origin of the Work of Art', *Basic Writings*, p. 202. See Adorno's critique of Heidegger's ontologization of historicity, to which reference was made in ch. 2, pp. 57–9, above.

65. Nancy, 'The Decision of Existence,' in *The Birth of Presence*, p. 405, n. 45.

66. Lacoue-Labarthe, *Heidegger, Art and Politics*, pp. 114, 108.

67. See the discussion of truth in $44 of *Being and Time*, pp. 256–73, where 'the disclosedness of [*Dasein*'s] ownmost Being' is seen to belong to its 'existential constitution' (p. 263). Its 'ownmost' Being is, of course, its status as an entity for which Being is in question.

68. See ch. 1, p. 27, above.

69. See, for example, Heidegger's appeal, 'German Students', of 3 November 1933, on the occasion of the plebiscite called by Hitler to sanction Germany's withdrawal from the League of Nations, which begins: 'The National Socialist revolution is bringing about the total transformation of our German existence (*Dasein*)', in Wolin (ed.), *The Heidegger Controversy*, p. 46. Cf. Karl Löwith, *My Life in Germany Before and After 1933: A Report*, trans. Elizabeth King, University of Illinois Press, Urbana and Chicago, 1994, pp. 34–44.

70. See pp. 111, 140, above.

71. As early as 1916, Benjamin judged the published text of Heidegger's *venia legendi* lecture at Freiburg, 'On the Concept of Time in the Science of History', to 'show precisely how not to deal with the matter'; while in 1930 he wrote to Scholem of his plan to 'annihilate' Heidegger 'in the context of a close-knit critical circle of readers', led by himself and Brecht. *The Correspondence of Walter Benjamin, 1910–1940*, pp. 82, 365. Brecht fell ill, and the plan was abandoned.

72. Caygill, 'Benjamin, Heidegger and the Destruction of Tradition', in Benjamin and Osborne (eds), *Walter Benjamin's Philosophy*, p. 4.

73. Ibid., p. 10.

74. Heidegger, 'The Origin of the Work of Art', in *Basic Writings*, p. 192; emphasis added.

75. Rabinbach, 'Between Enlightenment and Apocalypse', p. 105.

76. Caygill, 'Benjamin, Heidegger', p. 17; Derrida, 'Metaphysics and Violence', *Writing and Difference*, p. 81. For Heidegger, the existential subject is, of course, crucially, ungendered. It is the introduction of sexual difference which marks the passage from existentialism to psychoanalysis.

77. Caygill, 'Benjamin, Heidegger', p. 11. Anything, that is, except the angel of history. See above, pp. 149–50. Despite his concluding remarks about politics and 'the fundamental changes in subjectivity produced by modernity', Caygill consistently overstates the homogeneity of Benjamin's work, projecting the melancholy perspective of *The Origin of Tragic Drama* forward into the 1930s. He thereby impedes the development of his own dialectical project of reading Benjamin and Heidegger *together*, 'each against the other's grain'. Ibid., p. 30.

78. *Critique of Pure Reason*, p. 312. See the reading of Heidegger in Nancy, *The Experience of Freedom*, for which this quotation from Kant stands as the epigraph.

79. Andrew Benjamin, 'Time and Task', in Benjamin and Osborne (eds), *Walter Benjamin's Philosophy*, p. 243; emphasis added.

80. Walter Benjamin, 'N' (9a, 8), in Smith (ed.), *Benjamin*, p. 68. Cf. Andrew Benjamin, 'Time and Task', p. 231.

81. See ch. 4, n. 53, above.

82. Andrew Benjamin, 'Time and Task', pp. 229, 224. The text of Heidegger's being considered here is the concluding section of the part on 'European Nihilism' (1940) in the final volume of his *Nietzsche*.

83. Andrew Benjamin, 'Time and Task', p. 247. For the concept of *Nachträglichkeit*, see ch. 3, pp. 88–90, above.

84. See ch. 4, p. 131–2, above.

85. This is what Andrew Benjamin fails to see. He considers the 'after' to be 'unthinkable except as a form of repetition'. Ibid., p. 236.

86. 'N' (9, 5), in Smith (ed.), *Benjamin*, p. 63. Cf. Andrew Benjamin, 'Time and Task', p. 230.

87. These are the motifs of the 1935 exposé for the Arcades Project, 'Paris – The Capital of the Nineteenth Century', and the two works on Baudelaire – 'The Paris of the Second Empire in Baudelaire' (1938) and 'Some Motifs in Baudelaire' (1939) – which developed out of chapter five of the exposé, respectively. They are translated as Benjamin's *Charles Baudelaire*.

88. See Janet Wolff, 'Memoirs and Micrologies: Walter Benjamin, Feminism and Cultural Analysis', in *New Formations* 20, Summer 1993.

89. 'On the Program of the Coming Philosophy', in Smith (ed.), *Benjamin*, pp. 3–4.

90. Ibid., pp. 10–11; first emphasis added.

91. Scholem, *Story of a Friendship*, p. 59. See the discussion of Benjamin's interest in Walter Lehmann's lectures on the language and culture of ancient Mexico at the University of Munich in the academic year 1915–16, in Kraniauskas, 'Beware Mexican Ruins!', in Benjamin and Osborne (eds), *Walter Benjamin's Philosophy*. Benjamin's 'desire to speak "Aztec"' links his Jewish mysticism to his interest in Surrealism, via a fascination with ethnology which was common to both German and French modernisms of the period.

92. 'On the Program of the Coming Philosophy', in Smith (ed.), *Benjamin*, p. 12.

93. *One-Way Street*, p. 45.

94. 'Surrealism', in ibid., p. 237; emphasis added.

95. Marx, *Capital*, Volume 1, pp. 126, 165, 169, 173, 167. Scholem's claim that Benjamin's Surrealism essay is 'still dominated by an absolutely pre-Marxist line' (*Story of a Friendship*, p. 146) – with its implication that the kind of Marxist reading conducted here is illegitimate – is unconvincing, since, as Witte points out (*Walter Benjamin*, p. 106), the politicization of his discourse had already received 'tangible expression' in *One-Way Street*.

96. *Capital*, Volume 1, p. 165.

97. Sigmund Freud, 'Fetishism' (1927), in *On Sexuality: Three Essays on the Theory of Sexuality and Other Works*, Penguin Freud Library, Volume 7, Harmondsworth, 1977, pp. 345–57.

98. Clifford, 'On Ethnographic Surrealism', in his *The Predicament of Culture*, ch. 4; Marx, *Capital*, Volume 1, p. 165.

99. For a discussion of the conditions under which mass cultural hieroglyphs might attain the productivity of writing (*écriture*), see Miriam Hanson, 'Mass Culture as Hieroglyphic Writing: Adorno, Derrida, Kracauer', *New German Critique* 56, Summer 1992.

100. For an account of this overlapping of Marxist and psychoanalytical connotations of fetishism in the Surrealist image, see Theodor W. Adorno, 'Looking Back on Surrealism' (1954), in *Notes to Literature. Volume One*, trans. Shierry Weber Nicholson, Columbia University Press, New York, 1991, p. 89.

101. Hal Foster, *Compulsive Beauty*, MIT Press, Cambridge MA, 1993, p. 134. Foster reads Surrealism through the concept of the uncanny.

102. *One-Way Street*, p. 229.

103. See Margaret Cohen, *Profane Illumination: Walter Benjamin and the Paris of*

Surrealist Revolution, California University Press, Berkeley and Los Angeles, 1993. The issue of gender in Benjamin's representations of modernity is complex and disputed. Compare, for example, Christine Buci-Glucksmann, 'The Utopia of the Feminine: Benjamin's Trajectory', in her *Baroque Reason: The Aesthetics of Modernity* (1984), trans. Patrick Camiller, Sage, London, Thousand Oaks and New Delhi, 1994, Pt II, with Sigrid Weigel, '"The Female Has-Been" and the "First-Born Male of his Work": From Gender Images to Dialectical Images in Benjamin's Writings', *New Formations* 20, Summer 1993.

104. See, for example, Susan Rubin Suleiman, *Subversive Intent: Gender, Politics and the Avant-Garde*, Harvard University Press, Cambridge MA, 1990; and, for a broader view, reconnecting psychoanalytical feminist film theory with Marx's notion of commodity fetishism, Laura Mulvey, 'Some Thoughts on Theories of Fetishism in the Context of Contemporary Culture', *October* 65, Summer 1993.

105. See Benjamin, *'Traumkitsch'* (Dreamkitsch), *GS* II, pp. 620–2.

106. Benjamin, 'Paris – The Capital of the Nineteenth Century', in *Charles Baudelaire*, p. 176.

107. *One-Way Street*, p. 229.

108. Benjamin, 'Central Park', p. 35.

109. See the section on 'Modern Mythology and Dream Consciousness', in McCole, *Walter Benjamin and the Antinomies of Tradition*, pp. 229–40.

110. *One-Way Street*, p. 230.

111. It is because Benjamin's interest in the everyday is always, ultimately, a metaphysical as well as a political one – because politics and metaphysics, politics and truth, are always thought in his work together, through the middle term of history – that there is something question-begging about Janet Wolff's attempt to separate out the question of its interest for contemporary cultural analysis from that of its theoretical structure – what she calls 'getting Walter Benjamin "right"'. 'Memoirs and Micrologies', p. 113. For the philosophical terms of Benjamin's micrologies are radically different from those of their more recent Foucauldian cousins. In this respect, interest in Benjamin's cultural analyses involves, of necessity, a *critique* of contemporary cultural studies.

112. 'Setting to Work (Transnational Cultural Studies): An Interview with Gayatri Spivak', in Peter Osborne (ed.), *A Critical Sense: Interviews with Radical Philosophy*, forthcoming, Routledge, London and New York, 1996.

113. For the origins of modern élite theory in the reaction to the unification of Italy, see Richard Bellamy, *Modern Italian Social Theory*, Polity Press, Cambridge, 1987, chs 1–3.

114. *Being and Time*, p. 62.

115. Ibid., p. 37.

116. Ibid., p. 69

117. Ibid.

118. Ibid., pp. 168, 422.

119. Ibid., p. 168; Benjamin, 'The Program of the Coming Philosophy', in Smith (ed.), *Benjamin*, p. 11.

120. 'When Dasein is absorbed in the world of its concern – that is, at the same time, in its Being-with towards Others,' Heidegger writes, 'it is not itself.' *Being and Time*, p. 163.

121. Ibid., p. 164.

122. Jürgen Habermas, *The Structural Transformation of the Public Sphere: An Inquiry into a Category of Bourgeois Society* (1962), trans. Thomas Burger, Polity Press, Cambridge, 1989. See also Oskar Negt and Alexander Kluge, *Public Sphere and Experience: Toward an Analysis of the Bourgeois and Proletarian Public Sphere* (1972), trans. Peter Labanyi et al., University of Minnesota Press, Minneapolis and London, 1993.

123. *Being and Time*, p. 165.

124. Ibid., p. 164; emphasis added.

125. G.W.F. Hegel, 'Aphorismen aus der Ienenser Zeit', no. 31, in *Dokumente Zu Hegels Enturicklung*, ed. Johannes Hoffmeister, 2nd ed., Frommann, Stuttgart, Bad Cannstatt, 1974; quoted in Vincent Descombes, *The Barometer of Modern Reason: On the Philosophies of Current Events*, Oxford University Press, New York, 1993, p. 3.

126. Heidegger's hostility to the city was notorious. He refused the chair at Berlin in the early 1930s on the grounds that it was not possible to philosophize there, amid the 'rootless'. See Martin Heidegger, 'Why Do I Stay in the Provinces?', in Thomas Sheehan (ed.), *Heidegger: The Man and the Thinker*, Precedent Publishing, Chicago, 1981.

127. Heidegger, *The Concept of Time*, p. 9E. The German word *Tradition* stands here for tradition in a bad homogenizing sense, as opposed to *Überlieferung*, the handing-on through creative repetition.

128. See *Being and Time*, pp. 296–304.

129. Henri Lefebvre, *Everyday Life in the Modern World* (1968), trans. Sacha Rabinovitch, Allen Lane, London, 1971, p. 14.

130. Ibid., p. 13.

131. Henri Lefebvre, *Critique of Everyday Life. Volume One. Introduction*, trans. John Moore, Verso, London and New York, 1991, p. 252.

132. Ibid., p. 127. The gendering is unfortunate, since, as Lefebvre points out elsewhere, the 'generalised passivity' of the everyday 'weighs more heavily on women, who are sentenced to everyday life'. Henri Lefebvre, 'The Everyday and Everydayness', *Yale French Studies* 73, 1987, p. 10.

133. For an overview of the development of Lefebvre's project, see Michel Trebitsch, 'Preface', in Henri Lefebvre, *Critique of Everyday Life*, pp. ix–ixxviii. See also Lefebvre's autobiography, *La Somme et le Reste*, two volumes, La Nef de Paris, Paris, 1959.

134. Fredric Jameson, 'On "Cultural Studies"', *Social Text* 34, 1993, p. 17. Jameson is alluding to Jean-François Lyotard's use of the expression 'the desire called "Marx"' in his *Libidinal Economy*. The two desires are, of course, related.

135. *Critique of Everyday Life*, p. 267.

136. Ibid., pp. 130, 264.

137. See, in particular, Norbert Guterman and Henri Lefebvre, *La Conscience Mystifiée*, Gallimard, Paris, 1936, which was one of the first texts to draw explicitly on Marx's recently published Paris Manuscripts; and Henri Lefebvre, *Dialectical Materialism* (1939), trans. John Sturrock, Jonathan Cape, London, 1968. With its emphasis on a philosophical concept of praxis, beyond both 'idealism' and 'materialism' as conventionally understood, and its introduction of the concept of 'total man', this latter text may be read as the foundational text of Western (as opposed to Soviet-style) Marxism in France. See Mark Poster, *Existential Marxism in Postwar France*, Princeton University Press, Princeton, 1975, ch. 1 and Michael Kelly, *Modern French Marxism*, Blackwell, Oxford, 1982, ch. 2.

138. *Critique of Everyday Life*, chs 3 and 4.

139. Ibid., p. 49.

140. See in particular, Raymond Williams, 'Culture is Ordinary' (1958) and 'The Idea of a Common Culture' (1968), in his *Resources of Hope*, Verso, London, 1989. More specifically, one might compare the autobiographical opening of the former ('[t]he bus stop was outside the cathedral. . . . I was born and grew up halfway along that bus journey. Where I lived is still a farming valley. . . . Not far away, my grandfather, and so back through the generations, was a farm labourer until he was turned out of his cottage . . . ' [p. 3]), with Lefebvre's description of 'an ordinary village in France' in his 'Notes Written One Sunday in the French Countryside', in *Critique of Everyday Life*, pp. 210–24.

141. Cf. Williams's distinction between 'legitimating', 'academic' and 'operative' theory in 'Notes on Marxism in Britain Since 1945' (1976), in Raymond Williams, *Problems in Materialism and Culture*, Verso, London, 1980, p. 237. Lefebvre's

writings on Marx were primarily legitimating; while his work on everyday life was operative.

142. *Critique of Everyday Life*, p. 97; emphasis added.

143. Ibid.; final two emphases added.

144. Guy Debord, 'Perspectives for Conscious Alterations in Everyday Life' (1961), in Ken Knabb (ed.), *The Situationist International Anthology*, Bureau of Public Secrets, Berkeley, 1981, p. 69; emphasis added.

145. Lefebvre, 'The Everyday and Everydayness', p. 10.

146. *Critique of Everyday Life*, p. 30.

147. Ibid., p. 35.

148. For the Bakhtin of the 1930s, the everyday registers the 'authentic folkloric roots of the novel' in the 'low language of contemporaneity' to be found in the Greek demotic and Rabelais' representation of the medieval world. Bakhtin, 'Epic and Novel', in *The Dialogic Imagination*, p. 21. Ironically, however, such roots could only be manifest in their own day in the licensed compensation of the carnival, the very *opposite* of the medieval everyday. Interestingly, Lefebvre shared Bakhtin's interest in Rabelais (Henri Lefebvre, *Rabelais*, Les Editeurs Français Réunis, Paris, 1955) and in the carnival or festival as the site for the release of desires produced by, but repressed within, everyday life. In *Everyday Life in the Modern World*, '[t]he Festival rediscovered and magnified by overcoming the conflict between everyday life and festivity' appears as 'the final clause of the revolutionary path' (p. 206). For the later Bakhtin, on the other hand, '[[p]ure everyday life is a fiction.' Bakhtin, 'From Notes Made in 1970–71', in his *Speech Genres and Other Late Essays*, trans. Vern W. McGee, University of Texas Press, Austin, 1986, p. 154.

149. *Everyday Life in the Modern World*, pp. 40, 30. See also Henri Lefebvre, *The Survival of Capitalism: Reproduction of the Relations of Production* (1973), trans. Frank Bryant, Allison and Busby, London, 1974; and Theodor Adorno, 'Free time', in his *The Culture Industry: Selected Essays on Mass Culture*, Routledge, London, 1991, ch. 8.

150. *Critique of Everyday Life*, pp. 58, 131.

151. Lefebvre, *Everyday Life in the Modern World*, ch. 2; *Critique of Everyday Life*, p. 97.

152. See Lefebvre, 'Towards a Permanent Cultural Revolution', in *Everyday Life in the Modern World*, ch. 5; Debord, *The Society of the Spectacle*, (1967), Black and Red, Detroit, 1983; Raoul Vaneigem, *The Revolution of Everyday Life* (1967), trans. Donald Nicholson-Smith, Left Bank Book and Rebel Press, 1983; Gilles Deleuze and Félix Guattari, *Anti-Oedipus* and *A Thousand Plateaux: Capitalism and Schizophrenia* (1981), trans. Brian Massumi, University of Minnesota Press, Minneapolis 1987; Jean Baudrillard, *Seduction* (1979), trans. Brian Singer, Macmillan, Basingstoke and London, 1990 and *Simulations* (1981), trans. Paul Foss et al., Semiotext(e), New York, 1983. Lefebvre was probably as influenced by the Situationists as they were by him. For overviews of the transition, see Peter Wollen, 'The Situationist International: On the Passage of a Few People Through a Brief Period of Time', in his *Raiding the Icebox: Reflections on Twentieth Century Culture*, Verso, London and New York, 1993, ch. 4 and Sadie Plant, *The Most Radical Gesture: The Situationist International in a Postmodern Age*, Routledge, London and New York, 1992. It is interesting to compare the existentials in Vaneigem's phenomenology of everydayness (humiliation, isolation, suffering) with Heidegger's (idle talk, curiosity, ambiguity), to take the measure of the difference in character between the two critiques.

153. The reference to space here is far more than merely metaphorical. On Lefebvre's analysis the social is aways spatial; and space is always social. See Henri Lefebvre, 'Social Space', in *The Production of Space* (1974), trans. Donald Nicholson-Smith, Blackwell, Oxford, 1991, ch. 2. After 1968, Lefebvre's interest in the everyday became increasingly focused on questions of urbanization, making him one of the founders of the new 'urban geography', as well as a precursor of cultural studies.

154. *Being and Time*, p. 422.

155. Ibid., pp. 423, 64. This is one of a number of places in *Being and Time* where Heidegger shows his account to be mortgaged to an analysis of Being which never takes place.

156. Ibid., p. 477; emphasis added.

157. Lefebvre, *Everyday Life in the Modern World*, p. 24.

158. 'The Everyday and Everydayness', p. 10; emphasis added.

159. Lefebvre, *Everyday Life in the Modern World*, pp. 24, 19, 25. The most Benjaminian of these phrases ('the verso of modernity') is Lefebvre's summary of Hermann Broch. Cf. Benjamin's description of the relation of the metaphysical to the historical ('a stocking turned inside out'), and later, of Karl Krauss's writing ('a silence turned inside out'.) Walter Benjamin, 'Notes for the Trauerspeil Study', *GS* I, p. 918, quoted in this translation by Buck-Morss, *Dialectics of Seeing*, p. 21; and 'Karl Krauss' (1931), in *One-Way Street*, p. 262.

160. *Everyday Life in the Modern World*, pp. 25, 24. Cf. Bakhtin's argument that it is through the centrality of the present to the everyday that 'time and the world become historical' ('Epic and Novel', p. 30), with his description of the 'commonplace, philistine cyclical everyday time' of the provincial town in Flaubert's *Madame Bovary* ('Forms of Time and of the Chronotope in the Novel', in *The Dialogic Imagination*, pp. 247–8).

161. *Everyday Life in the Modern World*, p. 18.

162. Bakhtin, 'Epic and Novel', p. 30.

Epilogue

1. Moretti, *The Way of the World*, p. 35.

2. Bakhtin, 'Epic and Novel', pp. 15, 7, 30.

3. See, for example, Jameson, *Postmodernism*, ch. 1.

4. Ibid., p. 46. See also the Introduction and Part One of Fredric Jameson, *The Geopolitical Aesthetic: Cinema and Space in the World System*, Indiana University Press, Bloomington and Indianapolis and BFI Publishing, London, 1992, where the idea of postmodernism as the 'cognitive mapping' of an apparently 'unrepresentable' world system is developed through an allegorical reading of the logic of conspiracy. Jameson's postmodernism appears as a new type of conspiracy theory.

5. For the idea that it is war which disrupts the everyday, providing the third term for its mediation with history, see Karel Kosík, *Dialectics of the Concrete: A Study of Problems of Man and World* (1961), trans. Karel Kovanda with James Schmidt, Reidel Publishing Company, Dordrecht and Boston, 1976, pp. 42–9.

6. Bhabha, *The Location of Culture*, pp. 243, 247, 242. Cf. the quotation from Meschonnic in ch. 1, p. 14, above.

7. Cf. Gilroy, *The Black Atlantic*, chs 2 and 6, where it is 'the intimate association of modernity and slavery' which is the 'fundamental conceptual issue' (p. 53). Bhabha's recourse to the works of Toni Morrison to illustrate the representational possibilities of postcolonial memory-work elides the difference between the two perspectives.

8. See, in particular, the critique of Jameson's postmodernism in *The Location of Culture*, ch. 11 where, despite the derision of Jameson's totalizing ambitions, Bhabha's postcolonial alternative clearly occupies an equivalent, if alternatively articulated, conceptual space.

9. Gayatri Chakravorty Spivak, 'Who Claims Alterity?', in Barbara Kruger and Phil Mariani (eds), *Remaking History*, Dia Art Foundation Discussions in Contemporary Culture no. 4, Bay Press, Seattle, 1989, p. 274.

10. Ibid., p. 281. In my view, this danger is inherent in the Heideggerian structure of Bhabha's notion of the 'projective past', since it is unaccompanied by any account of the relationship of colonial to other forms of social difference, or of the referential constraints upon its alternative historiography – although it is the opposite of the politics explicit in the text.

11. Benjamin, 'Exposé: Paris, Capital of the Nineteenth Century', n. 15, *GS* V, p. 1218.

12. Pierre Bourdieu, *The Logic of Practice*, trans. Richard Nice, Polity Press, Oxford, 1990, p. 99.

Select Bibliography

Abrams, Philip, 'The Sense of the Past and the Origins of Sociology', *Past and Present* 55, 1972.

Adorno, Theodor W., 'The Idea of Natural History', trans. Bob Hullot-Kentor, *Telos* 60, Summer 1984.

——, 'A Portrait of Walter Benjamin', in *Prisms*, trans. Samuel and Sierry Weber, Neville Spearman, London, 1967.

——, *Minima Moralia: Reflections From Damaged Life*, trans. E.F.N. Jephcott, Verso, London, 1978.

——, 'Looking Back on Surrealism', in *Notes to Literature. Volume One*, trans. Shierry Weber Nicholson, Columbia University Press, New York, 1991.

——, 'Free Time', in J.M. Bernstein (ed.), *The Culture Industry: Selected Essays on Mass Culture*, Routledge, London and New York, 1991.

——, *Negative Dialectics*, trans. E.B. Ashton, Routledge and Kegan Paul, London, 1973.

——, 'On Tradition', *Telos* 94, Winter 1992–3.

——, 'Resignation', *Telos* 35, Spring 1978.

——, *Aesthetic Theory*, trans. C. Lenhardt, Routledge & Kegan Paul, London, 1984.

—— and Horkheimer, Max, *Dialectic of Enlightenment*, trans. John Cumming, Verso, London, 1979.

Althusser, Louis, 'Sur l'objectivité de l'histoire (Lettre à Paul Ricoeur)', *Revue de l'Enseignement Philosophique*, Volume 5, no. 4 , 1955.

——, *For Marx*, trans. Ben Brewster, New Left Books, London, 1977.

—— and Balibar, Etienne, *Reading Capital*, trans. Ben Brewster, Verso, London, 1979.

Anderson, Benedict, *Imagined Communities: Reflections on the Origin and Spread of Nationalism*, Verso, London, 1983.

Anderson, Perry, 'The Notion of Bourgeois Revolution', in *English Questions*, Verso, London and New York, 1992.

——, *Arguments Within English Marxism*, Verso, London, 1980.

——, 'Modernity and Revolution', in *A Zone of Engagement*, Verso, London and New York, 1992.

Arendt, Hannah, *Between Past and Future: Eight Exercises in Political Thought*, Penguin, Harmondsworth, 1977.

Aristotle, 'Physica', in *The Basic Works of Aristotle*; ed. Richard McKeon, Random House, New York, 1941.

Aron, Raymond, *Introduction to the Philosophy of History: An Essay on the Limits of Historical Objectivity*, trans. George J. Irwin, Weidenfeld and Nicolson, London, 1961.

Arthur, Chris, 'Hegel's Master-Slave Dialectic and a Myth of Marxology', *New Left Review* 142, November/ December 1983.

Asad, Talal, *Anthropology and the Colonial Encounter*, Ithaca Press, London, 1973.

Ashton, T.H. and Philpin, C.H.E., *The Brenner Debate: Agrarian Class Structure and Economic Development in Pre-Industrial Europe*, Cambridge University Press, Cambridge, 1985.

Bakhtin, Mikhail, *The Dialogic Imagination: Four Essays*, trans. Carly Emerson and Michael Holquist, Texas University Press, Austin, 1981.

——, *Speech Genres and Other Late Essays*, trans. Vern W, McGee, University of Texas Press, Austin, 1986.

Balibar, Etienne and Wallerstein, Immanuel, *Race, Class, Nation: Ambiguous Identities*, trans. Chris Turner, Verso, London and New York, 1991.

Barker, Francis et al. (eds), *Postmodernism and the Re-Reading of Modernity*, Manchester University Press, Manchester, 1992.

Barthes, Roland, 'Historical Discourse' (1967), in Michael Lane (ed.), *Structuralism: A Reader*, Jonathan Cape, London, 1970.

Bataille, Georges, 'Hegel, Death and Sacrifice', trans. Jonathan Strauss, in Allan Stoekl (ed.), *Yale French Studies 78: On Bataille*, Yale University Press, New Haven, 1990.

Baudelaire, Charles, *The Painter of Modern Life and Other Essays*, ed. and trans. Jonathan Mayne, de Capo Press, New York, n.d. (reprint of Phaidon Press ed., 1964).

——, *Intimate Journals*, trans. Christopher Isherwood, Black Spring Press, London, 1989.

Baudrillard, Jean, *Seduction*, trans. Brian Singer, Macmillan, Basingstoke and London, 1990.

——, *Simulations*, trans. Paul Foss et al., Semiotext(e), New York, 1983.

Beck, Ulrich, *Risk Society: Towards a New Modernity*, trans. Mark Ritter, Sage Publications, London and Thousand Oaks, New Delhi, 1992.

Benjamin, Andrew (ed.), *The Problems of Modernity: Adorno and Benjamin*, Routledge, London and New York, 1989.

——, 'The Unconscious: Structuring as a Translation', in Jean Laplanche, *Jean Laplanche*.

——, 'Time and Task: Benjamin and Heidegger Showing the Present', in Benjamin and Osborne (eds), *Walter Benjamin's Philosophy: Destruction and Experience*

—— and Osborne, Peter (eds), *Walter Benjamin's Philosophy: Destruction and Experience*, Routledge, London and New York, 1994.

Benjamin, Jessica, *The Bonds of Love: Psychoanalysis, Feminism, and the Problem of Domination*, Virago, London, 1990.

Benjamin, Walter, *Gesammelte Schriften*, 7 volumes, ed. Rolf Tiedemann and Herman Schweppenhauser, Suhrkamp Verlag, Frankfurt am Main, 1972–89.

——, 'On the Program of the Coming Philosophy', trans. Mark Ritter, in Smith (ed.), *Benjamin*.

——, *The Origin of German Tragic Drama*, trans. John Osborne, New Left Books, London, 1977.

——, *One-Way Street and Other Writings*, trans. Edmund Jephcott and Kingsley Shorter, New Left Books, London, 1979.

——, *Illuminations*, ed. Hannah Arendt, translated by Harry Zohn, Fontana, London, 1973.

——, *Charles Baudelaire: A Lyric Poet in the Era of High Capitalism*, trans. Harry Zohn, Verso, London, 1983.

——, *Understanding Brecht*, trans. Stanley Mitchell, New Left Books, London, 1973.

——, 'Central Park', trans. Lloyd Spencer, *New German Critique* 34, Winter 1985.

——, 'Theories of German Fascism: On the Collection of Essays *War and Warrior*, edited by Ernst Jünger', trans. Jerolf Wikoff, *New German Critique* 17, Spring 1979.

——, 'N [Re the Theory of Knowledge, Theory of Progress]', trans. Leigh Hafrey and Richard Sieburth, in Smith (ed.), *Benjamin*.

——, *The Correspondence of Walter Benjamin and Gershom Scholem, 1932-1940*, ed. Gershom Scholem, trans. Gary Smith and Andre Lefebvre, Schocken Books, New York, 1989.

——, *The Correspondence of Walter Benjamin, 1910–1940*, ed. Gershom Scholem and Theodor W. Adorno, trans. Manfred R. Jacobson and Evelyn M. Jacobson, University of Chicago Press, Chicago, 1994.

Benveniste, Emile, *Problems in General Linguistics*, trans. Mary Elizabeth Meek, University of Miami Press, Coral Gables, 1971.

Bergson, Henri, *Time and Free Will: An Essay on the Immediate Data of Consciousness*, trans. F.L. Pogson, George Allen and Unwin, London, 1910.

Berman, Marshall, *All That Is Solid Melts into Air: The Experience of Modernity*, Verso, London, 1983.

——, 'The Signs in the Street: A Response to Perry Anderson', *New Left Review* 144, March/April 1984.

——, 'Why Modernism Still Matters', in Scott Lash and Jonathan Friedman (eds), *Modernity and Identity*, Blackwell, Oxford, 1992.

Berman, Russell A., *Modern Culture and Critical Theory: Art, Politics and the Legacy of the Frankfurt School*, University of Wisconsin Press, Madison, 1989.

Bernasconi, Robert, *The Question of Language in Heidegger's History of Being*, Humanities Press International, Atlantic Highlands, 1985.

—— and Critchley, Simon (eds), *Re-Reading Levinas*, Athlone Press, London, 1991.

Bhabha, Homi, *The Location of Culture*, Routledge, London and New York, 1994.

Bloch, Ernst, *Heritage of our Times*, trans. Neville and Stephen Plaice, Polity Press, Cambridge, 1991.

—— et al., *Aesthetics and Politics*, New Left Books, London, 1977.

Bloch, Marc, *The Historian's Craft*, trans. Peter Putnam, Manchester University Press, Manchester, 1954.

Blumenberg, Hans, *The Legitimacy of the Modern Age*, trans. Robert M. Wallace, MIT Press, Cambridge MA, 1983.

Boothby, Richard, *Death and Desire: Psychoanalytic Theory in Lacan's Return to Freud*, Routledge, New York and London, 1991.

Borsch-Jacobsen, Mikkel, *The Freudian Subject*, trans. Catherine Porter, Macmillan, London, 1989.

Bourdieu, Pierre, *The Logic of Practice*, trans. Richard Nice, Polity Press, Oxford, 1990.

Braudel, Fernand, *On History*, trans. Sarah Matthews, Weidenfeld and Nicolson, London, 1980.

——, *The Wheels of Commerce: Civilisation and Capitalism, 15th–18th Century*, Volume 2, trans. Sian Reynolds, Collins, London, 1982.

Buck-Morss, Susan, *Dialectics of Seeing: Walter Benjamin and the Arcades Project*, MIT Press, Cambridge MA, 1989.

——, 'Aesthetics and Anaesthetics: Walter Benjamin's Artwork Essay Reconsidered', *October* 62, Fall 1992.

Bultmann, Rudolf, *History and Escatology. The Gifford Lectures 1955*, The University Press, Edinburgh, 1957.

Bürger, Peter, 'Walter Benjamin's "Redemptive Critique": Some Preliminary Reflections on the Project of a Critical Hermeneutics', in Peter Bürger, *The Decline of Modernism*, trans. Nicholas Walker, Polity Press, Cambridge, 1992.

Butler, Judith, *Subjects of Desire: Hegelian Reflections in Twentieth Century France*, Columbia University Press, New York, 1987.

——, *Bodies that Matter: On the Discursive Limits of "Sex"*, Routledge, London and New York, 1993.

Calinescu, Matei, *Five Faces of Modernity: Modernism, Avant-Garde, Decadence, Kitsch, Postmodernism*, Duke University Press, Durham NC, 1987.

Caputo, John D., *Demythologising Heidegger*, Indiana University Press, Bloomington, 1993.

Caygill, Howard, 'Benjamin, Heidegger and the Destruction of Tradition', in Benjamin and Osborne (eds), *Walter Benjamin's Philosophy*.

Clifford, James, *The Predicament of Culture: Twentieth Century Ethnography, Literature, and Art*, Harvard University Press, Cambridge MA, 1988.

—— and Marcus, George E. (eds), *Writing Culture: The Poetics and Politics of Ethnography*, California University Press, Berkeley, 1986.

Cohen, Margaret, *Profane Illumination: Walter Benjamin and the Paris of*

Surrealist Revolution, California University Press, Berkeley and Los Angeles, 1993.

Cooper, Frederick, 'Colonising Time: Work Rhythms and Labour Conflict in Colonial Mombassa', in Nicholas B. Dirks (ed.), *Colonialism and Culture*, University of Michigan Press, Ann Arbor, 1992.

Critchley, Simon, *The Ethics of Deconstruction: Derrida and Levinas*, Blackwell, Oxford, 1992.

——, 'Black Socrates? Questioning the Philosophical Tradition', *Radical Philosophy* 69, Jan./Feb. 1995.

Debord, Guy, 'Perspectives for Conscious Alterations in Everyday Life', in Ken Knabb (ed.), *The Situationist International Anthology*, Bureau of Public Secrets, Berkeley, 1981.

——, *The Society of the Spectacle*, Black and Red, Detroit, 1983.

de Certeau, Michel, *The Practice of Everyday Life*, trans. Steven Rendall, University of California Press, Berkeley, Los Angeles and London, 1984.

——, *The Writing of History*, trans. Tom Conley, Columbia University Press, New York, 1988.

Deleuze, Gilles and Guattari, Félix, *Anti-Oedipus: Capitalism and Schizophrenia*, trans. Robert Hurley, Mark Seem and Helen R. Lane, University of Minnesota Press, Minneapolis, 1983.

——, *A Thousand Plateaux: Capitalism and Schizophrenia*, trans. Brian Massumi, University of Minnesota Press, Minneapolis 1987.

Derrida, Jacques, *Writing and Difference*, trans. Alan Bass, University of Chicago Press, Chicago, 1978.

——, *Margins of Philosophy*, trans. Alan Bass, Harvester Wheatsheaf, Hemel Hempstead, 1982.

——, 'At this Very Moment in this Work Here I am', trans. Ruben Berezdivin, in Bernasconi and Critchley (eds), *Re-Reading Levinas*.

——, *Aporias*, trans. Thomas Dutoit, Stanford University Press, Stanford, 1993.

——, 'The Deconstruction of Actuality: An Interview with Jacques Derrida', trans. Jonathan Rée, *Radical Philosophy* 68, Autumn 1994.

Descombes, Vincent, *Modern French Philosophy*, trans. L. Scott-Fox and J. M. Harding, Cambridge University Press, Cambridge, 1980.

——, *The Barometer of Modern Reason: On the Philosophies of Current Events*, trans. Stephen Adam Schwartz, Oxford University Press, New York and Oxford, 1993.

Dews, Peter, 'Power and Subjectivity in Foucault', *New Left Review* 144, March/April 1984.

——, *Logics of Disintegration: Post-Structuralist Thought and the Claims of Critical Theory*, Verso, London and New York, 1987.

——, 'Hegel in Analysis: Slavoj Zizek's Lacanian Dialectics', *Bulletin of the Hegel Society of Great Britain*, nos 21–2, 1990.

Dilthey, Wilhelm, *Selected Writings*, ed. and trans. H.P. Rickman, Cambridge University Press, Cambridge, 1976.

Elias, Norbert, *The Civilising Process. Volume One. The History of Manners*, trans. Edmund Jephcott, Blackwell, Oxford, 1978.

——, *Time: An Essay*, trans. Edmund Jephcott, Blackwell, Oxford, 1992.

Elliott, Gregory, 'Cards of Confusion: Historical Communism and the End of History', *Radical Philosophy* 64, Summer 1993.

Fabian, Johannes, *Time and the Other: How Anthropology Makes its Object*, Columbia University Press, New York, 1983.

Fanon, Frantz, *Black Skin, White Mask*, trans. Charles Lam Markmann, Paladin, London, 1970.

——, *The Wretched of the Earth*, trans. Constance Farrington, Penguin, Harmondsworth, 1967.

Farias, Victor, *Heidegger and Nazism*, trans. Paul Burrell and Gabriel Ricci, Temple University Press, Philadelphia, 1989.

Feuerbach, Ludwig, 'Towards a Critique of Hegel's Philosophy', in *The Fiery Brook: Selected Writings Of Ludwig Feuerbach*, trans. Zawar Hanfi, Anchor Books, Garden City NY, 1972.

Forrester, John, *The Seductions of Psychoanalysis: Freud, Lacan and Derrida*, Cambridge University Press, Cambridge, 1990.

Foster, Hal, *Compulsive Beauty*, MIT Press, Cambridge MA, 1993.

Foucault, Michel, 'Georges Canguilhem: Philosopher of Error', trans. Graham Burchell, *Ideology and Consciousness* 7, Autumn 1980.

——, 'Kant on Enlightenment and Revolution', trans. Colin Gordon, *Economy and Society* Volume 15, no.1, Feb. 1986.

——, 'What is Enlightenment?', trans. Catherine Porter, in Paul Rabinow (ed.) *The Foucault Reader*, Penguin, Harmondsworth, 1986.

Fraser, Nancy, 'Foucault on Modern Power: Empirical Insights and Normative Confusions', in *Praxis International* 1, 1981.

Freud, Sigmund, *New Introductory Lectures on Psychoanalysis*, Pelican Freud Library, Volume 2, Penguin, Harmondsworth, 1973.

——, *The Interpretation of Dreams*, Penguin Freud Library, Volume 4, Penguin, Harmondsworth, 1976.

——, *The Psychopathology of Everyday Life*, Penguin Freud Library Volume 5, Penguin, Harmondsworth, 1975.

——, *On Sexuality: Three Essays on the Theory of Sexuality and Other Works*, Penguin Freud Library, Volume 7, Penguin, Harmondsworth, 1977.

——, *On Psychopathology: Inhibitions, Symptoms and Other Works*, Penguin Freud Library, Volume 10, Penguin, Harmondsworth, 1970.

——, *On Metapsychology: The Theory of Psychoanalysis. Beyond the Pleasure Principle, The Ego and the Id and Other Works*, Penguin Freud Library, Volume 11, Penguin, Harmondsworth, 1984.

——, *Civilisation, Society, Religion: Group Psychology, Civilisation and its Discontents and Other Works*, trans. James Strachey, Penguin Freud Library, Volume 12, Penguin, Harmondsworth, 1985.

Frisby, David, *Fragments of Modernity: Theories of Modernity in the Work of Simmel, Kracauer and Benjamin*, Polity Press, Cambridge, 1985.

Fukuyama, Francis, *The End of History and the Last Man*, Penguin, Harmondsworth, 1992.

Gadamer, Hans-Georg, *Truth and Method*, Sheed and Ward, London, 1979.

Gardiner, Patrick (ed.), *Theories of History*, Free Press, New York, 1959.

Gilroy, Paul, *The Black Atlantic: Modernity and Double Consciousness*, Verso, London and New York, 1993.

Goldman, Lucien, *Lukács and Heidegger: Towards a New Philosophy*, trans. William Q. Boelhower, Routledge & Kegan Paul, London, 1977.

Gould, Stephen Jay, *Time's Arrow, Time's Cycle: Myth and Metaphor in the Discovery of Geological Time*, Penguin, Harmondsworth, 1988.

Gramsci, Antonio, *Selections from the Prison Notebooks*, trans. Quinton Hoare and Geoffrey Nowell Smith, Lawrence and Wishart, London, 1971.

Griffen, Roger, *The Nature of Fascism*, Routledge, London and New York, 1993.

Guterman, Norbert and Lefebvre, Henri, *La Conscience Mystifiée*, Gallimard, Paris, 1936.

Habermas, Jürgen, *The Structural Transformation of the Public Sphere: An Inquiry into a Category of Bourgeois Society*, trans. Thomas Burger, Polity Press, Cambridge, 1989.

——, 'A Review of Gadamer's Truth and Method', in Fred R. Dallmayr and Thomas A. McCarthy (eds), *Understanding and Social Inquiry*, University of Notre Dame Press, Notre Dame, 1977.

——, 'Walter Benjamin: Consciousness-Raising or Rescuing Critique', in Smith (ed.), *On Walter Benjamin*.

——, 'Modernity – An Incomplete Project', trans. Seyla Benhabib, in Hal Foster (ed.), *Postmodern Culture*, Pluto, London, 1985.

——, *Theory of Communicative Action*, 2 volumes, trans. Thomas McCarthy, Polity Press, Cambridge, 1991, 1987.

——, *The Philosophical Discourse of Modernity: Twelve Lectures*, trans. Frederick Lawrence, Polity Press, Cambridge, 1987.

——, 'Taking Aim at the Heart of the Present: On Foucault's Lecture on Kant's What is Enlightenment?', in *The New Conservatism: Cultural Criticism and the Historians Debate*, ed. and trans. Shierry Weber Nicholson, Polity Press, Cambridge, 1989.

Hall, Stuart (ed.), *Understanding Modern Societies: An Introduction*, 4 volumes, Polity Press/Open University, Oxford, 1992.

Harvey, David, *The Condition of Postmodernity: An Inquiry into the Origins of Cultural Change*, Blackwell, Oxford, 1989.

Hassan, Ihab, *The Postmodern Turn: Essays in Postmodern Theory and Culture*, Ohio State University Press, 1987.

Hegel, G.W.F., *Phänomenologie des Geistes*, Ullstein, Frankfurt am Main, 1970.

——, *La Phenoménologie de l'Esprit*, trans. Jean Hyppolite, 2 volumes, Paris, 1939.

——, *Phenomenology of Spirit*, trans. A.V. Miller, Clarendon Press, Oxford, 1977.

——, *Science of Logic*, trans. Johnston and Struthers, George Allen and Unwin, London, 1929.

——, *Philosophy of Mind*, trans. William Wallace, Clarendon Press, Oxford, 1971.

——, *Philosophy of Nature*, trans. William Wallace, Oxford University Press, Oxford, 1970.

——, *Reason in History: A General Introduction to the Philosophy of History*, trans. Robert S. Hartman, Bobbs-Merrill, Indianapolis, 1953.

——, *Lectures on the Philosophy of Religion*, trans. E.S. Haldane, Routledge and Kegan Paul, London, 1952.

Heidegger, Martin, 'The Concept of Time in the Science of History', trans. H.S. Taylor and H.W. Ufflemann, *Journal of the British Society of Phenomenology*, Volume 9, no. 1, 1978.

——, *The Concept of Time*, trans. William McNeill, Blackwell, Oxford, 1992.

——, *The Basic Problems of Phenomenology*, trans. Albert Hofstader, Indiana University Press, Bloomington, 1988.

——, *Being and Time*, trans. John Macquarrie and Edward Robinson, Blackwell, Oxford, 1962.

——, *History of the Concept of Time: Prolegomena*, trans. Theodore Kisiel, Indiana University Press, Bloomington, 1992.

——, *Kant and the Problem of Metaphysics*, trans. Richard Taft, Indiana University Press, Bloomington and Indianapolis, 1990.

——, 'The Self-Assertion of the German University', in Wolin (ed.), *The Heidegger Controversy*.

——, 'Why Do I Stay in the Provinces?', in Thomas Sheehan (ed.), *Heidegger: The Man and the Thinker*, Precedent Publishing, Chicago, 1981.

——, 'The Origin of the Work of Art', in David Farrell Krell (ed.), *Basic Writings*, Routledge, London, 1993.

——, *Nietzsche*, 4 volumes, ed. David Farrell Krell, trans. David Farrell Krell, Frank Capuzzi and Joan Stambaugh, Harper, San Francisco, 1979–87.

——, *Hegel's Concept of Experience*, Harper and Row, New York, 1970.

——, 'Letter on Humanism', in David Farrell Krell (ed.), *Basic Writings*, Routledge, London, 1993.

——, *An Introduction to Metaphysics*, trans. Ralph Manheim, Yale University Press, New Haven and London, 1959.

——, 'Time and Being', in his *On Time and Being*, trans. Joan Stambaugh, Harper Torchbooks, New York, 1972.

——, '"Only a God can Save us": *Der Spiegel*'s Interview with Martin Heidegger', in Wolin (ed.), *The Heidegger Controversy*.

Heller, Agnes, *Everyday Life*, trans. G.L. Campbell, Routledge and Kegan Paul, London, 1984.

——, *A Philosophy of History in Fragments*, Blackwell, Oxford, 1993.

Herf, Jeffrey, *Reactionary Modernism: Technology, Culture, and Politics in Weimar and the Third Reich*, Cambridge University Press, Cambridge, 1984.

Hewitt, Andrew, *Fascist Modernism: Aesthetics, Politics, and the Avant-Garde*, Stanford University Press, Stanford, 1993.

Hobsbawm, Eric, *Age of Extremes: The Short Twentieth Century, 1914–1991*, Michael Joseph, London, 1994.

—— and Ranger, Terence (eds), *The Invention of Tradition*, Cambridge University Press, Cambridge, 1983.

Honneth, Axel, 'A Communicative Disclosure of the Past: On the Relationship between Anthropology and Philosophy of History in Walter Benjamin', *New Formations* 20, Summer 1993.

Husserl, Edmund, *Cartesian Meditations*, trans. Dorion Cairns, Kluwer, Dordrecht, 1993.

Hyppolite, Jean, 'A Spoken Commentary on Freud's *Verneinung*', Appendix to Jacques Lacan, *The Seminar of Jacques Lacan, 1*.

——, 'Hegel's Phenomenology and Psychoanalysis', in W. Steinkraus (ed.), *New Studies in the Philosophy of Hegel*, Holt, Rinehart and Wilson, New York, 1971.

Jacoby, Russell, *Dialectic of Defeat: Contours of Western Marxism*, Cambridge University Press, Cambridge, 1981.

Jameson, Fredric, *Fables of Aggression: Wyndham Lewis, the Modernist as Fascist*, University of California Press, Berkeley, 1979.

——, *The Political Unconscious: Narrative as a Socially Symbolic Act*, Methuen, London, 1981.

——, *Postmodernism, or, The Cultural Logic of Late Capitalism*, Verso, London and New York, 1991.

——, *The Geopolitical Aesthetic: Cinema and Space in the World System*, Indiana University Press, Bloomington and Indianapolis, and BFI Publishing, London, 1992.

——, 'On "Cultural Studies"', *Social Text* 34, 1993.

Kant, Immanuel, *Critique of Pure Reason*, trans. Norman Kemp-Smith, 2nd edn, Macmillan, London and Basingstoke, 1933.

——, *Perpetual Peace and Other Essays*, trans. Ted Humphreys, Hackett Publishing Co., Indianapolis and Cambridge, 1983.

Kelly, Michael, *Modern French Marxism*, Blackwell, Oxford, 1982.

Kermode, Frank, *The Sense of an Ending: Studies in the Theory of Fiction*, Oxford University Press, New York, 1967.

Kern, Stephen, *The Culture of Time and Space, 1880–1918*, Harvard University Press, Cambridge MA, 1983.

Kisiel, Theodore, *The Genesis of Heidegger's 'Being and Time'*, University of California Press, Berkeley and London, 1993.

Kittsteiner, H.D., 'Walter Benjamin's Historicism', *New German Critique* 39, Fall 1986.

Kojève, Alexandre, *Introduction à la lecture de Hegel*, Gallimard, Paris, 1980.

——, *An Introduction to the Reading of Hegel*, ed. Allan Bloom, trans. James H. Nichols Jr., Basic Books, New York and London, 1969.

Koselleck, Reinhart, *Critique and Crisis: Enlightenment and the Pathogenesis of Modern Society*, Berg, New York, 1988.

——, *Futures Past: On the Semantics of Historical Time*, trans. Keith Tribe, MIT Press, Cambridge MA, 1985.

Kosík, Karel, *Dialectics of the Concrete: A Study of Problems on Man and World*, trans. Karel Kovanda with James Schmidt, Reidel Publishing Company, Dordrecht and Boston, 1976.

Kracauer, Siegfried, *History: The Last Things Before the Last*, Oxford University Press, New York, 1969.

Kraniauskas, John, 'Beware Mexican Ruins!: *One-Way Street* and the Colonial Unconscious', in Benjamin and Osborne (eds), *Walter Benjamin's Philosophy*.

Kristeva, Julia, 'Women's Time', in Toril Moi (ed.), *The Kristeva Reader*, Blackwell, Oxford, 1986.

——, *Powers of Horror: An Essay on Abjection*, trans. Leon Roudiez, Columbia University Press, New York, 1982.

——, *Tales of Love*, trans. Leon S. Roudiez, Columbia University Press, New York, 1987.

Lacan, Jacques, *Écrits: A Selection*, trans. Alan Sheridan, Travistock, London, 1977.

——, *The Four Fundamental Concepts of Psychoanalysis*, trans. Alan Sheridan, Penguin, Harmondsworth, 1979.

——, *The Seminar of Jacques Lacan, 1: Freud's Papers of Techniques, 1953–1954*, trans. John Forrester, Cambridge University Press, Cambridge, 1988.

——, *The Seminar of Jacques Lacan, 2: The Ego in Freud's Theory and in the Technique of Psychoanalysis, 1954–1955*, trans. Sylvanna Tomaselli, Cambridge University Press, Cambridge, 1988.

Lacoue-Labarthe, Philippe, *Heidegger, Art and Politics: The Fiction of the Political*, trans. Chris Turner, Blackwell, Oxford, 1990.

—— and Nancy, Jean-Luc, 'The Nazi Myth', trans. Brian Holmes, *Critical Inquiry* 16, Winter 1990.

Laplanche, Jean, *Life and Death in Psychoanalysis*, trans. Jeffrey Mehlman, Johns Hopkins University Press, Baltimore, 1976.

——, 'A Metapsychology Put to the Test of Anxiety', *International Journal of Psychoanalysis* Volume 62, 1981.

——, *New Foundations for Psychoanalysis*, trans. David Macey, Blackwell, Oxford, 1989.

——, *Jean Laplanche: Seduction, Translation, Drives*, ed. John Fletcher and Martin Stanton, Institute of Contemporary Arts, London, 1992.

—— and Serge Leclaire, 'The Unconscious: A Psychoanalytic Study', *Yale French Studies* 48, 1972.

—— and J.-B. Pontalis, *The Language of Psychoanalysis*, trans. Donald Nicholson-Smith, Karnac Books, London, 1988.

Larrain, Jorge, *Theories of Development: Capitalism, Colonialism and Dependency*, Polity Press, Cambridge, 1989.

Lefebvre, Henri, *Dialectical Materialism*, Jonathan Cape, London, 1968.

——, *Critique of Everyday Life. Volume One. Introduction*, trans. by John Moore, Verso, London and New York, 1991.

——, 'The Everyday and Everydayness', *Yale French Studies* 73, 1987.

——, *Introduction to Modernity: Twelve Preludes, September 1959–May 1960*, trans. John Moore, Verso, London and New York, 1995.

——, *Everyday Life in the Modern World*, trans. Sacha Rabinovitch, Allan Lane, London, 1971.

——, *The Survival of Capitalism: Reproduction of the Relations of Production*, trans Frank Bryant, Allison and Busby, London, 1974.

——, *The Production of Space*, trans. Donald Nicholson-Smith, Blackwell, Oxford, 1991.

Le Goff, Jacques, *Time, Work, and Culture in the Middle Ages*, trans. Arthur Goldhammer, Chicago University Press, Chicago, 1989.

——, *Memory and History*, trans. Steven Rendall and Elizabeth Claman, Columbia University Press, New York, 1992.

Levinas, Emmanuel, *Time and the Other and Other Essays*, trans. Richard A. Cohen, Duquesne University Press, Pittsburgh, 1987.

——, *Totality and Infinity: An Essay on Exteriority*, trans. Alphonso Lingis, Duquesne University Press, Pittsburgh, 1969.

——, 'The Trace of the Other', trans. Adolfo Lingis, in Mark C. Taylor (ed.), *Deconstruction in Context: Literature and Philosophy*, Chicago University Press, Chicago, 1986.

——, *Otherwise than Being or Beyond Essence*, trans. Adolfo Lingis, Kluwer Academic Publishers, Dordrecht, 1991.

——, 'Wholly Otherwise', trans. Simon Critchley, in Bernasconi and Critchley (eds), *Re-Reading Levinas*.

Loone, Eeero, *Soviet Marxism and the Analytical Philosophies of Histories*, trans. Brian Pearce, Verso, London and New York, 1992.

Löwith, Karl, 'The Political Implications of Heidegger's Existentialism', in Wolin (ed.), *The Heidegger Controversy*.

——, *Meaning in History: The Theological Presuppositions of the Philosophy of History*, University of Chicago Press, Chicago, 1949.

——, *My Life in Germany Before and After 1933: A Report*, trans. Elizabeth King, University of Illinois Press, Urbana and Chicago, 1994.

Lukács, Georg, *Theory of the Novel*, trans. Anna Bostock, Merlin Press, London, 1971.

Lyotard, Jean-François, *The Postmodern Condition: A Report on Knowledge*, trans. Geoff Bennington and Brian Massumi, University of Minnesota Press, Minneapolis, 1984.

McCarney, Joseph, *Social Theory and the Crisis of Marxism*, Verso, London and New York, 1990.

——, 'The True Realm of Freedom: Marxist Philosophy After Communism', *New Left Review* 189, September/October 1991.

——, 'Endgame', *Radical Philosophy* 62, Autumn 1992.

——, 'Shaping Ends: Reflections on Fukuyama', *New Left Review* 202, November/December 1993.

McCole, John, *Walter Benjamin and the Antinomies of Tradition*, Cornell University Press, Ithaca and London, 1993.

Macey, David, *Lacan in Contexts*, Verso, London, 1988.

——, *The Lives of Michel Foucault*, Hutchinson, London, 1993.

Marcuse, Herbert, *Hegel's Ontology and the Theory of Historicity*, trans. Seyla Benhabib, MIT Press, Cambridge MA, 1987.

——, 'Heidegger's Politics: An Interview with Herbert Marcuse', in Robert Pippin et al. (eds), *Herbert Marcuse, Critical Theory and the Promise of Utopia*, Bergin and Garvey, South Hadley MA, 1988.

Marx, Karl, *Contribution to a Critique of Political Economy*, Progress Publishers, Moscow, 1970.

——, *Grundrisse: Foundations of the Critique of Political Economy (Rough Draft)*, trans. Martin Nicolaus, Penguin, Harmondsworth, 1973.

——, *Capital: A Critique of Political Economy*, 3 volumes, trans. Ben Fowkes and David Fernbach, Penguin, Harmondsworth, 1976–81.

—— and Frederick Engels, *Collected Works*, Lawrence and Wishart, London, 1975–.

Massey, Doreen, 'Politics and Space/Time', *New Left Review* 196, November/December 1992.

Melville, Stephen W., *Philosophy Beside Itself: On Deconstruction and Modernism*, University of Minnesota Press, Minneapolis, 1986.

Merleau-Ponty, Maurice, *Phenomenology of Perception*, trans. Colin Smith, Routledge and Kegan Paul, London, 1962.

Meschonnic, Henri, 'Modernity, Modernity', *New Literary History*, Volume 23, 1992.

Meszaros, Istvan, 'The Cunning of History in Reverse Gear', *Radical Philosophy* 42, Winter/Spring 1986.

Milbank, John, *Theology and Social Theory: Beyond Secular Reason*, Blackwell, Oxford, 1990.

Moretti, Franco, *The Way of the World: The 'Bildungsroman' in European Culture*, Verso, London, 1987.

Mosse, George L., *The Crisis of German Ideology: Intellectual Origins of the Third Reich*, Schocken Books, New York, 1981.

——, 'Fascism and the French Revolution', *Journal of Contemporary History*, Volume 24, no. 1, January 1989.

Mulvey, Laura, 'Some Thoughts on Theories of Fetishism in the Context of Contemporary Culture', *October* 65, Summer 1993.

Nancy, Jean-Luc, *The Experience of Freedom*, trans. Bridget McDonald, Stanford University Press, Stanford, 1993.

——, *The Birth of Presence*, trans. Brian Holmes et al., Stanford University Press, Stanford, 1993.

Negt, Oskar and Kluge, Alexander, *Public Sphere and Experience: Toward an Analysis of the Bourgeois and Proletarian Public Sphere*, trans. Peter Labanyi et al., University of Minnesota Press, Minneapolis and London, 1993.

Niethammer, Lutz, *Posthistoire: Has History Come to an End?*, trans. Patrick Camiller, Verso, London and New York, 1992.

Nietzsche, Friedrich, *Uses and Abuses of History*, trans. Adrian Collins, Bobbs-Merrill, Indianapolis, 1957.

Osborne, Peter, 'Adorno and the Metaphysics of Modernism: The Problem of a "Postmodern" Art', in Andrew Benjamin (ed.), *The Problems of Modernity*.

——, 'Overcoming Philosophy as Metaphysics: Rorty and Heidegger', *Oxford Literary Review*, Volume 11, 1989.

——, 'A Marxism for the Postmodern? Jameson's Adorno', *New German Critique* 56, Spring/Summer 1992.

——, 'Small-scale Victories, Large-scale Defeats: Walter Benjamin's Politics of Time', in Benjamin and Osborne (eds), *Walter Benjamin's Philosophy*.

Ott, Hugo, *Heidegger: A Political Life*, trans. Allan Bluden, HarperCollins, London and New York, 1993.

Patterson, Orlando, *Slavery and Social Death*, Harvard University Press, Cambridge MA, 1982.

Paz, Octavio, *Children of the Mire*, trans. Rachel Phillips, Harvard University Press, Cambridge MA, 1974.

Perloff, Marjorie, *The Futurist Moment: Avant-Garde, Avant Guerre, and the Language of Rupture*, Chicago University Press, Chicago, 1986.

Plant, Sadie, *The Most Radical Gesture: The Situationist International in a Postmodern Age*, Routledge, London and New York, 1992.

Plato, *The Dialogues of Plato*, 4 volumes, trans. B. Jowett, Clarendon Press, Oxford, 4th edn, 1953.

Pöggeler, Otto, 'Heidegger's Political Self-Understanding', in Wolin (ed.), *The Heidegger Controversy*.

Popper, Karl, *The Poverty of Historicism*, Routledge, London, 1960.

Poster, Mark, *Existential Marxism in Postwar France*, Princeton University Press, Princeton, 1975.

Rabinbach, Anson, 'Between Enlightenment and Apocalypse: Benjamin, Bloch and Modern German Messianism', *New German Critique* 34, Winter 1985.

Rancière, Jacques, *The Names of History: On the Poetics of Knowledge*, trans. Hassan Melehy, Minnesota University Press, Minneapolis, 1994.

Randoti, Sandor, 'Benjamin's Politics', *Telos* 37, Fall 1978.

Rickert, Heinrich, *Science and History: A Critique of Positivist Epistemology*, ed. Arthur Goddard, trans. George Reisman, D. Van Nostrand, Princeton, 1962.

Ricoeur, Paul, *History and Truth*, trans. Charles A. Kelbley, Northwestern University Press, Evanston, IL, 1965.

——, *Husserl: An Analysis of his Phenomenology*, trans. Edward G. Ballard and Lester E. Embree, Northwestern University Press, Evanston, IL, 1967.

——, 'Althusser's Theory of Ideology', in Gregory Elliott (ed.), *Althusser: A Critical Reader*, Blackwell, Oxford, 1994.

——, *The Contribution of French Historiography to the Theory of History*, Clarendon Press, Oxford, 1980.

——, *Time and Narrative*, 3 volumes, trans. Kathleen McLaughlin and David Pellauer, Chicago University Press, Chicago, 1984–8.

Rose, Gillian, *Hegel Contra Sociology*, Athlone Press, London, 1981.

——, *Judaism and Modernity: Philosophical Essays*, Blackwell, Oxford, 1993.

Rose, Jacqueline, 'Kristeva – Take Two', in *Sexuality in the Field of Vision*, Verso, London, 1986.

Rosenberg, Harold, *The Tradition of the New*, University of Chicago Press, Chicago and London, 1982.

Sakai, Naoki , 'Modernity and its Critique: The Problem of Universalism and Particularism', in Miyoshi, Masao and Harootunian, H.D. (eds), *Postmodernism and Japan*, Duke University Press, Durham NC, 1989.

Samuel, Raphael, *Theatres of Memory. Volume 1: Past and Present in Contemporary Culture*, Verso, London and New York, 1994.

Sartre, Jean-Paul, *Being and Nothingness: An Essay on Phenomenological Ontology*, trans. Hazel Barnes, Methuen, London, 1958.

——, *Existentialism and Humanism*, trans. Philip Mairet, Methuen, London, 1973.

——, *Search for a Method*, trans. Hazel Barnes, Vintage Books, New York, 1968.

——, *Critique of Dialectical Reason. Volume 1. Theory of Practical Ensembles*, trans. Alan Sheridan-Smith, New Left Books, London, 1976.

——, *Critique of Dialectical Reason. Volume 2. The Intelligibility of History*, trans. Quintin Hoare, Verso, London, 1991.

Schmidt, Carl, *Political Theology: Four Chapters on the Concept of Sovereignty*, trans. George Schwab, MIT Press, Cambridge MA, 1985.

Scholem, Gershom, 'Walter Benjamin and his Angel', in Smith (ed.), *On Walter Benjamin*.

——, *Walter Benjamin: The Story of a Friendship*, Faber and Faber, London, 1982.

Schottler, Peter, 'Althusser and Annales Historiography – An Impossible Dialogue?', in Michael Sprinker and E. Ann Kaplan (eds), *The Althusserian Legacy*, Verso, London and New York, 1992.

Schürmann, Reiner, *Heidegger on Being and Acting: From Principles to Anarchy*, trans. Christine-Marie Gross, Indiana University Press, Bloomington, 1987.

Sluga, Hans, *Heidegger's Crisis: Philosophy and Politics in Nazi Germany*, Harvard University Press, Cambridge MA and London, 1993.

Soja, Edward W., *Postmodern Geographies: The Reassertion of Space in Critical Social Theory*, Verso, London and New York, 1989.

Smith, Gary (ed.), *On Walter Benjamin: Critical Essays and Recollections*, MIT Press, Cambridge MA, 1988.

—— (ed.), *Benjamin: Philosophy, Aesthetics, History*, Chicago University Press, Chicago, 1989.

Spivak, Gayatri Chakravorty, 'Remembering the Limits: Difference, Identity and Practice', in Peter Osborne (ed.), *Socialism and the Limits of Liberalism*, Verso, London and New York, 1991.

——, 'Who Claims Alterity?', in Barbara Kruger and Phil Mariani (eds), *Remaking History*, Dia Art Foundation Discussions in Contemporary Culture no. 4, Bay Press, Seattle, 1989.

——, *Outside in the Teaching Machine*, Routledge, New York and London, 1993.

——, 'Setting to Work (Transnational Cultural Studies): An Interview with Gayatri Spivak', in Peter Osborne (ed.), *A Critical Sense: Interviews with Radical Philosophy*, forthcoming Routledge, London and New York, 1996.

Theunissen, Michael, 'Metaphysics' Forgetfulness of Time: On the Controversy Over Parmenides, Frag. 8, 5', in Axel Honneth et al. (eds), *Philosophical Interventions in the Unfinished Project of Enlightenment*, MIT Press, Cambridge MA, 1992.

Thompson, Edward, 'Time, Work-Discipline, and Industrial Capitalism', *Past and Present* 38, 1967.

Vajda, Mihaly, *Fascism as a Mass Movement*, Allison and Busby, London, 1976.

Vaneigem, Raoul, *The Revolution of Everyday Life*, trans. Donald Nicholson-Smith, Left Bank Book and Rebel Press, 1983.

Vilar, Pierre, 'Marxist History, A History in the Making: Towards a Dialogue with Althusser', *New Left Review* 80, July/August 1973.

Wallerstein, Immanuel, *The Modern World-System*, 2 volumes, Academic Press, London and New York, 1974, 1980.

White, Hayden, *Metahistory: The Historical Imagination in Nineteenth Century Europe*, Johns Hopkins University Press, Baltimore and London, 1973.

Williams, Raymond, 'Notes on Marxism in Britain Since 1945', in his *Problems in Materialism and Culture*, Verso, London, 1980.

——, *The Politics of Modernism: Against the New Conformists*, ed. Tony Pinkney, Verso, London and New York, 1989.

——, *Resources of Hope*, Verso, London and New York, 1989.

Witte, Bernd, *Walter Benjamin: An Intellectual Biography*, trans. James Rolleston, Wayne State University Press, Detroit, 1991.

Wolff, Janet, 'Memoirs and Micrologies: Walter Benjamin, Feminism and Cultural Analysis', *New Formations* 20, Summer 1993.

Wohlfarth, Irving, 'On the Messianic Structure of Walter Benjamin's Last Reflections', *Glyph* 3, 1978.

——, 'Re-fusing Theology: Some First Responses to Walter Benjamin's Arcades Project', *New German Critique* 39, Fall 1986.

——, 'On Some Jewish Motifs in Walter Benjamin', in Andrew Benjamin (ed.), *The Problems of Modernity*.

Wolin, Richard, *Walter Benjamin: An Aesthetic of Redemption*, Columbia University Press, New York, 1982.

——, *The Politics of Being: The Political Thought of Martin Heidegger*, Columbia University Press, New York, 1990.

—— (ed.), *The Heidegger Controversy: A Critical Reader*, MIT Press, Cambridge MA, 1993.

Wollen, Peter, 'The Situationist International: On the Passage of a Few People Through a Brief Period of Time', in *Raiding the Icebox: Reflections on Twentieth Century Culture*, Verso, London and New York, 1993.

Young, Robert, *White Mythologies: Writing History and the West*, Routledge, London and New York, 1990.

Zerubavel, Eviatar, 'The Standardisation of Time: A Sociohistorical Perspective', *American Journal of Sociology*, Volume 88, no. 1, 1982.

——, 'The Benedictine Ethic and the Modern Spirit of Scheduling: On Schedules and Social Life', *Sociological Inquiry* 50.

Zimmerman, Michael E., *Heidegger's Confrontation with Modernity: Technology, Politics, Art*, Indiana University Press, Bloomington and Indianapolis, 1990.

Žižek, Slavoj, *The Sublime Object of Ideology*, Verso, London and New York, 1989.

Index

action xii, 53–4, 66, 118, 124, 126,
    146, 150, 152, 154–6, 170–71
Adorno, Theodor W. 9, 14, 39, 54,
    57, 59, 123, 127, 145, 150
  Minima Moralia 145
aestheticisation
  of commodities 194
  of ontology 161
  of politics 154, 160
afterwardsness (*Nachträglichkeit*)
    88–90, 93, 102, 106–7, 178–9
alienation 84–7, 97–8, 154, 182, 188,
    190–91, 193–4
alterity *see* other(s)/otherness
Althusser, Louis, 3, 13, 23–9, 31, 139
  Reading Capital 28
anarchism 176
Ancients 9, 10, 12
Anderson, Perry 5–9, 13–15, 17, 19,
    23, 26
Annales 23, 25–8, 134
anthropology 2, 16–18, 25, 27, 32,
    147, 166, 182, 184, 191
anti-semitism 165
anxiety 79, 103
  sexual 183
antiquity 9, 10, 137, 184
apocalypse 144, 150, 157–9
aporia 137, 154
  of dual perspective 45, 46, 52,
    62–3
  of time 45, 47–8, 67
  of totality 46, 52, 54, 60
Aragon, Louis 1, 153, 184
Aristotle viii, 46, 48–52, 54, 62–6,
    110, 170, 172–3
  Physics 45, 48

Aron, Raymond, 209–210
astronomy 65–7
atheism 173
Augustine, Saint 47–9, 54,
  Confessions 45, 47
aura 135–6
Auschwitz 39
authenticity xii, 52, 57, 62–5, 69,
    113, 116, 161, 168, 170–7, 185,
    188–9, 195
authority 127, 170, 174, 193
auto-eroticism 91, 98
avant-garde ix, 160, 196
  reactionary 165, 174
  see also experience, avant-garde

Bachelard, Gaston 31
Bakhtin, M.M. 193, 197
Balibar, Étienne 165
Bataille, Georges 40, 43,
Baudelaire, Charles x, 12, 138, 141–2
Baudrillard, Jean 194
Beck, Ulrich 204
Benjamin, Andrew 232, 239
Benjamin, Jessica 97–102, 110
  Bonds of Love 97
Benjamin, Walter, xi–xv, 3, 5, 12, 43,
    64, 113–16, 124, 127, 133–59,
    160–61, 168, 175–85, 187–8, 190,
    196, 200
  Arcades Project 136–7
  'On the Concept of History' 115,
    184
  'On Some Motifs in Baudelaire'
    180
  'On the Programme of the Coming
    Philosophy' 180

Benjamin, Walter, *cont.*,
  'One-Way Street' 181
  Origin of German Tragic Drama
    146, 176
  'Surrealism' 180
  'The Storyteller' 134–5, 141, 156
  'Theological-Political Fragment'
    184
  'Theses on the Philosophy of
    History' 147
  'Work of Art' 134, 154
Benveniste, Emile 66, 133,
Bergson, Henri 214–15
Berman, Marshall viii, 5–10,
  14, 15
  All That is Solid Melts into Air 5
Bhabha, Homi, 198–9
Blanqui, Auguste 143
Bloch, Ernst 146, 206
Blumenberg, Hans 11
Bourdieu, Pierre 201
Braudel, Fernand 25–6,
  'History and the Social Sciences' 25
Breton, André 182–4
Buck-Morss, Susan 151–2
Bultmann, Rudolf 173

Canguilhem, Georges 31
capitalism 29, 34, 39, 136, 162,
  164–5, 182–4, 192–4, 199–200
  see also modernization, capitalist
castration complex 89, 103
Catholicism 172–3
Caygill, Howard 127, 176
child development 83–108, 110
Christianity 10, 127 *see also*
  eschatology, Christian; time,
  Christian; tradition, Judaic-
  Christian
chronology xii, 14, 15, 19, 66,
  141–4, 152–3 *see also* time,
  chronological
civilization 162
classical, the 127–31, 141–2
classicism 138, 142
Colletti, Lucio 31
colonialism 13, 16, 17, 21, 22, 29,
  34, 72, 199
  decolonization 1, 39, 72
  postcolonial 199
commodity 137, 141, 182–4, 188,
  191
  fetishism 182

commodification 193–4, 197
communication 102, 106, 132–3,
  135–7, 147–8, 168, 172, 180, 197
  situation 101, 110,
communism x, xiii, 2, 39, 116, 148,
  154, 159, 162, 182
Communist Party of France 190
community 66, 127, 135
Comte, Auguste 3
conjuncture 8, 13, 23–9
conservatism ix, 38
  Burkean 130
  see also revolution, conservative
constructivism xii
criticism/critique 100, 130, 134,
  189–90
  of historical reason 31–2
crisis 11, 135, 139, 141–2, 157, 163,
  172, 200
culture viii, 142, 162, 166, 176, 201
  cultural analysis xiii, 180, 191
  cultural change viii, 1–2, 5, 14, 114
  culturalism 199
  European 41, 126
  cultural experience ix
  cultural form ix, xi, xii, 7, 114,
    121, 133–4, 136, 197
  cultural history vii, xiii, 133
  cultural logic 122, 202
  cultural practice xi
  cultural studies 185, 190
  cultural theory ix, xiv, 185
  cultural pessimism 38
  political x
  cultural politics 200
  Western 157
  see also modernity, culture of; time,
    culture of

Dasein 11, 48, 50, 52, 56–61, 63–6,
  69–71, 74, 79, 88, 110, 115, 117,
  160, 167–73, 175, 177, 185–9
death x–xii, 43, 46, 54–71, 73–80,
  83, 95, 97, 102–3, 106, 113,
  117–18, 120, 124–5, 137, 147,
  154, 168, 173, 184, 189–90, 200
  anticipation of 57–8, 60, 62–3, 68,
    70, 79–80, 88–90, 104–5, 107–8,
    110–11, 113, 125, 131, 158, 168,
    176–7, 185
  being-towards 57, 61, 70, 82, 88,
    103, 108, 117, 198
  denial of xiv, 141

fear of 78–9, 88–9, 102–3, 108,
  freedom for 58, 77
  historical xii, 177
  insignia of 95
  physical 76–7, 80
  social 77
  trial by 73–4, 83–8, 108–9
death drive xi, 88–90, 102–5, 107–8,
  110–11, 175, 179, 198
Debord, Guy 160, 192
decline 19–20, 163, 172
decision 169
  of existence 171, 198
  resolute 116, 167, 186, 195, 198
decisionism 168–74, 179
deconstruction 120, 124, 169–70,
  185
  see also Derrida
Deleuze, Gilles 194
Della Volpe, Galvano 31
democracy 125, 147, 157, 174, 188,
  193, 200
Derrida, Jacques viii, 36, 43, 55–6,
  61, 116, 119–20, 122, 124–5,
  147, 176, 185
Descartes, René 121
  Meditations 121
desire xi, 73, 75, 77, 79, 84, 103,
  110, 117, 121, 125, 182, 184,
  190, 194
  mother's 91–8
destiny (Geschick) 161, 168–91,
  196–7
development 11, 16, 17, 21, 23
diachrony see synchrony
dialectic 36, 41–2, 44, 47, 61, 76,
  109, 134, 145, 150, 155, 184,
  189, 194
  of identification 86
  master-slave 71–3, 77–81, 83–4, 98
  of modernity and tradition 114–15,
    135, 198
  pseudo- 190
  of recognition xi, 70–4, 77,
    90, 103, 107, 109, 117
  of self-consciousness 82
  specular 90, 102, 107
  speculative 138
  temporal 86, 110, 183
  of traditionality 132
  see also image, dialectical
difference 40, 61, 111, 119–20, 191
  colonial 199

cultural 219
  infinite 124
  original 199
  sexual 89, 92–4
  social 198–9
  temporal 128, 168–9, 179 (see also
    time, differential)
Dilthey, Wilhelm 31–2, 138, 176
disavowal 182, 184, 199
discourse 133–4
doomsday 11, 21
Droysen, J.G. 138
Durkheim, Emile 200
duration 14, 49–51, 128, 141, 153
  see also time, phenomenological
durée, long 28

economy 24, 182
  political 39, 121, 190
ecstatic, the 150, 156, 159, 175–6
  see also exteriority; now; time,
    ecstatic-horizonal
ego 80, 82, 86–7, 91–2, 95–7, 101,
  119–20
Eliot, T.S. 166
empiricism 4, 187
end see history, end of; time, end of
Engels, Freidrich 31, 164
enigmatic signifier see signification,
  enigmatic
Enlightenment viii, 10, 21–3, 128–9,
  138, 162, 173
environmentalism 177
epic 135–6, 141
epoch see periodization
equality 99, 122, 158
eschatology 35, 61, 116–20, 124–5,
  147
  Christian 11,
  Jewish 114
  see also time, eschatological
eternity 11, 14, 19, 32, 42, 108,
  112–13, 127–8, 130, 141–3, 145
  see also present, eternal;
    timelessness
ethics/the ethical xii, 52, 57, 62,
  118–19, 121, 127, 170 see also
  authenticity
ethnology 18, 182, 184
eugenics 166
Europe 135, 185
everyday xiii, 23, 52–3, 64, 155–6,
  180–96

everyday, *cont.*,
  everyday life xiii, 104, 116, 155–6,
    160, 180, 182, 189–97
  everydayness xii, 185–9, 193–5
existence see *Dasein*
existentialism 122, 161, 166, 168,
    170, 173, 190
  linguistic 185
experience 5, 7, 117, 120–2, 135,
    152, 157–8, 180–81, 190–91
  aesthetic 185
  avant-garde 150, 185, 198
  communicable 133, 156
  cultural 183
  hermeneutical 115, 132
  historical x, xiii, 7, 39, 41, 82, 96,
    109, 113–14, 131–5, 141, 143,
    148–9, 151–3, 168, 172–3, 175,
    177, 180, 183, 185, 189, 194,
    196, 200
  metaphysical 143
  political 179, 185
  religious 147, 185
  revolutionary 183
  social 136–7, 180
  space of 53, 132, 152
  surrealist 153, 183–5
  temporal 114, 135, 174, 200
  see also modernity, as quality of
    experience
exteriority 65, 107, 111, 113–14,
    116–21, 128, 146–7, 177, 180,
    198
  absolute 61–2, 119–21, 124–5, 155
  messianic 147–8, 152, 177–8
  vertical 176

Fabian, Johannes 17, 27–8
Fanon, Frantz 72,
fallibilism 35–6, 41–4
falsificationism 31, 36
familialism 109, 222
fantasy 101, 103, 158, 167, 182
fascism xii, 39, 59, 154, 157, 159–62,
    166, 174
  see also National Socialism; Nazis
fashion 12, 137, 142, 184
fate 168, 177
fatalism 171
father
  imaginary 91, 94, 97–8, 106
  of personal prehistory 91–3, 98
Febvre, Lucien 25

feminism 19, 183
fetish 137, 182, 184
feudalism 34
Feuerbach, Ludwig 42, 44, 71
  'Towards a Critique of Hegel's
    Philosophy' 42
film 136, 138
finitude 44, 58, 61, 64, 120–21, 125,
    132
  original 122
First World War 39, 162–4
Flaubert, Gustave 12
forgetting 50, 63, 65, 134, 137,
    140
Forrester, John 83
Foster, Hal 182
Foucault, Michel vii, 21–3, 41, 139,
    173
freedom 61, 72, 77–9, 95–6,
    99, 102–3, 124, 128, 168, 170,
    177
Freud, Sigmund 79–80, 82–3, 85–6,
    88, 90–94, 98, 101–6, 108–9,
    178–9, 181–2
  The Ego and the Id 92
  Psychopathology of Everyday Life
    181
Freudianism, neo- 87
Fukuyama, Francis 37–9, 81
future/futurity x, xii, 6, 11,
    19, 23, 33, 58, 117, 131, 142,
    145, 153, 159, 163–4, 169,
    174, 180 *see also*
    past/present/future
futurism 161, 166

Gadamer, Hans-Georg xii, 55, 115,
    127–133, 138, 151
  Truth and Method 46, 128
gender 18, 19, 98
genetics 166
geography 13, 16
Germany 154, 163 *see also* people,
    German
Gilroy, Paul 78, 243
God 10, 118, 120–23, 126, 139
Goethe, J. W. 6
  Faust 6
Gramsci, Antonio 228–9
Granel, Gerard 50
Great Slump 163
Guattari, Felix 194
Guterman, Norbert 190

Habermas, Jürgen vii, viii, 21–3, 32,
    115, 129, 131–3, 153–4, 163,
    188, 230
    *Philosophical Discourse of
    Modernity* 132–3
happiness 141, 143
Hegel, G.W.F. viii, xi, 33, 36–7,
    40–44, 63, 70–85, 88–90,
    95–104, 108–9, 113, 115, 117,
    120, 122, 138, 151, 167, 174,
    187–8
    Phenomenology of Spirit xi, 36, 40,
    44, 70–81, 83–5, 104, 109, 187
    Philosophy of Nature 44
    Philosophy of Right 37
Hegelianism x, xi, 23, 25, 27, 31, 36,
    40–44, 54, 61, 82, 89, 119, 128,
    134, 145
    anti- 82, 138
    Christian 177
    Left 37–8, 40
    Marxist 37–9 (*see also* Marxism,
    Hegelian)
    neo- 176
    post- x, 44, 113–14
    Right 39–40
Heidegger, Martin x–xiii, xv, 31, 43,
    46, 48, 50–52, 54–71, 74, 79–80,
    82, 88–9, 102, 104, 107–8, 110,
    114–18, 122, 124–5, 128, 130,
    138–9, 144, 147, 156, 158–80,
    185–9, 191, 193–5, 198–9
    Being and Time xi–xiii, 45, 55–7,
    65, 71, 74, 104, 130–31, 160–2,
    167–76, 186–7, 189, 194–5
    'The Concept of Time' 188
    'The Concept of Time in the Science
    of History' 31
Heideggerianism xi, 89
    quasi- 156
    see also Marxism, Heideggerian
Hellenism 167
    neo- 173
Heraclitus, 176
Herf, Jefferey, 163
heritage 59, 116, 131, 140, 142, 168,
    172, 174
    see also tradition
hermeneutics 31, 52, 55, 127–32, 186
    of historical consciousness 46–7
    of historical existence 47, 55, 57,
    90, 114, 126, 154, 191
    of narrative 60

ontological 46, 55
philosophical 46
of tradition 115
Hiroshima 39
Historical School 138
historicality (*Geschichtlichkeit*) xii,
    52, 56, 58–9, 64, 130, 168,
    171–2, 174–5, 177–8, 195
historicism xii, 31, 67, 116, 124, 126,
    129, 134, 138–44, 148–50, 152,
    156–7, 167, 175–7, 179, 189
historiography 32–3, 67, 115–16,
    124, 126, 132–5, 137, 141–2,
    186, 193
    modernist 134
historization 59–60, 123, 126–7, 155,
    168, 186, 197
    co-historizing 161–2
history viii–xi, 2, 11, 13, 19, 21,
    24, 28, 30, 34–5, 41, 55–61,
    83, 109–10, 112, 117–27,
    136–59, 168–9, 173–80, 189,
    198
    of Being 160, 171–2
    cultural vii
    end of 36–44, 53, 81, 152
    materialist conception of xiv, 3, 5
    (*see also* materialism, historical)
    natural 119, 123
    new 35
    ordinary conception of 116, 124,
    156
    philosophy of ix–xi, 33, 36, 41,
    54, 81, 112–13, 138, 150
    pre- 38
    science of 33
    social 123
    space of 153
    total 26
    universal 54, 113
    world 34–6, 40, 59–60, 171
    see also time, historical
Hitler, Adolf, 162, 166
Hobsbawm, Eric 166
Hofmannsthal, Hugo von 162
homogenization
    of time 5, 13–20, 29
    see also time, homogeneous
Horace 9
humanism 44, 56
Husserl, Edmund 48–52, 57, 61, 63,
    65–7, 117–20, 122, 145, 172–3,
    186, 197

Lectures on the Phenomenology of Internal Time-Consciousness 45
Hyppolite, Jean 72

idealism 31–2, 57, 65, 80
  German ix
idealization 87, 97, 99, 109, 193
identification 14, 43–4, 50, 54,
    81–99, 109–11, 113, 117, 154,
    156, 172, 185, 199
  with authority 170
  communal 170
  means of 166
  phallic 87
  primary xi, 85–6, 90–98, 102, 110,
    118
  secondary 86
identity xii
ideology 2, 3, 5, 7, 19, 37, 157,
    160–62, 164 *see also* time,
    ideological
image/*imago* 87, 88–90, 94–5, 97,
    127, 138, 146, 180, 192, 197,
    199
  after- 154, 158
  dialectical 145, 147–52, 155,
    157–8
  fetishistic 182
  surrealist 190
imaginary 82–98, 106–7
  hegemonic 87
  see also father, imaginary; mother,
    imaginary; other, imaginary
imagination 44, 133
  transcendental 105
immanent method 30, 33–9, 44, 126,
    179
imperialism 35
individualism 59, 70, 82, 89, 109,
    170, 194
infinity 32, 61, 65, 118–23, 125, 141,
    145
  bad 167, 223
  false- 122
  positive- 122
instant 124, 143, 145, 196
  Aristotelian 48–51, 55, 64, 144
intentionality 50–52, 61, 122–3,
    125, 174–5, 178, 180, 185,
    193
internalisation theory 100
interruption 139, 142, 145,
    150–59

messianic 114
  quasi-messianic 144
irony 37, 41–2,

Jacoby, Russell 31
Jameson, Fredric 17, 35, 190, 198,
    202, 209
Japan vii, 18
Judaism 144 *see also* Messianism,
    Jewish; tradition, Judeo-Christian
Jünger, Ernst 162–3, 176

Kafka, Franz 135
Kant, Immanuel 21, 22, 33, 102,
    104–5, 122, 129, 133, 177
  Critique of Pure Reason 45, 105
Kantianism 32, 44, 47
  neo- 31, 65, 138, 173
Kermode, Frank 157
Kierkegaard, Soren 134, 162, 173
Kisiel, Theodore 173
Kittsteiner, H.D. 139
Klee, Paul 149
Kojève, Alexandre 40, 44, 71–2, 77,
    81
  Introduction to Reading of Hegel
    71
Koselleck, Reinhart 5, 9–14, 132–3
Kracauer, Siegfried 3
Kristeva, Julia 18, 19, 90–98, 102,
    106, 110
  Tales of Love 90

Labrousse, Ernest 25, 28
Lacan, Jacques 69, 77, 80–90, 92–4,
    97, 99–103, 106–10
  'The Mirror Phase' 81
  Rome Discourse 81, 88
Lacoue-Labarthe, Philippe 165,
    174
language 124, 146, 149 *see also*
    linguistics
Laplanche, Jean 82–3, 90, 96, 98,
    100–108, 110, 189, 198
Lefebvre, Henri, xiii, 189–96
  Critique of Everyday Life 190
  L'Existentialisme 190
Le Goff, Jacques 9, 10
Lenin, V.I. 26, 28
Levinas, Emmanuel xi, xii, 61, 114,
    117–25
  Totality and Infinity 121–2
  'The Trace of the Other' 123

Lévi-Strauss, Claude 17, 25-7, 175
  The Savage Mind 175
Lewis, Wyndham, 166
Liberation 72
liberalism
  radical 7
linguistics 113
  structural 82, 108
  see also structuralism
Löwith, Karl 161
Lukács, Georg 134-5, 162
  Theory of the Novel 134
Lyotard, Jean-Francois vii, 13,
  157

Marburg Theological Society 188
Marcuse, Herbert 56, 217, 234
Marx, Karl viii, xiii, xiv, 3, 5-8,
  12, 29, 31-4, 37-8, 56, 67,
  72, 164-5, 182-4, 190-92,
  199
  Communist Manifesto 6
  The Geman Ideology 31
  Paris Manuscripts 56
Marxism ix, xiii, xiv, 2-4, 7, 23-4,
  28-9, 31-2, 141, 149, 180, 182,
  188, 190-91
  classical 35
  Gothic 183
  Hegelian 31, 37, see also
    Hegelianism, Marxist
  Heideggerian 56
  post- 35,
  right-wing 81
  Western xiii, 6, 31, 185
materialism 114, 147
  historical xiii, 2, 3, 25-6,
    37, 114, 139, 146, 148-9, 154,
    158 see also history, materialist
    conception
  psychic 80
mediation 150, 158
  narrative 46, 52-5, 109, 111
memory 43, 49, 51, 80, 132-3,
  136-7, 140, 149, 158
  see also remembrance
Mensheviks 39
Merleau-Ponty, Maurice, 61, 66
Meschonnic, Henri, 14, 133-4
messianic, the xii, 113, 116, 143-9,
  152-3, 176
  quasi- 143-4
Messianism 146

Jewish 115-16, 177
  materialist 116, 177, 185
metaphysics 61, 80, 109, 114,
  119-22, 124, 130, 138, 144,
  147-8, 160, 166, 168, 170,
  180-81
  modernist 142
Michelet, Jules 13
Middle Ages 9, 10
mimesis 53-4, 146, 155-6, 175
mirror phase 82-90, 94-5, 97, 99,
  102, 106-7
mode of production 2, 3, 7, 24, 26,
  34, 182
modernism ix, 6-9, 13, 23, 116, 136,
  138, 142-3
  aesthetic 7, 12,
  anti- 164
  artistic 166
  bad 167
  philosophical viii, xii, 166
  political xii, 166
  reactionary xii, 159, 162-8,
    174-5
modernity viii-x, xii, xiv, 1-29, 40,
  50, 81, 113-16, 127, 132-43,
  145, 147, 156-63, 166, 188-9,
  192, 194-9, 201
  aesthetic concept of 12
  bad 67, 115, 167, 223
  culture of x, 177
  as periodizing category 1-13
  phenomenological concept of 5,
  philosophical 172
  philosophical discourse of vii-ix,
    21-3
  as project 15, 20-23
  as quality of experience 13-20,
    141
  as temporalization of history 5, 29,
    34, 45
  secular 114
  sociological concept of 1-5,
    188
  temporal dialectics of viii
  theories of 17, 20, 21,
modernization 1, 8, 9, 15, 16, 17, 19,
  21, 116
  capitalist 6, 7
Moderns 9, 10, 12, 13
money 14, 34, 191
montage 115-16, 150, 197
Morrison, Toni 78

mother 83–4, 86, 88, 90–98, 102
  imaginary 95
  see also desire, mother's
myth xii, 8, 149, 157, 162, 164, 167,
    178, 184, 198
  of Being 175
  of nation 174
  Nazi 165
  of people 175

Nancy, Jean-Luc 61, 165, 169, 174
Napoleon 81
narcissism 82–3, 85, 87–8, 98
  primary 91–3, 96–7
Narcissus 85
narrative x–xii, xiv, 35, 45–8,
    60, 66, 113, 115–16, 125,
    133–6, 150, 155–9, 172–3, 175,
    178, 197
  anti- 155, 158
  apocalyptic 157–8, 177
  completion 158, 180
  closure 60, 158
  grand 157
  historical 133
  metanarrative ix
  novelistic 141
  see also mediation, narrative; poetics
National Socialism 56, 58, 154,
    160–62, 165–7, 174
  see also fascism; Nazis
nationalism 163, 166, 173–4, 186
  neo- 166
  revolutionary 174
naturalism 42, 67, 83, 107, 177, 179
nature 32, 44, 46, 57, 62–3, 65, 67,
    80, 108, 111, 113, 118–19, 123,
    126–7, 129, 145, 149, 154, 158,
    198
  second- 127
  suppressed
  see also exteriority
Nazis/Nazi Party 161–3, 165–7, 171,
    176
  see also National Socialism
negation 75–8, 80, 115, 128, 137,
    144, 155, 184, 199
Neo-Kantianism *see* Kantianism, neo-
Neuzeit 9–13, 115–16
new, the xii, 12, 14, 15, 17, 20, 115,
    136–7, 139–40, 142–3, 150, 159,
    164, 177, 179, 184, 195–6, 200
newspapers 188

New World 11
Niethammer, Lutz 36–8
Nietzsche, Friedrich viii, 12, 20, 22,
    39, 71, 81, 127, 137, 142–3, 166,
    171, 176
nihilism 58, 150, 166, 183
nominalism 4
novel 135–6, 158, 197
now, the 14, 27–9, 48–50, 64, 66–7,
    143–7, 149–58, 176–7, 196
now-being (*Jetztzsein*) 143, 150,
    152
now-time (*Jetztzeit*) 64, 115–16,
    144–50, 152–8, 178–80

Occupation 71
Oedipal complex 91–4
old, the xii,
ontology 52, 55, 57–60, 80, 109–10,
    113, 118–20, 132, 155, 161, 169
    172–3, 178, 186
  ancient 170, 173
  existential 58
  hermeneutical 65
  of historical time x, 46–7, 114
  of misrecognition 109
  modernist 7
  phenomenological 30, 44–7, 65,
    75, 109, 118–19, 126, 186
  social 80, 179
  temporal 175
  see also hermeneutics, ontological
other(s)/otherness 42–3, 68, 75,
    77, 79–80, 83, 95, 103,
    117–25
  absolute 42, 82, 85, 107–8,
    117–20, 122, 189, 224
  Being-with- 59, 63, 66, 69–74,
    107, 175
  concrete 98–101
  imaginary 95–7, 102, 111
  inside- 106
  outside- 106
  of personal prehistory 106
  self- 109
Ovid 9

Paik, Nam June vii, xiv
Pannwitz, Rudolf 149
Paris 180
Pascal, Blaise 36, 104
past, the 2, 10, 33, 115, 146, 149,
    153

past/present/future ix, 5, 14, 18, 33,
  42–4, 49–51, 59, 109, 127–8,
  132, 143, 150–52, 158, 172,
  176–9, 198–200
Paz, Octavio 16
people (*Volk*)
  German 166, 173–4, 177
periodization vii–ix, xiii, 1–14, 16,
  19, 35, 114
phallus 87, 91–4,
phenomenology x, 117–21, 125
  Husserlian 57, 65, 120, 172
  of the everyday 186
  existential 191
  neo–Hellenic 173
  of sociality 118
  of social life 193
  of 'the they' 194
  transcendental 119
  see also ontology,
    phenomenological; time,
    phenomenological
philosophy ix, xiv, 31, 42, 60, 114,
  120, 123–4, 134, 181, 186
  anti-practical 176
  as criticism of life 189
  of desire 194
  end of 171
  fascistic 161
  first 170
  of freedom 170
  history of xiii, 123
  ordinary language 187
  practical 169, 176
  of science 31, 36
  systematic 170
  Western 123
Plato 121, 187
  Parmenides 121
poetics x
  of narrative 45–7, 52
  see also narrative
politics 43–4, 58, 116, 118, 127, 148,
  153–4, 160–67
  anti- 176
  of the everyday 185
  of the fetish 184
  of memory 150
  of modernity 13–20
  of time, *see* time, politics of
Pontalis, Jean-Bernard 96
Popper, Karl 31, 36, 229
positive science 31

positivism 31
posthistoire 36–8
possibility 58, 65–6, 77, 79, 107,
  168, 170, 173, 177, 179, 182,
  198, 200
postmodernism vii–ix, xiv, 13, 17,
  18, 35, 114, 198
  philosophical vii, viii
postmodernity vii, ix, 2–4, 9, 15, 20
poststructuralism 18
Pound, Ezra 166
power 171, 174
present, the viii, xiv, 2, 4, 6, 9–10,
  19, 21–6, 28, 135, 140
  eternal 42, 53, 128, 151
  Augustinian 48
  historical 143, 145, 149
  phenomenological 145, 152
  threefold 49–51, 54
  see also past/present/future; today
progress 3, 11, 16, 17, 19–21,
  115–16, 138–41, 150, 157, 200
  inverted 149
protention 49–51, 117
psychoanalysis xii, 82, 117
  psychoanalytic theory xi, 54,
    81–112, 118, 182
psychology 100–101
  meta- 80, 109, 112
publicity/public sphere 188

race 162, 164, 166–7, 199
  racism 165–6
radicalism 130
Rancière, Jacques 134
Ranke, Leopold von 31, 138–9
rationalism 31
reaction ix, xii 164, 166, 200
  radical 162, 167
  revolutionary 164 *see also*
    modernism, reactionary
reason viii, 21, 22, 36, 41–2, 72,
  128–9
  post-secular 114
  realization of 37–40, 61
recognition xi, xii, 5, 7, 20, 37–8, 44,
  63, 69–90, 95–103, 108–10, 185,
  189, 199
  struggle for 71, 81, 83, 113,
    117–18, 174
  see also dialectic, of recognition
redemption 42, 113, 115, 138,
  143–7, 149, 152–3, 156

reduction 77
  Husserlian 65–6
  reflection 129–32
Reformation 10
religion 37, 114, 116, 118, 122, 164,
    167, 177, 181
  positive 123
  popular 182
  see also Christianity; Judaism;
    tradition
remembrance 49–51, 135, 137,
    140–43, 175–9
  see also memory
Renaissance 9, 10
repetition xii, 19, 59, 93, 111, 128,
    131, 137, 168–80, 186, 195, 199
  cyclical 195
  exact 143
  linear 195
repression 100, 103, 106, 110–11
resoluteness 160, 168, 170–3, 176
retention 49–51
revolution 7, 11, 129, 146, 154, 197,
    199
  anti-Jewish 167
  conservative 159, 162–7 see also
    modernism, reactionary
  counter- 154
  French 11
  Industrial 11
  national 163, 167, 174
  social 8
Rickert, Heinrich 31
Ricoeur, Paul x–xii, xiv, 30, 40, 41,
    44–68, 108–9, 111, 115–16,
    131–3, 155–6, 158, 179
  Time and Narrative 45–7
Roman Empire 9
Romanticism 128, 162, 190, 192
Sakai, Naoki 16, 18
same 119, 121, 123–5, 137, 140,
    143, 179, 195
Sartre, Jean-Paul 3, 54, 57, 72, 78,
    82
  Being and Nothingness 78
  Critique of Dialectical Reason 54,
    78
Saussure, Ferdinand de 27, 108
Scholem, Gershom 146, 150, 154,
    181
Second International 3, 149
Second World War 71–2, 165
secularization 35, 148

seduction 101
self-consciousness 70–85, 97,
    100–102
serfdom 72–3, 76
sexual difference see difference, sexual
sexuality 100–101, 111, 182
signifiance 94
signification 102, 199
  enigmatic 83, 90, 100, 102–8, 110
  primary 94
Simmel, Georg 12
situation 168, 171
Situationism 194
slavery see dialectic, master-slave
social, the 62–8, 108, 111, 118–19,
    121–2, 125–6
socialism xiii, 190
socialization 111, 199
  primary xi, 67
sociology ix, 1–4, 8, 32, 121, 134–5,
    156, 169, 174, 180
  of the everyday 188–92
  right-wing 186, 188
Socrates 82
space/spatial relations 13, 15–19, 26,
    28, 87, 106, 124, 157, 198
  existential 126
  social 194
species 123, 125, 127
  -being 191
  death of 177
speculation 35, 42–5, 120
Spengler, Oswald 162
spirit (Geist) 72–3, 80
  European 40
Spivak, Gayatri Chakravorty 35, 185,
    244
Stalin, Joseph 81
Stern, Daniel 100
  The First Relationship 100
structuralism 25, 27–8 see also
    linguistics, structural
subject/subjectivity 14, 48, 70,
    82–111, 115, 124, 129, 133, 168,
    171, 187, 197, 201
  existential 176
  heterosexist 182
  see also Dasein; ego;
    self-consciousness
subjectivism 171
suffering 141
Surrealism x, 153–4, 175, 180–85,
    190, 196

symbolic   82–9, 94, 97–8, 100, 102,
    107
synchrony/diachrony   27–9, 108, 175

technology   136, 153, 160, 162–4,
    177
    planetary   161
temporality *see* time
temporalization   xi, xii, 45, 54, 58,
    60, 80, 102–11, 117, 124, 127,
    131, 194
    existential   198–9
    hierarchy of modes   52, 63, 197
    historical   ix–xii, 5, 61, 108, 111,
        113–16, 121, 123, 126, 128, 130,
        134, 137–8, 155, 169, 178,
        197–200
    human   117
theology   112–14, 118, 120, 122, 130,
    138, 141, 145, 147–9
    Christian   173
Third World   39,
time
    calendrical   64, 66–7
    of capital   196
    Christian   11, 16
    chronicle   66–7
    chronological   10, 15, 19, 23, 26,
        28, 140
    of circulation   29
    clock   34, 64
    cosmic/cosmological   44–55, 60–68,
        71, 81, 96, 108, 111, 118, 143,
        155, 175
    culture of   x, 157
    differential   xi, 7, 8, 15, 16, 23–30
    ecstatic-horizonal   52, 56, 64, 167
    end of   40, 124, 149, 157–8
    eschatological   16
    of everydayness   195, 198
    existential   61–8, 80, 83, 88, 97,
        102, 125, 177, 189
    historical   viii–xii, 3, 5, 7, 9,
        15, 16, 18–29, 31–2, 40, 44–7,
        50–62, 67, 93, 96, 111, 113–17,
        124–5, 139, 143–4, 146, 149,
        152, 155–6, 159, 168, 175–7,
        180, 184, 196, 198, 200
    homogeneous   1, 24, 27, 67,
        139–40, 143–4, 149
    human   105, 110
    ideological   25, 27
    of initiative   53, 60, 155–6, 158

    labour-   14, 34
    lived   46–8, 51, 53, 60, 67, (*see also*
        time, phenomenological)
    men's   19
    messianic   149, 151
    of modernity   114–15, 136, 169,
        175 *see also* modernity, as quality
        of experience; modernity, as
        temporalisation of history
    multiple   24–8, 30
    narrative   xii, 154
    natural/of nature   44, 63, 143, 196
    objective   49–54, 62 *see also* time,
        cosmic/cosmological
    ordinary conception of   25, 52,
        62–8, 144–5, 188
    of the other   117–18, 124–5, 189,
        194
    perceptual   104–5
    phenomenological   ix, 28, 45–55,
        60–68, 81, 96, 155
    philosophy of   viii–x, 45, 60, 83,
    physical   49 *see also* time,
        cosmic/cosmological
    politics of   viii–ix, xii, xiii, 116,
        199–200
    primordial   52, 63, 67
    public   194
    psychoanalytical ideas of   97
    of questioning   106 *see also*
        afterwardness
    of renewal   163
    revolutionary   165
    of shock   136
    social   27–8, 30, 93
    of the soul   46–7, 49 *see also* time,
        phenomenological
    subjective   52, 62 *see also* time,
        phenomenological
    of tradition   115, 165, 189
    of truth   144
    universal   48, 67
    women's   19
    of the world   46–7 *see also* time,
        cosmic/cosmological
    world standard-   34
timelessness   104–8, 110–11, 113,
    116–17, 120, 125, 128, 130,
    152
today   2, 9, 50, 168
Tönnies, Ferdinand   134
    Community and Society   134
totalitarianism   34, 61

totality   23, 26, 54, 56–8, 60–61, 69,
    107, 117–19, 121, 123–4, 141,
    146–7, 168, 190–92
  expressive   24
  finite   124–5
  see also aporia, of totality
totalization   x, 34, 36, 42, 111, 118,
    126
  de-   53, 109–10
  historical   viii–xi, 28–68, 109, 198,
    200
  re-   53, 109, 115, 117, 156
  infinite   124
  narrative   115–16
tradition   xii, 2–4, 11, 12, 21, 55, 81,
    113–16, 127–42, 164, 173,
    176–7, 179, 184, 188
  blank   116
  destruction of   115, 133–4, 138,
    147–8, 156
  invention of   157
  Judaic–Christian   113–14
  mystical   114
  philosophical   xiv
  political   xiii
  religious   122
  see also heritage; time, of tradition
traditionalism   ix, xii
traditionality   131–2, 178–9
traditionalization
  de-   4
  re-   4
tragedy   176, 190
  Elizabethan   157
transcendence   61, 70, 117, 119–24,
    138, 141
  finite   168–9
transcendental (method)   30–33, 36,
    45, 126, 128, 130, 132, 138

aesthetics   161
translation   83, 105–7, 110–11,
    148–9
  de-   106
  re-   106

unconscious   xi, 100–11, 113,
    136–7, 158, 175, 189,
    198
universality   191–3
utopia   125, 147, 192, 194

values   129–31, 140, 174
Vilar, Pierre,   34–5
voluntarism   171, 174

war   136, 153, 198
  after-   163
  theory of   163
Weber, Max   200
Weimar Republic   163, 181
West, the   16, 18, 41, 193 see also
    culture, Western; Marxism,
    Western; philosophy,
    Western
will   124
  not to will   171
  to power   166
  to will   166
Williams, Raymond   13, 191
within-timeness (Innerzeitigkeit)   52,
    62–5, 194
Wohlfarth, Irving   148
Wolin, Richard   161, 164

Young, Robert   17
youth   135

Žižek, Slavoj   85